D1390993

A HODDER CHRISTIAN PAPERBACK OMNIBUS

CATHERINE MARSHALL

Beyond Our Selves
Meeting God at Every Turn
A Closer Walk

BEYOND OUR SELVES

Beyond Our Selves

Catherine Marshall

Hodder & Stoughton
LONDON SYDNEY AUCKLAND

British Library Cataloguing in Publication Data
A record for this book is available from the British Library

Beyond Our Selves

To Len

Printed and bound in Great Britain by
Cox & Wyman Ltd, Reading, Berks

Hodder and Stoughton
A Division of Hodder Headline PLC
338 Euston Road
London NW1 3BH

Contents

Acknowledgments

I wish to express my appreciation to Elizabeth Sherrill for her constructive criticism and wise counsel; to my husband, Leonard Earl LeSourd, who has assumed responsibility for my manuscript as though it were his own; to Dr Dudley Zuver, who has checked the manuscript for Biblical and theological accuracy; to Miss Patricia Harris, who has done a herculean job of typing and retyping manuscript; to the Fleming H. Revell Company for their generosity in loaning me Hannah Whitall Smith's out-of-print books, to the kind ladies at the Chappaqua Library; and to Mr Robert F. Beach and his associates at the Union Theological Seminary Library; finally, my lasting gratitude to the friends who have been so gracious in allowing me to share their personal experiences with the readers of this book.

Thanks are due to those who have kindly given permission for quotations from the following works: *The Faith That Rebels* by D. S. Cairns, published by S. C. M. Press Ltd.; *The Dignity of Man* by Russell Davenport, published by Harper & Brothers; the writing of Arthur John Gossip in *The Interpreter's Bible*, published by Thomas Nelson & Sons Ltd.; *Modern Man in Search of a Soul* by C. G. Jung, published by Routledge & Kegan Paul Ltd.; *How Character Develops* by Fritz Künkel and Roy E. Dickerson, published by Charles Scribner's Sons; *Beyond Personality* by C. S. Lewis, published by Geoffrey Bles Ltd.; *The Bible: A New Translation* by James Moffatt, published by Hodder & Stoughton Ltd.; "Twenty Minutes of Reality" by Margaret Prescott Montague in *Atlantic Monthly*; *Why I Know There Is a God* by Fulton Oursler, published by The World's Work (1913) Ltd.; *The Gospels Translated into Modern English* by J. B. Phillips, published by Geoffrey Bles Ltd.; *The Gospel of Healing* by A. B. Simpson, published by Marshall, Morgan & Scott Ltd.

Foreword

SEVENTEEN years ago, when illness hemmed me within the four walls of my bedroom, certain questions presented themselves to me with terrible urgency:

Is it really possible for us to get in touch with the God who created our world?

Why does God allow evil, if He has the power to destroy it?

Can God heal where medicine fails?

Can prayer affect the outward circumstances of our lives?

Does God guide people today?

The search for the answers to these questions has brought adventure beyond anything I could have imagined. *Beyond Our Selves* is the story of that search.

Many others have shared in the explorations that made this book possible. Three persons especially have had a part in it, the first being a woman who died before I was born. I first met her in the pages of one of her own books.

It was in the fall of 1944 that a copy of Hannah Whitall Smith's *The Christian's Secret of a Happy Life* fell into my hands. Superficially the volume was anything but inviting. The print was small and cramped, the language quaint, the writing style outdated. All of this was understandable, as the book had been written in 1870. Since then—with almost no advertising—this little volume had sold about three million copies. I wondered why.

I soon found out. Here was a practical how-to book written in the days before there was any such thing. The chapter headings read like a table of contents still damp with printer's ink: "How to Enter In" (that is, into the Christian life); "Difficulties Concerning Guidance"; "Difficulties Concerning Doubts"; "Difficulties Concerning Faith" . . .

The zest and decisiveness of her writing revealed Hannah

Smith as a woman who knew what she believed and why she
believed it. In her day, hell and damnation were still major
emphases across Christendom. Instead, her emphasis was that
the Christian life is the happiest of all lives. Yet hers was no
easy cult-of-happiness teaching, for she insisted that Christian
joy could not be bought cheaply. There was no evading the
total surrender of one's life and resources, no avoiding the
giving up of doubt and the giving in to a costly obedience.

I read the book through, then read it again. Certain chapters
I returned to, over and over. If I had a spiritual problem
puzzling me, I could always find an answer in *The Christian's
Secret,* provided—provided I meant business about getting
straightened out. Some day, I told myself, I would like to write
the same kind of helping book for my time. In it I would want
to share, as Hannah Smith had, the discoveries—great and
small—which had been of value to me in my Christian walk.

The second person whose mark is indelibly on *Beyond Our
Selves* is Peter Marshall. When I was a college girl in Atlanta,
Peter first caught my attention by the recurring note in his
preaching of conviction based on personal experience. In a
hundred different ways he said, "I know this is so, because
I have experienced it."

He talked often of God's guidance, since he was an example
of one whom the Lord had guided. He spoke ringing words
about God's ability to provide material needs; God had provided his needs.

He had much to say about Christianity being a joyous life.
Those who bowled with him or accompanied him on fishing
trips or to baseball games saw the joy first hand. He insisted
that a man need not be a sissy to love the Lord. Other men
listened to him, because he was walking proof.

To us college girls, the surety of his conviction and first-hand
faith was more fresh and more impressive than any preaching
we had ever heard.

Then after he became my husband, he continued to mould
me. Here was the love of God pouring through as warm and
vivid a personality as I have ever known. Through Peter I
saw that our love for God should involve the emotions. Why

not? For emotion need not be maudlin. It can also have a virile strength.

He taught me, and many another, the difference between going through the mechanical motions of a church service and the art of corporate worship. Through him I learned what worship is.

Peter imparted to me his knowledge of immortality. His sureness about it was a trumpet call of faith. He was certain of the continuation of life beyond this one, certain in a way that few persons ever are.

He took my tendency toward snap judgments of people and situations and taught me that "there, but for the grace of God, go I."

And I can never forget his insistence that women should be women, that in our femininity is our glory.

All of this Peter did for me. Not often is there such a combination of husband and teacher. So far as Christianity is concerned, I sat at his feet as did thousands of others. I find now that his ideas, his convictions, even his word-pictures, have become a part of me, tissue and sinew. That is why any book I write is Peter's book too.

I also owe to Peter, in a strange sort of way, my present happiness. For he engrafted into me the truth that in God's scheme of things there is no place for rivalry or jealousy. Each beloved person's place is secure, his own for this life and for eternity. No one can take it from him, nor does it impinge on anyone else's place. That is why Peter is and always will be a part of my life. It is also why Len can share him with me and is as grateful as I for Peter's influence on our life together.

For the third person whom I want to mention in connection with the writing of *Beyond Our Selves* is, of course, Leonard LeSourd, whom I married in 1959, almost eleven years after Peter's death.

I find that having an editor in the family has many compensations, along with a few drawbacks. As the editor of *Guideposts* and a writer himself, Len understands the hours that every writer must keep, the needed isolation. He is patient with me when I fall into a black mood because ideas are not flowing, sentences are wooden, and what I am turning out is just plain terrible. Always he gives me unstintingly of his fine editorial judgment.

There are times, however, when I want to slam the office door on my manuscript and not think or speak of it until the next day.

But ideas do not keep hours for Len. "Now, Catherine, if you shifted this section from the middle of Chapter Six to the end—" Or, "I hate to mention it, but the material slows down here." Once he even telephoned me from a toll booth along the New Jersey Turnpike: "I've been thinking about that chapter on forgiveness all the way down here. The opening paragraph still isn't quite right—" Then of course, like all editors, he is ruthless with the blue pencil.

But somehow he always knows when I need to shut the door on my writing for longer periods of time. "I want you to write FUN on your calander for x number of days," he will say every so often. "See what you think of this plan for a trip?"

Some day perhaps I shall write about the adventure of rearing a second family. Just at the point when I thought childrearing was over, Len's three children have joined Peter John in calling me "Mother".

There is Jeffrey, a mischievous and lovable five-year-old. Standing beside Peter John's six feet, five-and-a-half inches, Jeff appears even tinier than he is. Chester, all of eight now, has enormous deep brown eyes and a well-developed passion for baseball. Peter John has earned his adoration by coaching him for Little League. Then there is Linda, who is at that about-to-grow-up age of twelve. She has always wanted a big brother, and looks on the one she acquired as a dispensation straight from heaven. Linda is also ecstatic over having a writer "for a mommy". She will be even more ecstatic, I hope, when she finds something about herself in this book.

The sprawling white house with red shutters that is home is set in the rocky, tree-shaded countryside of Westchester County. We have a rural mailbox, a school bus route, and moles in the lawn.

Many experiences have tested me in my lifetime, but none

more than this one. And none has made me happier. But writing about it must come later. A man swimming a horse across a turbulent stream does not stop to take a picture of the experience. I'll get my colts across the stream, see them thoroughly dried off, well fed, and on their way—then perhaps, the picture.

Thus, with these three people—Peter, Len and Hannah—always at my shoulder, *Beyond Our Selves* has been written. Though so different, each of them has one characteristic in common: enthusiastic delight in what Peter Marshall liked to call "spiritual research unlimited". All too often this enthusiasm is the missing ingredient in Christian circles. So if I have succeeded in transferring to the pages that follow one one-hundredth part of the excitement that I feel about Christianity, I shall have achieved my purpose.

CATHERINE MARSHALL

Chappaqua, N.Y.
July 25, 1961

1: *Something More*

IF you are satisfied with your life and feel no need for any help outside yourself, this book is not for you. The search for God begins at the point of need.

Most of us feel this need either because of some problem for which we have no answer or because of a nagging consciousness that we should be getting more out of life or putting more into it. There is the realisation that we are going through but the motions of living. Surely our half-somnolent existence is not living as it was meant to be! We yearn for something more.

I first felt this need for something more during my college days. Recently I came across these comments, written in a journal that I began about the middle of my freshman year:

> People bustle and strive and hurry. Their eyes are mostly on material considerations. They die, and apparently it's all over. What are we here for anyway? There must be some purpose in living, but I haven't found it yet.
>
> All of my life I've thought that I was possessed with a wanderlust. Now I know that the trouble lies within myself, and I cannot escape myself. I'm restless and unhappy.

Some of the restlessness may have been typical of late adolescence. But not all, for this search for something that I had not yet experienced lasted for ten years or more—into my late twenties.

I think of many of all ages who are on the same search. For example, a man named Alex. He is tall and lean, with the high forehead of the intellectual, the eyes of a thoughtful man. Alex is the product of one of the best of the Ivy League colleges and is now a successful free-lance writer.

Where religion was concerned, until a few years ago Alex

was an agnostic—and proud of it. With a mind trained in materialism and rationalism, he suspected in all religion a form of elaborate self-deception.

"The truth is that my god has been reason," Alex told me recently. "And reason seemed a god worth worshipping until—"

Until Alex came squarely up against problems in his family life that no amount of reasoning could solve.

"It was hard for me to admit that there are areas in life for which reason has no answers—like man's emotional life and the knotty problem of human relationships. Realising that shook me," he said. For the first time, he was encountering the indisputable truth that there must be something more.

And I think of Sheila Goshen, a housewife in Birmingham, Alabama, who asked for my help in her search:

. . . After ignoring God for fifty years, I recently got a new look at myself and, believe me, I did not like what I saw, So now I've been trying to change myself into what I want to be, but I find that I can't make myself over.

For the first time I know that I need God and faith. So now the question is, how does an ordinary person like me go about gaining an "intimacy" with God?

This is an easy question to ask, a hard one to answer. I puzzled for weeks, then months over it. In a way, this book is my answer.

There is abundant proof that vocational and material success fail utterly to satisfy the inner hunger. The famous Hollywood actress, Mary Astor, has known the fairy-tale magic of movie stardom. An Academy Award, glamorous marriages, two children, several Beverly Hills mansions, furs, jewels, publicity—what more could any woman want?

Yet Mary Astor admitted in print that "for years—even in the midst of fame and glamour—I yearned for contentment, happiness. It took me almost twenty years to go from idle curiosity about religion . . . to meeting God as a Person and a Father, and knowing that walking in faith meant growing up."

I have seen this search in college students, especially during their senior year. One such incident happened recently during one of my week-end visits to Yale University to see my son, Peter John. Three of Peter's friends and I had been chatting over lunch in the cafeteria. The tall, dark-haired boy directly across from me rose. "Sorry to have to rush like this, but I have a one-o'clock class. This has been an interesting conversation—"

An odd look, one that I could not interpret, crossed his face, and he hesitated before he spoke again. "Now that I'm a senior, I'm spending quite a lot of time these days trying to figure out what life is all about. Isn't it queer that we get so little help with this in college? I mean why we're here and how to handle life and all that. Well—g'bye, all."

Often the inner hunger catches up with those most immersed in materialism. One day I was talking with a man in the investment business. "During the last year," he told me, "I've experienced a kind of restlessness that baffles me. I've tried working late at the office, even plunged in the stock market so that I won't have time to think about myself. I've gone out on the town more, trying to have some fun. Even tried drinking more than usual. Nothing is ever as gratifying to the taste, sight and touch as I hope it will be. I've tried to find some satisfaction in new sports equipment, two expensive cars. Nothing helps.

"What I'm about to ask may sound strange—especially from a Wall Street broker who spends his time thinking about Dow-Jones averages rather than religion. But I wonder— could this gnawing inside be ... well, my inner spirit crying out for its Maker and refusing to be satisfied with anything less? If this is a possible explanation, what can I do about it? How does one go about finding God?"

In every community, in every land, at every social and economic level, are individuals just as eager as the investment broker to find their way to God, though many are too shy to voice it as he did. They have questions to ask, problems to solve. They wonder if Christianity really does have answers for them.

To know where answers cannot be found is at least a step in the right direction. Until the first world war, many people were certain that the Something More was right here on earth. Of course, we thought it wise to give lip-service to a Higher Power. *In God We Trust* was stamped on our coins. A sentence or two mentioning a Supreme Being appeared in most political speeches, rather like a sprig of parsley for garnish. But through all this there was the tacit understanding that we could work out our destinies, both personal and national, by ourselves. We did not really need God.

In fact, as the twentieth century dawned, Americans were probably the most optimistic people on earth. Industry, stimulated by mass production and distribution, made the end of poverty seem in sight. Eventually all the inhabitants of earth could be provided with at least minimum requirements of food, clothing, and shelter. Given time, medicine would virtually stamp out disease. More inventions and gadgets would give us leisure time for fun and culture, perhaps even a little self-examination.

Best of all, education would finally convince men that war was folly. During the late 1920s, in high schools across the United States, boys and girls were studying about the League of Nations. I know, because I spent many a winter evening curled up in an easy chair near a gas heater, preparing for a stiff examination on the subject. The prize (which I did not win) was a trip to Geneva, Switzerland, to see the League in action. My generation was confident that intelligent arbitration guided by the League and the World Court would soon replace the senseless outrage of war. It was all a part of the doctrine of inevitable progress.

Without realising what was happening, most of us gradually came to take for granted the premisses underlying this philosophy of optimism. We proceeded to live these propositions, though we would not have stated them as blandly as I set them forth here:

Man is inherently good.
Individual man can carve out his own salvation with the

help of education and society through progressively better government.

Reality and the values worth searching for lie in the material world that science is steadily teaching us to analyse, catalogue, and measure. While we would not deny the existence of inner values, we relegate them to second place.

The purpose of life is happiness. And happiness we define in terms of enjoyable activity, friends, and the accumulation of material objects.

The pain and evil of life—such as ignorance, poverty, selfishness, hatred, greed, lust for power—are caused by factors in the external world. Therefore the cure lies in the reforming of human institutions and the bettering of environmental conditions.

As science and technology remove poverty and lift from us the burden of physical existence, we shall automatically become finer persons, seeing for ourselves the value of living by the Golden Rule.

In time, the rest of the world will appreciate our demonstration that the American way of life is best. They will then seek for themselves the good life of freedom and prosperity. This will be the greatest impetus toward an end of global conflict.

The way to get along with people is to beware of religious dictums and dogma. The ideal is to be a nice person and to live by the Creed of Tolerance. Thus we offend few people. We live and let live. This is the American way.

So we believed. So we acted.

So, in fact, the Americans had believed and acted since the turn of the century.

Then came the first world war and its hideous aftermath. In Europe and the British Isles, the disillusionment was deep and real. Europeans were no longer convinced of the inherent goodness of man.

But in the Western Hemisphere we had had no cities shelled, no countryside devastated. The ink was scarcely dry on the Versailles Treaty before our philosophy of optimism reasserted itself. The trouble that caused the 1914–1918 war, we assured ourselves, was not unredeemed human nature but the munitions-makers and kindred institutions inherited from an unenlightened nineteenth century. On college campuses, lecture platforms, and in church groups our indignation was loud and vociferous. I remember taking part in inter-collegiate debates—some of them with international teams from Oxford, Cambridge, and the University of London—in which we aired our loathing for the armament-makers and the peddlers of war propaganda.

The fault was never in ourselves. No, this had nothing to do with man and his God. It was just a matter of ironing the kinks out of our society. Meanwhile technological developments rose to ever greater heights. The Golden Twenties gave certitude to the doctrine of inevitable progress. And while the depression that struck in late October 1929 was, for a time, a shattering experience, once again most people felt that the trouble was not in man but in his institutions—in this case, monopolies, the stock market, buying on margin, greedy big business. Franklin Delano Roosevelt's New Deal with its relief, recovery, and reform would take care of all that.

Suspicions that mankind might not be working out salvation for our world came with Adolf Hitler. Czechoslovakia, Poland, Denmark, Norway, the Netherlands, Belgium, France —one by one they fell before the tide of Nazism. But it was not so much the war itself as the Nazi atrocities that finally shattered our philosophical optimism about man. These shocked us to our depths, destroying once and for all the pretty picture of man as inherently good. Certain pictures can never be erased. . . .

The year was 1941. The scene a Polish village called Minsk. Adolph Eichmann, Hitler's specialist for Jewish Affairs for the Third Reich, had been sent to witness the extermination of five thousand Jews.

The morning was cold. The condemned men, women, and children undressed down to their underwear or their shirts. They walked the last hundred yards and jumped into a pit that had been prepared for them. Eichmann was impressed by the fact that they offered no resistance, apparently by this time reconciled to death.

Then the rifles and machine pistols opened fire. Children in the pit were crying, clinging to their parents. Eichmann saw one woman hold her baby high above her head, pleading, "Shoot me, but please let my baby live. Take my baby. Please take my baby—"

Eichmann had children of his own. For a moment he felt a twinge of compassion. He almost opened his mouth to order, "Don't shoot. Hand over the child." Then the baby was hit.

"I scarcely spoke a word to the chauffeur on the trip back," he reported later. "I was thinking. I was reflecting about the meaning of life in general. . . ."

What conclusions did Eichmann reach? Years later he summarised how he felt about the mass execution programme that destroyed some six million Jews. "I was a little cog in the machinery of the Reich. I merely carried out orders. Where would we have been if everyone had thought things out in those days?

"After all, the people who were loaded on trains and buses [for extermination] meant nothing to me. It was really none of my business."[1]*

What had happened to the German people? Americans who had travelled in Germany between the two world wars remembered the charm of the tidy countryside, the friendliness of the people on the city streets and in the shops, the love of music, the gaiety. We had acquired a healthy respect for the typical German businessman; his approach seemed so akin to ours. And so more and more Americans had roamed the globe, one conclusion had seemed paramount: surely men everywhere are much the same.

So it was not only the enormity of the Nazi cruelties that appalled us but the ugly suspicion that imperfect man might commit other brutalities—anywhere, at any time. Was it really true that man is innately good, that education, science,

---

* Numbers refer to notes (beginning on page 252), where sources for quotations will be found. Notes are numbered consecutively within each chapter.

technology, and a better environment will ultimately perfect him? The German people had had all those advantages.

But there was still one corner in which we as Americans might hide from the truth about human nature, so we fled to it. It was undeniable that evil things had happened in the rest of the world. But Americans, we reasoned, are different. We are people of goodwill. We hate war. We covet no empire. Our intentions are of the best. We are a generous people.

And then, just at the close of the second world war, a bomb was dropped on Hiroshima. It made dubious our carefully drawn distinction between us and the evil of the rest of the world. It had not been merely German evil that had been responsible for unspeakable brutalities: it was human evil. And we too were a part of that humanity.

Some occurrences during the Korean conflict threw further light on man's potential for weakness, evil, even depravity.[2] There were events involving Americans. Take, for example, an incident that took place in February 1951, just ten years after the mass murders of the Minsk pit. It happened in the mountains of North Korea, near Pyoktong. Forty-three American prisoners were huddled in a hut trying to keep warm. Two of the men had severe cases of diarrhoea, not pleasant in the close quarters.

In the course of the evening, an American corporal suddenly got to his feet, picked up one of his sick comrades and dumped him outside. Then he came back and threw the other sick soldier out. Not a man stirred, not a voice was raised in protest. It was thirty degrees below zero outside; the exposed men were dead within minutes.

The merciless corporal who was thus responsible for the death of two fellow countrymen was tried after the war, convicted of manslaughter, and sentenced to life imprisonment.

But what of the forty witnesses? All of these were questioned about the incident by Army psychiatrists. The typical interview, as reported by the psychiatrists, went something like this:

"Soldier, did you see that man throw the two sick soldiers out of the hut?"

"Oh, yes, sir."

"What were you doing at the time?"

"Oh, I was huddling together with the rest of the guys, trying to keep warm. That's the only way you could stay alive."

"Then you knew that it would destroy these men to be exposed?"

"Well—sure."

"But what were you doing about it?"

"I wasn't doing anything—except trying to keep warm."

"Why *didn't* you do something about it, soldier?"

"Because," the reply would come, "it wasn't any of my business."

The words echo strangely: "It was really none of my business."

To be sure, there were many examples of American self-sacrifice and heroism in the Korean war, as in every war in which Americans have been involved. Yet something about the attitudes and conduct of a large percentage of men in the Korean conflict has seriously disturbed our military leaders. An exhaustive study made by the Army to determine what happened to some nine thousand Americans in Korean prison camps and how they reacted to imprisonment is weighted with frightening material:

1. At the beginning of the Americans' imprisonment, the Chinese Communists screened out all soldiers with leadership qualities and kept them apart from the rest. These included anyone with overt religious faith, anyone who showed "poisonous individualism". When only 5 per cent of the Americans had been segregated from the rest, there was no leadership left among the remaining 95 per cent.

2. One of every three American prisoners in Korea was guilty of some kind of collaboration with the enemy—was willing to make a deal. This, in spite of the fact that torture was virtually non-existent; nor were drugs, hypnotism, or magic used by the Communists, according to Army psychiatrists. There seems to have been little about the so-called

"brainwashing" that could not have been successfully resisted by any man who had strong personal convictions and who wanted to resist.

3. Among our prisoners there was *not one* permanent escape from the prison camps. This has never happened before in any war in American history. The reason appears to have been in the will of the men themselves, for there were only six armed guards to every five hundred to six hundred Americans; no guard dogs; no machine-gun towers; no electric fences or searchlights. By contrast, in order to guard the Chinese Communists we took prisoner, we were eventually forced to keep three fully armed airborne regiments, that is, a total of fifteen to eighteen thousand men, away from the front.

4. American prisoners had the highest death rate of any war in our history—including the American Revolution. About 38 per cent of the prisoners died. This was not because of starvation or epidemics or any mass executions. Rather, most of the men died from a psychological disease for which the Medical Corps had no name. The soldiers themselves called it "give-up-itis". It happened to the boy who was dependent and homesick, the boy who brooded, the boy who had no beliefs to which to cling. He would crawl into a corner by himself, pull a blanket over his head, and turn his face to the wall. He was making the most profound of all human surrenders. Often within forty-eight hours he was dead.

Medicine had never before recorded anything like this on such a scale among eighteen to twenty-two-year-old adult males. The conclusion of the Army's study was that these boys had few inner resources that could give them the courage to rise above these obstacles.

5. The Americans were largely ignorant about their own history, heritage, or the principles upon which our nation was founded. They were equally ignorant about Communism and about what was happening elsewhere in the world.

Yet these were American boys from all across the nation— a nation presumed to be "under God". They had come up through our public school system, a percentage of them also through our Sunday schools. Since childhood they had heard about the worth of the individual, about liberty and human rights, and "loving thy neighbour". How was it that these values had not become a part of them?

Obviously something had happened back home, something that had allowed them to grow up insecure children of an Age of Anxiety, with a sense of isolation and a desperate need to make contact with other human beings. As prisoners in the cold wasteland of North Korea, they found that the Something More was not where they had thought it. Materialism had provided them pleasure, but it had given them no answers about the meaning of life.

These boys were part of the generation of youth that likes to call itself the "cool, the uncommitted" generation. What is there worth getting excited about, worth crusading for, worth believing in?

On the other side, the Communists do believe in something, believe so strongly in a set of ideas that they have long since seized the initiative in the world-wide ideological warfare. And they are getting results, because even wrong ideas passionately believed are more effective than cool lack of commitment. The result is that one-third of the peoples of the earth now live under the domination of Communist ideas.

Could it be that we in the Western world are still deceiving ourselves into hanging on to a pre-nuclear, Maginot-line kind of thinking? We act as though our security lies in stockpiling bigger and better atomic weapons, while simmering just under the surface is the knowledge that this is not security at all.

We act as though we still believe that a materialistic ideology can stem the tide of Communism engulfing the world, even though we have had abundant evidence that this ideology which ignores the spirit has failed time and again. We act as though we believe that pinning our hopes on fear alone will be a final deterrent to atomic holocaust, even though we know that a policy based on fear has never brought about a better world.

Then our real defence must be on the battleground of ideas and inner values. Why is man on earth? What are his goals?

What about the backward nations on the march, searching for meaning to life? Have we anything to offer them beyond the gadgets of our materialism and our great god science? If the American Dream is all that we have assumed it to be, then why are we unable to articulate it in a convincing way for the rest of the world?

"The truth is," as the late Russell Davenport commented, "our idea of freedom does not seem to fit either the needs or the ideals of most of the people of the globe. There is something lacking in it that people want, something that they need. ... And we had better find out what that 'something' is. For unless we can produce it, Communism will wholly capture ... the cause of all mankind."[3]

Let us admit that most of us, reflecting the inner poverty of so many of our boys in Korea, are equally responsible for the fact that our nation is steadily losing the Cold War to the Communists. Something more is needed.

Where are we to look for it? Humanism has failed us: we have had abundant evidence that we cannot save ourselves. And since the nuclear physicists have proved that matter is, so to speak, non-material, we cannot find ultimate truth in materialism. It is true that science has given us great material gifts. But it has also handed us our greatest problem: super-weapons in the hands of unredeemed human nature.

And so our only hope lies in a change inside man. Are we finally at the place where we know that only with the help of a power greater than ourselves can any man, can any nation, be redeemed?

Is this too slow a way, now that civilisation has arrived at the eleventh hour? No, for we have tried all other ways. And the influence that can be wielded by a single great man in the grip of a spiritual passion can never be measured. Even as a handful of leaders in the grip of evil have wrecked the lives of millions, so other leaders who are willing to put themselves into the mainstream of God's power may yet be able to grant us a reprieve.

The stakes are higher than they have ever been. For the first time mankind faces the possibility of self-extermination.

But in these stakes there are challenge and high adventure, along with the danger.

A few years ago, there were those who said that the atom could not be split. The atom has been split. Why should we not go forward in the same spirit to explore the spiritual world where lies the answer to a greater riddle—the riddle of the nature of man and his relation to the universe?

This spiritual world is a real world. Of that some of us have abundant evidence. There is terrain there still to be discovered; there are peaks yet to be scaled; new truth to be mined; in short, the spiritual atom to be split.

We can learn much from the spiritual explorers who have sought and found some of that truth. They can lead us at least a part of the way, to the foothills beyond which rise the mountains that challenge our time. Some of them, like Hannah Whitall Smith, lived in other centuries, and we have the privilege of sharing their discoveries through the written word. Many are contemporaries. A number are friends whom I have found eager to share anything that they have learned, so that others can go on to further discoveries. Some of their stories are in the pages that follow.

This book, then, is the story of a pilgrimage. The end has not yet been written. In a sense, you and I will be doing that in the days and years ahead. What I have written here is for anyone who longs for something more and who wants to be a part of the quest.

2: The Unselfishness of God

I KNOW a young scientist who admits he does not believe in God. He is warm-hearted and likeable, is good to his family, but has a restless uncertainty about the meaning of life.

From talking to him I know that at intervals he goes through a certain cycle. Some experience or reasoning process will bring him to the conclusion that there has to be "something more" in life than birth, struggle, death, nothingness. He will thirst for things of the spirit, hunger to believe in God. Then just at the point where there could be a spiritual breakthrough, he encounters tragedy somewhere—possibly the death of a child, the disfigurement of a beautiful girl, cancer in someone well known and well loved.

"How can a good and loving God permit this, if He made and runs the world?" he asks then. Rather than seek an explanation, he shrugs off religion as something too baffling to comprehend.

If there is a Creator, what could His nature be? That is what the scientist wants to know. It is a question over which many would-be believers stumble. It is the question with which all of us who want the adventure of exploring the spiritual world must begin. Its answer is pertinent to our happiness. Unless each of us can find answers that satisfy, we cannot trust that Creator with our dearest hopes, and so we shall have no basis for faith in God.

All of us have had contradictory experiences of the nature of God. I know I have. They run like threads through my childhood. In the very beginning, the love of my father and mother taught me of the fatherliness of God lying at the heart of the universe. Looking back at that childhood, feelings of glorious freedom and of rushing joy rise even now to meet me. Safe and loved we were, in God's world.

My brother, Bob, and sister, Emmy, and I used to roam the

woods and mountains that surrounded our small West Virginia town. We waded mountain streams to pick mint and watercress and violets on far banks. We skipped smooth stones across the water, dared one another to run across swinging bridges. There is the memory of struggling up a mountainside, gulping deep drafts of the cool air, all of the aching effort worth that moment when we would stand on the summit to survey the world we knew so well lying at our feet, with more mountains beyond pushing back the horizon.

There was the exhilaration of lying on our stomachs, coasting down long, snow-packed hills in the winter; skimming down the same hills on our bicycles in the summer, the wind in our faces. There was the way we would stand and "pump" in our swing: Begin slowly. Bend the knees in rhythm with the swinging. Make it go higher ... higher ... up and down. Now again, swishing through the air, until finally the jerk of the chains told us that the swing had gone as high as it could. Then "let the cat die. . . ."

There were the twilight hours of long summer evenings when all the children of the neighbourhood gathered to play "Kick the Can . . ." The breathless dash out of hiding to give the can a swift kick and listen to the music of its careening, crashing, clinking progress down the street.

This was the freedom of the child who is loved and knows that he is loved. It was not that we children were free to disobey or to do as we pleased. But neither did we have to strain to earn love by being good. For we had constant evidence that Mother and Father would keep on loving us even when they disapproved our actions.

How well I recall one spring day when an irate neighbour called upon Father to inform him that a portion of the wall in his back yard had collapsed. The neighbour was sure that this was no act of God; the Wood children were mixed up in it somewhere.

Father's investigation proved that the man was right. We had been using a coal house behind the neighbour's property as a clubhouse. All our spare time for several weeks had been used in digging a secret tunnel. Soon, our toy wagon had hauled out quite a mound of dirt. As a result the tunnel which had begun underneath the coal house had veered too close to the neighbour's stone wall.

At such times the parental temper could flare. Em and I, being girls, knew better than Bob how to placate this one weakness of Father's. What usually developed was a highly dramatic scene with Bob and Father in the leading roles, Em and I standing by trying to give Bob support.

"You know perfectly well," Father would begin in that strong booming voice he had developed in seminary, "that you had no business doing all that digging in someone else's yard. The mere fact that you kept it a secret proves that—"

Already Bob was in tears, his cowlick jerking. "But—we *had* to keep it secret. All three of us had signed a pledge in blood—"

"In *what*? Never mind—I don't care *what* you signed the pledge in. I have warned you over and over—"

By now, Em was behind Mother's back, signalling to Bob. All of us were a captive audience for Father's eloquent oration. Like his well-organised sermons, the oration had several clear points: first, reminder of previous warnings; second, our total lack of respect for parental authority; third, the uncertain destiny of the younger generation; fourth, the futility of trying to raise good, obedient children; fifth, this time was the last straw.

By the time the rising crescendo of the fifth point had been reached, Mother was saying, "Pl-lease-e, John, *lower* your voice. Must we tell all the neighbours?"

Father's mien was that of a wounded lion. "Leonora, it *so* happens that in this case, the neighbours already know *only* too well." Then, with giant stride, the great man would storm out of the back door, decisively snap a small switch off the privet hedge, re-slam the back door, and stalk back in.

This was the cue for Bob to increase the anguish of his wails: "I'm sorry, Dad, I'll never do it again—never—never—" And for me to try to make myself heard: "Father, Bob wasn't the only one. Em and I—" And for Em to burst into tears: "Don't switch Bob, Dad. I dug the tunnel, too—"

But after the tempest had subsided and peace was restored, it was Father who patiently helped us rebuild the stone wall. Through his lecture and even the punishment that followed, his love (which was God's love to us then) shone through. Thus even in our wrongdoing we discovered that our father and mother would always be beside us in the midst of trouble, still loving us.

As a younger child, I can remember the warmth and strength of Father's arms as I nestled there, content to sit silent while he carried on leisurely conversations with grown-ups. Just as clearly I can remember Mother's firm hand on my forehead when I was sick, the deliciousness of ice-cold apple scraped with a silver spoon for a fevered tongue, the stories she read aloud during bouts with the measles or chicken pox. I learned early that stories were experiences, entrancing lands to which the gates were always invitingly open.

In the same awareness of God's love at its simplest and most profound, I remember the fragrance of the first hyacinths in the spring and of the reddish-brown blossoms of the sweet scrub. ... The feel of bare feet on moss under our giant oak trees. ... The luxuriance of the purple wistaria that made beautiful even the old coal house. ... The way we children would bite off the tip of a honeysuckle blossom and suck out the honey. ... And, toward the turn of the year, the smell of balsam Christmas trees, of candle wax and wood smoke.

One day my mother and I stood at a window watching the fury of a thunderstorm of near-hurricane strength. It seemed drama on a cosmic scale—the clash of cymbals in the sky, the rolling of drums, fireworks of lightning. Rather than being afraid, I felt like shouting and applauding as the ferocious wind shook the great trees backward and forward as though they had been twigs clenched in the jaws of a dog. All the while, my mother's arm lay protectively around my shoulders.

Only in retrospect would I one day see the connection between these childhood experiences and my understanding of the nature of God. Then I would know that it made no sense at all that God would create my parents with a greater capacity for loving than He has Himself.

At the same time, there was another strand of experience in my childhood. As I grew up, I could not but become aware of the evil and suffering in the world. In any clergyman's home, as in any physician's, the raw drama of life passes steadily before the eyes.

I vividly recall my first encounter with suffering—the winter's night Father was called to the local hospital to minister to a woman who was dying of first-degree burns over most of her body. A stove had exploded when she had tried to start a fire with kerosene. When, after a vigil of many hours, Father wearily returned home, we children found ourselves backing away from him. The odour of burned flesh clung to his clothes. For days Father was so haunted by what he had seen that he had difficulty in eating.

Then there was the night the mayor of our town banged on our door at three A.M. to tell Father that the body of our friend and neighbour, Mr Fisher, had been discovered on the Baltimore and Ohio railroad tracks near Harpers Ferry. Apparently he had lost his balance and had fallen off the rear platform of the Capitol Limited.

"I just can't bear to be the one to break this awful news to Mrs Fisher," the mayor said. "You're a minister. You'll know what to say."

But Father was also a human being. His family knew that he found it just as hard as anyone to be the bearer of such tidings.

In a sense, Mother was as much a minister as Father. She had been appointed by the mayor to serve on the Board for County Relief because she had a reputation for always being on the side of the down-and-outers. Every Christmas she supervised the assembling of a hundred-odd baskets of food, clothes and toys for the poor. And a spot like Radical Hill—the chief slum district of our town, where most of the baskets were taken—lay heavily on her conscience. There many families lived in shacks with no plumbing and little heat.

Then came the afternoon when Mother's deep conviction that something must be done spilled over into action. She spent the day tramping over Radical Hill surveying the situation. When she returned home, we children were awed to see her weep at the remembrance of what she had seen. Then she gingerly stripped herself of every garment, dumped her clothes in the washing machine, took a bath, even washed her hair.

Later, during my undergraduate days at Agnes Scott College, I was to have an experience reminiscent of Mother's. A group of college men and women were asked to give an afternoon to the Syrian Mission in Atlanta, Georgia. I was among the volunteers.

The mission was in the heart of Atlanta's worst slum district, close to the state capitol building, as is often the case. The afternoon was to include a short service at the mission and visiting afterward—two by two—in some of the homes. It was the visiting that brought the revelation. I had dimly realised that such squalid, dirty places did exist, but I had never been personally exposed to them.

Pictures still came back: Men around a fireplace, slinking away as we went in. . . . Broken window panes stuffed with rags and paper. . . . A sick child doubled up on a dirty bed in a corner. . . . Air so stale that we felt polluted to breathe it. . . . An absurdly young mother wearing ankle socks, nursing her baby before us. . . . In another room an old woman who had been ill, she told us, for six months, her yellow skin stretched tight over gaunt cheekbones. . . . A lamp on an old-fashioned dresser made grotesque shadows on flyspecked walls.

I wanted to flee. But even as we headed back toward college, I wondered—was this, too, God's world?

It was some time during my teens that I received my first clear shaft of light on the riddle of evil. There was growing larger and larger in my mind the contrast between my loving, compassionate parents and a God who allowed such terrible things. One day I took this puzzling question to a woman who had become a very special friend.

Mrs MacDonald was one of those remarkable people who love all young people. Because she never talked down to teenagers, many of us gave her our complete confidence. She was married to a Scotsman, a successful lawyer. On occasions when he had to be away from home on law cases, I would spend the night with her. Those evenings were talkfeasts.

The flavour of Mrs Mac's life was reflected in her home. Windows were filled with African violets. On the stair landing stood a grandfather clock whose musical chimes marked the quarter-hours. There were current books of history and travel lying about. Just before bedtime Mrs Mac and I would always have heaping bowls of ice cream,—more ice cream than I could eat. Then she would tuck me under an eiderdown in a mahogany bed with tall pineapple posts.

On one of these evenings I found myself spilling out my inner rebellion against a God Who permitted suffering and evil when He had the power to stop it.

"Catherine," she said thoughtfully, "you know how often I speak of Kenneth?"

I nodded. Quickly my mind reviewed what I knew about Kenneth. He had been the MacDonald's only son, had died of diabetes as a teenager. It had compounded their sorrow that insulin had been discovered just a few months too late to save their boy. Here then, close at home, was an example of the kind of tragedy that made me question the love of God.

"Well," my friend went on, "if I had reasoned as you suggest, I could have railed bitterly against God for allowing Kenneth's death. God has power. He could have prevented it, so why didn't He?

"Even now, I can't give you a complete answer to that. But I can't be bitter either, because during Kenneth's long illness, I had so many examples of God's tender father-love. Like that time soon after Kenneth himself suspected that he was going to die and asked me, 'Mother, what is it like to die? Mother, does it hurt?'"

Even as Mrs Mac repeated the questions, tears sprang to my eyes. "How—did you answer him?"

The white-haired woman seemed to be seeing into the past. "I remember that I fled to the kitchen, supposedly to attend to something on the stove. I leaned against the kitchen cabinet. Queer, I'll never forget certain tiny details, like the feel of my knuckles pressed hard against the smooth, cold surface. And I asked God how to answer my boy.

"God did tell me. Only He could have given me the answer to the hardest question that a mother can ever be asked. I knew—just knew how to explain death to him. 'Kenneth,' I remember saying, 'you know how when you were a tiny boy, you used to play so hard all day that when night came, you would be too tired to undress—so you would tumble into Mother's bed and fall asleep?

"'That was not your bed. It was not where you belonged. And you would only stay there a little while. In the morning —to your surprise—you would wake up and find yourself in your own bed in your own room. You were there because someone had loved you and had taken care of you. Your father had come—with his great strong arms—and carried you away.'

"So I told Kenneth that death is like that. We just wake up some morning to find ourselves in another room—our own room, where we belong. We shall be there, because God loves us even more than our human fathers and takes care of us just as tenderly."

We were both silent for a moment. Then Mrs Mac said softly. "Kenneth never had any fear of dying after that. If— for some reason that I still don't understand—he could not be healed, then this taking away of all fear was the next greatest gift God could give us. And in the end, Kenneth went on into the next life exactly as God had told me he would— gently, sweetly." There was the look of profound peace on my friend's face as she spoke.

After Mrs Mac tucked me in that night, I lay in the mahogany bed under the eiderdown, pondering her words. What she had really been telling me was that those on the inside of tragedy are often initiated into something that out-siders may not experience at all: the love of God—instant, continuous, real—in the midst of their trouble. With the presence of the Giver, they have something more precious than any gift He might bestow.

Not until years later, after my marriage to Peter Marshall,

did I experience this for myself. During our first happy year in Atlanta, we had a close friend who had known much trouble—the death of children, financial reverses, the misunderstanding of friends. She used to look quizzically at us—young, so in love, fresh in our faith in the goodness of God.

"Neither of you has really had any trouble," she would say.

"You're bound to have some sooner or later. Everyone does. When trouble comes to you, I wonder if you will feel as you do now?"

The friend's prediction was right. We did have trouble—much illness, and finally Peter Marshall's death at forty-six. So now I am in a better position to answer the friend's question. The answer is yes, I still believe in God's love, believe more firmly than ever, because my faith has stood trial.

A few hours before Peter's death I found out what the Hebrew poet meant when he wrote about "the everlasting arms."[1] I experienced the comfort of those arms. It happened in the early morning hours after Peter had been taken by ambulance to the hospital. I was forced to stay behind, so that our young son Peter John would not be in the house alone.

There was no doubt that Peter's life hung in the balance. I sank to the floor by the bed, put my head in my arms, pondering how should I pray. Suddenly there was the feeling of being surrounded by the love of God the Father—enveloped in it, cradled with infinite gentleness.

Awe swept through me, followed by the conviction that it was not necessary to *ask* for anything. All I had to do was to commit Peter and me and our future to this great love. At the time I thought this meant that Peter's heart would be healed.

Much later—when I had trodden the long way through the Valley of the Shadow—I realised that God had given me this experience in the hours preceding Peter's death so that I might have absolute assurance that He was beside Peter and me every minute, loving us, sharing Peter's glory and my grief.

That is how I came to know personally that the Apostle Paul's glowing assertion is literally true that nothing—neither death, nor life, nor tribulation, nor peril of any sort shall be able to separate us from the love of God. . . .[2]

Then, in the years that followed Peter Marshall's death, I thought I glimpsed another shaft of light illuminating the dark night of human sorrow. Not only is God always beside us in trouble, identified with our suffering, but He can also make everything—even our troubles and sorrows—"work together for good."[3]

How many times I have received letters from readers whom I have never met, who marvelled at how God accomplished this in our case . . . "How I wish that I might have heard Dr Marshall preach! But so far away here in New Zealand, I would never have known about him at all, had it not been for *A Man Called Peter*. And now, to think that he is preaching to more people than ever today."

This is not to say that God willed Peter's death in order that He might bring about a widened ministry. Rather that, given his death, God could turn even that to good.

I remember a poignant letter I received from a reader posing a difficult question—why small children must be taken:

Our little boy was hit last spring in the street in front of our home by a truck. He died a week later. Billy was our only child. He had seemed like a gift from God, because we had hoped and prayed for a baby for two years. . . .

Then was it God's will that this little boy die such an unnecessary death? In trying to bring themselves to say with honesty, "Thy will be done", these parents found themselves confused. For along with the best physicians and surgeons they could find, they tried everything medical science knew to save their child. Then had they been working during those days against the will of God?

I understood the questions of this mother, because I had faced them all when death had invaded my life. Surely there is a difference (and it is not just a quibble) between God's ideal will and His permissive will. Thus, in my case, I cannot believe that it was God's ideal will that Peter Marshall die at forty-six.

But given a certain set of circumstances—among them Peter's inherited physique, so fine that he was inclined to overtax it—God had an alternate plan by which He could bring unimagined good even out of early death.

In the same way I could not believe that it was God's ideal will that three-year-old Billy die in such a cruel way. But given a motorised society, given our congested cities, given human free will that resulted in a driver's and a child's carelessness, God would still not suspend the operation of His universe to violate the free will that conspired to bring about this tragedy.

And so illumination came to me. By giving humans freedom of will, the Creator has chosen to limit His own power. He risked the daring experiment of giving us the freedom to make good or bad decisions, to live decent or evil lives, because God does not want the forced obedience of slaves. Instead he covets the voluntary love and obedience of sons who love Him for Himself.

This, then, is a large portion of the answer to my early question: Why does not a compassionate God hasten to remedy every wrong? I remember the way Peter Marshall answered this in a memorable sermon, "God Still Reigns", preached in Washington during the second world war:

> There is no use trying to evade the issue.
> There are times when God does not intervene—
> The fact that He does nothing is one of the most
>   baffling mysteries in the Christian life.
>
> If was H. G. Wells who voiced the dilemma
> that many troubled hearts have faced in war-time:
> "Either God has the power to stop all this
> carnage and killing and He doesn't care,
> or else He does care, and He doesn't have the
> power to stop it."
>
> But that is not the answer. . . .
> As long as there is sin in the world.

As long as there is greed
   selfishness
  hate in the hearts of men
there will be war. . . .

It is only because God is God that He is reckless
enough to allow human beings such free will as has led
the world into this present catastrophe.

God could have prevented the war!
Do you doubt for a moment that God has the power?
But suppose He had used it?
Men would then have lost their free agency . . .
They would no longer be souls endowed with the
ability to choose . . .

They would then become puppets
                 robots
              machines
       toy soldiers instead.

No, God is playing a much bigger game.
He is still awaiting an awakened sense of the
responsibility of brotherhood in the hearts of
men and women everywhere.
He will not do for us the things that we can do
for ourselves. . . .

A few years ago I was asked to conduct a Sunday evening
seminar at an exclusive girls' boarding school in the Virginia
countryside outside Washington, D.C. When I arrived I found
the high school sophomores grouped informally around a large
living room, some sitting on the Oriental rugs before a blazing
fire.

The students had been told that they might ask any questions they wished. After the first few minutes it became
obvious that, while these were intelligent girls, their questions
uncovered the most basic misunderstanding of God. One girl
voiced the query that is always asked at every church young

people's conference: "What about people in remote parts of Africa or certain jungles of South America who have never heard of Jesus Christ? Will they be condemned to eternal torment? What would be fair about that?"

Another girl, who had obviously been studying sociology, chimed in, "Let's bring the question closer home. What about individuals who become criminals because they were born into slums or other terrible surroundings where they had no chance from the beginning? How could God be just and blame them?"

A beautiful fifteen-year-old posed the one that really tugged at my heart: "There's something that really bothers me. . . ." I saw that she had tears in her eyes as she tried not to make obvious what she most wanted to ask: "My mother and father seldom go near any church. Will God condemn them to eternal damnation for that?"

I was shocked at the terrifying illusion of God that those questions revealed. The mother and father of the fifteen-year-old were dear to her. Did God love them less than she? And how would she ever be able to trust her Creator with her own happiness so long as her only emotion toward Him was terror?

The family love that was so implicit in this girl's questioning reminded me of what my own joyous childhood had taught me: God would scarcely give fathers and mothers a greater capacity for loving their children than God Himself has for loving all his children. I suggested to the girls that God would not have bothered to create father-love and mother-love in the first place, if He Himself did not have it in great abundance.

Then as I told them of my own gropings toward this answer, I thought of how grieved God must be that any of His children should cower before Him in fright. And I realised how often we attribute emotions and deeds to God that we would ascribe only to the most depraved of human minds. Probably no personality in the universe is so maligned as that of the Creator.

Soon after the evening at the girls' school, I came across this same thought in one of Hannah Whitall Smith's books:

... The amazing thing is that all sort of travesties on the character of God and libels on His goodness can find a welcome entrance into Christian hearts. ... Nothing else matters as much as this, for all our salvation depends wholly and entirely upon what God is; and unless He can be proved to be absolutely good, and absolutely unselfish, our case is hopeless. ...[4]

Then Hannah Smith relates how she discovered for herself the unselfishness of God. Between the ages of sixteen and twenty-six, she had passed through a period of scepticism. During this period God had seemed far off, an unapproachable Being, a stern and selfish Taskmaster, an Autocrat. She asked exactly the same questions that the sophomores in the girls' school asked me that Sunday evening: What about those born into circumstances for which they are not responsible and from which they cannot escape? Would vast numbers of fellow human beings therefore be doomed to eternal punishment for what they cannot help? Most of the church groups of her day taught that they would be. But, Mrs Smith wondered, would that be justice from a Creator whose tender mercies were said to be "over *all* His works"?[5]

Hannah Smith began to see in every face the anguish which resulted from sin's entrance into the world. She came to be grateful that the fashion of her day dictated veils for women in public; at least the faces before her would be blurred.

One day she was riding in a tram-car along Market Street in Philadelphia. Two men came in and sat down opposite her on the straw seat. When the conductor came for the fare, she was forced to raise her veil to count out change.

She looked up and saw clearly the faces of the two men opposite her. They were lost, debauched-looking. Not only that, but one of them was blind. A new flood of emotion rose to engulf her. In her thoughts she railed against God: "How can You bear it? You might have prevented all this misery, but You did not. Even now You might change it, but You do not. How can You go on living and endure it?"

Suddenly, there in the tram car, God seemed to answer her.

The word *lost* blazed with a tremendous illumination: nothing can be lost that is not first owned. Just as a parent is compelled by civil law to be responsible for his family and property, so the Creator—by His own divine law—is compelled to take care of the children He has created. And that means not only caring for the good children, but for the bad ones and the lost ones as well.

So the word *lost* came to be for Mrs Smith a term of greatest comfort. If a person is a "lost sinner", it only means that he is temporarily separated from the Good Shepherd who owns him. The Shepherd is bound by all duties of ownership to go after all those who are lost until they are found. For Hannah Smith the question about the plight of individuals who have had little chance in life was for ever answered. "Who can imagine a mother ever dropping a search so long as there is the least chance of finding a lost child?" Mrs Smith wrote. "Then would God be more indifferent than a mother? Since I had this sight of the mother-heart of God, I have never been able to feel the slightest anxiety for any of His children. We can trust Him . . . trust Him."

In my dealings with people I have been surprised to find that so many honestly do not believe that God wants our happiness and fulfilment. We have heard all our lives that God is Love, but we insist on "spiritualising" this. Many Christians have been taught that God's love is different from ours—not the kind His creatures understand. Deeply imbedded in our consciousness is the idea that God is primarily interested in our spiritual and moral rectitude; that, therefore, most of what He requires of us will be about as welcome as castor oil.

Of course God is concerned about our growing into mature spirits. And the God I know sometimes asks diffcult things of us, it is true. But His will also includes a happiness here on earth abundant enough to float every difficulty.

But when men persist in these mistaken and tragic ideas of the Creator, how can God show us what He is really like? This is the problem that He had with men. And He solved it in the Incarnation. If God were to break into the stream of history—come to earth as a man and demonstrate that He loved people, weep with them when they suffered, rejoice with them in moments of gladness—then there might be a closer relationship between God and His children.

A story that I first read in my late twenties helped me see why the Incarnation had to be:

One day a British scientist discovered a large anthill in his kitchen garden. These were different from any ants he had observed before, so he was eager to study them. But each time his shadow fell across the anthill, the terrified ants scurried off.

"I stepped back," the scientist wrote in his diary, "and sat down on the grass to think out the situation. I had only good will for the ants, did not wish to harm one of them. But how could I make the ants aware of my good will?

"My imagination played with the problem. To those tiny ants, I was an all-powerful creature 'somewhere up there', whose thoughts they could not guess, whose ways and intentions they could not know.

"If only I could communicate," the scientist wrote. "But even that wouldn't be enough. Even then, I would be a gigantic being to the ants, and they would never believe that I understood their problems—the minute organisation of the hill, their struggles for food, their battles with other ants.

"Only one thing could give them complete confidence. That is, if, by some alchemy, I could—for a time—become an ant—"

The gap between our understanding of the nature and the intentions of the Creator is far wider than the gap between those of ant and man. Only as much of God as could be contained in human flesh would suffice to demonstrate to us what the Father is like. That was why the Incarnation was necessary.

That was why Jesus insisted, "I have come down from heaven not to carry out my own will but the will of him who sent me. . . ."[6] and that "He who has seen me has seen the Father."[7]

Then, in watching Jesus, what did His disciples learn about God?

The most obvious thing they observed was the daily intimacy of Jesus' relationship with His Father. At first this must have puzzled them. For always He appeared to be listening to a Voice beyond Himself. There is no record of His ever having argued with anyone about the existence of God; this was fact. Also there was no doubt that God was always present to help, to guide, to succour.

Jesus acted as if there was never any question of the Father's willingness to supply all needs—even such material ones as appeasing hunger. God was concerned about men's bodies along with their souls: Divine love delighted in dispelling pain, in restoring sanity, in straightening crooked limbs and opening blind eyes, even in banishing premature death. Jesus said that in heaven there was an instant readiness to forgive and great joy over finding the lost. And are not these the things that ordinary human father-love or mother-love would delight in doing, if it could?

At every turn, Christ Himself made the comparison between human families and the Fatherhood of God. There is the unforgettable story of the universal Father dealing with the prodigal son.[8] And in the Sermon on the Mount, Jesus asked:

> Why, which of you, when asked by his son for a loaf, will hand him a stone?
> Or, if he asks a fish, will you hand him a serpent?
> Well, if for all your evil you know to give your children what is good,
> how much more will your Father in heaven give good to those who ask him?[9]

The gospels make it clear that to Jesus the Father is all-loving, is of the essence of love, cannot help loving. Moreover, this love includes the attributes of love known to all of us—good will, unselfishness, consideration, justice, wanting only good things for us, desiring our happiness. It is not a love dependent on our earning it. God is "for us" first, last, and always. By every word and action, by all the force of His personality, Christ sought to tell us that the Father is always nearer, mightier, freer to help us than we can imagine.

There were those who said that any man who held such

ideas must be mad. But the disciples who tramped the dusty roads with Jesus day after day, who witnessed His decisiveness in dealing with people, His fearlessness of criticism, His sense of the sacredness of human personality, the realism with which He faced evil, knew that this One was not mad. Indeed He was more beautifully sane than anyone they had ever known.

And so the central issue became sharper and sharper. As the late D. S. Cairns has put it so memorably in his book, *The Faith That Rebels*, "Either Jesus Christ was a dreamer about God. . . . or they and all men were dreamers, walking in the darkness and deeming it to be light. Either He alone was awake to reality . . . in His incessant summons to faith and the staking of everything upon God and His purpose of good for all mankind . . .,"[10] or else Jesus was a liar, a madman, a charlatan. There was no alternative. And the disciples were right in concluding that this was the all-important question which they and all men have to resolve.

The issue is as sharp today as it was then. I have come to believe that only if we can depend upon the Creator as a God of love (not an obscure, ethereal love, but love as you and I know it) shall we have the courage and confidence to turn our life and affairs over to Him. Hannah Smith once wrote this pithy sentence: "Perfect obedience would be perfect happiness, if only we had perfect confidence in the power we were obeying."

What builds trust like that in the Creator? Only knowing Him so well—His motives, His complete good will—being certain that no pressures will make Him change, knowing Him for a long enough time to be sure of these things.

There are many persons who claim that they have broken through to that kind of knowing—from the Apostle Paul down through spiritual adventures in every century, even to our day. "I know whom [not *what*] I have trusted," is Paul's ringing assertion, "and I am certain that he is able to keep what I have put into his hands. . . ."[11]

And we who long for an equally confident and solid base to life, how do we go about entering into that kind of relationship with God?

3: How to Enter In

SOME time before I was ten, evangelist Gypsy Smith, Junior, came to hold revival services in our town—Canton, Mississippi. A large tent was pitched on a vacant lot near the town limits. It did not prove large enough to hold the crowds that flocked there. On a platform of raw wood, from which the resin still oozed, sat the massed choirs gathered from all the churches. Their favourite anthem was "Awakening Chorus":

> The Lord Jehovah reigns, and sin is backward hurled!
> Rejoice! Rejoice! Rejoice! . . .

The "Rejoicings" reverberated so shrilly that they always raised goosebumps along my spine. As the congregation sang, the waving arms of the music director would beat out the rhythms of hymns like

> *Stan*-ding on the *prom*-i-ses of *Christ* my *king*—

> or

> *Sing* them o-ver a-*gain* to me,
> *Won*-der-ful *words* of *Life*. . . .

Each time we collectively took a breath, the pianist would run in scales, chords, and flourishes marvellous to my childish ears.

Then would come the preaching. Gypsy Smith would lean far over the crude pulpit, pausing from time to time to whip out a handkerchief and wipe his flushed, perspiring face or to take a drink of water. His was a sincere testimony. The emotion in his preaching would steadily mount, tranferring itself to the congregation. And finally a hush would fall over the tent, as the choir sang almost in a whisper.

> Softly and tenderly Jesus is calling,
> Calling for you and me. . . .

"Believe on the Lord Jesus Christ, and thou shalt be saved," the evangelist would thunder. "That's all you have to do. Accept the Lord Jesus as your personal Saviour."

Soon at the far edge of the tent someone would rise and slowly make his way down the aisle toward the front. Then another person—and another—and another—and another.

From those evangelistic meetings of my childhood, I thought that "believing on the Lord Jesus Christ" simply meant being fully persuaded that what the church believed about Christ's divinity was true.

This did not seem difficult. In fact, it was not long after the revival tent had been packed up and moved to another town that I decided to join the church. One Sunday at the close of the regular morning service in our church, my preacher-father issued "the invitation". On an impulse, I rose, marched down the aisle, and so became a member of the First Presbyterian Church of Canton. Because I had marched spontaneously, I remember my father was so moved that he stood in front of the altar and looked at me through eyes swimming with tears behind his spectacles.

Years passed. Not until my college days did I recognise that something was missing in this inherited Christianity based on an untested assent. By that time I had acquired a parallel King James—Moffatt New Testament. Moffatt's translation brought the ancient words alive for me.

I found that the evangelist of my childhood had been right in insisting that the only way we can really know God is by looking at Jesus Christ. Christ is the centre of Christianity. To pretend anything else—that we need think of Him only as a good man who was also a great teacher, for instance—is not Christianity, whatever else it may be.

But I was also astonished to discover that no mere intellectual acceptance of Christ's divinity would have satisfied Jesus as a way of entrance into His kingdom. He will settle for nothing less than making Him the ruler of one's life, with the inevitable result of a practical day-by-day obedience: "Why call ye me Lord, Lord, and do not the things which I say?"[1]

No wonder marching down the church aisle had not changed me one whit.

I feel that I have come to a crisis in my life [I wrote in the journal I was keeping during these college years]. It's very easy for me to see how people can lose their so-called religion when they have gotten enough education to make them think at all. That is very likely to happen to anyone whose religion is simply an inheritance or a habit. Unless something intervenes, it could happen to me.

My religion is not on a very firm basis, I'm afraid I have had no vital experience. God doesn't seem real to me. I believe now—because of people I know who do have something vital and real, like Peter Marshall. But I can't go on like this. What are we here in this world for anyway?

This questioning may have seemed like a prelude to change, but the fact is that I did "go on that way" for many years, even after my graduation and marriage to the young preacher, Peter Marshall.

During those years I was an active, interested minister's wife. In addition to my home making, I attended women's meetings, led Bible studies, made talks, called on parishioners, and took part in programme-committee meetings. Obviously most of this work was on the organisational level. Even when I led Bible studies for small groups of women or gave a talk or book review, I was still relying mostly on other people's ideas about the Christian life. Those who listened carefully must have missed the authentic note of personal experience.

During all this time, I never stopped struggling to find the way to God for myself. Peter's preaching was a never-ending challenge to me:

The Christian Church in its early days grew in numbers and in influence because God used the testimonies of men and women who had something to say about Jesus. What they had to say was that this Jesus, who had died on a cross, was alive and spiritually present every day to the disciples.
And they proclaimed everywhere they went, with enthusiasm

and conviction, the good news of the gospel. It was to them
the thrilling and exciting story of how life had been changed
for them,
  and how they had been changed for life.
They could no more keep silent than a flower can withhold
its fragrance or the sun keep back its light. This power that
had made them different, they said, was available to anyone
who would believe . . .
Sins could be forgiven: Christ could come into human life
to change natures and dispositions
 to change moods and temperaments
  to banish fear and worry
  to remove shame and guilt
 to provide a new dynamic, a new purpose in life,
a new joy and a peace that nothing could destroy.
The early disciples were thrown into prison.
They were persecuted
   boycotted
   hounded from place to place.
Yet thousands joined their fellowship and discovered the
truth they were proclaiming, and found life becoming a new
and thrilling experience. . . .

Why—under preaching like that, and especially when the
preacher was so close at hand to answer my questions and to
help—could I not make contact with the Christ whom Peter
knew so well? Perhaps I was still not ready. So often this
personal encounter with God comes through crisis. Peter's had
been a vocational crisis, when he had had to decide whether
or not he would leave his native Scotland to enter the ministry.
So far my life had been protected, serene, free of urgent need.
There was only that deep gnawing ache for Something More
that I had known since college days.

Then, in March 1943, came the event that was to change my
life. A routine physical check-up brought bad news. Chest
X-rays showed a soft spotting over both lungs. Specialists were
unable to make a conclusive diagnosis, but the trouble appeared
to be tuberculosis. *Tuberculosis!* Hated word, hated disease. I

was ordered to bed twenty-four hours a day for an indefinite period.

Fifteen months later I had gained some fifteen pounds; otherwise nothing was changed. The area of infection was as widespread as at the beginning. When other specialists were consulted, they rejected the usual pneumothorax treatment, as well as surgery, or even the use of the drugs that were then beginning to be used in TB cases. Their only advice was "More bad rest." When we asked "How long?" they said frankly they had no idea.

Despair settled in. After almost a year and a half in bed, I could see few gains. My husband and four-year-old son needed me. Our household situation was becoming more difficult with every month that passed.

Often during those discouraging days there was a vivid picture in my mind: I was groping my way along a pitch-black tunnel. There were passages, twistings and turnings off the main tunnel. I tried this way and that. Repeatedly I found only dead ends and was forced to grope my way back to the black centre shaft. I clung to the hope that somehow, sometime, I would emerge from darkness into the sunlight again. But in order to get there, I had to proceed resolutely straight ahead. I knew by now that there were no short cuts. Did this mean that I had to deal directly with God, who was insisting through circumstances that He alone knew the shortest way to the sunlight of His presence?

There was in me a desire for an all-out effort to reach Him, born of desperation. Sloughed off now were all the trappings of religion, most of them concerned with the ceremonial or organisational aspects of churches that so often confuse the central issue. I began to see wholeness as more than the search for physical health. As I understood the viewpoint of Jesus, it was that physical soundness is merely part of a more profound wholeness. In this sense, wholeness can only come about as inner cleavages are healed, as man is joined to the Source of his being. Thus, for me, the search for health became the search for a relationship with God. The question was, what was blocking that relationship?

I stood before my Maker starkly, stripped of pretences. My unworthiness shrieked at me. My tendency to over-criticalness, to harsh, hasty judgments. My little jealousies, the self-centredness that had made me a poor one for teamwork of any kind. Lying in bed I summoned up the dishonesties of my past. Once in high school I had cheated on an algebra test. Another time, when I had been treasurer of a school organisation, I had "borrowed" some money from the fund and then paid it back ten days later.

There were dishonesties of a different sort: I had not always been candid with my husband. I saw in myself a streak of secretiveness, a tendency to bar him from a corner of my mind and heart. I well knew that this was no way to build a solid marriage.

Through agonising days I made methodical notes on these ignoble traits and deeds. Then I asked Peter to hear me out on the ones that affected him. He listened, looking pained, not so much at what I was confessing as at the spiritual anguish he saw in me.

I then felt it necessary to write two letters—one to the high school principal who had taught algebra, the other to the teacher who had been faculty adviser to the school organisation. Since the last thing I wanted was to be considered a religious crackpot, I laboured over the wording of the letters. In each case, as matter-of-factly as I could, I told why I felt it necessary to write the letter: that this was one of the steps which would help me to enter into a new and total Christian experience. Three days passed before I could muster enough courage to mail those letters. In the end, I posted them only because I knew that my relationship with God now meant more to me than the reputation that I had once thought all-important.

Both recipients of the letters turned out to be as generous and forgiving as people usually are when confronted with honest confession.

Then Peter, through his preaching, taught me the next step to God. Facing up to ourselves in confession is therapeutic, provided we move on to forgiveness and do not wallow in our wrongdoing. It is possible to over-emphasise the self-centred-ness, the me-first angle, even in relation to our sins: "Look at me, what a great sinner I've been. My case is worse than most. God is going to have to do a special job on me . . . *I* . . . *I* . . . *I*. . . ."

Having confessed every wrong that had surfaced to my conscious mind, I then specifically claimed God's promise of I John 1:9: "If we confess our sins, He is faithful and just to forgive us our sins, and to cleanse us from all unrighteousness." Then I proceeded to burn the list and the notes I had made as a symbol that everything was, from that moment, forgiven—forgotten—gone for ever.

No doubt the burning was a childish procedure. Yet in this way I stumbled on the value of dramatising and thus making more real—that is, more real for myself—a definite transaction with God.

So now the house cleaning was over—except for one thing. I was aware that a psychiatrist would scarcely regard my amateur self-probing as a thorough enough job of analysis. So I prayed that God would see to it that any residue of debris in the subconscious would eventually come to light, or that He would deal with anything left by pouring His cleansing and healing Spirit into those subterranean levels.

In subsequent months more of the debris did come into my consciousness. For instance, I became aware of a compartment in my being in which I had locked certain persons whom I disliked. They could go their way; I would go mine. But now Christ seemed to be standing by the locked door saying, "That isn't forgiveness. It won't do. No closed doors are allowed. The Kingdom of God is the kingdom of right relationships. Remember what I said—'If ye forgive no men their trespasses neither will your Father forgive your trespasses?' If you cannot forgive, you cannot enter the kingdom. This unforgiveness grieves me more than any cheating on an algebra test."

By the time I had faced up to this, it was the summer of 1944, time for our annual trek back to the Cape Cod cottage. I got there only by Peter's special arrangements—a compart-ment on the train and an ambulance to meet me at the station.

Later that June, early one morning I was reading Jesus' parable about the cleansed house:

> When an unclean spirit leaves a man, it roams through dry places in search of refreshment and finds none. Then it says "I will go back to the house I left," and when it comes it finds the house vacant, clean and all in order. Then it goes off to find seven other spirits worse than itself; they go in and dwell there, and the last state of that man is worse than the first. . . .[2]

There was danger, then, in my attempts to clean house unless the Spirit of God took over the house. The keys and the management of my house had to be turned over to Christ. For how could I ask Him to heal me until He was completely in charge? Any human physician requires the surrender of a given case into his care; he can do nothing unless the patient agrees to follow his orders. Common sense told me that exactly the same was true of the Great Physician.

So that sunshiny June morning, I got out of bed and stood at the bedroom window looking out at the garden that Peter had so lovingly planted . . . Roses and white hollyhocks, yellow day lilies, zinnias, all a riot of colour . . . A blue, blue sky above . . . The sea just over the brow of the hill. There I stood and took the plunge. It amounted to a quiet pledge to God, the promise of a blank cheque with my life:

"It is ten-twelve A.M. on the twenty-second of June 1944," I said. "From this moment I promise that I'll try to do whatever You tell me for the rest of my life, in so far as You'll make it clear to me what Your wishes are. I'm weak and many times I'll probably want to renege on this. But, Lord, You'll have to help me with that too."

I took a deep breath; I was trembling. I had entered in. Yet nothing seemed different. The hollyhock faces still nodded at the window. Fluffy clouds still floated in that blue, blue sky. I turned and noted in my journal the date and the hour of the promise I had just made. There would be moments in the future when this pledge would not seem real to me. But it was real, and writing it down would help to remind me.

I felt no emotion other than the relief of knowing that I had completed my part so far as I knew it. This brought me a peace of mind I had not known during the tortuous days of self-probing and writing the letters of confession.

The proof of the reality of the pledge I had made began coming during the next six weeks. My physical condition was improving. Each morning I would lie in the yard, soaking up sunshine. Next I tried joining the family for dinner each night. That did not tire me over much. Then I began taking short walks some afternoons with Jeffrey, our cocker spaniel, trotting beside me. It was a joy to stand at the top of the rise in the road and see the sea again, feel the tangy salt air on my cheeks, laugh at the sea-wind blowing back Jeffrey's floppy ears as he stood poised, watching the circling gulls. It was even good to feel sand in my shoes. As of old, I began taking an interest in the garden and the kitchen. Perhaps I could take it as my job to arrange some flowers each day for the house. And would it be possible for the family to gather some beach plums for jelly? I could not help much with the jelly-making, but perhaps a little. It was like coming to life again. And life was good, so good. The speck of light at the other end of the tunnel was becoming a steady beam.

God deals differently with each of us. He knows no "typical" case. He seeks us out at a point in our own need and longing and runs down the road to meet us. This individualised treatment should delight rather than confuse us, because it so clearly reveals the highly personal quality of God's love and concern.

At the same time, there is one central core of the entering-in or commitment experience that is common to everyone who undergoes it. It is the act of putting oneself—past, present, and future—into God's hands to do with as He pleases.

A girl once asked me, "But isn't that a terrible risk?"

Yes, it certainly would be, if we had a God who wanted to deprive us of joy rather than add joy to our lives, if He were not a God who cares supremely for us and our welfare. But what He wants for us is exactly what every thoughtful parent wants for his child—that pure, deep-flowing joy that springs out of maturity and fulfilment.

That God is like this, each of us must discover for ourselves. There is only one difficulty. The discovery comes second, the act of will first. The order of events can never be reversed: action on our part, that is, the decision to hand our life over to God and the promising of obedience; then, and only then, come understanding and the unfolding knowledge of the character of God.

This decision need not be dramatic or emotional. It is just as real, though it be but a quiet assent without any emotion whatsoever. This has been vividly demonstrated to me recently by John Sherrill, now a dear friend.

As with most of us, it was personal need that brought John to the point of commitment. My need had been a long illness. John's was a more immediate physical crisis. Three years before he had had a malignant mole removed from his ear which had been diagnosed as melanoma, one of the most vicious killers of all types of cancer. Miraculously—everyone felt—it had been caught in time. But now the doctor had discovered a small lump on John's neck that was suspect.

The details of the physical problems and the prayers for healing are not the point that I want to make here. Suffice it to say that as soon as I heard about the situation, I knew that John's crisis was also my crisis—part of "my bundle" of responsibility, as the Quakers express it so vividly. Then—how were we who were so concerned to pray about John?

A series of thoughts kept pounding at me and would not be put aside: healing is not an end in itself; it is a dividend of the gospel. Physical health is but one part of total wholeness. Then came the inevitable question: had John ever made an act of turning his whole being over to God?

Who was I to ask John a question like that? He was an intellectual—an editor and successful writer. Any emotional approach to Christianity as well as the usual religious clichés and shibboleths, were repugnant to him. Considering all this, would not any question about his relationship to God be gross presumption on my part and anathema to him?

Still, time was running out. Only twenty-four hours remained until John would enter New York's Memorial Hospital for surgery. After all, what he thought of me did not matter at a time like this. The fact that a life was at stake gave me the courage to telephone John and tell him that I had to see him.

His wife, Tibby, came with him. The three of us found a quiet room and shut ourselves in. There was no attempt at a subtle approach. I explained what had led up to my telephone call, what I had learned about the process of entering in, and why this seemed important as a foundation for any prayer for healing. My heart was in what I was saying, so that several times my voice broke.

When I had finished, John asked wonderingly, "Do you mean that I can just decide that I am willing for God to take over my life, and tell Him so—as blandly and as matter-of-factly as that—and have it work?"

"That's right," was my reply. "Do it as matter-of factly as you please. You do not have to have all your theological beliefs sorted out either. Nor do you have to understand everything. You just come to Christ as you are—questions, complexes, contradictions, doubts, everything. After all, how else can any of us come? You make a definite movement of your will toward God. After that, the next move is up to Him. The feelings, the proof that He has heard and has taken you on, even the understanding will come later."

At that point John and Tib had to rush away for their last hasty preparations for the hospital. It was not until later that I found out what happened immediately after they left me.

"After we told you good-bye and backed out of your driveway," John told me. "I did the simple thing you had suggested —just said 'Yes' to God while driving the car. I can show you the exact spot on Millwood Road where it happened, right by a certain telephone pole.

"Then because it had been such a quiet, interior thing, I felt that I ought to go on record by telling someone. So I said to Tib, I suppose a bit ruefully, 'Well, I'm a Christian now.'

"And she asked curiously, 'Do you feel any different?'

"'Not a bit different,' I told her."

Yet John is different now—so different. The quiet transaction at that certain spot on Millwood Road was real enough because never have I seen so much action on God's part in the life of one man in one short year. That too, is another story—an exciting one which is his to tell, not mine. Some day I hope he will. But I can at least add that, when the famous New York specialist operated, all he could find was a dried-up *nodule,* easy to remove. There was no malignancy.

Church folk often give the impression that there are only two ways of entering into the Christian life: being born into a Christian family or stumbling into a dramatic religious experience as an adult. Either approach to Christianity seems to have two unfortunate factors in common: the initiative was apparently not with the individual and the way to God was clouded in vagueness.

I am convinced that God never meant for anything about the Christian life to be vague, least of all the steps by which we enter into a meaningful relationship with Him. The obscurity must surely be on our side, not God's.

Growing up in a believing family is not to be under-valued. It is still the ideal beginning, because it is the foundation of the happiest possible childhood. Yet I know now that something more is needed: each human being must enter into Life for himself. There is, therefore, no such thing as inheriting Christianity.

David du Plessis, a minister from South Africa and a new friend, recently told me a fascinating story about himself and this matter of an inherited Christianity.

"It happened one cold January night, really cold—in fact five degrees below zero. I had been sleeping soundly, then woke suddenly about four in the morning. I thought that a voice had wakened me. But as I lay there listening, there was no sound except the creak of snow-laden branches outside the bedroom window and the measured breathing of the children in the adjoining room.

"Then the voice came again. This sounds peculiar, I realise, but I don't honestly know whether it was an audible voice or not. At any rate, the words were clear enough, though they seemed nonsensical: 'God has no grandsons.' Just that—nothing more.

"Well, I snapped on my bedside light and reached for a Bible with a concordance in the back. I looked up the word *grandson*. No such reference anywhere in the Scriptures. Then I looked up *grandfather*. Not there.

"Sons? Yes, lots of references. 'Behold what manner of love the Father hath bestowed on us, that we should be called the sons of God. . . .' 'For as many as are led by the Spirit of God, they are the sons of God.' And lots more, a long list of them.

"But," I wondered, "what did these references have to do with God having no grandsons? Yet this one sentence had been clearly imprinted on my consciousness. More puzzled than ever, I finally turned off the light and went back to sleep.

"I didn't find out myself until ten days after the sentence was first given to me," he said. "I was aboard a plane, *en route* from Milwaukee to Chicago—when suddenly I knew.

"When Christ's apostles first started preaching, they insisted that every individual had to have a personal encounter with Christ and make the decision to accept His way—for himself. Judging from history, there must have been plenty of vitality in that first-century church—enough to shake the sophisticated Roman world to its depths.

"Well, the years passed. After a while those first followers of Christ began to reason. 'These children of ours were born into a Christian family. They have grown up in the church and have been instructed in the faith. They were born Christians. Surely they don't need any special experience of repentance as we did.'

"The church pews were soon filled with the sons and daughters of those first followers. But since the children had inherited their belief in Christ, they knew Him only second-hand.

"Perhaps it was not surprising that by the second century the vitality of the church had begun to decline. Proofs of God's power, like healing through faith, became the exception rather than the rule.

"Sure, in every century, there are always some who have

had a personal confrontation with Christ. During revival periods—like the time of Luther in Germany, or the Wesleyan Revival in England—large numbers have had the personal experience of being truly born again to become sons of God.

"But then in the following generation, the same sad process starts over. And soon the pews are filled again largely with secondhand believers—grandsons and granddaughters."

My friend had unintentionally stated what had been my own case. I understood why my inherited faith had not been enough. I had been a prime example of a "granddaughter". *And God has no grandsons or granddaughters.*

I wonder how many others there are who have thought of formal church membership as a substitute for that direct Father-child relationship that God really wants of us? No wonder much of our religious life today is plagued by vagueness. Let us not mistake it: Entering in does take childlikeness. The door through which we enter into Life is a low door. And sometimes it is the humble and the needy who can show the rest of us the way.

So a group of ministers recently discovered. One of them, Bruce Larson of *Faith at Work* magazine, told me this story. They had gathered for a two-day retreat at a church in New Jersey to discuss mutual problems and to pray about them. As so often happens, the discussion part predominated. It was late afternoon of the final day when a startling event occurred.

Suddenly the door of their meeting-room opened and a stranger walked in. The minister of the host church knew him, had seen him often around the neighbourhood. Self-consciously the man seated himself at the fringe of the circle. Though there was no more than a momentary pause in the discussion, the experienced eyes of the other clergymen present took in the situation—the watery eyes, the sagging shoulders, the seedy clothing. Obviously the man was an alcoholic.

The discussion continued, while the stranger listened. "It seems to me," a crisp voice said, "that all we have been talking about these two days can be summed up in our need for God's power—the kind of power that changes lives, heals, restores that—"

He stopped, his attention arrested by the agitated movements of the stranger.

"That's it! That's what I need. I could use some of that."

There was sudden silence. While everyone watched, his bleary eyes filled a bit more and the quavering voice continued.

"My name is Ernie. I drink too much. People have tried to help me ... doctors, hospitals, clinics, missions, and all that. But I ... I can't seem to stop. How do I get this power you're talking about?"

The question hung, quivering in the silence. Despite the fact that these men were experienced in dealing with people in need, the intrusion was embarrassing. There was a time schedule for the meeting, trains and planes to be caught, families to get back to, next Sunday's sermons to think about. Closing time was at hand.

Finally, a white-haired man spoke up. "Ernie, all of us have problems too. It's a problem-filled world. ..." The voice of the elderly minister was gentle, suave, as he sought to identify with the stranger. All of the men knew that the pastor who was speaking had had professional training in counselling.

"As to how we can get God's help. Well, that isn't always too easy. It takes patience, time. There are many roads to God many avenues by which—"

"Damn!" The interruption was explosive, passionate.

"Damn ... Damn ... Damn ... Damn!"

The quiet of the room was suddenly being blasted by Ted, a young minister and a former businessman, anger and impatience written clearly on his face. Again and again he beat his fist down on the seat of the empty chair beside him.

"This man doesn't want to hear about our problems," Ted said vehemently. "He's asked us a question—how can he get God's help to stop drinking? We haven't answered him. If we don't know the answer, then let's adjourn this meeting, stop our endless talking, go home and tell our people that the church hasn't any answers for today. In that case, we'd better stop being hypocrites and shut the church doors for good."

There was a shocked silence, but the impassioned words had cleared the air. Almost simultaneously, five or six men—

including the angry young preacher and the white-haired minister—rose and walked over to Ernie.

Ted knelt in front of the alcoholic. "Ernie, do you believe that Jesus Christ can come into your life and change it?"

The watery eyes looked down, childlike. "Yes . . . Yes, I do."

"Then we're going to pray right now, Ernie, that He will do this for you."

The young minister took both of Ernie's hands in his. The white-haired preacher stood behind, placed both hands gently on top of the alcoholic's head. The others stood around in a semi-circle, each one with his hands on the stranger.

Ted's prayer was short, hard-hitting, impassioned. He asked for Christ's healing power for Ernie, for the forgiveness of sins, for the beginning of a new life.

"Now, Ernie," Ted said, "you pray too. Just thank God that He has heard you and healed you."

"I hope so," Ernie quavered.

"Not hope so. He *has!*"

"I—Well, I'd like to believe that."

The answer was gentle, but firm. "Ernie, thank Jesus that He has already come into your life."

The room became completely still. And then in wavery sentences Ernie's voiced reached up to God. "God, I'm a tired, weak old man. I don't see what use I am to anyone. But I'd like to find the new life they talk about. Please help me."

It was real. It was vital. Every man in the room knew it, felt it. They had been talking about power. This *was* power.

Forgotten were train schedules, plane reservations, other obligations. For the first time in two days, real contact had been made with God through one of the least likely of persons. The air was charged with emotion. Out from the depths came some of the deep needs of the ministers themselves.

A pastor from New England began it. At first his words seemed unrelated—"I was driving down here several days ago, feeling lonely and apart from God. While crossing over Bear Mountain Bridge, I looked in the ice-clogged river and saw a small boat locked in the ice some distance off shore.

"That boat fascinated me. For my life has been like that.

Frozen, isolated, shut within myself. I'm frozen with the fear of other people's opinions, the fear of not being a success, the fear of not pleasing people."

Suddenly his eyes filled with tears. "Would you pray for me, that I'll get thawed out so I can really help people again?"

There was no hesitation now. The men quickly gathered around him. All but Ernie, who hung back, shyly. But the young minister walked over to him.

"Ernie, come on over and pray with the rest of us."

"Oh no! I couldn't do *that*. . . ."

The minister took him by the hand. "Look, Ernie, you've received; now you must give. And *we* need *you* now."

So Ernie knelt beside the minister and prayed with the others. The prayer was very simple. And in this room miraculously filled with power, every one of the ministers made his way back to God with a childlike renewal of commitment.

Later the minister from New England was marvelling to the young preacher at the turn of events. "As long as I live, I'll never get over it," he said. "What had happened to Ernie minutes before was the real thing. The proof was that it was Ernie, with his winey breath in my face, who was God's channel for transmitting the power. It was like electricity flowing through him to me." And he added with awe in his voice, "Except ye become as little children ye shall not enter into the kingdom of heaven. . . ."

And so we enter in, each of us, up our own secret stairs into the most joyous and rewarding relationship of our lives. The good news is that this is no experience meant just for the saints. God welcomes us no matter what our lives have been, no matter what we have done or have failed to do, whether we feel adequate or broken or merely empty.

And the rest of the good news is that the way into the Christian life need not be vague. Sometimes laymen who approach Christianity with few preconceived ideas can be surprisingly specific and helpful. A case in point is the twelve steps toward God outlined by Alcoholics Anonymous. Out of great need and hard experience, the men who were the founders of this movement hammered out the steps. When I

first read them, years after my own entering-in experience, I
was astonished to find that this path to sobriety was precisely
the road I had travelled on my way to a personal commitment
to Christ. I have changed only a few words:

1. We admit helplessness in one or more specific areas of
   our lives.
2. We believe that there is a Power greater than ourselves.
3. We make a decision to turn our lives over to the care of
   God as we understand Him.
4. We make a searching and fearless inventory of ourselves.
5. We admit to God, to ourselves, and to another human
   being the exact nature of our wrongs.
6. We are ready for God to change us, to remove these
   defects of character.
7. Humbly we ask Him to do so.
8. We make a list of all the people we have harmed, and we
   become willing to make amends to them all.
9. We make direct amends to such people when possible,
   when to do so would not injure them or others.
10. At intervals we continue to take personal inventory, and
    when we are wrong, promptly admit it.
11. Through daily prayer and meditation, we seek to improve
    our conscious contact with God as we understand Him,
    praying only for the knowledge of His will for us and for
    the power to carry it out.
12. We try to carry this message to others and to practice
    these principles in all our affairs.

The way to God is a clearly marked, well-travelled road.
Only one question remains to us: Do we really want to find
our way down that road?

Do we really want to enter in?

4: The Secret of the Will

SOME years before Peter Marshall's death, a man approached him on the sidewalk outside the church following a Sunday-morning service. The stranger introduced himself as a visitor to Washington, a used-car dealer from St. Paul, Minnesota. He had a direct blunt manner. What he had to say so impressed Peter that he told me about their conversation as we were driving home.

As I remember, the point that the man was making went something like this: "Dr Marshall, you challenged me this morning to want to apply Jesus' teachings to life. But as a business man, I'm puzzled by what appears to be a lack of realism in what Christ told us to do—such as in the Sermon On the Mount. Have you ever known anyone who loved his neighbour as much as himself? Or who's willing to turn the other cheek all the time? Or who never has a lustful thought? I'll even make a special trip back to Washington to hear you, if you'll promise to preach a sermon telling *how* we can do what Christ asked."

Like the used-car dealer, many of us are puzzled about the *hows* of Christianity. For some years, I too wondered if there were some principle involved here, some secret that I had somehow missed.

The day that I found the answer—in the book mentioned so often in these pages, *The Christian's Secret of a Happy Life*— I felt like someone who had stumbled on buried treasure. Hannah Smith, in turn, had learned the secret from a book called *Spiritual Progress*, written by the Frenchman, François Fénelon, who lived during the seventeenth century. Fénelon was a cleric with an extraordinary insight into human nature. He was spiritual adviser to the lowly and the great, including Madame de Maintenon and the Duke of Burgundy, heir to the throne of France.

Where Fénelon and others learned the secret, stretching back to the New Testament writers, I do not know. But this I do know: in my life this formula has been the answer to the how.

The secret is simply this: that the Christian life must be lived in the will, not in the emotions; that God regards the decisions and choices of a man's will as the decisions and choices of the man himself—no matter how contrary his emotions may be. Moreover, when this principle is applied, the emotions must always capitulate to the will.

At birth, as I have pointed out, God gives each human being the gift of freedom of will. Under no circumstances will God ever violate this central citadel of man's being. The picture in the book of Revelation of Christ standing, knocking, outside the closed door of the human heart, I believe to be a literal picture:

> ... if any man hear my voice, and open the door,
> I will come in to him, and will sup with him,
> and he with me.[1]

But the latch of the door is on the inside. It is our hand that must open the door. It is our voice that must invite Christ in. Genuine freedom of will permits no door crashing, not even from the Lord of glory!

Before the entering-in decision, we have probably thought that we belonged to ourselves, that what we did with ourself was our business. We reasoned that, since God gave us intelligence, He intended that we use it for all those decisions that go to make up a life—a career, whom we shall marry, where we will live, how we shall rear our children. Self-interest, what the self thought it wanted, what seemed best to the self —these have been the deciding factors.

But if the man is to enter in, he must decide that, while this intelligent self-interest may seem good, there is a better way. A man must will that self abdicate its throne; that henceforth Christ's will determines action. And this movement of the will —that decision-making part of man—must be made without paying any attention to the emotions.

It is important that we should not gauge the reality of spiritual experience by our feelings. A sixteen-year-old girl posed this question to me in a letter: "How can one be sure he is a Christian? If a person has asked Christ with sincerity to come into his heart, but still doesn't feel any different, well—how can he know whether He has or not?"

The key to her quandary, it seemed to me, was the word *feel*. We petition, we pray, we wait, but we do not "feel" any different. Feelings are at the bottom of most of our Christian difficulties. Our emotions are often painfully misleading, and at best we have imperfect control over them. This should come as no surprise, for psychology tells us that these emotions often rise up out of the depths of the subconscious, even out of the emotional set of ancestors long dead, out of the race consciousness. Our feelings can be affected by such irrelevant matters as the mood of those around us, by whether we have a good night's sleep, by hunger or indigestion, or by a morning in which the rain blew through the open window, spattered the wallpaper, and the neighbourhood dogs turned over the garbage pail. "I don't feel God's presence today," we wail.

What is the remedy? It is simplicity itself: Our emotions are not the real us. The motivating force at the centre of our physical being is our will. The dictionary describes *will* as "the power of conscious deliberate action". The will is the governing power in us, the rudder, the spring of all our actions. Before God we are responsible only for the set of that will—whether we decide for God's will or insist on self-will. Our Maker knows that our feelings are unruly, unreliable gauges. So if we see to it that our intentions (our motives) are right, we can trust God to see to the results.

If the girl who is not sure that she is a Christian will make a definite act of giving her will to God, even though she feels nothing at all, in God's eyes that is a real transaction—done, finished. As soon as she accepts the truth of this, God will handle her emotions. Eventually she *will feel* different. Eventually she *will feel* God's presence. The emotions trail behind the will. In the interval, she must not be led astray by ephemeral emotional responses to a date that turns out badly or ants that invade the picnic basket.

Does this sound too simple? Actually, I believe it to be the only principle that makes entering the Christian life possible.

It is a theory that works in real life. I think of what happened in the case of the late Fulton Oursler—for years editor of *Liberty* magazine and senior editor of *Reader's Digest* at the time of his death. Perhaps best known for his *The Greatest Story Ever Told,* Oursler was for years a close friend and associate of my husband Len.

At thirty Mr Oursler was a self-styled agnostic. He believed in no absolutes of right and wrong, certainly not in anything approaching the supernatural. As he described himself, he was "genially loyal to ethical standards when they did not interfere too much with what I wanted to do. But I sneered at God as an elaborate self-deception and did all that I could to tear down the faith of those close to me."[2]

Then trouble surrounded Fulton Oursler in all phases of his life. *Liberty* went under, so he was out of a job. At the same time there were health and marriage difficulties. There came the day when he realised that he was absolutely helpless to do one thing for himself.

What happened then is vividly described by Oursler himself in a book he later wrote, *Why I Know There Is a God.* On a blustery day with dark clouds lowering, the distraught man wandered down Fifth Avenue in New York City. He stopped in front of a church—self-conscious, filled with conflicting emotions, but knowing that unless he got help he had come to the end of the way. For the first time in years, he ventured inside a church. Let him tell the rest of it in his own words:

"In ten minutes or less I may change my mind," he prayed. "I may scoff at this—and love error again. Pay no attention to me then. For this little time I am in right mind and heart. This is my best. Take it and forget the rest; and if You are really there, help me."

What Mr Oursler did in the quiet church was what Hannah Smith meant by setting the rudder of the will and diregarding everything else—conflicting thoughts, contrary feelings. And God must have accepted this as the real decision of the real man, exactly as Hannah insisted that He always does. Within two weeks Fulton Oursler's problems began to resolve.

"Only chance would explain it to the unbelieving," he said later, "because nothing either I or anyone else did contrived the events. The complications dissolved ... by what the rationalist would call a series of beautiful coincidences God literally took over my life, took it out of my hands."

The more impressive proof that God accepted Fulton Oursler's gift of his will that day in the church is the massive contribution to the religious life of the nation that Mr Oursler made during the remainder of his life. A knowing, spirited faith replaced his former agnosticism. Lost in emptiness, he found direction. His enthusiasms, his intensity, his insatiable love of a good story that had once poured into murder mysteries, plays, and movie scripts he now dedicated to the building up of faith in others. Since that experience his work includes some eighteen books, an endless succession of articles, and his column "Modern Parables", syndicated in about a hundred newspapers. When he was stricken with a heart attack on May 23, 1952, his *The Greatest Faith Ever Known* was interrupted in mid-sentence.

The principle of the will has the most practical sort of application to numerous everyday difficulties. At the moment we have a home-grown illustration of it with our twelve-year-old daughter, Linda. She is having corrective dentistry to straighten her teeth. After she wore braces for a year, the dentist fitted her with a retainer, a complicated and expensive plastic device to correct the bite. The trouble is that the retainer is removable.

On too many evenings we have had a scene like this:

"Linda, where is your retainer?"

Silence. Then a slightly bewildered expression on her pretty freckled face. "I don't know."

"Did you wear it to school this morning?"

"Yes—but I took it out during lunch."

"And then?"

"Some of the girls started passing it around from hand to hand under the table . . . just in fun, of course."

We give her a glassy stare. "Fun? But not very sanitary! Don't you know that—"

Linda, sensing that a real outburst is coming, adds quickly, "It's in my purse. I'm sure it is. Pretty sure, that is."

"Would you mind looking?"

Linda soon returns, holding the troublesome item aloft. There is a mild note of triumph in her voice. "See—all safe. It wasn't in the purse though. It was in the glove compartment of the car."

We bite our lips helplessly, make no comment. Then— "Linda, how *are* we going to get you to wear it regularly?"

"I don't know" (the stock answer for everything).

More months pass. More hairbreadth rescues of retainer from cars, a doctor's office, the front lawn. Once it had to be mailed back from her grandmother's. Then one day Linda bequeathed it to the Pennsylvania Railroad by leaving it in a ladies' room on one of their trains. She remembered it hours later, after the train was hundreds of miles away. Correspondence with the railroad revealed that my English—even with a thesaurus—was not up to an adequate description of a retainer. Anyway they had not seen it. So back Linda went to the dentist to be fitted for a new one, while her Daddy ground his own teeth thinking about the bill.

The dentist warned Linda that if she kept forgetting, she would undo his two years of work. Neither warnings nor naggings helped. Finally, I decided to try out on her the principle about the will.

One night before her prayers I suggested that because the retainer was clumsy and uncomfortable, something deep inside her had decided "I don't want to wear it, so I won't remember."

"Do you know what it is to have will-power, Linda?" I asked.

"Yes, I think so."

"What does it mean to you?"

"To do something I don't want to do," she answered after some hesitation.

"That's pretty good. You remember that we have told you that all through your life you will have to do certain things that you may not enjoy doing. You can try to make yourself do these hateful things by will-power. But Linda, there's a much better way. If you tell God that you're willing to have Him change you, so that you'll like doing what you must do, then He will. It really works!"

That night Linda added to her bedtime prayers, "God I hate the old retainer. But I know that if I don't wear it, I won't have pretty teeth. So I'm willing to have You change me on the inside, so that I *want* to wear, want to remember—and then I will."

After praying this way several nights in a row, the problem of the retainer was on its way to being solved. When Linda set the rudder of her will in the right direction, so that God's will became her will, then she no longer had trouble remembering, and she was no longer miserable wearing it.

Remembering a retainer may seem unimportant beside the big issues of life. Yet I have seen this principle of the will operate just as successfully in some of the knottiest, most soul-rendering situations life can hand us.

Several years ago a veteran pilot was forced to land a passenger plane in a dense fog in California. The instructions from the tower were apparently not clear to him. To the horror of all who were there to meet the plane—mostly wives and children—the plane crashed at the edge of the landing field and burned. All aboard were killed.

The Civil Aeronautics Board's investigation and findings fixed the blame on the pilot. Many who knew the circumstances felt that this was unfair. In any case, it compounded the widow's grief. It was devastating enough to lose her husband, but it seemed more than she could bear to have him blamed for the death of twenty-three other human beings.

I am acquainted with the pilot's widow and her three daughters. The problem she posed to me was: "How *can* I let go my resentment at the unfairness of this and find peace again?"

Nothing in my experience approached the bitterness of this woman's problem. I pondered it and then wrote her about what had helped me to handle smaller resentments . . . . Grudges or resentments are emotions. We cannot get rid of them by saying, "I will no longer feel that way. I shall now love this person who harmed me."

Recognising the principle of the will, I pray something like this: "Lord, You have plainly told me that all vengeance is thine, not my business at all. You have said that I must forgive. I am willing to, but I've tried over and over, and the resentments keep surging back. Now I *will* this bitterness over to You. Here—I hold it out to You in my open hand. I promise only that I will not again close my fist and reclaim the resentment. Now I ask You to take it and handle these emotions that I cannot handle."

There I leave the matter. When thoughts return to it, there is the quiet inner assertion that it has been turned over to God, and that He is taking care of it. Always for me, in a matter of hours or days, I find the resentment has evaporated and in its place has come peace. The pilot's widow had a long struggle, but she wrote me that eventually she did find a peace of mind that led her into a creative new life.

I once had success in applying this secret of the will to a neighbour who invariably irritated me. Ann Sheldon (not her real name, of course) had not wronged me. Indeed, any reasons I could have given for not liking her were not reasons at all . . . such things as her ceaseless chatter, and that habit of asking you a direction question and then never pausing to hear the answer. Her personality affected me like scratching fingernails across a blackboard. My human inclination was to avoid her. Let Ann Sheldon go her way, and I'd go mine, I told myself. The world was plenty big enough for the two of us.

But then a curious thing happened. Each time I tried to pray, the thought of this woman popped into my mind. About the fourth time it happened, I concluded that God was trying to tell me something. With a sinking heart, I was afraid I knew only too well what the message was. "Avoiding Ann will not do. It is not good enough. Have you forgotten that we are to love one another?"

Love Ann Sheldon? The idea seemed ludicrous. Nevertheless I knew I had to try. First, I recognised that it would have been most unlike Jesus Christ if by "love" He had meant billowing waves of gushing sentimentality. By love He meant something more substantial—respect for another human being, caring about him and his problems, being sensitive to his needs, wanting him to prosper and to be happy.

As soon as I faced up to my defective relationship with Ann, I saw that everything turned on my will. I had to be *willing* to like this woman. Suppose that by some miracle God could replace my irritation with congeniality, even affection? (That *would* be a miracle, I thought glumly.) But all that God was asking of me was a shift in consciousness at the centre of my will to include this possibility.

For help I went back to Hannah Smith's illustration in which she compared the will to a wise mother in a nursery and the feelings to clamouring, crying children. "The mother makes up her mind to a certain course of action which she knows to be best. The children rebel, declare they will not obey. But the mother, knowing that she is mistress and not they, pursues her course lovingly, firmly, never giving in for a moment to their contrariness. Eventually the clamouring ceases; the children do what they're told. All is harmony in the nursery."

So, in essence, my prayer was, "Lord, let me admit that my every clamouring emotion rebels at the thought of liking Ann Sheldon! But I put my will over on the side of what is best. So I ask You to handle my feelings."

The first result of my prayer was that I stopped avoiding Ann. On closer contact, I began to realise that her chatter was a camouflage for a desperate unsureness about herself. Ann had always seemed to me a hopeless sentimentalist—witness the way she kept a memory book on the level of a teen-ager. She even pasted into it paper cocktail napkins and poetry

clipped out of women's magazines! Then I saw the reason.
She and her husband had always wanted children and had had
none. Her affectionate nature had never had enough of an
outlet. Soon I had evidence that underneath the sentimentality
was a rare capacity for staunch friendship. Then one day I was
astonished to realise that Ann Sheldon no longer irritated me.

She never got over her habit of asking questions and interrupting the answer. But there came the time when without
malice I could say freely, "Ann, do you want me to answer
that—or don't you?" And we would laugh about it together.

Ann died at forty-three—suddenly—of a brain haemorrhage.
I had seen her only two days before her death, and we had
parted with real affection.

The secret of the will is particularly effective in those areas
where emotionally we are divided personalities. We know
perfectly well what we should do. We want to do it; at the
same time we do not want to.

The tangled emotions of grief often accentuate this divided
self. This is the way one widow from a small town in Arkansas
analysed it in a letter to me:

*It is five years since my husband died at the age of forty-nine, just
half an hour after the doctor told him he would recommend him
for insurance any time.*

*For months, I was so numbed and crushed with grief that I
couldn't even realise what had happened to me. Yet in my heart I
knew that a big part of this was feeling sorry for myself.*

*My husband had always praised me for being a sensible person
in whatever situation I had to face, and in time I came to know
that if I persisted in this self-pity I would be failing him in the
worst kind of way. So—how can I handle this?*

I think there are several reasons why, in grief, the will is so
stubbornly at odds with itself. In the first place, the ego is
deeply involved. Love has been wounded, and in the process
part of us had died too. Also, like Queen Victoria who made a
production of mourning for forty years for her Albert, most
of us have a lingering pagan suspicion that those who do not

exhibit strong and continuing sorrow are dishonouring the dead.

We take a long time to face up to the fact that no amount of grieving will bring the one we love back to our side. And since life must go on, we are faced with simple alternatives: will it be a good life or a miserable, snivelling existence? At this juncture the secret of the will can take over and steer us down the right road.

After the publication of my book *To Live Again*, which was about my own experience of grief at my husband's death and my subsequent recovery, letters poured in from the bereaved—both men and women. Often the letters were disconcerting, for in effect many of them said, "I have read your book. But let me tell you the peculiarities of *my* case. Do you have something more to say to me?"

Since I had poured myself out in *To Live Again*, I thought I had shared everything that might be helpful. But now I find there is something more. The secret—Hannah Smith's secret —is simple recognition of the fact that sorrow is an emotion and that you have little control over it. You know that God loves your loved one, who is now with Him, and that He loves you. You know that God has a plan for your life. So you admit to God that you are divided. One part of you is clinging to grief almost as an indulgence; another part knows well that until you are willing to let grief go, happiness and a good life cannot be yours again.

The principle of the will can handle this division, though we have to begin farther back. Our prayer here must be, "Lord, I am willing to be made willing."

And there one lets the matter rest for days or weeks, doing no forcing or straining, giving God time to change the emotional climate at deep levels in the personality.

A clergyman friend of mine from St. Louis once told me how he had applied this same principle to a broken marriage. The young woman, Marty, who came to see him at his church office, began by saying that she no longer loved her husband, Bill. He had been unfaithful and had lost her respect.

"Did you love him once?" the minister asked.

"Yes, I did."

"And how does your husband feel now? Is he unchanged, or contrite—or what?"

"We've been separated for a year. Two months ago Bill came to me. He said he'd been a fool, that the affair was all over, and asked my forgiveness. Now he's pleading for a reconciliation."

"Well, can you forgive him?"

The woman hesitated. "I've heard you say often enough from the pulpit that we have to forgive, no matter what. But that isn't my worst problem. When respect goes, love goes. What I really came to ask is: Is it right, even fair to Bill for me to live with him again when I don't love him?"

"Marty, what do you think God's will is for you and Bill?"

She thought for a while. "I suppose that in God's sight Bill *is* my husband. I took him 'for better or for worse'. Then it must be God's will for me to love my husband."

The counsellor smiled at her. "But your difficulty, Marty, is that love can't be summoned like whistling for one's dog. Is that it?"

"Yes, that's it."

"There is an answer, Marty. If you are willing to do what you deeply feel God wants you to do, then He will attend to your emotions, give you back your love for Bill."

"How can you be so sure of that?"

"I can guarantee it, if you'll fulfil certain conditions." Then the minister explained to the young woman the principle of the will. As he talked, he shoved across his desk a crude diagram. "This is not original with me," he explained. "I got the idea from Dr Glenn Clark."

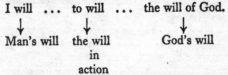

Marty studied the diagram. When she finally looked up, her eyes were hopeful. "I begin to see a way out of my box!

You mean that love is an emotion, and I can't control *that*, but I can control my will. And if I set my will right, then the emotions *have* to come right too. Is that it?"

"That's it."

"Then," Marty continued, "my part is to decide to go back to him."

"A little more than that," the clergyman corrected. "You have to go back, not reluctantly or half-heartedly, but willing to find joy and a new love for Bill. You can supply the willingness; God will do the rest."

That was five years ago. The marriage has not only lasted, but according to this minister Bill and Marty—now more mature and tested—are happier than they ever were before.

Surely we have misunderstood Christianity if we think God wants us to obey Him reluctantly—resisting, bucking, hating every step of the way. In fact the New Testament tells us that this reluctant obedience growing out of fear of punishment was the old way, the Old Covenant. Jesus came to show us a new way by which God promises to work in us "both to will and to do of His good pleasure".[3] This means that God will bring about such a change in us that His plans and desires for us will be our delight.

God's will gets written in our hearts by the simple application of the principle of the will to each life situation as we meet it. Christ would indeed be unrealistic if He asked us to do the impossible. He does not. His "secret" not only tells us how, but speeds us on our way with joy.

5: Dare to Trust God

"Now don't push the term *faith* at me," a lawyer told me bluntly at a dinner party recently. "The word is like a red flag."

"Why such a violent reaction?" I asked.

"Well, because I object to the way Christianity uses faith as a theological gimmick to duck all rational problems. At every point where a man wants to understand, they say, 'You just have to have faith', or 'Reason can only go so far'. I resent it! I see nothing wrong with 'Prove it to me first, then I'll believe'."

As we talked, I realised that it had never occurred to this intelligent, well-educated man that in his everyday life he often follows the reverse order—belief and acceptance first, then action. Every day he lives, he acts on faith many times with little proof or none at all, and he does not feel that he is being impractical.

He demonstrates an act of faith each time he boards a plane. He believes that it will take him to his destination, but he has no proof of it. He entrusts life itself to several unknown mechanics who have serviced the plane, as well as to a pilot about whom he knows nothing.

Each time he eats a meal in a restaurant he trusts some unknown cook behind the scenes and eats the food on faith, faith that it is not contaminated. He enters a hospital for an operation and signs a release giving permission for surgery. This is an act of faith in an anaesthetist whose name he may not even know and a surgeon who holds in his hands the power of life or death.

He accepts a prescription from a doctor and takes it to a druggist, thus acting his faith that the pharmacist will fill the prescription accurately. The use of the wrong drug might be deadly, but he is not equipped to analyse the contents before swallowing the pill.

It is obvious that were we to insist on the "proof first, then faith" order in our daily lives, organised life as we know it would grind to a screeching halt. And since life together among men is possible only by faith, as we act our trust in other people, it should not seem odd that the same law applies to our life with God.

The New Testament makes it clear that in the spiritual realm, when for some reason or other we refuse to act by faith, all activity stops just as completely as it does in the secular realm. There is no way for us even to take the first steps toward the Christian life except by faith, any more than a baby can get launched on his earthly life without blind baby-trust in his parents and other adults. We have to accept the fact of a personal relationship with Jesus Christ by faith, even as our young children accept the fact of parental love. For the child, as for the new Christian, understanding and proof come later.

In the same way, every step in our Christian walk has to be by faith.

In Jesus' ministry of healing the spirit, the mind, and the body, faith seems to have been necessary before the divine act, not (as logic would have it) afterward. The gospels are studded with statements of this:

And he said to the woman, Thy faith hath saved thee, go in peace.[1]

Then touched he their eyes, saying, According to your faith be it unto you.[2]

... Jesus said ... all things are possible to him that believeth.[3]

All that ever you ask in prayer, you shall have, if you believe.[4]

Much of my own problem with faith arose from an early misunderstanding of what faith is. First of all, I used to believe that faith had something to do with feeling. For example, when I had messed up some situation and had asked God for forgiveness, then I would peer inside myself to see if I *felt* forgiven. If I could locate such feelings, then I was sure that God had heard and had forgiven me. Now I know that this is an altogether false test of faith.

We would not be so foolish as to go to a railroad station, board the first car we saw, then sit down and try to feel whether or not this was the train that would take us where we wanted to go. Our feeling would obviously have no bearing on the facts. Yet I know now that at times my actions in the spiritual realm have been just that foolish.

Another misconception I once had was that faith is trying to believe something one is fairly certain is not true. But faith is not hocus-pocus, opposed to knowledge and reality. In fact, faith does not go against experience at all; rather it appeals to experience, just as science does. The difference is that it appeals to experience in a realm where our five senses are not supreme rulers.

Nor is faith a kind of spiritual coin which you and I can exchange for heaven's blessings. Nor is it simply believing doggedly in some particular doctrine. One can believe in the divinity of Jesus Christ and feel no personal loyalty to Him at all; indeed, pay no attention whatever to His commandments and His will for one's life. One can believe intellectually in the efficacy of prayer and never do any praying.

Perhaps one reason that the real meaning of faith eluded me personally for so many years was that it is so surprisingly simple, so practical. Faith in God is simply trusting Him enough to step out on that trust.

My first lesson in stepping out on trust came in connection with the problem of financing a college education. We were then living in a little railroad town in the eastern Panhandle of West Virginia. By the time I reached my senior year in high school, the town had for some years been struggling through the long aftermath of the 1929 crash. Its only industry—the Baltimore and Ohio railroad shops—was all but shut down. The church my father served as minister was suffering along with everything else. Father had voluntarily taken several cuts in his already meagre salary. Even grocery money was scarce. It was fortunate that Mother knew how to prepare fried mush in a way that made it seem like a rare delicacy.

Something I had dreamed of as far back as I could remember—a college education—now seemed out of the question. The dream even included a particular college—Agnes Scott in Decatur, Georgia.

Agnes Scott accepted me. Although the school was accustomed to ministers' and missionaries' daughters whose ambitions outstripped their pocketbooks, the financial burden nevertheless looked hopelessly heavy. Even with the promise of a small work scholarship and the $125 I had saved from high school essay and debating prizes, we were several hundred dollars short.

It was frightening to see that my parents were helpless in this situation. It was in their faces, in their voices. Through all my growing-up years, in every childish emergency they had been equal to anything. What now? Did this mean that I was going to have to relinquish my heart's desire?

One evening Mother found me lying across my bed, sobbing. She sat down beside me, put her cool hand on my forehead. No words were needed. She knew what the trouble was.

Presently she said quietly, "You and I are going to pray about this. Let's go into the guest room where we won't be disturbed." And she took me firmly by the hand.

We sat down on the old-fashioned golden-oak bed, the one that Mother and Father had bought for their first home. "Let's talk about this a minute before we pray," Mother said slowly. "I believe that it is God's will for you to go to college, or else He would not have given you the mental equipment. Furthermore, all resources are at God's disposal. Do you believe that, Catherine?"

"Yes—yes—I think I do."

"All right. Now here's another fact I want you to think about. Everybody has faith. We're born with it. Much of what happens to us in life depends on where we place our faith. If we deposit it in God, then we're on sure ground. If we place our trust in poverty or failure or fear, then we're investing it poorly. So keep that in mind while I read something to you." She opened a Moffatt Bible to I John 5: 14, 15:

> Now the confidence we have in him is this,
> that he listens to us whenever we ask anything
> in accordance with His will; and if we know that he
> listens to whatever we ask, we know that we obtain the
> requests we have made to him.

"Note how the thought goes in that promise, Catherine. Whenever we ask God for something that is His will, He hears us. If He hears us, then He grants the request we have made. So you and I can rest on that promise. Let's claim it right now for the resources for your college." And so we knelt by the bed and prayed about it.

I shall never forget that evening. During those quiet moments in the bedroom, I was learning what faith is and how it works. It is true that my faith was immature and weak, but the strength of Mother's was contagious. She had helped me take my first step in faith. The answer would come. We knew it would, thought neither of us had any idea how.

When it came, it was the offer of a job for Mother with the Federal Writer's Project. Would she be willing to write the history of the county? Would she! Her salary would cover the amount needed for my college expenses with a little to spare. Since history has always been one of Mother's loves, no job could have been more to her liking. Moreover, she could work at home and, along with her writing, keep a hand on all of the family projects.

That was the way I learned that we must have faith *before* the fact, not after, if we are to function as human beings at all. The only question is—faith in whom? Faith in what?

God challenges us to place it in Him rather than in fallible human beings: "Taste and see that the Lord is good."[5] In my experience this is not an ivory-tower approach. It is the only effectual one.

I have seen faith in God vindicated many times in stirring

ways. No story every captured my imagination so much as George Müller's. My children will read it and—if I have anything to say about it—my grandchildren.

In the year 1828 a man sat in a room in Teignmouth, England, struggling with a problem. A German, George Müller was then twenty-three years old. His father was a collector of excise taxes in Prussia, and the son had inherited the father's preoccupation with figures, his adding-machine mind, his astute business sense. During this period in England the Industrial Revolution was well under way. George Müller felt he could become a successful industrialist. Yet he hesitated.

Only three years out of the University at Halle, George had been mostly preoccupied with taverns, women, cards, and occasional study. He certainly had not been at all interested in religion. Then there had come a turning point. It had come through Müller's unexpected discovery one night at a friend's party that he could have fun in a Christian group—a different, deeper kind of pleasure than he found in his favourite tavern.

To his own surprise, George Müller began to think about the meaning of life. Often he pondered the fact that all through the Gospels there kept recurring Jesus' plea for us to have faith, to ask . . . ask . . . ask:

> Hitherto you have asked nothing in my name;
> ask and you will receive, that your joy may be full.[6]

> If for all your evil you know to give your
> children what is good, how much more will
> your Father in heaven give good to
> those who ask him?[7]

Had Christ meant those words literally? If so, then why—generation after generation—did mankind continue to ignore them or water them down?

Müller thought of several individuals he had recently met. One was a man who had to work at his trade fourteen to sixteen hours a day. He had no time for his family, no time to enjoy life. Concerned, Müller had spoken to him only a week before: "Henry, you simply have to work less. Your family needs something more of you than your pay. Your body's suffering and your soul is starving."

But the reply had been, "But if I work less, I won't earn enough for the support of my family."

When Müller had quoted him the promise, "Seek ye first the Kingdom of God, and His righteousness, and all these things shall be added unto you,"[8] Henry had said with a wry grimace, "I wish I could believe that applies to my situation, George. Guess I just need more faith."

Müller now sat chin in hand, staring out the second-storey window over the chimney-pots of the town to the sea in the distance, foaming and curling at the base of the red cliffs of Parson Rock. But he was not seeing the beauty of a sunset on Teignmouth's coast now. Instead he was thinking of an old woman, Marie, so frightened of old age without a pension, so terrified of the poorhouse waiting for her at the end of the road. Where was her faith in God's ability to take care of her? And then he was thinking of Lawrence, a man now in his early thirties and in a business he hated. But he dared not switch to where his heart was—medicine. "How would I take care of my family while I complete my studies?" He too had merely shrugged when Müller had mentioned faith in God as the solution.

So what could he—George Müller—do about it? How could he define this matter of faith and prove to these people that Jesus had meant it when He bade us *ask*.

At that moment he saw through the window two ragged little girls on the cobblestone walk. He had seen them before. Their father was a merchant seamen whose ship had been lost last year off Desolation Island in the Magellan Straits. Two weeks ago their mother had died of tuberculosis. Müller recalled the pathetic funeral, the raw pine casket, the lost look on the faces of the children. He knew that the eleven-and thirteen-year-old girls were trying to take care of three younger children. And these were not the only destitute children in the town, either. There seemed to be no institutions for needy children in England. He wondered why not.

The thoughts went round and round. And then he noticed his Bible open on the table beside him. It was open to the Psalms: suddenly he was reading a verse he had never noticed before: "Open thy mouth wide, and I will fill it."[9] Müller suddenly found himself quietly praying, "All right, I'm opening my mouth to ask. If you want me to do something about all this, You'll have to show me how and where to begin."

George Müller began by offering his services to a local mission. His drive and imagination soon revitalised it. The records show that he met and married Mary Groves in 1830. The two of them consecrated their marriage vows with a rather remarkable demonstration of Jesus' words ... "Sell what you possess and give it away in alms. . . ."[10] Just so, did George and Mary part with their household goods. Like many daring experiments, Müller wanted to go all the way. His desire was to make himself and his wife dependent for everything on God alone. Their motive was sincere, above all suspicion. At the time he and his wife kept the act of giving away their possessions a secret from all who knew them.

The next step was even more daring. Müller refused all regular salary from the people of the small mission he had been serving. He and his wife would henceforth tell their needs to God alone in prayer. Theirs would be a test case for the world to see.

Then George found his thoughts centering on the idea of founding an orphan's home. It would not be just a place to care for a few homeless children, but a vast institution—built and operated on faith. He would make it, too, a pure example of trust in God.

On April 21, 1836, the first Orphan Home was dedicated in a rented building. Within a matter of days there were forty-three children to be cared for. Müller and his co-workers decided that the controlled experiment would be set up along these lines:

1. No funds would ever be solicited. No facts or figures concerning needs were to be revealed by the workers in the orphanage to anyone, except to God in prayer.

2. No debts would ever be incurred. The burden of experiment would therefore not be on local shopkeepers or suppliers.
3. No money contributed for a specific purpose could ever be used for any other purpose.
4. All accounts would be audited annually by professional auditors.
5. No ego-pandering by publication of donor's names with the amount of their gifts; each donor would be thanked privately.
6. No "names" of prominent or titled persons would be sought for the board or to advertise the institution.
7. The success of the institution would be measured not by the numbers served or by the amounts of money taken in, but by God's blessing on the work, which Müller expected to be in proportion to the time spent in prayer.

When the first building was opened, George Müller and his associates stuck to their principles, spending time in prayer that ordinarily would have gone to fund-raising. An un-believing public was amazed when a second building was opened six months after the first. Müller concentrated on prayer, and the money kept coming in. Eventually, there were five new buildings, with 110 helpers taking care of 2,050 orphans.

Before opening his first orphanage Müller had said that he would consider the experiment a failure if ever the orphans had to go for a single day without food. They never did. Nor were these children taken care of in minimal fashion. Part of George Müller's conviction was that God not only provides, but that He provides bountifully. For their time, his orphanage buildings were constructed with remarkable details—built-in cupboards with a large pigeonhole for each child's clothes; sunny playrooms with shelves and cupboards for the toys that were not yet there. Each child must always have not one but three pairs of shoes. Each boy, three suits; each girl, five dresses. There must always be white tablecloths for the evening meal and flowers whenever possible. Behind the scenes were the latest labour-saving devices available: one of the first American washing machines in England and an early type of centrifugal dryer.

After each year's audit a detailed report was made public showing how the Lord had provided for that year. Soon it became apparent that all around the world people were watching this experiment with fascination. Businessmen were particularly interested. One executive travelled a considerable distance for an interview with Müller. His firm was threatened with bankruptcy. In his methodical manner, Müller wrote out for his visitor a prescription of five parts—advice as applicable today as it was then:

1. Each day you and your wife are to spread your business difficulties before the Lord.
2. You are then to watch for answers to prayer and expect them.
3. Absolute honesty necessary; avoid all business trickeries.
4. Beginning immediately, a certain proportion of your income must be given to God.
5. Keep a record—month by month—how the Lord is dealing with you, what's happening.

The man did keep a record; in face he sent a monthly report to Müller, and in his journal Müller recorded that during the first year the man's business came out of the red and up some three thousand pounds over the previous year. For as long as George Müller recorded the figures, the businessman's profits continued to mount.

The results of his amazing orphanage experiment have been published in detail in the four volumes of George Müller's *Journals*. For more than sixty years he recorded every specific prayer request and the result. His mathematical mind kept meticulous books on every penny received and all money expended.

So great did public interest in the orphanage become that, when Müller was seventy, he felt that the time had come to tell the story himself. So over a number of years he travelled 200,000 miles, lecturing in forty-two countries. For hundreds of thousands of people he became a living demonstration of the fact that faith is nothing more or less than believing God, not just intellectually but actually.

Faith is only worthy of the name when it erupts into action. Unlike George Müller, most of us can show few trophies won through faith. Were we to use the muscles of our legs as little as we do the muscles of our faith, most of us would be unable to stand.

Then what can we do to strengthen them?

First, we cannot trust God until we know something about Him. The way to begin is by reading His word and thinking about it. The Bible acquaints us with the nature and character of God: His power: His unselfish, unchangeable love; His infinite wisdom. We read instance after instance in which God has exercised His power and wisdom in helping and delivering His people.

Second, faith is strengthened only as we ourselves exercise it. We have to apply it to our problems: poverty, bodily ills, bereavement, job troubles, tangled human relationships.

Third, faith has to be in the present tense—now. A vague prospect that what we want will transpire in the future is not faith, but hope.

Fourth, absolute honesty is necessary. We cannot have faith and a guilty conscience at the same time. Every time faith will fade away.

Fifth, the strengthening of faith comes through staying with it in the hour of trial. We should not shrink from tests of our faith. Only when we are depending on God alone are we in a position to see God's help and deliverance, and thus have our faith strengthened for the next time.

This means that we must let Him do the work. Almost always it takes longer than we think it should. When we grow impatient and try a deliverance of our own, through friends or circumstances, we are taking God's work out of His hands.

George Müller was faithfully reflecting the New Testament in his blunt, realistic insistence in depending on God alone. The Epistle of James declared that "faith, unless it has deeds, is dead in itself."[11] And John added more bluntly still, "He who will not believe God, has made God a liar. . . ."[12]

Believe what? Believe the consistent testimony in Scripture of the unfailing love and goodwill of our God, of His ability to help us, and of His willingness—indeed eagerness—to do so.

The adventure of living has not really begun until we begin to stand on our faith legs and claim—for ourselves, for our homes, for the rearing of our children, for our health problems, for our business affairs, and for our world—the resources of our God.

6: The Prayer of Relinquishment

AFTER the discovery that faith in God can make life an adventure, comes the desire to experiment with prayer. Like most people, I was full of questions, such as why are some agonisingly sincere prayers granted while others are not?

Many years later I still have questions. Mysteries about prayer are always out ahead of present knowledge—luring, beckoning on to further experimentation.

But one thing I do know; I learned it through hard experience. It is a way of prayer that has consistently resulted in a glorious answer, glorious because each time power beyond human reckoning has been released. This is the Prayer of Relinquishment.

I got my first glimpse of it in the fall of 1943. The illness that I have mentioned before in these pages had kept me in bed for many months. A bevy of specialists seemed unable to help. Persistent prayer, using all the faith I could muster, had resulted in—nothing.

One afternoon a pamphlet was put in my hand. It was the story of a missionary who had been an invalid for eight years. Constantly she had prayed that God would make her well, so that she might do His work. Finally, worn out with futile petition, she prayed, "All right. I give up. If You want me to be an invalid for the rest of my days. that's Your business. Anyway, I've discovered that I want You even more than I want health. You decide." The pamphlet said that within two weeks the woman was out of bed, completely well.

This made no sense to me. It seemed too pat. Yet I could not forget the story. On the morning of September fourteenth (how can I ever forget the date?) I came to the same point of abject acceptance. "I'm tired of asking" was the burden of my prayer. "I'm beaten, finished. God, You decide what You want for me for the rest of my life. . . ." Tears flowed. I had no faith as I understood faith. I expected nothing. The gift of my sick self was made with no trace of graciousness.

The result was as if windows had opened in heaven; as if some dynamo of heavenly power had begun flowing, flowing into me. From that moment my recovery began.

Through this incident and others that followed, some of which I want to tell later, God was trying to teach me something important about prayer. Still I got only part of the message. I saw that the demanding spirit—"God, I must have this and so; God, this is what I want You to do for me—" is not real prayer and hence receives no answer. I understood that the reason for this is that God absolutely refuses to violate our free will and that therefore, unless self-will is voluntarily given up, even God cannot move to answer prayer. But it was going to take more time and more experience for me to begin to understand the Prayer of Relinquishment.

Part of that understanding has come through learning of other people's experiences with this type of prayer. It has been exciting to uncover in contemporary life, in the Bible, and scattered through the writings of men in other centuries the infallible power of this prayer technique.

Some years ago, I stumbled across one example in the life of the New England writer, Nathaniel Hawthorne. In 1853 Hawthorne had decided to take his family abroad for an extended stay. He wanted a broadening of his horizons, contact with other writers in England and Italy. By then he was already recognised as a master of the craft of the short story through his *Twice Told Tales* and was famous as the author of the successful novel *The Scarlet Letter*.

In late 1858, the Hawthornes were settled in a villa in Rome. February 1860 found them in the midst of a grave crisis. Una, their eldest daughter, was dying of a virulent form of malaria. The attending physician, Dr Franco, had that afternoon warned the distraught parents that unless the young girl's fever abated before morning she would die.

As Sophia Hawthorne sat by her daughter's bed, her thoughts went to her handsome husband in the adjoining room. She could picture him—his troubled blue eyes, that splendid head with its mop of dark hair, bowed in grief. She recalled what he had said earlier that day, "I cannot endure the alternations of hope and fear, and therefore I have settled with myself not to hope at all."

But Sophia could not share Nathaniel's hopelessness. Una could not, must not die. This daughter strongly resembled her father, had the finest mind, the most complex character of all the Hawthorne children. Why should a capricious Providence demand that they give her up?

Moreover, Una had been delirious for several days and had recognised no one. Were she to die this night, there would not even be the solace of farewells.

As the night deepened, the young girl ceased her incoherent mutterings and lay so still that she seemed to be in the ante-room of death. The mother went to the window and looked out on the piazza. There was no moonlight; heavy clouds scudded across a dark and silent sky.

"I cannot bear this loss—cannot—cannot." Then suddenly, unaccountably, another thought took over. "Why should I doubt the goodness of God? Let Him take Una, if He sees best. I can give her to Him. No, I won't fight against Him any more."

Then an even stranger thing happened. Having made the great sacrifice in her mind, Sophia expected to feel sadder. Instead she felt lighter, happier than at any time since Una's long illness had begun.

Some minutes later she walked back to the girl's bedside and felt her daughter's forehead. It was moist and cool. The pulse was slow and regular. Una was sleeping naturally. Sophia rushed into the next room to tell her husband that the crisis seemed to be past. She was right, Though Una was months getting the malaria out of her system, she did recover completely.

A contemporary answer to prayer reminiscent of the Hawthornes' experience was related to me by a friend in a letter:

. . . Three years ago our son was born. At first he seemed a normal, healthy baby. But when he was not quite twelve hours old, while

*I was holding him in my arms, he had a convulsion. More
convulsions followed in the next few days.*

*The only explanation the doctors had was that he must have
suffered a brain injury of some kind at birth. This only added to
my terror. . . . If he lived, perhaps he would be blind, deaf, dumb,
or a cripple, or with his mind affected.*

*I've never felt so alone as during the time that followed. I
prayed, but I couldn't feel that God cared about me any more
Why had this had to happen to my baby?*

*I know now that my prayers were not prayers at all, but accusa-
tions. I was demanding that God heal my child.*

*Then out of sheer exhaustion of body and soul, I stopped
commanding God and gave in to Him completely. I just said,
"Take him if that's what You want. Anything You decide will
be all right with me. Even if You want him to be a cripple, or
deaf, then I will just have to learn to accept it and live with it."
I put myself and the baby entirely in His hands.*

*From that instant, not only did Larry begin to improve,
but suddenly my tears left, and my fears went with them. An
inexplicable peace filled my heart, and I knew, just knew, that
Larry would not only live but would have a normal useful
life. . . .*

*Well, the end of the story is that Larry is now as normal and
healthy as any little boy. He's very very intelligent, and if he were
any more active, well I'd be the one to be a cripple.*

Larry's story and Una's have several points in common. In
each case, the mother wanted the same thing desperately—life
and health for her child. Each mother commanded God to
answer her prayer. While the demanding spirit had the upper
hand, God seemed remote, unapproachable.

Then, through a combination of the obvious futility of the
demanding prayer plus weariness of body and spirit, the
mother surrendered to the possibility of what she feared most.
At that instant there came a turning point. Suddenly and
inexplicably fear left and the feeling of soul-strain with it.
Peace crept into the heart. There followed a feeling of light-
ness and joy that had nothing to do with outer circumstances.

This marked the turning point. From that moment the prayer began to be answered.

The intriguing question is: What is the spiritual law implicit in this Prayer of Relinquishment? I think I know at least part of it. ... We know that fear blocks prayer. Fear is a barrier erected between us and God, so that His Power cannot get through to us. So—how does one get rid of fear?

This is not easy when the life of someone dear hangs in the balance, or when what we want most in all the world seems to be slipping away. At such times, every emotion, every passion, is tied up in the dread that what we fear most is about to come upon us. Obviously only strong measures can deal with such a powerful fear. My experience has been that trying to overcome it by turning one's thoughts to the positive or by repeating affirmations is not potent enough.

It is then that we are squarely up against the law of relinquishment. Was Jesus showing us how to use this law when He said, "Resist not evil"? In God's eyes, fear is evil because it is acting out of lack of trust in Him. So Jesus is advising "Resist not fear".

In other words, Jesus is saying: "Admit the possibility of what you fear most. And lo, as you stop fleeing, as you force yourself to walk up to the fear, as you look it full in the face, never forgetting that God and His power are still the supreme reality, the fear evaporates." Drastic? Yes. But effective.

One point about the Prayer of Relinquishment puzzled me for many years. There seemed to be a contradiction between the Prayer of Faith and that of relinquishment. If relinquishment is real, the one praying must be willing to receive or not receive his heart's desire. But that state of mind scarcely seems to exhibit the faith that knows that one's request will be granted. And as I read the gospels, Jesus placed far greater stress on the Prayer of Faith than on the Prayer of Relinquishment.

Now I believe I have the explanation. The fact is that I went through a period of misunderstanding faith. Once I thought that faith was believing this or that specific thing in my mind

with never a doubt. Now I know that faith is nothing more
or less than actively trusting God.

Peter Marshall liked to illustrate what such active trust
means by a homely example:

Suppose a child has a broken toy.
He brings the toy to his father, saying that he
    himself has tried to fix it and has failed.
He asks his father to do it for him.

The father gladly agrees ...
    takes the toy ...
    and begins to work.

Now obviously the father can do his work most quickly
and easily if the child makes no attempt to interfere, simply
sits quietly watching, or even goes about other business,
with never a doubt that the toy is being successfully
mended.

But what do most of God's children do in such a situation?
Often we stand by offering a lot of meaningless advice and
some rather silly criticism.

We even get impatient and try to help,
and so get our hands in the Father's way,
generally hindering the work ...

Finally, in our desperation, we may even grab the toy
out of the Father's hands entirely, saying rather bitterly
that we hadn't really thought He could fix it anyway ...
that we'd given Him a chance and He had failed us.

Grabbing the toy away is certainly not trust. But what does
demonstrate trust is to put the thing or the person one loves
best into the Father's hands to do with as He pleases. Thus
faith is by no means absent in the Prayer of Relinquishment.
In fact this prayer is faith in action.

And that is why this prayer is answered, even when the one making the relinquishment has little hope that what he fears most can be avoided. For I have always felt that God is not half so concerned about our having a few negative thoughts as He is concerned with what we do. And the act of placing what we cherish most in His hands is to Him the sweet music of the essence of faith.

This kind of faith can be used to solve any type of problem. I remember an attractive young girl, Sara Bradford, who sat in my living-room and shared with me her doubts about her engagement.

"I love Jeb," she said, and there was deep feeling in her words. "And Jeb loves me. But there are problems. He had an unhappy childhood. His mother and father were divorced when he was ten. His mother was a great beauty. She's still a beautiful woman at sixty-two. She married again, and that marriage was unhappy, too. Jeb is most defensive of her."

"Does this make you feel that Jeb is a poor risk for marriage?"

Sara hesitated. "Well, it's left a lot of marks. There are other problems, too. At twenty-four, Jeb is still restless—"

"You mean he hasn't settled on a career?"

"No, he hasn't. Then, too, it bothers me that religion doesn't mean much to him. Oh, a few times he's gone to church with me. But his heart isn't in it. I don't really want to establish the kind of a home in which God will be left out. And then there is his drinking . . . What should I do? Do all these doubts mean that God is trying to tell me to give Jeb up?"

As she talked on and on, Sara reached her own conclusion. It was that she would lose something infinitely precious if she did not follow the highest and the best that she knew. Her voice broke as she said, "I'm going to have to break the engagement. Then if God wants me to marry Jeb, He will find some way of showing me."

Right then, simply and poignantly, she told God her decision. Her prayer was a true relinquishment. She was putting her broken dreams and her now-unknown future into God's hands.

I remained interested in Sara and in knowing how her future turned out. Jeb did not change, so Sara did not marry him. But a year later Sara wrote me an ecstatic letter. "Something wonderful happened that afternoon in your living-room. It nearly killed me to give Jeb up. Yet God knew that he wasn't the one for me. Now I've met The Man. He's terrific and we're to be married in October. Now I *really* have something to say about trusting God."

The Prayer of Relinquishment also helps us in small matters. A friend confided that she had been suffering from insomnia. Her doctor had prescribed sleeping pills.

"I've been reading so much lately about how the sales of sleeping pills rise and rise. Are we becoming a nation of addicts?"

"Not you, certainly," I reassured her.

"Thanks. But the principle of this bothers me. I'm not sure I want this crutch."

Later we met again and she told me what happened.

"I decided nix on the pills. So that night I lay and prayed, 'All right, God, I put myself and my sleep into Your hands. If you want me to stay awake most of the night, fine. You decide'."

"And did you stay awake?"

.. There was a sheepish look on her face. "No, I slept like a baby."

No doubt psychologists, as well as the sleep experts, could comment knowingly on this incident. But I relate it here only because it illustrates the Law of Relinquishment not in a dramatic crisis but in an ordinary situation.

My own latest adventure with the Prayer of Relinquishment came in connection with the mundane problem of household help. In the weeks prior to my marriage to Leonard LeSourd, I was happily excited but at the same time panicky at the thought of taking on three young children. After all, I had thought myself finished with child-rearing. Peter John had then been out of the home nest for three years, away at school. At the same time I wanted to keep on with my writing. What if I was not adequate to the situation?

In his efforts to reassure me, Len made solemn promises of household help. But after our marriage, the help was slow in materialising. Three months passed, four. One maid stayed for three weeks, then decided to go back to her home in North Carolina. Then a cleaning woman who was helping me one day a week had to stop when she fell and injured her leg.

Many a morning Len and I prayed about it. Soon after our marriage, we had hit upon a pleasant way to begin our day with quietness and prayer. An automatic coffee pot attached to a clock would waken us with the fragrance of percolating coffee. Then we would sit propped up in bed, sipping coffee, reading a portion of Scripture together, thinking through the day ahead.

One morning I was particularly discouraged. I was caught between all my blessings—a wonderful husband, three lovely children at home and a fourth in and out, a big new house, and my daily writing. I was, quite frankly, exhausted. We had tried everything we knew: agencies, the suggestions of friends and relatives, the Help Wanted columns in the local and New York newspapers. Just the evening before a promising candidate from Boston with whom we had been corresponding had telephoned that she could not come.

So once more we took the situation to God. ... "Lord, we've tried everything we can think of. Every road has seemed a dead end. Doors have been so consistently shut in our faces that You must be trying to teach us something. Tell us what it is—"

There followed the illumination that prayer often brings. In this case, it was not pleasant. I had been trying to dictate the terms of my life to God—what I wanted: help in the home so that I could get on with my writing. A thought stabbed me. What if—for this period of my life—I was supposed to give up the writing? Immediately this possibility brought tears. Why should I have to relinquish something which I had from the beginning dedicated to God—and something from which I also got such intense satisfaction? Still it was obvious that our home and the children had to come first. So, knowing that I would get no answer from God until I was willing to surrender the writing, I set myself to the task.

At that point, Hannah Whitall Smith's practicable principle of the will came to my rescue. Resolutely I set my will to accept what had to be accepted. Though my emotions were in stark rebellion, I knew that sooner or later they would fall into line.

I plunged into homemaking, completing the furnishing and decorating of the house ... meals ... laundry ... groceries ... creating an atmosphere of security for children who badly needed it.

Then I realised that, beyond the writing, there had been another reason why I had wanted help. It was the haunting fear that I would be physically and emotionally unable to handle all the housework, take care of the children, be a good wife to my husband—all at one time. But now I was learning that I could cope with it. With that knowledge came the self-assurance that washed away all fears. And I would never have had this sense of security and confidence if we had started our marriage with domestic help.

When the relinquishment was complete, the breakthrough occurred. Unexpectedly a letter came from Boston. The woman who had refused us before said that she was now available. Lucy Arsenault came to us. Lucy—settled, reliable, a superb cook, a rare person. As always, a loving God had planned so much better than we ever could have.

The morning mail frequently holds surprises for me. On one particular morning a few months ago I noticed that the tissue-thin air mail letter was postmarked Quito, Ecuador. After glancing over the first two paragraphs, I turned to the second sheet to see the signature—and gasped. Betty Elliot! Only a few days before I had been reading about her in *Life* magazine. Her husband had been one of the five missionaries brutally massacred by the Auca Indians on January 8, 1956. I was curious to know why she should be writing to me.

I have just spent Christmas alone here in an Auca Indian settlement reading your book, To Live Again. *Though my present circumstances could hardly be more remote from those you describe, I responded deeply to much of your message, and I felt I wanted to thank you. . . .*

Then she went on to tell me what her circumstances were. Betty and her small blonde daughter, Valerie, together with Rachel, the sister of Nate Saint (another of the murdered men) are now living in the midst of the South American Auca tribe. The two women and the tiny girl are altogether at the mercy of the same men who killed their husband and brother. They have no weapons; there are no other white people within miles of jungle, inaccessible except on foot or by airlift. How did such circumstances come about "God led us here, opened the way through Dayuma, an escaped Auca woman. . . ." Betty explains simply.

Yet Betty Elliot is a realist. "It is possible for us to lose our lives any day. The Aucas are still savages, who do not even think of killing as wrong. Fear can drive them to kill in a twinkling. What the future holds for Rachel and Valerie and me is God's business. . . ."

I found my imagination straining as I thought of how the pages I held in my hand had been written. She had penned them seated in the doorway of the palm-thatched hut that Betty calls home. The muddy Tewaenon River flows near by. Her husband's body, a broken spear still imbedded in it, had been found three years before floating face down in the same river. And closer, the lush green jungle for ever impinges on the natives' clearing.

All around her as she wrote those words were the short savages with their tea-coloured skins and straight black hair. Both men and women go naked except for the vines tied tightly around waists, ankles, and wrists. Valerie near by chattered animatedly with a pet parrot. . . .

I was awed at the evidence of such a love for God as these two women were demonstrating. Then my eye fell on the last paragraph of the letter:

Your solution to grief is just another way of giving the same answer that God gave me in the first empty days—Accept this. Only in acceptance lies peace—not in forgetting nor in resignation nor in busy-ness. His will is good and acceptable and perfect. . . .

So this woman, in the midst of such cruel events, had discovered the secret, too: there is a difference between acceptance and resignation. One is positive; the other negative. Acceptance is creative, resignation sterile.

Resignation is barren of faith in the love of God. It says, "Grievous circumstances have come to me. There is no escaping them. I am only one creature, an alien in a vast unknowable creation. I have no heart left even to rebel. So I'll just resign myself to what apparently is the will of God; I'll even try to make a virtue out of patient submission." So resignation lies down quietly in the dust of a universe from which God seems to have fled, and the door of Hope swings shut.

But turn the coin over. Acceptance says, "I trust the good-will, the love of my God. I'll open my arms and my understanding to what He has allowed to come to me. Since I know that He means to make all things work together for good, I consent to this present situation with hope for what the future will bring." Thus acceptance leaves the door of Hope wide open to God's creative plan. This difference between acceptance and resignation is the key to an understanding of the Prayer of Relinquishment.

Obviously Betty Elliot's acceptance left the door open to a creative plan so daring that only God could have conceived it. Can two women and a tiny girl succeed in taking Christianity to Stone-age savages where many men have failed? For other white men died violently at the hands of the Aucas before the five missionaries. In 1942 the Shell Oil Company lost three men by Auca spears, in 1943 eight more. Since then the tribe has repaid with death any invasion of their territory by white men.

So now the world watches while an adventure story unfolds, In the plan that God gave Betty Elliot, I have never seen a better example of the "foolishness" of God being wiser than men, and the "weakness" of God being stronger than men.[1]

To the disciples of Jesus Christ, His actions during the last week of His life on earth must have seemed equally nonsensical. Their Master had a great following among the common people. His disciples were hoping that He would use this following to overthrow the Roman grip on their little country and move, at last, to establish His earthly kingdom.

Instead He deliberately set His feet on the path that would lead inescapably to the cross. For let us not mistake it. Christ could have avoided that cross. He did not have to go up to Jerusalem that last time. He could have compromised with the priests, bargained with Caiaphas. The disciples were probably right in thinking that He could have capitalised on His following, appeased Judas, and set up the beginning of an earthly empire. Later Pilate would all but beg Him to say the right words so that he might release Him.[2] Even in the Garden of Gethsemane on the night of betrayal, Christ had plenty of time and opportunity to flee.

But He would not flee. Instead He knelt to pray in the shadowy Garden under the grey-green leaves of the olive trees. And in His prayer that night, Jesus gave us, for all time, the perfect pattern for the Prayer of Relinquishment.

Jesus had been given genuine humanity, as well as divinity. Part of that humanity was His free will. He chose to use His free will to leave the decision to His Father as to whether He must die by execution.

It was agony, such agony that as He knelt there He could not have been aware of the beauty all around Him. The valley under the brow of the hill was washed in moonlight. Below Him the brook Kedron rippled and sang over stones and through rushes. Around Him were the myrtle trees, palms, and fig trees that melted into the olive groves. And in the enclosed Garden of Gethsemane, all around His prostrate figure were the leaves and trunks of the olive trees silvered by filtering moonlight. ... This was not a world that Christ, the man, wanted to leave.

Was there a moment when He wondered *how* to pray about

the terrible alternatives before Him? If so, in the end He knew that only one prayer could release the power that was needed to lift a sin-ridden world:

"Dear Father, all things are possible to You. Please—let me not have to drink this cup. Yet it is not what I want, but what You want."[3]

In these words Jesus deliberately set himself to make His will and God's will the same. The prayer was not answered as the human Jesus wished. Yet power has been flowing from His cross ever since.

God has given you and me free will, too. And the voluntary giving up of our self-will always has a cross at the centre of it. It is the hardest thing human beings are called on to do.

When we come right down to it, how can we make obedience real, except as we give over that self-will in reference to each of life's episodes as they unfold? That is why it should not surprise us that at the centre of answered prayer lies the Law of Relinquishment.

7: *Forgive Us Our Sins ...*

AT the heart of the Christian gospel lies forgiveness, the greatest miracle of all. Only as each of us opens himself to receive this most wondrous of gifts can the inner self deep within us be freed to become the happier, finer person we are meant to be. Whenever I think of our desperate need for forgiveness and of how difficult it is for some of us to accept it, my thoughts go back to Margaret Stanley—Meg, as some of us call her.

It is a long story covering some four years. It begins in the drab living-room in a government housing project called Lillypond in Washington, D.C. Meg was musing, letting her mind roam over the previous evening. Every detail remained vivid. From the street the building had looked like a Victorian stone mansion. Only the polished brass plate beside the door had revealed that this was a church. Meg had not been near a church in years. She had let her sister, Alice, talk her into going this Wednesday night only because she had been assured that she would meet some interesting people.

She recalled the moment when they had pushed open the green door and a turbulence of voices, humming and buzzing, rising and falling, had beaten upon them. She shut her eyes to recapture her first impression of the large entrance hall. There were stairs, with curving arches above them forming a backdrop. The bare parquet floor had been polished to mirror brightness. A square, old-fashioned grand piano stood to one side. People had been clustered in little groups talking animatedly. Alice had linked an arm through hers and had taken her from group to group. Names ... so many names. There had been an obvious affection for Alice, a warmth that had flowed from her and back to her. Meg thought of that now with envy. She wondered if anyone had ever really loved *her*.

Then there had been dinner at small candle-lit tables, with

music in the background; afterward they had assembled in the little chapel to the left of the hallway. The chapel must have been made, Meg thought, by forming together two rooms of the old mansion.

Alice had tried to reassure her that this was not a church service. "Just a class," she had said lightly. "Meets every Wednesday. Arnold teaches it. He's the minister."

But he had not been Meg's idea of what a minister should look like. He was young, with a crew cut. His clear blue eyes had laughter crinkles at the corners. His clothes were preposterously casual. He even wore loafers.

If Meg had known that the class was called "What Christians Believe and Do" she probably would have fled before it started. As it was, the young minister had startled her into listening. "Christ requires a toughness to follow Him that frightens us," he began. "He asks that we deal decisively with all the things that keep us petty and make us ineffective.

"This is not just 'religious stuff'. It is practical. It works. In fact, if you are willing to try Christ for even six months, I'll guarantee that your life will be changed."

Back in her drab housing-project living-room, Meg grimaced as she thought back to those words. Then she lifted one foot, kicked disgustedly at the ridiculous-looking coal stove in the centre of the living-room. Changed? Maybe some people, but not *her*. If those people at the church knew about her past, they would never ler her set foot in the place!

She and her sister had come from a broken home. After years of dissension, their parents had been divorced. As a little girl Meg had been so unhappy that she had been unable to adjust to any school. There had been eighteen of them in all. After her second year in high school, she left school and found a job.

Her need for affection drew her to friendships with men. Many of them were nice enough fellows and they had needs, too. If she could give them a little pleasure, why not? Then she discovered that liquor helped to dull the feelings of guilt that always went with the affairs. There were a succession of men, then an illegitimate baby.

The Florence Crittenton home placed the baby for adoption, and a few months later she met Maynard. He seemed even nicer than the other men she had known. So she married him, because she thought marriage would change her. It had not.

Maynard had gone into the service and was sent to the West Coast. For Meg back home there began again the round of parties, heavy drinking, and now extra-marital affairs. A psychiatrist later analysed her behaviour not so much as wanton depravity but as a type of "sloppy kindness" brought on by her desire to please. Without a spiritual morality it quickly got out of hand.

Eventually Meg began spending every Saturday night at a down-at-the-heel dance hall. She found the young men there quick to take advantage of her weakness. Almost always there would be a drunken brawl, most Saturday nights the patrol wagon had to be called. Though Meg was disgusted by the brawls and managed to stay out of them, the police in the vicinity came to know her well.

Tales of what was going on at home got to Maynard. By this time, 1944, he was in a psychiatric ward in a veterans' hospital in Texas. There he tried to commit suicide. Hearing of this, Meg had been jolted enough to try and pull herself together. Eventually Maynard came home and fourteen months later a daughter was born to the couple. But their marriage was in no better shape. Finally, Maynard asked Meg for a divorce.

The young minister's words rang now in her mind: "If you are willing to try Christ for six months, I'll guarantee that your life will be changed." Guarantee! How could he guarantee? One part of Meg's mind said, "Better not go near that group again, if you want to hang on to the old life." But another part of her wanted to see those people again. There were things she wanted to figure out. For instance, what was the vitality that flowed from them? Why did they get so excited about ideas? Why did she feel a warmth—yes, that was it, warmth—in their presence? Suddenly Meg realised how starved she was for love. Love! All her affairs and her attempts at love had not touched the aching need that gnawed at her.

So on other Wednesday nights Meg did go back to "the church in the house", as she came to call it. After several dinners with the group, she decided that hypocrisy must be lurking somewhere: nobody could be *that* nice. But how could she accuse the folks at the church of hypocrisy when they kept saying that the church was meant for sinners, that those who thought themselves good were not yet ready for a church.

Moreover, there was a closeness in their relationships that Meg had never seen before. It was more than friendship. For instance, she marvelled at the way Steve, once a seemingly hopeless alcoholic and now a successful piano salesman, was helping Phil, a painfully shy man who worked in the Interior Department. Ben, who drove a bread truck, would at times minister to Betts, an interior decorator. There was Martha, a secretary; Sam, an oceanographer; Jane, a beautician; Bill a former Harvard professor; Estelle, a publicity girl; Karl, who had spent forty years as a sailor—drunk most of the time. All saw a great deal of one another and shared each other's problems. Their lives were transparently open to the fellowship. In this transparency it seemed the natural thing to reveal their faults freely and to ask for help.

Nevertheless Meg was sure that she had a margin on all of them when it came to sin. She went through a period of trying to shock them. Over the years she had developed a hard line of talk. Increasingly she tried it out at the church. Once she let out some oaths in the chapel. No one batted an eyelash.

Then she had a conference with the minister, Arnold, and tried out on him raw statements of disbelief liberally sprinkled with profanity. She was dismayed to find him shockproof. He seemed neither surprised nor impressed by anything she said.

"Why should any of us be startled," he commented to her one afternoon, "to find out that human nature is capable of anything? There aren't any new sins, Meg. Just variations on old ones. Besides, the sort of thing you've been telling me is pale stuff compared to the adventure that Christ brings into life." He grinned at her discomfiture, and it was a disarming grin.

"Christ doesn't want to condemn you. He didn't come to earth to deepen our sense of moral defeat. He came to deliver us from what defeats us. All He wants, Meg, is to lift the weight of your past from you, so that you'll be free—really free. It's His love that makes that possible, Meg, His love—"

Meg burst into tears and fled from the office.

There were times when Meg was sure that Arnold and all the people at the church were crazy. Then there was a period when she thought they were rich—how else could they give so much money to the church? Finally there came the time when Meg did not care what they were. She knew only that she wanted what they had. She needed their love, needed to know that she belonged. Still—how could they love *her*?

Meanwhile Meg had asked Maynard to delay the divorce. She was now actively enrolled in a course called "Christian Growth" and there was the outside chance that she might get some help toward saving their marriage. Maynard was distant and unimpressed, but agreed to postpone divorce action for a few weeks. He even began dropping in at the church to see what it was all about.

One evening Arnold was talking about sin. "Sin is not simply the violation of a code." he told the class. "Sin is an affront by one spirit against another—an outrage of love.

"That's bad enough, but it's even worse when we try to deny our sin to God and ourselves. Because that shuts off forgiveness and the peace that comes with a reconciliation with the God of love.

"Why does the Bible tell us that sin is so deadly?" As Arnold talked on, Meg began taking notes:

1. Our sins come between us and God and make it difficult to feel His presence. They are like mud and dirt thrown up on a window pane, shutting out the sunlight.
2. Even small sins narrow down the channel by which life and vitality flow to us, thus choking off creativity. But often we don't understand the connection between our lack of productivity and sin.

3. Sin divides us on the inside, splits us asunder. It separates conscious mind from subconscious, so that we are a personality in conflict with ourselves.

4. Our wrongdoings cut us off from other human beings. God reaches down to hold my hand. With my other hand I touch the lives of fellow human beings. Only as both connections are made can the power flow. And sin will break the connection every time. Isn't that why Jesus warned us that if we want forgiveness for ourselves, we'd better forgive others?

Outside the classroom a bell rang. The young minister picked up his notes, put them in the pocket of his coat. "Now that we are all aware, I hope, of our need for forgiveness, next Wednesday we'll try to answer the question how can we go about getting it."

Meg sat there for a moment staring at him. That was what she most wanted to know.

The following Wednesday, Meg had her notebook out and her attention riveted on getting down the steps in forgiveness as Arnold outlined them:

1. We have to be honest—candid and above board with God about all our sins and failures.

   Drop all excuses and explanations; these are not important.

   Be as specific as possible in confession.

2. We claim for ourselves one of God's promises for forgiveness. Here are some to choose among:

   "If we confess our sins, he is faithful and just to forgive us our sins, and to cleanse us from all unrighteousness."[1]

   "Him that cometh to me I will in no wise cast out."[2]

   "Come now, and let us reason together, saith the Lord: though your sins be as scarlet, they shall be as white as snow; though they be like crimson, they shall be as wool."[3]

   "For Thou, Lord, art good, and ready to forgive; and

plenteous in mercy unto all them that call upon thee."[4]

3. We accept Christ's forgiveness *right now*, by faith—even though we feel no different yet.

    We also accept an initial entering into a personal relationship with Him, or an instantaneous return to fellowship with Him, as the case may be.

4. God may ask you to make some restitution. (This is not always possible. Some wrongs can never be righted by us.) If He does ask restitution, obey—no matter what the cost to your pride.

5. Now turn from the past to face the future. No more wallowing in remorse. God has forgiven you and wiped out your sins. Now you must forgive yourself. "Forgetting those things that are behind" is the only healthy way.

"When you've gone through these five steps," Arnold continued, "you're ready to begin living. Remember that it's everyday life that Christ wants to sanctify. Sometimes a new Christian makes the mistake of thinking he ought to be mystical, of wanting a sort of ivory-tower faith. Believe me, when you let Christ order your days, you won't spend your time reading spiritual books while your children are on the street and your house in disorder—"

Meg raised her hand. Her face was flushed, her voice trembling a little. "I've taken notes on all this, but there's still something I don't understand."

"Ask any question you'd like," Arnold encouraged.

"Well, Maynard and I have a coal stove in our living-room. It's the bane of my life. Shake it down once and coal dust covers the whole house. Talk about disorder! I hate it almost as much as I hate myself." Meg hesitated, then blurted out, "How in th' hell can you sanctify a coal stove?"

When the friendly laughter had subsided, Arnold's answer seemed inspired: "In other words, the hated stove has become a sort of symbol to you. Think of it like this, Meg. When the coal is placed in the stove to come in contact with the flames, there's always an initial burning off of surface dust, gases, the superficial debris. The coal is not yet united with the flame. We are the coal. The flame is God's love.

"Once the superficial things are burned off; then a more fundamental change takes place. The coal itself catches fire. Finally it glows red-hot, even at its heart. This is a depth transmutation in which the coal and the flame are fused—"

"What about all the ashes which I have to dust and which Maynard has to keep carting away?" Meg asked.

"The ashes, Meg? All during your lifetime ashes will be sifting off. . . ."

On Good Friday of that year Meg and Maynard slipped into the back of the chapel to find a play going on. During their drive to the church, Meg had been talking about how stupid Good Friday seemed to her. Why did the churches make such a commotion about it? What did Jesus' death and ressurrection have to do with them?

There was little space at the front of the chapel, so the stage set had to be simple. The play had been written by Elizabeth Ann Campagna, one of the group. It consisted of a conversation between two middle-aged woman about their sons, their hopes for them, the trials and joys of raising children. In the end it turned out that one woman was the mother of Judas, the other the mother of Christ. It was direct and powerful. And something profound got through to Meg. When she left the chapel an hour and a quarter later, for her Jesus Christ had passed from a historic figure who had lived and died long ago to a Person alive now.

Meg described later how she felt after that performance. She saw that she had a choice. She could say to Him, "Yes I will let You live in my heart." This would be disturbing, unsettling to her existence. Or she could say, "No, I will not let you into my life." In that case, she felt she would be a part of the mass of people who crucified Him. She would, in effect, be pounding in some nails herself. And as far as she was concerned, Christ's agony would have been for nothing.

As she walked down the stone steps into the Washington

spring, she whispered an interior "Yes" to this Christ of whom she was now acutely aware. All along Massachusetts Avenue the trees were a delicate chartreuse lacework of green. Azaleas flamed here and there in the yards—fuchsia and coral and magenta. She sniffed the fragrant air. Soon all across Haines Point and the Tidal Basin the Japanese cherry trees would be budding—rose and pink, flesh and white. Meg tried to let the spring seep into her spirit.

But something was wrong. Even the "Yes" she had whispered had left her no feeling of relief—only the dead weight of wrong, so much wrong.

Late that spring Meg became pregnant again. During the previous two years she had had two miscarriages. The doctors at the George Washington University Hospital could find no physical cause for her problem.

After talking with Meg at length and after several examinations, one of the gynaecologists summed up their findings for her: "Our conclusions will probably surprise you. We believe that on occasion a deep-seated sense of guilt can bring about a spontaneous abortion. Let me explain that a woman's emotions are a powerful factor, especially in the first months of pregnancy.

"You've been amazingly frank with us about your past. Because of certain actions resulting in guilt, your subconscious mind has persuaded you that you aren't fit to be a mother. Understand, I'm not saying that is true. That's your verdict about yourself. But the result is that each time you become pregnant, you abort the foetus."

Meg, abrupt as usual, merely asked, "So what can I do about it?"

"This is where medicine has to join hands with psychiatry or religion—maybe both. There are several possible approaches," the doctor answered cautiously. "I'm going to stick my neck out here a bit because your situation is unusual. Psychoanalysis might help. Or if you're a Catholic, the confessional might do it. If you're a Protestant, you could seek out a minister. But if you are intent on bringing this baby to term, we do urge something in addition to the drugs and the help we're going to give you."

The doctor stood up and held out his hand. "Good luck. You know we will do everything we can here at the clinic."

Now that it was imperative that she find the way to accept forgiveness, Meg felt desperate. The baby's life depended on it. Apparently guilt could kill. But she and Arnold had talked so often about getting rid of guilt. What more could he tell her? Nevertheless she set up a conference with him for the first afternoon he had some free time.

"The problem as the doctor analysed it," Arnold reflected, "is how to persuade yourself at deep levels of consciousness that God has forgiven you. This may take time, Meg. What I suggest now is that you try the game of 'acting as if—'"

"I don't understand—"

Arnold rose and stood in front of the fireplace, his hands behind his back. "Meg, do you believe that God is so eager to have us as His children that He accepts us the minute we come asking for forgiveness?"

"Yes, I think I can believe that."

"All right, then. You have asked, and He has forgiven. But there is something in you that dies hard, that refuses to feel clean. So from now on try disregarding that soiled feeling. Act the truth—that the past is wiped out. And if that sometimes seems like hypocrisy, like acting a lie, tell yourself you're playing the game of 'acting as if'."

"All right, I'll do it. I'll try anything, I've got to have this baby! I've got to!"

In the days that followed Meg found a technique that helped her with the 'act as if' game. Each time a self-despising thought assaulted her, she would counter by reading over one of the Scripture verses she had typed on cards. Some of the friends at the church who were more familiar with the Bible than she had helped her cull them:

Nòw ye are clean through the word which I have spoken unto you.[5]
We know that we belong to God. . . . We reassure ourselves

whenever our heart may condemn us; for God is greater
than our heart, and he knows all.[6]
We do know, we have believed, the love God has for us. ..
Love has no dread in it. ....
So you must consider yourselves dead to sin and alive to
God. ....
Let us enjoy the peace we have with God through our Lord
Jesus Christ.

There were more verses. Meg found them living words,
weapons against the still-lurking shadows. After a time she
scarcely had to glance at the cards. Her hope was that as she
memorised the words, spoke them over and over, that stubborn
core inside would finally yield to the love of Christ.

The nine months of her pregnancy seemed endless. On two
occasions when self-loathing rose strongly to haunt her, she
came close to losing the baby. Each time she took a firmer
grip on 'acting as if' and on the healing words of Scripture.
Even so, final victory was to come only after the baby's birth.

It happened in the hospital, three nights after Jacqueline was
born. Meg awoke about midnight. The room looked as it had
a few minutes before—pale moonlight streaming across the
polished linoleum floor. Scrim curtains billowed gently into
the room on an evening breeze. Three pink roses drooped in
a vase on the dresser, yet there was a Presence in the room.
Meg felt it, knew it. This was Christ, and He had come to take
her on a journey.

The journey took her back to her childhood. All that long
night Christ helped her emotionally to re-live episode after
episode from her past. Through part of this she appeared to be
dreaming. Then she would emerge into consciousness and
would cringe and weep over the vivid pictures that had
risen to haunt her, the faces of those whose lives she had soiled
—no detail too tiny to recall.

Yet she was aware that something wonderful was happening. Into each painful memory there was flowing the healing
of the Spirit of God. Then she would sink again into the
dreaming state, and she and Christ would move on to the next

episode—and the next. It was a falling and rising, a falling and rising, and in the process the recalcitrant subconscious was being healed and made of one piece with the conscious.

She knew now that Christ did not minimise her sins. He loathed the deeds that had soiled and betrayed her. Yet how tenderly He loved her!

As light flooded the hospital room Meg knew that she would never again see a sunrise so beautiful. She wept once more, this time not from shame, but to think that Christ had cared enough about her—after all she had done and been—to seek her out and to make complete the forgiveness she and Arnold had begun by faith. For the first time in her life Meg felt clean.

One of the fascinating sidelights of her experience was that, although on that memorable night the name and face of every man with whom she had been sexually involved were vividly remembered, she was to discover a few years later that she could not recall a single name. Thus it was literally true that her transgressions were wiped out, removed from her.

Almost immediately her friends saw the transformation. Meg's hardness and profanity died in her. The expression on her face was different; her manner altered. Even her taste in clothes changed.

And how she looked forward to seeing her friends at church and to listening to Arnold's teaching! Step by step she moved ahead. "If we don't keep our window panes clean," Arnold told her and the others one night, "the excitement that we feel when we first enter the Christian life will fade. Even an accumulation of small sins can make life seem like a bottle of ginger ale from which all the fizz is gone. So here are some hints.

"Discouragement about our failures and stumblings is never the way to handle them. In an old book I found this statement, 'All discouragement is from the devil'. Whether you believe in the devil as a personality of evil in the world or not, ponder that one.

"Some kind of methodical cleaning out at intervals is necessary if we are to have an uninterrupted fellowship with God.

We in the Protestant churches don't make enough provision for this, though certain high Episcopal churches do offer the Confessional.

"In trying to keep cleaned out, beware of things that you have an instinctive desire to keep hidden—no matter how insignificant these may seem to you.

"In this connection, I want to read to you a paragraph from Carl Jung's *Modern Man in Search of a Soul:*

> "To cherish secrets and to restrain emotions are psychic misdemeanours for which nature finally visits us with sickness. ... It is as if man had an inalienable right to behold all that is dark, imperfect, stupid and guilty in his fellow beings—for such of course are the things that we keep private to protect ourselves. It seems to be a sin in the eyes of nature to hide our insufficiency—just as much as to live entirely on our inferior side. There appears to be a conscience in mankind which severely punishes the man who does not somehow and at some time, whatever cost to his pride, cease to defend and assert himself, and instead confess himself fallible and human. Until he can do this, an impenetrable wall shuts him out from the living experience of feeling himself a man amongst men. ..."[7]

For Meg came the final step toward forgiveness that Christ sometimes requires—restitution. She knew that she could never undo all the wrong she had wrought. Yet now that Christ had offered her the love that would never let go, He was making it clear to her that neither would that love let her off.

"Christ told me," Meg said later, "to go back to the spot where I'd shared degradation with so many youngsters and show them some real fun. It was a case of 'Go home to thy friends'."

So each Saturday night she went. About the fifth week a burly Irish cop met her at the door of the dance hall. "Lady, it's wonderful what you're doing for these kids," he confided.

"You know, there used to be the most awful woman down here—"

"My head went down and I stared at my shoes," she recalls. "I breathed a quick little prayer. 'God, when you gave me a new life, I hope that you gave me a new face. Please don't let him recognise me. I couldn't take that—yet!'

"I guess that there wasn't much danger that the cop would recognise me. Already God had done a pretty thorough job. The man just patted my hand in a fatherly way and said, 'Lady, the police force is sure glad you're here!'"

The new person that is Meg became an integral part of the small church that had lured her away from the old life. It was there that I came to know her. Of course, Margaret Stanley is not her real name. I have cherished her friendship for something over ten years. I have marvelled at her ceaseless striving for growth in her new life, have been astonished at the flashes of insight that come to her.

Often as I have witnessed her unwavering compassion for the failures and foibles of all human beings, I have remembered that nameless woman of long ago. Out of her shame a group of Scribes and Pharisees had dragged her before Christ. For me, the scene is for ever etched as Peter Marshall's words painted it:

> . . . The woman lies before Christ in a huddled heap,
>   sobbing bitterly. . . .
>   shivering as she listens to the indictment.
> The penalty for adultery is stoning.
>
> Jesus' steady eyes take in the situation at a glance.
> He sees what they try to hide from Him—
>   the hard faces that have no mercy or pity.
> Every hand holds a stone and clutching fingers run
> along the sharp edges with malicious satisfaction.
> They have brought the woman to Christ as a vindictive
> afterthought, not for formal trial,
>   (for they have already tried her)
> but in a bold effort to trap Him.

Either He will have to set aside the plain commandment of
the law, or tacitly consent to a public execution. . . .
And has He not said often, "Be ye therefore merciful"?
How can He condemn the woman and still be merciful?
The circle of bearded men wait impatiently for His
answer. . . .

Christ looks into the faces of the men before Him, and
steadily—with eyes that never blink—he speaks to them:
  "He that is without sin among you,
   let him first cast a stone at her."

His keen glance rests upon the woman's accusers one by
one. . . .
There is the thud of stone after stone falling on the
pavement.
Not many of the Pharisses are left now.
Looking into their faces Christ sees into the yesterdays that
lie deep in the pools of memory and conscience. He sees
into their very hearts . . .

                 Idolater . . .
                  Liar . . .
                Drunkard . . .
               Murderer . . .
               Adulterer . . .

One by one, they creep away—like animals—slinking into
the shadows. . . .
  Shuffling off into the crowded streets to lose
  themselves in the multitudes.

"He that is without sin among you, let him cast the first
stone at her."

But no stones have been thrown.
They lie around the woman on the pavement.
She alone is left at the feet of Christ.

The stillness is broken only by her sobbing.
She still has not lifted her head. . . .
And now Christ looks at her.
He does not speak for a long moment.

Then, with eyes full of understanding, He says softly:
  "Woman, where are those thine accusers?
  Hath no man condemned thee?"
And she answers,
  "No man, Lord."

That is all the woman says from beginning to end.
She has no excuse for her conduct.
She makes no attempt to justify what she has done.
And Christ looking at her, seeing the tear-stained cheeks,
                    seeing further into her heart,
                    seeing the contrition there,
says to her, "Neither do I condemn thee:
                        go, and sin no more . . ."

And His voice is like a candle at twilight,
  like a soft angelus at the close of the day. . . .
    like the singing of a bird after the storm. . . .
It is healing music for the sin-sick heart.

All is quiet for a while.
If she breathes her gratitude, it is so soft that only He
hears it.
Perhaps He smiles upon her, as she slowly raises her eyes.
  a slow, sad smile of one who knows that He Himself has
  to pay the price for that absolution. . . .

She has looked into the eyes of Christ.
She has seen God.
She has been accused
            convicted
        judged but not condemned.

She has been forgiven!
And now her head is up.
Her eyes are shining like stars, for has she not seen
the greatest miracle of all?

It is more wonderful than the miracles of creation. . . .
    more mysterious than the stars. . . .
    more melodious than any symphony. . . .
      more wonderful than life itself. . . .
that God is willing, for Christ's sake, to forgive sinners
like you and me. . . .[8]

And that is the miracle that came to Meg.

8: ...As We Forgive Those Who Sin Against Us

FORGIVENESS has two sides that are inseparably joined: the forgiveness each of us needs from God, and the forgiveness we owe to other human beings. Most of us prefer not to face up to the fact that God's forgiveness and man's are for ever linked.

Jesus warned us that if we want the Father's forgiveness, there is only one way to get it: Start the flow of forgiveness between heaven to earth by forgiving our brother from the heart. The story of Harvey Smith, a friend of my husband Len, is an extraordinary example of man's need to forgive those who have wronged him.

This young minister recently wrote Len that he would soon be passing through New York. "I'm resigning my pastorate in Danielsville, Georgia, to move to Boston for some graduate work. With a wife and four children, you can imagine that this has been a hard decision. I could come out to Chappaqua to see you late Saturday afternoon." So it was arranged.

When our guest arrived, I found him as curious about me as I was about him. At first, I put this down to his interest in how I might be adjusting to my new situation: a husband, a new household, and three young children in addition to Peter John. But as Harvey Smith shook my hand firmly and looked me straight in the eyes searchingly, he said, "Before I leave, I want to tell you the main reason that I've been so eager to meet you."

"Then that makes two stories for me to hear," I told him.

Harvey and Len had been friends in 1950 when they were both attending the Marble Collegiate Church in New York. Len had told me the bare outlines of Harvey Smith's story—

his experience with forgiveness—but I wanted to hear it directly from him.

Our guest settled himself in a lounge chair and crossed his long legs. He had an easy manner and soft speech of the southerner. "Forgiveness? I used to think I knew a lot about that subject." Suddenly Harvey Smith's thoughts seemed far away.

"Every time my congregation repeats that one sentence in the Lord's Prayer, I stand there in the pulpit wondering if they realise the terrible condition of forgiveness that they are acknowledging."

"How do you mean?" I asked.

"The sentence 'Forgive us our trespasses as—that is, in proportion as—we forgive those who trespass against us.'"

"Christ was even more specific after He had finished teaching them the prayer," Len added, "when He says that if we do not forgive other men, God will not forgive us.[1] That seems rugged."

"I've had good reason to ponder that teaching," Harvey continued, "It certainly doesn't mean that God is threatening to punish us by paying us back in kind."

"But Jesus must have meant what He said," I added. "He could not have been more clear-cut or emphatic about it."

As the three of us discussed the sentence in the Lord's Prayer, we came to the conclusion that the terrible condition is there, not because Jesus willed it but because it states an inescapable fact, a law. When we hold unforgiveness or malice in our hearts, then we cannot possibly have our hearts open to the love of God. We are the ones who have shut the door, not God.

And then Harvey Smith spoke several memorable sentences which I hope I can quote accurately:

"In forgiveness, there has to be a flow. It is the law of the tides; the law of seedtime and harvest. No receiving without giving; no dead-sea hearts are possible. As we give, it is given unto us—in money, in health, in love, in forgiveness. We just cannot have forgiveness in any other way, because that is the way life works."

And then Harvey told us his story.

In the autumn of 1950 Harvey Smith had come to New York City from La Grange, Georgia, to attend Columbia University. Soon after arriving, he had met a boy named Jack in one of his classes. Jack was a young man with an unhappy background, reared in a broken home. He had just done a miserable stint in the Navy, and now was confused about his future. He seemed to need a friend, so Harvey let him share his apartment. It was a basement apartment in the shadow of the Cathedral of St. John the Divine.

What the Southerner did not know was that Jack had always been an emotionally disturbed person. This unhappy truth came out soon enough. Periods of seeming normalcy would be followed by uncontrollable temper tantrums. As these become more frequent and Jack's drinking bouts grew heavier, Harvey realised that he was in a situation he could not handle. Moreover, his unhappy friend refused to go to a counsellor.

Finally Harvey knew what he had to do. He would move out and leave the apartment to Jack. His plan was to find a room near by, so that they could still be friends. Perhaps then he could be more objective and so be of more help.

It was on a Thursday morning just as he was about to leave for school that Harvey told his apartment-mate of his decision. It was only later that he realised how shattering this was to the distraught man. Apparently he had become Jack's only security. Now love was being withdrawn, and his whole world was collapsing.

The agitated Jack pleaded at first. Then rage took over. He struck out at Harvey, who protected himself from the flailing arms and held them until the other boy quieted down.

When the anger seemed to be spent, Harvey went over to the mirror to tend to a cut on his nose. At that moment he heard a noise like a snarl behind him. As he wheeled, Jack shoved the door to with one foot. In one hand he was brandishing a hammer.

Harvey was not frightened. He was a larger man than his apartment-mate; he was sure he could disarm him easily. But as he grabbed for the hammer and kicked it under the dresser, he felt a heavy blow in the back. Then as the two men grappled, there were two more sharp thrusts in Harvey's back.

This was the worst tantrum yet. He must get Jack out of the room. He shoved his antagonist back to the door, then held him with one hand, while with the other he turned the latch. Suddenly there were two more lunges at him, one to the abdomen and one to the chest. And at that moment Harvey's eyes caught the flash of a knife.

Summoning all his strength, he shoved Jack into the hall, threw the latch, and stood leaning against the door, trying to understand why he could not get his breath.

Through the closed door, he called for help. Mr Rogers, the building superintendent, had a workshop just down the hall. Perhaps he would hear. Then Harvey realised that his voice did not sound right. Feeling something sticky on his sweater, he looked down. Red-tinged bubbles were seeping through the sweater from his chest. A sickening realisation swept him. "I've been stabbed. My lungs are punctured." He swayed, then steadied himself against the door.

Immediately there was a knock. *Must be Mr Rogers*. The wounded man managed to open the door, then collapsed in a heap on the floor.

The superintendent took one horrified look. Blood-specks had spattered the young man's face and sweater. A red stain was spreading across his chest. Colour was draining from Harvey's face, his eyes were glazing.

Fear gripped Mr Rogers. Without realising what he was doing, he left Harvey where he was and ran to get the police, leaving the apartment door open.

Jack appeared again in the doorway. He stood over his helpless victim, the bloody knife still in his hand. Lying there, Harvey knew that there was nothing he could do to prevent Jack from finishing the job. One more stab would probably be enough.

Instead, Jack half-lifted half-dragged Harvey to the bed. From far away, his assailant's voice came to him, "Harvey, can you forgive me?"

Harvey tried to open his eyes. Jack's face swam hazily above him. *Jack was sorry.* The haze cleared a bit. He saw Jack raise the knife to plunge it into his own chest. *Must stop him—must.* With his last strength, Harvey half-raised himself, grabbed the knife, and dropped it behind the bed.

Now the blackness began to close in. But Jack's request for forgiveness lay like a stone on Harvey's mind. He heard his own voice from a great distance, "Yes, Jack, I forgive you."

Mind and spirit seemed to be separating from body. *That's not me, the natural man speaking. That came as a response from all the thing's I've ever learned in my Christian faith. . . .*

There were no more thoughts.

In the operating theatre of Knickerbocker Hospital on New York's West Side, Dr Ruth Selznick was examining Harvey Smith's multiple chest wounds. This skilled physician, a specialist in chest surgery, had never seen a worse case. Five deep knife wounds . . . lungs rapidly filling with blood . . . patient in a state of deep shock . . .

She set to work. Hours went by. Then suddenly there was a new crisis. The patient's breathing stopped. A split-second decision required a new incision, then alternate pressure and suction on the lungs. No response from the inert form on the table. Minutes passed . . . four . . . six. Suddenly a tremor went through the patient's body. Harvey began to breathe again.

Seven hours and fifty minutes after having been placed on the table, Harvey was wheeled from the operating room. But the struggle to live had only begun. The doctor sat by his bed and laboured over him all that night.

For a week Harvey hung between life and death. Most of the time he was conscious and thinking clearly, but he had to lie still. With both lungs punctured and collapsed, the least movement might cause haemorrhaging.

There was pain too—much pain, and at moments, self-pity. *Do I really know the meaning of forgiveness? I told Jack I had forgiven him. I gave it all I had. And it wasn't enough, because I still feel resentful.*

Harvey lay very still, thinking. His thoughts roamed over the weeks prior to the stabbing. Then an idea came to him. Are any of us ever blameless? Maybe it had been out of pride and not a little self-righteousness that he had been trying to help Jack. Perhaps his "goodness" had actually been a stumbling block to Jack.

Then the pain would come back again. Harvey would gasp for a breath that was slow in coming. Nothing but a gurgling sound deep in his chest. And in his heart, fear.

This isn't easy. Forgiveness is costly. Am I really willing to pay the price? Do I really forgive him?

It seemed even more costly that day when Harvey heard that Jack was building his testimony on the basis of self-defence. Harvey's fingerprints were on the hammer. Of course they were! So Jack had decided to plead that he had been attacked first, had struck with the knife only to protect himself. Grimly Harvey pondered the irony of it. *Forgiveness is costly...*

He thought back to that moment when he had lain on the bed with Jack standing over him brandishing the bloody knife. "Yes, Jack I forgive you...." The instinct that had told him that this was not really him speaking had been right.

He had not the ability to get rid of the surging resentments, the bitterness, the self-pity, the temptation to compare Jack's conduct to his. He could not cleanse himself of those emotions, but the One who had spoken those words of forgiveness for him that day in the apartment could complete the job for him now. All he had to do was to be willing to let the resentment go and to set his will toward forgiveness. Christ would do the rest. *But forgiveness is costly: it cost Christ a great deal.*

As he lay in his hospital bed, near death, Harvey found the meaning of life. Out of new understanding, once more from the depths of his being, came the words "Jack, I forgive you." And at last there was peace in his heart.

Meanwhile during those weeks in the hospital, Harvey's friends at the Young Adult Group of the Marble Collegiate

Church were donating blood—a great deal of it. Over and over they met to pray for Harvey and for Jack. One member of the group was Ann Hougasian, whom Harvey had met some months before.

Quietly the young people raised the money to pay all Harvey's hospital expenses. Daily they inquired about him, sent flowers, fruit, showered small kindnesses on him. Through them Christ's love was flowing to him. He dared not dam up any of that love and prevent it from flowing to the one who needed it most—Jack.

Then Harvey learned something else about forgiveness. It was his red-haired doctor who taught him.

"You're going to get well," she told him one morning.

The patient smiled at her. "I've known that for several days. It's mostly thanks to you, too."

"No-o. There's another reason. Your condition has been so precarious that anything could have tipped the scales."

"What do you mean?"

"I've watched you closely. You're been at peace with yourself, especially the last ten days. If you had held on to any hate at all, that negative emotion would have sapped so much of your energy that you probably would not have pulled through."

Throughout the rest of the day, Harvey pondered the doctor's words. In this case, hateful unforgiving thoughts would literally have destroyed him.

The doctor was right. Her patient eventually did make a complete recovery. And Harvey, convinced that his life had been spared for some purpose, became intent on finding that purpose.

It was more than three years before he knew. In the meantime, he had taken a full-time job with the Boy Scouts of America. On Christmas Day 1952 he and Ann Hougasian were married in a quiet ceremony in La Grange, Georgia.

Len and I had listened to this gripping story through part of the morning and during lunch. Immediately after lunch our twelve-year-old Linda appeared in the doorway. "Daddy, I've spilled something on the rug by my bed and need to use the vacuum sweeper. But it won't work. Something's wrong. Will you—?"

"I'll have a look at it," Len said. Soon he and Harvey were down on hands and knees taking the plug apart. In the end, it was Harvey who found the loose wire and reconnected it. I remember this little incident because what to some might have been an annoying interruption was to Harvey Smith a pleasure: he was helping someone.

After that, Harvey told us the second part of his story. "This is the part I really came here to tell you," he said to me. "It happened one Saturday night in mid-April 1955. I was then completing my third year as a district Boy Scout executive in New York City. Ann and I and another couple had gone to the Roxy to see the movie of your book, *A Man Called Peter.*

"I sat there completely absorbed in the story. There came that scene at the Naval Academy in Annapolis where Dr Marshall had decided at the last minute to change his sermon and preach about death. He didn't know why; it seemed an odd topic for the young cadets. But that same afternoon he discovered why. Over the car radio came the news that Pearl Harbour had been bombed. We were at war.

"In that scene God got through to me. Nothing spectacular —no visions, mind you. Just a simple message to heart and brain, 'Harvey, I want you to give up Boy Scout work. I led Peter Marshall. I can lead you. You're to go back to school and prepare for the ministry.'

"My response was immediate. No struggle, in spite of the fact that I loved Scout work. No indecision, though going back to school would mean a financial struggle. By then, Ann and I had a year-old son.

"I just said to myself, 'All right, Lord, if that's what you want for me.' I remember trying to hold back the tears. Ann sensed my emotion because she reached for my hand.

"The rest of the movie was lost to me. I had to go back a few weeks later to see how it ended.

"Later that evening, when I told Ann what had happened

in the theatre and asked her how she would feel about being the wife of a minister, she was jubilant. 'Why, darling, now I can tell you. I thought you were studying to be a preacher when I first met you. Be a minister's wife? Nothing could please me more.'

"The decision had to go through a time-testing period to make certain that this was no ephemeral emotionalism. But months later I was as sure as ever, the call as clear, my enthusiasm just as great. So I entered seminary in the fall. You know the rest of the story."

The three of us marvelled at the events that had dovetailed and conspired to bring Harvey to the place where God wanted him.

Then I asked "But what happened to Jack?"

"He was sentenced to several years' treatment in a corrective institution. I understand that now he is out again." Harvey was silent a moment. "There is so much to learn the hard way about forgiveness."

Then he repeated again the steps.

"First, came the realisation that I was not without blame, that none of us ever are. Second, that forgiveness isn't easy—it's costly. And then I learned that, from God's point of view, forgiveness isn't complete until a severed relationship has been mended. It took me a while to see that this is the point of that Scripture verse, 'If thou bring thy gift to the altar, and there rememberest that thy brother hath aught against thee; Leave there thy gift before the altar ... first be reconciled to thy brother, and then come and offer thy gift.'[2]

"This means that we won't feel that our prayers are getting through, or our gifts being accepted, until we have done something to try to heal the broken relationship. So you see, actually the forgiveness process between Jack and me is not finished yet."

"But, Harvey," Len interrupted, "after all that has happened and considering Jack's emotional situation, do you really think a constructive relationship could be established now?"

"It takes faith to think so," Harvey answered slowly. "I

can't honestly say I relish trying it. But it's unfinished business, so only God can tell me how to finish it."

_ _ave a feeling that Harvey will get back to Jack. Some day I shall learn the final chapter of this extraordinary story.

Jesus had a great deal to say about forgiveness. Take the scene recorded by Matthew in which the subject is under discussion: The disciples know that according to old Jewish law, one must forgive three times. After that, a man can be as hostile to another as he wishes.

But impetuous Peter is feeling expansive. He draws his striped robe about him and asks, "Lord, how oft shall my brother sin against me and I forgive him?" A smug look creeps across the disciple's face. He will be overly generous in answering his own question and so win a word of approval from the Master: "Until *seven* times?"

Christ looks at His disciple, His eyes showing amusement. Peter is so transparent, always ready to talk. "Your arithmetic is all wrong, Simon, as wrong as that of the scribes and Pharisees. Forgive seven times? Nay—seventy times seven."

Then seeing Peter's face screwed up, obviously working on the sum in his head, the Master says, "Let me tell you a story:

"A certain King had a servant who owed him ten thousand talents—"

Immediately Matthew, the former customs collector with the mathematician's brain, exclaimed, "Ten thousand talents! Why, the total annual taxes of all five provinces of our land are but eight hundred talents. That's—that's twelve and a half times that much!"*

Jesus continued. "Of course the king knew that a debt like that was impossible of repayment, so he ordered the servant, his wife, and children sold into slavery.

"But the miserable servant prostrated himself, bowing his head in the dust before the king. 'Lord, have patience with me. I will pay thee all.'

---

* About £714,000 sterling; the purchasing power of that sum was many times what it would be today.

"It was so preposterous as to be touching. The King's amusement was tinged with pity. This servant had many lovable qualities. With sudden compassion, he said, 'All right, I release you from the debt. Rise up. Be gone!'

"The servant leapt to his feet, rejoicing. He would have kissed his master, had he dared. He was free—free!

"Later on the same day, the servant went to the bazaar to purchase fresh pike for the master's household. Suddenly down the street, opposite the linen draper's shop, he spied Nahum's retreating back. Nahum had owed him a hundred shillings for half a moon. Was the rascal trying to avoid him?

"The servant drew his robe about him and ran down the cobblestone street, ducking women with baskets and pails, side-stepping donkeys and asses. He caught up with Nahum at the dove stall. Roughly he reached for his throat. 'You've been running from me long enough! You'll pay what you owe me right now.'

"Nahum fell at his feet. 'Look, I'll pay. I promise. Just have patience. If you'll give me till the sun goes down tomorrow—'

"'Patience, indeed! I will not! I've caught you now, and I'm not going to let you go again or else it will be another moon. A few days in jail may sharpen your conscience.' And he summoned the magistrate, who had no choice but to throw the debtor into jail.

"Soon word of the episode got back to the King. His own generous forgiveness had wrought no gratitude after all! He summoned his servant to him. 'Thou wicked servant! I forgave thee all that great debt. Could you not have had like mercy on your fellow servant? Your heart is hard, incapable of receiving forgiveness. Torment is always the end of the hard heart. Torment will be yours until you learn that only as you forgive, shall it be forgiven you.' "

The Master finished. His penetrating eyes circled the group, looked into each man's face in turn. For once even Peter was silent. The message of the story was sinking into their hearts: Our debt to the Heavenly Father is inordinate, unpayable so we are at the mercy of the Father's compassion. In comparison with our debt to Him, the most any human being can owe another is trifling.

Every one of us is guilty before God. There are sins of the mind and the spirit as well as of the body. There are unworthy motives. There are all the opportunities that have gone begging away. There are all the times we have chosen second best. Yet God is willing freely to forgive us, no matter what we have done, *provided* we are willing to be "kind one to another, tenderhearted, forgiving one another, even as God for Christ's sake hath forgiven you."[3]

Today our civilisation cries out for forgiveness. Husbands and wives need it ... Parents and children ... Friends ... Statesmen. Businessmen and labour leaders need it.

Yes, and nations. Jesus would tell us that we Americans must forgive the Japanese for Pearl Harbor, just as the Japanese must forgive us for Hiroshima. The Jews have so much for which to forgive the Germans. And the Germans have much to forgive the Russians; and the Russians the Germans. Have the Ethiopians forgiven the Italians? And what about the Israelis and the Arabs with so much bitterness on both sides? If the wounds of millions are to be healed, what other way is there except through forgiveness?

Jesus, at least, gives us no alternative. The command is stern. The terms are set. "But if ye forgive not men their trespasses, neither will your Father forgive your trespasses."[4]

God's forgiveness and man's are one.

9: How to Find God's Guidance

In a popular magazine some years ago, I read a story whose broad outlines have haunted me ever since. The author followed a man through one day of his life. First we saw him on a May morning, walking down the tree-shaded Main Street of his home town. He passed children on their way to school. Already some of the housewives were busy with their spring cleaning.

Up ahead on the left was the white frame cottage of a girl he knew well. All at once, he longed to push open the iron gate and stroll up the uneven brick walk for a chat with her.

For a moment he hesitated. The upstairs shades had been raised; she must be up. But no—he really should get on down to the bank. So he walked on.

Then the author interrupted his own story to show us how different the rest of this man's life would have been had he followed that impulse to push open the iron gate and walk through.

Ah—but that was not the way he decided it. And so the story went on through the trivia of the rest of the man's day.

It is a parable of our lives. At the time of each choice, we stand at one of life's crossroads. How many examples each of us could cite of seemingly insignificant decisions that changed the course of a life! The plane reservation cancelled a few hours before the plane crashed. . . . The strange timing that led to meeting the man one later married . . . and so on.

Then, if decisions—large and small—can be so important, on what basis shall we make them? Without God, most of us muddle through somehow, often with better hindsight than foresight, and sometimes with poor to disastrous consequences. To make decisions, we employ a pot-pourri of common sense, what we have learned through past experience, immediate circumstances, the weighing of factors for and against, the advice of others—all with a dash of emotion and another of prejudice.

Christianity from the first has taught that a better way for making decisions is available: the direct guidance of God to the individual. The promise that God can guide us is the clear teaching of Scripture, both in its total sweep and in its specific promises.

This Scriptural teaching rests on three pillars: (1) that God has all wisdom, hence knows the past and the future and what is best for His children; (2) that He is a God of love who cares about the individual enough to want to direct him right; (3) that He can communicate with men. As Abraham Lincoln once commented, "I am satisfied that when the Almighty wants me to do, or not to do any particular thing, He finds a way of letting me know it."

As for specific promises, there are many in the Bible, among them:

In all thy ways acknowledge him and he shall direct thy paths.[1]

He calleth his own sheep by name, and leadeth them out. . . . He goeth before them, and the sheep follow him: for they know his voice.[2]

If any of you lack wisdom, let him ask of God, that giveth to all men liberally, and upbraideth not; and it shall be given him.[3]

Howbeit when he, the Spirit of truth, is come, he will guide you into all truth . . . and he will show you things to come.[4]

Then the Bible goes on to show us how these promises were fulfilled in the lives of men and women. Take, for example, the incident concerning Paul and Ananias, as told in the ninth chapter of Acts. Let me put the story in modern language. . . .

One morning in the city of Damascus about the year A.D. 34, God spoke to a man named Ananias. "I want you to get up and go to number 38 Straight Street. That is the home of one Judas. There you are to ask for a man named Saul—"

"But, Lord—"

"This Saul has lost his sight. You will know why later. I want you to lay your hands on him, and he will recover his sight."

Suddenly a thought stabbed Ananias. "Lord, you can't be sending me to Saul of Tarsus! Appalling reports are abroad about that man. He's a murderer! He stood by and watched Stephen's death and did not lift a finger to save him. He's even had men and women who claim to be Your disciples put in chains. Why Lord, he's one of Your worst enemies—"

So Ananias, wondering if he had heard God aright, tortured with the thought that his mind might be playing tricks on him, started out for Straight Street. He found that number 38 was indeed the home of Judas and that a man named Saul was there.

But the moment he walked into the room where Saul sat, all doubts and fears left him. Whatever this Saul had been before, he was now a broken man—stunned, bewildered, lost. In a wave of compassion and confidence which Ananias scarcely understood himself, he heard himself saying, "Saul, my brother, I have been sent by the Lord to let you regain your sight and to tell you the next step—"

What if Ananias had refused to follow God's directions that day? Was this one of those hinges upon which history turns? For Saul was to become Paul, saying "I have been wrong", one of the most dramatic turnabouts any man has ever made. He was to become Paul of the towering mind, of the blazing convictions, giant of an apostle to the Roman empire, impelling advocate of Christianity to the Western world.

There are many such instances of direct guidance in Scripture. Apperently the first-century Christians expected to receive their marching orders from God, regarded this kind of inner guidance as the rule rather than the exception.

But what about today? Can we expect the same sort of direct word from God?

It would seem so, for the New Testament attaches no time tags to its promises of guidance. When I first became interested in this subject, I could not ignore Peter Marshall's oft-reiterated conviction that God can and does communicate His will to modern men and women just as He did to those in Biblical times. In his life, Peter had not often had the guidance of the inner Voice. More frequently his direction had come through providential circumstances plus a strong inner feeling or rightness about a particular decision. He had thus been led from Scotland to the United States to enter the ministry when he had thought he wanted to go to China. When the door to China had been shut in his face, he had tried for home-mission work in Scotland. That door closed, too. Through a series of remarkable circumstances, the way to the United States then opened. Certainly this was God's guidance to an extraordinarily fruitful life.

I, too, knew more of this type of guidance by circumstance than that of the inner Voice. But it was of inner guidance that Peter and I both longed to know more.

About two years after we moved to Washington, the matter was further brought to our attention by a certain group of friends in the old Oxford Group, which was the forerunner of Moral Rearmament. They believed that quietness, a receptive mind, and a pad and pencil would result in God's Voice speaking to the inner man. Since this technique was obviously meaningful to some people, I decided to try it.

Each morning after Peter left for the church office, I would shut the bedroom door and sit quietly, trying to still my churning thoughts. My thoughts were usually unruly: those two thank-you notes that should be written ... Don't forget to telephone for the pick-up of the dry cleaning ... What are we going to have for dinner tonight?

Impatiently I would break away from such trivialities, trying to make my mind a blank again. No use! Morning after morning no mighty inspiration came, no inner Voice made itself heard. The notebook on my lap had little written on it other than lists of household tasks.

Peter and I had close friends, however, who often experienced inner direction. Sometimes the guidance they received was of quite a dramatic nature.

For instance, we had two women friends who customarily spent their winters together in Florida. On Sunday they went to separate churches, because Tay is a Catholic and Fern is an Episcopalian. On one particular Sunday, after Mass in Palm Beach was over, Tay picked up Fern on the corner nearest her church. As Fern got in the car, Tay said, "I've got news for you. We're going to run down to see Grace." Whereupon she started backing into a driveway to turn around.

"You mean now? Before lunch?" They both knew that Grace's home was in Delray Beach, twenty-two miles away.

Tay nodded. "I know it's an odd time to go visiting. I may as well tell you the truth, Fern. During Mass it came to me strongly that Grace needs us desperately, right away."

"I—see. Well I'm not going to argue with that." Fern sensed an authority behind her friend's words. There had been a long series of similar guidances in the past, most of them uncannily correct. And Fern herself had often experienced a similar sort of inner direction.

As the women drove into their friend's yard, the screen door of the house burst open, and Grace came to meet them. "Am I glad to see you! I've been trying to reach you for hours by phone."

Then she told them of the emergency. During the night her husband had suffered a stroke. Already the doctor had warned her that the sick man could not possibly recover. His distraught wife was anxious to get him home to Akron, Ohio, where their married children and their families were. If the doctor's prediction was correct, then above all else her husband would want this final reunion with his family. But it was now a race against time. Tay and Fern spent the rest of the day making the arrangements.

Not until a month later, after Grace and her husband had got safely home and the dying man had had six days of joyful reunion with his children and grandchildren before the end, did Grace think to ask Fern how it was that she and Tay had driven by her house that Sunday.

At the time I wondered how to analyse such a dramatic happening. Some might call the direction Tay received in church that Sunday an example of extrasensory perception. I suspected that the first Christians would have said, "There is more to it than that."

It is true, of course, that as the church grew and spread across the centuries, some of the ideas that had meant most to those first-century disciples were almost forgotten—sturdy practical beliefs like the communion of the saints, healing, and God's direct leading. As often in the history of Christendom, it is the rebellion of small segments or fringe groups that points unerringly to the dead spots in the organised church.

Thus it was in the England of 1647 that George Fox, the son of a weaver of Drayton-in-the-Clay, conceived some strong convictions about the formalism and deadness of the churches of his day. Fox had no thought of forming a separate religious sect; he simply wanted to see the church revivified. He and his cohorts called themselves the society of friends (not even with capital letters) and among other convictions they held strongly to the "perceptible guidance of the Holy Spirit", "the inward light", meaning the distinct and conscious voice of God in the heart and mind.

During this period of my searching out the question of guidance I became especially interested in the experiences of the Society of Friends, since this is one of their strongest teachings. One memorable story of a visiting Friend, a woman who was talking to a weekday meeting in a suburb of Philadelphia, appeared in one of Hannah Smith's books.[5] The visitor knew no one in the room except those to whom she had been introduced a few minutes before.

Suddenly she interrupted her talk to say, "A young man has come into this room who has in his pocket some papers by which he's about to commit a great sin. If he will come and see me this afternoon [and she told where she was staying] I have a message from the Lord for him that will show him a way out of his trouble." Then the woman resumed her sermon.

Hannah Smith, who was present that day, followed up this case. A strange young man did call that afternoon at

the house where the woman preacher was stopping. He had
a forged cheque in his pocket. He was on his way to cash it
when something made him stop and slip into a seat in the back
of the meeting house. His name was not asked for or given,
but he tore up the cheque in the presence of the woman. Later
it was discovered that he had been so impressed with this
message from God that, from that hour, he determined never
to attempt such a dishonesty again.

On another occasion the same woman preacher was staying
with a cousin of Mrs Smith. The guest came down to breakfast
one morning saying that during the night God had told her
to take a message to a man living some miles away. She had
been given neither name nor directions. Yet her faith was such
that she asked the cousin to get out his carriage and take her.
"God will show us the way," she insisted.

At each crossroad the woman would point the direction
they were to go. Finally, after about six miles in countryside
which neither of them knew, she pointed to a farmhouse in the
distance. "That is the house and, when we get there, I'll find
the man in the garden. Thee may wait for me at the gate."

It was as she said. She delivered her message to the man in
the garden: "Thee art contemplating a wrong action that will
bring great trouble on thee and thy family. The Lord so wants
to deliver thee that He told me to come and try to open thy
eyes to the danger."

At first the man was too startled to reply. Then he haltingly
admitted that what his strange guest had said was true. This
was the day on which the plan was to have been carried out.
Now he dared not go on with it. If God had cared that much
about him, then surely He could be trusted to work out the
problem. And subsequently this man's problem was resolved
in a much simpler way than he had thought possible.

I could have no reasonable doubt as to the authenticity of
these stories because I appreciated Hannah Smith's Yankee
hard-headedness. In fact, so clear-eyed was she that throughout
her work she warns against the dangers of delusion and
fanaticism if one does not apply certain common-sense checks
to these inner impressions.

It was not until after my entering-in experience in 1944 that the inner Voice became a reality to me. Apparently this surrender of self is necessary groundwork, since not even God can lead us until we want to be led. It is as if we are given an inner receiving set at birth, but the set is not tuned in until we actively turn our lives over to God.

Then, too, most of us think of our lives in compartmentalised fashion—home life, business life, social life. Actually the various aspects of a truly creative life must dovetail. God will not direct a man's business life, for example, when the man insists on running his family life his own way. Any such partial surrender or halfway commitment will not work.

Next I discovered that, for a beginner like me, it was important that I concentrate on one or two questions on which I needed light, and ask God for directions on those. This selectivity proved more effective than trying to make my mind blank, ready to receive any message on any subject.

Also, I found that I had to be willing to obey—no matter what. Otherwise no directions would be forthcoming. Receiving guidance is definitely not a matter of telling God what we want and hoping that He will approve.

A further finding was that the inner Voice was more likely to speak to me at the first moment of consciousness upon awakening, or during some odd moment of the day as I went about routine tasks, than while I waited expectantly with pad and pencil in hand.

I experienced this one day when I was working on a curtain for our kitchen door. In a woman's magazine I had seen a picture of an hourglass-shape curtain, so attractive that I decided to copy it. It looked easy, but I soon discovered that when I pulled the curtain together in the middle, the rods bowed at top and bottom.

I worked and struggled, trying without any success to figure it out. Some sort of mathematical problem seemed to be involved, and I am not good at mathematics! I grew more and more exasperated at my own stupidity. How silly to be nonplussed by such a small problem!

Then I called a friend in, but she could not solve it either.

Finally, in great disgust, I gave up, went upstairs and flopped down on a bed. After I had been lying there a few minutes, the inner Voice said very quietly, "You do it this way." There followed a set of simple directions involving graduated tucks. The directions worked easily, perfectly.

Does this seem trivial? Of course it is. Moreover, it might be argued that it is not unusual for a solution to be served up *in toto* from the subconscious when the mind is relaxed. People experience this constantly. Then how can I justify connecting God with it?

In the first place, I think it a mistake to think of God's intervention only in terms of great events and dramatic circumstances—a sudden healing or the saving of a life in jeopardy. After all, most of our days are full of ordinary events and common experiences. Are we to believe that God has no interest in these?

Secondly, who knows what the subconscious, or the unconscious, really is? Psychologists admit that they do not. For example, here is what the late Carl Gustav Jung had to say on the subject:

> . . . in so far as anything is unconscious it is not definable. Since we cannot possibly know the limitations of something unknown to us, it follows that we are not in a position to set any limits to the self. . . .

Since a scientific man like Jung admits that we cannot set limits to the self, the Christian may be permitted to wonder whether somewhere in the deeps of personality—still beyond the reach of our scientific probing and measuring—there is not a place where the Spirit that is God can impress upon the spirit that is man a thought, a direction, a solution. Certainly it is neither plausible nor scientific to say that such things "just happen". Or if so, then many things have "just happened" to me during the course of my ordinary days.

One Sunday, our whole family (including a small guest of Peter John's), went to a Washington Hotel for Sunday dinner. After dinner, Dr Marshall lingered in the lobby of the hotel to talk to an acquaintance. Since the grown-up talk went on for some time and the two little boys got restless, they asked to go out and play. The hotel was set safely back from the street in wide lawns, so I let them go.

Minutes passed. Then, gently but clearly, that still small Voice gave me a message, "The boys need you. Better go out to them immediately."

I excused myself and went. The two boys were standing hand in hand on the curbing just ready to try to cross 16th Street—one of Washington's busiest and most dangerous thoroughfares.

Such happenings make me wonder whether God does not try more often than we know to save His children from the accidents and disasters of our lives on this earth. But many of us do not practice the art of listening to the inner Voice with regard to small everyday matters. Because we are not tuned in, He cannot get His message through to us even in emergencies.

Sometimes these emergencies are a matter of life and death. On the evening of December 7, 1946, a businessman, Stuart Luhan (he prefers that his real name be not used), checked into the Winecoff Hotel in Atlanta, Georgia. He asked for and got a room on the tenth floor above the city's traffic.

Some time after retiring, Mr Luhan was wakened by noise in the corridor. A strange red glow was reflected in the sky outside his window. *Fire!* Heart pounding, he opened his bedroom door into the corridor only to have billowing clouds of suffocating smoke all but engulf him. Backing into the room, he hastily shut the door and the transom and rushed to the window to fill his lungs with air.

What he saw there was even more terrifying. Ten storeys below a crowd was gathering, milling around fire trucks. Behind him, he could hear screams and cries for help.

Fear so consumed him that it was like a weight on his chest. But years before he had formed the habit of setting aside a time each morning for prayer and practice in listening to the Voice inside. From long experience, he knew that he could rely on God in any emergency, even in a burning building.

He retreated to the centre of the room and forced himself to begin speaking slowly the Ninty-first Psalm: "Because thou hast made the Lord, which is my refuge, even the most High, thy habitation, there shall no evil befall thee. . . ."

No evil befall thee? In this situation? How could he claim that for himself?

As he repeated this verse, suddenly his thoughts cleared. God is my very life, he reasoned. Therefore that life is eternal. "I hereby put myself in Your care and keeping," he prayed. "Let Your presence be my fortress. I await Your instructions as to the way out of this crisis."

"The first sure sign that God was with me in that fire-surrounded room was that after this prayer my fear just left me, siphoned off like poison," Mr Luhan wrote me later. "Judging from the sounds around me and the increasing heat in the room, the situation was getting worse by the minute. Yet on the inside was a centre of calm, such calmness that I really could hear that inner Voice."

The first instruction was that he should pull on his clothes. The next clear suggestion was to make a rope of the sheets, all blankets, even the bedspread. As he tied the knots, he knew that the rope would not reach more than a third of the way to the street. But he followed instructions, sure he would be told what to do next.

As he put the rope out the window, he heard the Voice say, "No—not yet, Trust Me—"

It seemed as if the delay might be fatal. Again the man started to throw the rope out of the window. Again the clear order came, "Not yet. . . . Wait."

It took will power to obey, because now black smoke was seeping into the room. But long ago he had learned to trust the Voice of God; it had led him out of other predicaments. Finally the Voice said, "Now is the time. Put the rope out the window. Tie it around the centre part of the window frame and climb out."

As Mr Luhan climbed over the sill, the wood was getting hot. In his mind rang the words, "God is my life and my salvation . . . I shall not fear. . . . God is my life—"

Down the twenty feet he slid, but his rope reached only to the eighth-floor level. What could he do now? Once again he deliberately turned his thought to God, his fortress. "God is my life. . . . My life. . . . God is my life. . . ."

Across the face of the building he saw a fireman extending a ladder to the eighth floor. That was as far as the ladder would reach. Even so it was still too far away, one room to the right.

Suddenly the fireman saw Mr Luhan hanging there. He signalled him and swung a rope hanging from a window above toward him. The first time the rope came close, the next time not so close. How could he grasp the swinging rope and still cling to the knotted bedclothes? Once again the rope hurtled through the air. This time Mr Luhan caught it.

He took a deep breath, twisted the rope around his right hand, let go the knotted bedclothes, and swung in a wide arc across the burning wall. The fireman at the top of the ladder leaned over as far as he dared, caught the end of the rope on which the man dangled, pulled it over. For a moment both men balanced precariously on the slender ladder. Then Stuart Luhan climbed down to safety.

He looked up. His improvised rope was already burning. Flames billowed from the window of the room he had just left. Yet here he was, safe on the ground with no injuries except some rope burns on the palms of his hands. God's timing had been perfect.

The next day the nation's newpapers carried ghastly pictures of the disaster and its victims, calling it one of the nation's worst fires. One hundred and twenty-seven people lost their lives; many more were injured. The details that I have put down here have been checked in correspondence with Mr Luhan.

Why was one man saved by such split-second timing when so many others died? Did God love them less? Not at all. A loving God plays no favourites, is "no respecter of persons". Could it not be that God was unable to get through, to make His voice heard and His help tangible to those who lost their lives? On the other hand, Mr Luhan was one of those rare individuals who was not only aware of the inner Voice, but had practised using his "receiving set" in tranquil days—before crisis struck.

The guidance Stuart Luhan received, as well as most of the other instances I have mentioned, came to the individual concerned at the psychic level. Or, expressed in theological terms, these people are what the New Testament calls "the sons of God ... who are guided by the Spirit of God".[6]

There is, however, a warning or corollary teaching to be seen in the New Testament. I have already mentioned it in passing: the guidance or inspection that reaches us via the unconscious should be subjected to certain tests.

The reason that guidance must be tested is one that many find difficult to believe. The writers of Scripture insist that, at the unconscious level, we are open to influences not alone from the Holy Spirit but also from perverse and evil spirits. Even those who cannot credit this in the Bible have no trouble accepting the same point when a psychological interpretation is put on it. Every one has experienced thoughts and impulses rising out of the subconscious that are selfish rationalisations or so wrongly motivated as to be evil. The end result is the same, to whatever source we credit the evil.

What are these tests to which we should subject inner messages? There are at least four of them: that of Scripture, the advice of trusted friends who are also seeking God's leading, providential circumstances, and the application of our judgment and what we might call sanctified common sense.

Testing our inner impressions by Scripture is important. Our generation is rediscovereing the Bible. Modern translations, many making use of newly discovered ancient manuscripts, have made the Scriptures more readable and understandable. Anyone who means business about God's leading will need to turn again and again to the Bible as a textbook. There are several reasons why this is important. We cannot really know what God is like until we know how God incarnate in human flesh acted, what Jesus' attitude was and is with regard to every facet of the human experience—sin, sickness, disasters, and so on. For this we have to study the

Bible intelligently, not as if the Scriptures were a sort of holy rabbit's foot, but for its wisdom in the broad sweep of its teaching about the nature of God and of man.

Then, too, the Bible has more explicit guidance for us than most of us are willing to obey. It gives clear directions about money, lawsuits, racial prejudice and social snobbery, marriage and divorce, the discipline of children, how to treat servants, advice about avenging injuries, about scruples, and much more.

Especially important, God's voice will never contradict itself. That is, He will not give us a direction through the inner Voice that will ever contradict His voice in the Scriptures.

Hannah Smith once cited a humorous example of this. A Quaker, actually a woman of integrity, stole some money because she had opened her Bible at random and put her finger on I Corinthians 3:21: "... For all things are yours. ..." Obviously the woman would have done better to have considered the consistent voice of Scripture on the side of total honesty, and its thundering "Thou shalt not steal".

The point is that, in the main, the Bible deals in principles —not disjointed aphorisms or superficial rules of conduct. These principles are valid checks: God is love, so He will not tell us to do anything unloving. God cares about other people as much as about us, so He will not tell us to do something selfish or harmful to others. His true guidance works for the benefit of all persons concerned. God is righteous, so He will not guide us to any impure act or dishonest act.

The check of a close fellowship is the next most important one. Christianity was never meant to be a lone-sheep experience. One reason the first Christians received so much guidance was that they had the *koinonia*, a corporate fellowship which made them "of one heart and soul". It was in this setting that illumination, inspiration, and guidance flourished.

Every one of us needs as much of the *koinonia* as he can find. We must seek out mature Christian friends with whom we can share questions, problems, and the joys of discovery. Ideas will often come to our corporate mind that would not come to us in isolation. And sometimes God does speak directly through these friends. At the very least, their love, perspective, and common sense will help to steer us clear of wild tangents.

Then there is the check of providential circumstances. We are most fortunate in having this test. When we have asked God to guide us, we have to accept by faith the fact that He is doing so. This means that when He closes a door in our faces (as when Peter Marshall wanted to go to China and was turned down by the London Missionary Society), then we do well not to try to crash that door.

Sensitivity is needed here. When God is guiding us, we need not ride roughshod over other people's viewpoints, lives, and affairs. The promise is that the Shepherd will go ahead of the sheep; His method is to clear the way for us.

Fourth, there is the check of our judgment and common sense. It is true that sometimes God asks us to do something the reason for which we cannot understand at the time—as in the case of Ananias in the Bible or my friend in Florida. On the other hand, neither individual was being asked to do anything that violated basic principles of right and wrong, or indeed that violated anything except personal convenience. God does not ask us to cancel out the minds or ignore the common sense He has given us, except in most unusual circumstances.

In relation to the matter of inner judgment, the Quakers were fond of saying, "Mind the checks". They meant that when we feel a strong doubt that a particular course is right, then wait. Don't move on it. Or, to put it positively, we should always move forward in faith—never out of fear.

If a strong inner suggestion is from God, it will strengthen with the passing of time. If it is not from Him, in a few days or weeks it will fade or disappear entirely.

In addition to these four checks, there are other truths about guidance that have accumulated through the centuries. Here are a few time-tested suggestions I have found useful:

Obey one step at a time, then the next step will come into view. God will not give us a blueprint of the future; He still insists that our walk be step by step in faith.

As we practice obedience, the Voice becomes clearer, the

instructions become more definite. Perhaps it should not surprise us that with guidance, as with anything else, we learn through practice.

That is why it is wise to give God a chance to speak to us each day, perhaps the first thing in the morning when the mind is freshest. A few minutes of quietness helps us focus on the areas where we most need God's help. And we need to remember that even God cannot get His word through to us when our prayers are limited to self-centred monologues.

Do not rule out God's help with the small details of life. After all, details make up the totality of life. If we do not let God into our everyday lives, He may not be able to intervene in the crises.

Finally, if you are one of those individuals who does not believe that the Creator can possibly be interested in your little affairs, then you are just the person to experiment with guidance. A few personal experiences of finding God's wisdom (a wisdom easily recognised as beyond your own), a few proofs of His personal solicitude; and your doubts, too, will melt away.

But you will never know until you try.

10: *The Power of Helplessness*

WHEN I lived in the nation's capital, I used to notice how often the Washington papers reported suicide leaps from the Calvert Street Bridge over Rock Creek Park. In fact, this happens so repeatedly that the site is often called "suicide bridge".

It was easy to sense the human tragedy behind these brief notices—the plunge of the young wife of an Air Force major who had learned that she had an inoperable cancer, or that of the elderly man whose wife had just died. These were people in the grip of circumstances which they felt helpless to change. They saw no way out of their predicaments except the way that lay over the bridge.

Helplessness is a terrifying thing to most of us. We resist it, deny it, and when we are finally face to face with it, a few of us find that we are unable to endure it.

Yet I often thought that if I could speak with such persons at the zero hour, I would use one thought to try to stop them in their mad race toward death. That thought would be that helplessness is actually one of the greatest assets a human being can have. In clichés like "God helps those who help themselves" there is but half truth. Of course, if there were no God and if we could expect no help outside ourselves, then naturally we would do well to work up all the self-confidence and self-sufficiency possible. When we could no longer muster it, we would react as did those people who took their last walk to the Calvert Street Bridge.

But since God does exist, then the cult of self-sufficiency is mistaken—tragically so in some instances, misleading in all. In my case, the most spectacular answers to prayer have come following a period when I could do nothing for myself at all.

The Psalmist says, "When I was hemmed in, thou hast freed me often."[1] Gradually I have come to recognise this hemming-in process as one of God's most loving and effective devices for teaching us that He is gloriously adequate for our problems.

This was first brought home to me at the time of Peter Marshall's death. On that chilly January morning in 1949— as I looked at my husband's face for the last time, then turned to leave the bare little hospital room—it seemed like whistling in the dark to believe that God could bring good out of such tragic loss. For to me and others in Washington and across the nation, the stilling of this effective, prophetic voice at forty-six seemed tragic waste indeed.

Here was the ultimate in helplessness—death. Sometimes life finds us powerless before facts that cannot be changed. Then we can only stand still at the bottom of the pit and claim for our particular trouble that best of all promises, that God will make even this to "work together for good to them that love God".[2] So that is what I did, and the Great Alchemist set to work.

I, who was a novice at writing and editing, put some of Peter's sermons together to form the book, *Mr Jones, Meet the Master*. From the work I got immense satisfaction and some assuagement for my sore heart. Then there came the thought of a book I might write myself. Bit by bit my childhood dream of becoming a writer seemed to be coming true. This only began to happen after God had underscored for me again—so that I would never forget it—the creative power that can begin at the point of helplessness.

It happened about halfway through the writing of *A Man Called Peter*. While I had always had a penchant for writing, I had had no training except in college English courses. I knew nothing about the technique of putting a book together. I was also on shaky economic ground because I had resigned a teaching position in order to give full time to the book.

Events reached a climax on the day that I received devastating criticism from a man whose judgment I trusted: "The manuscript lacks warmth, emotion. The facts are here"—my critic thumped the pile of pages in his lap—"but not the heart. You haven't even begun to get inside the man Peter Marshall."

Back in the apartment Peter John and I shared in Washington, the gravity of this criticism shattered what little self-confidence I had. Yet I knew that my friend had spoken the unvarnished truth. I remember standing at the bedroom window looking out through a blur of tears at a group of children playing in the courtyard, then throwing myself across the bed to cry it out.

What I did not realise then was that this was the crucial point at which the book and my future could have gone either way. Every human inclination was pulling me toward the trap of self-pity.

And why not? It is easy to rationalise self-pity. How much can one person take? My husband was gone at the prime of his career, leaving me with a small boy to rear alone. There was no over-abundance of money. And what made me think that I could write, anyway? I had no training except as a preacher's wife.

My thoughts went back to lines from one of Edna St Vincent Millay's poems that I had been fond of in college:

> My spirit sore from marching
> Toward that receding west
> Where Pity shall be governor. . . .

What does one do when the spirit is sore from marching? Give up? Let Pity be governor? Yet I knew that this kind of thinking was self-indulgence. It was settling down to a self-centredness that shuts God out, blocks His power, cuts the nerve of creativity.

And so I faced my crossroads. Perhaps I should put the manuscript aside for a while. That would give my thoughts time to jell, I would tell myself. Meanwhile, the practical solution was a job that would provide a steady income for Peter John and me. Looking back now I wonder whether, if I had yielded to this urge, I would ever have got back to the writing.

Some time during the next hour, out of some dusty pigeonhole of my mind, rose words to haunt me from Brother Lawrence, a seventeenth-century French Carmelite monk. I had read his tiny *Practice of the Presence of God* so often that many of the archaic sentences were for ever mine.

. . . When an occasion of practising some virtue offered, he addressed himself to God saying, "Lord, I cannot do this unless Thou enablest me."

. . . When he had failed in his duty, he simply confessed his fault, saying to God, "I shall never do otherwise if Thou leavest me to myself; it is Thou who must hinder my falling, and mend what is amiss."

"It is Thou who must mend what is amiss. . . ." For me, a great deal was amiss. Odd that I should think of those words now! Yet not so odd, because it was Brother Lawrence who had first called my attention to the power of helplessness. He, like so many other seekers through the centuries, had finally seen his human helplessness as the crucible out of which victory could rise.

And so I was able to turn from my sense of failure enough to put the writing project into God's hands. I was inadequate, but God was adequate. He knew the secret of successful creative effort. I did not. Without realising what I was doing, I prayed the Prayer of helplessness. I asked that God should guide the creation of *A Man Called Peter* and that the results should be His, too.

And they were. I still regard as incredible the fact that from time to time I hear of lives changed by that book, of men entering the ministry because of the inspiration of Peter Marshall's life, and of Peter's voice reaching now to a world-wide audience. And significantly, in the years since, no one has ever commented to me about *A Man Called Peter* without mentioning—often ruefully, referring to their own involuntary tears—a quality in the book that irresistibly reached in to touch their emotions.

Out of this experience I learned that, when achievement has come because of our helplessness linked to God's power, it has a rightness about it that no amount of self-inspired striving can have. Furthermore, when achievement comes this way, it does not bear in it the seeds of increasing egocentricity that success sometimes brings. Because we know that ideas and the ability to implement them flowed into us from somewhere beyond our selves, we can be objective about our good fortune.

We know, too, that if, in the future, the connection with the Source of creativity is broken, there will not be success the next time.

Since then God has never allowed me the fulfilment of a soul's sincere desire without first putting me through an acute realisation of my inadequacy and my need for help.

It should not surprise us that creativity arises out of the pit of life rather than the high places. For creativity is the ability to put old material into new form. And it is only when old moulds and old ways of doing things are forcibly broken up by need or suffering, compelling us to regroup, to rethink, to begin again, that the creative process starts to flow.

Fritz Künkel, German physician-psychiatrist noted among other things for his attempts to unify the findings of Freud, Adler, and Jung, puts it this way: "The way to real creativeness is through danger and suffering. Thus we see that each creative act must be preceded by a certain time of need, distress, or even despair. ... Nor should anyone say, 'I am clever enough to overcome all the difficulties of my crises. I can bring myself through all their changes.' Such statements reflect egocentric thinking. ... He who relies upon his own small private consciousness must fail, for the source of creativity is not the individual but the We, or to state it another way, not the individual but God who manifests Himself in the We, of which the Self is a part. ..."[3]

Crisis brings us face to face with our inadequacy and our inadequacy in turn leads us to the inexhaustible sufficiency of God. This is the power of helplessness, a principle written into the fabric of life.

At this point some realist will surely say, "I cannot accept this helplessness theory. It goes against everything I have been taught about rugged individualism. Where would our nation be now, if it were not for the pioneer spirit of our forefathers who refused to admit defeat in the face of tremendous odds? America was built by men who scorned weakness and helplessness."

It is precisely here that the realist misses the point about this principle. For the realisation of helplessness in no sense precludes a courageous pioneer independence. Being adventuresome does not mean that we cannot admit our need for God. To be sure, if by a rugged individualist one means a man who says, "I can by myself do all things", then he violates the principle. But as I read American history, our nation was not built by men who denied their dependence on their Creator.

Preachers and patriotic speakers mention glibly "the faith of the Founding Fathers". How much do most of us really know about their faith? Anyone who has stood on the deck of the *Mayflower II* (the modern replica of the tiny original) has some inkling of what a terrifying voyage it was to America in the seventeenth century. Those who sailed on the first *Mayflower*, or any other sailing ship, had to want to come in the most ardent way. Powerful motives beyond self-gain must have been involved. The settlers' trepidation and awe, along with their spirit of adventure, are reflected in such documents as the Mayflower Compact, the Fundamental Orders of Connecticut (1639), the Rhode Island Colonial Charter, the Articles agreed on at Jamestown in 1651, and other ringing statements of purpose.

In the summer of 1787 in Philadelphia, the Constitutional Convention was in full swing. The sessions were long and wearying. May and a part of June had come and gone. There were marked differences and long debates. At a critical point, Benjamin Franklin, the oldest delegate in the assembly, rose and made a daring and impassioned speech:

Mr President: The small progress we have made after four or five weeks close attendance ... is, methinks, a melancholy proof of the imperfection of human understanding. We indeed seem to feel our want of political wisdom, since we have been running about in search of it. ...

In this situation ... how has it happened, Sir, that we have not hitherto once thought of humbly applying to the Father of Lights to illumine our understanding? In the beginning of the contest with Great Britain, when we were sensible of danger, we had daily prayer in this room. Our prayers, Sir ... were graciously answered. ... And have we now forgotten that powerful Friend? Or do we imagine we no longer need His assistance?

Thereupon the Constitutional Convention waited upon God in prayer—with results that have stood the test of time.

It was George Washington's habit to begin and close each day with a time of prayer, alone in his room. How important this was to him is reflected in statement after statement of his public speeches: "No people can be bound to knowledge and adore the Invisible Hand which conducts the affairs of men more than those of the United States. Every step by which they have advanced to the character of an independent nation seems to have been distinguished by some token of providential agency. . . ."

.Abraham Lincoln is considered the classic example of the rugged individualist, the frontiersman, the rail-splitter who went from log cabin to the White House by the most prodigious feats of energy and application.

Yet this is the same man who prowled the White House corridors at night, pleading for direction from God for a nation in mortal struggle. This is the same man who went on record as saying, "I should be the veriest shallow and conceited blockhead . . . if I should hope to get along without the wisdom that comes from God and not from man."

Thus through hard experience Americans have learned the truth of that towering Biblical statement, "Apart from me, ye can do nothing."[4]

Nothing? That seems a trifle sweeping. Perhaps Jesus meant simply that we shall be more effective with His help than without it.

But when we go back to the context in which the statement is made, we find that Jesus meant precisely what He said. This is the allegory of the vine and the branches: "I am the vine, you are the branches." The point is not that the branches will do better when they are attached to the vine. Unless attached, the branches must wither and die.

Dr Arthur Gossip, famous Scottish theologian who wrote the exposition on John for the *Interpreter's Bible*, calls the statement "Apart from me, ye can do nothing" the *most hopeful words in Scripture*. "For it is on the basis of that frank recognition of our utter fecklessness apart from Him that Christ enters into His covenant with us, and gives us His tremendous promises. . . ."[5]

In the complex world of today, just how self-sufficient are we? We had nothing to do with our being born—no control over whether we were male of female, Japanese, or Russian, or British, or American, white or yellow or black. We did not control our ancestry or the basic mental or physical equipment with which we started life.

Even after birth an autonomic nervous system controls the vital processes of life. A power that no one understands keeps our hearts beating, our lungs taking in air, our blood circulating, our body temperature up.

A surgeon can cut human tissue, but he is helpless to make the severed tissue heal. We grow old relentlessly and automatically. In the end, despite all the so-called miracles of modern medicine, every one of us must die.

Self-sufficient? Hardly!

The planet on which we live rotates on an axis tipped at the angle of $23\frac{1}{2}$ degrees, the necessary angle for the climatic conditions that support life. Were the earth not tilted, continents of ice would lie at the poles and probably deserts between them. Moreover, the earth is exactly the right distance, some ninety-two million miles, from the sun. Any nearer, we would be consumed with solar radiation; any farther away, we would be frozen to death. Were this angle and this distance somehow to change, we would all be instantly destroyed.

The natural balance of oxygen and nitrogen in the air we breathe is exactly right for men and animals. The law of gravity which holds the world together operates independently of us. And is man—little man who struts and fumes upon the earth—self-sufficient? Not at all. . . .

The Scriptures say that you and I are helpless even in relation to our own spiritual lives. We want to feel that God is real. We think that we are reaching out for Him. This is an illusion. "No one," Jesus said, "is able to come to me unless he is drawn by the Father."[6] "Ye have not chosen me, but I have chosen you."[7]

We want salvation from our sins and we yearn for eternal life. We think that we can earn these things; Saul of Tarsus thought so, too, Then we find out, as Paul did, that we cannot pile up enough good marks and merits to earn anything from God. No, salvation "is the *gift* of God: not of works, least any man should boast".[8]

Indeed, not a single spiritual quality—faith, peace of mind, joy, patience, the ability to love the wretched and the unlovely —can we work up by self-effort. Anyone who has tried knows that he cannot.

Moreover, Christ tells us that the same human dependence applied equally to Him while He wore His human flesh. "I can of mine own self do nothing," He told His apostles.[9]

I came across a dramatic example of this human helplessness of God several years ago in the writings of Dr A. B. Simpson, a famous New York City clergyman. While in his twenties, Dr Simpson had developed serious heart trouble. His preaching and pastoral work were done at great physical expense. Usually it took him until Wednesday to get over the effects of his Sunday sermons. Climbing stairs or even a slight elevation was suffocating agony.

Dr Simpson was only thirty-seven when he was told by his physician that he might not have long to live. On his doctor's advice, he went for a long rest to the resort town of Old Orchard Beach, Maine. There he happened into an unusual religious meeting conducted by a Boston physician, Dr Charles Cullis. Dr Cullis was then having much success with treating tubercular patients through prayer and common-sense health measures alone.

Several statements made in the meeting about healing through prayer sent Dr Simpson back to the Bible to find out what Jesus had to say on the subject. He soon became convinced that Jesus had always meant His gospel to include healing of the body along with healing of the mind and the spirit.

In the quiet of his room, Dr Simpson reviewed his life. He

was always struggling desperately for even his minimal needs
—for enough health to keep going, for enough ideas and
intellectual resources to write talks and sermons, for enough
caring about other people. It was almost as if his creed was
"Of myself I must do everything". But somehow he always
fell short of his objectives. Was God now trying to reach him
with a new idea? Had he ever really given God a chance to
run his life?

One Friday afternoon shortly after that, Dr Simpson went
for a walk. Since he was always out of breath, he was forced
to walk slowly. The path led into a pine wood, and he sat
down on a fallen log to rest. All around him was that thick
carpet of moss so often seen in the Maine woods. Sunlight
filtered through the tall pines, laying striped patterns across
the emerald green floor. Simpson pulled out his watch and saw
that it was three o'clock.

"All things in my life looked dark and withered," Simpson
wrote afterward. "The doctors had made it clear that they
could do nothing for me. Intellectual life and spiritual life were
also at a low ebb. So there in the woods I asked God to become
my life for me, including physical life for all the needs of my
body until my life work was done. And I solemnly promised
to use His spiritual and physical strength in me for the good
of others. God was there all right, because every fibre of my
body was tingling with His Presence. He had come to meet
me at the point of my helplessness."

A few days later, Simpson took a long hike and climbed
a mountain three thousand feet high. "When I reached the
mountain top," he related joyously, "the world of weakness
and fear was lying at my feet. From that time I literally had a
new heart in my breast."[10]

He also had a new source of creativity. For the first three
years after his heart was healed, he kept count and found that
he had preached more than a thousand sermons, had held
sometimes as many as twenty meetings in a week—and
without exhaustion. Simpson's output of literary work was
equally prodigious. He lived as vigorously as any man could
and died at seventy-six. To this day much of his work,

including the Christian and Missionary Alliance, is still a vital force.

An experience like Dr Simpson's points up the other half of the Prayer of Helplessness. For in helplessness alone there would be no value, our situation would be intolerable if Jesus had left us there. But He went on to add, "With God all things are possible."

"All things!" This is as audacious a statement as the opposite was, "Apart from me, ye can do nothing." Jesus must be saying that there is nothing in heaven or in earth over which God does not have control.

Most of us can believe that God can control us, provided we are willing. Thus if we are in the hole because of our own foolishness, misjudgment, or sin, we can concede God's ability to help.

But there is another type of life situation at which faith often staggers. This is when heartbreak has come to us because of other people's sins and failures—what might be called "second causes".

The tragedies most difficult to take are those that come through the failures, ignorance, carelessness, or hatred of other human beings. These are times when men seem to be working havoc with God's plans. I had a friend, for instance, a well-known man in the District of Columbia, who died because of an error made by a pharmacist in filling a prescription. Another friend's husband is an alcoholic. No amount of institutional or religious help can seem to cure him. But it is my friend and the children who are the real victims.

It is important that we believe that God is adequate even for these situations. Otherwise the Prayer of Helplessness will fall to the ground. In order to fly, the bird must have two wings. One wing is the realisation of our human helplessness, the other is the realisation of God's power. Out faith in God's ability to handle our particular situation is the connecting link.

What the Bible says about this is worth listening to, if we are to find a creative way out of the holes into which life so often throws us. For if we cannot believe that God can help us recover from troubles shaped by human beings as well as those we bring upon ourselves, then we have a narrow basis indeed for our faith in Him.

The Old Testament story of Joseph illustrates perfectly how God can operate in and around and in spite of the sins and shortcomings of men. When Joseph was a seventeen-year-old boy, he was literally at the bottom of a pit. He had been thrown there by his own brothers. Their act was the climax of years of hostility arising out of envy.

Joseph was the favourite child of their father's old age. To his brothers, the boy seemed over-protected and spoiled, a threat to their futures. So they bargained with some Ishmaelite traders and sold him into slavery for twenty pieces of silver.

A bewildered boy found himself being carried to the slave market of Egypt's capital. He was forced to stand, stripped, on the slave block, while he was measured and scrutinised. He was finally bought by Potiphar, one of the Pharaoh's officials.

The years went by swiftly. Transplanted from his simple, nomad world, the boy adjusted to the sophistication of Egypt. For him it was a new world of city streets and chariots, of pleasure barges on the Nile, of elaborate tombs and great granaries, of clean-shaven men in white pleated garments and women with painted eyes and heavy jewels.

The boy made the adjustment by coming to terms with himself. Since his fate was to be a slave and he was helpless to change it, he determined to be the best slave Potiphar had ever had. Thus the Israelite soon found himself chief steward, in charge of his master's house.

Adversity had changed a spoiled boy into a mature man. And Potiphar's wife found the man attractive. Undoubtedly a sensualist and a woman with too much leisure and too much luxury, she propositioned the slave.

Joseph could have reasoned that, when in Egypt, he might as well do as the Egyptians. Their flexible standards knew few scruples and little morality. But since his master had trusted him so completely, the Israelite could not bring himself to betray that trust. Day after day he turned away from her allurements so brazenly displayed.

Joseph did not reckon with the fury of a woman scorned. Unable to seduce the handsome young slave, Potiphar's wife turned violently against him. One day she caught and tore a piece of the slave's garment, made a scene, and then cried out to her husband, "The Hebrew servant . . . came in to mock me: and . . . as I lifted up my voice and cried, he left his garment with me, and fled out."

Potiphar believed his wife and promptly had Joseph thrown into prison. Egypt's prisons were terrible beyond belief. In the midst of filth and despair, Joseph must have faced his supreme moment of truth.

He had lived up to the best he knew. He had resisted temptation when giving in to it would have been easy. Goodness had not been rewarded. Bitterness and self-pity must have clamoured for possession of him. Betrayed by his own kinsmen, now he languished in prison, not through any sin he had committed, but because he had refused to commit one. He remained in prison for more than two years.

How many times during those years Joseph must have prayed the Prayer of Helplessness and, by so doing, overcome the bitterness and self-pity. The captain of the guard found something about the young man's spirit so appealing that he put Joseph in charge of some of the other prisoners.

When the answer to Joseph's prayer finally came, it was marvellous beyond belief. Through a talent he had possessed from childhood—the gift of dream-interpretation—he caught the attention of the Pharaoh. Then through a series of remarkable events, Joseph at thirty suddenly found himself prime minister of Egypt.

The suffering through which he had passed reaped its harvest in a burst of creativity. Joseph conceived a workable plan by which the Land of the Nile piled up a crop surplus while neighbouring countries run by less imaginative men were in the grip of famine.

The final testing of Joseph's character came when his own brothers came from the land of Canaan and stood before him, begging to buy grain. They could not possibly have recognised the strong-jawed, bronzed Egyptian as their kinsman.

But the fires of despair had done their work well. Joseph had no thought of vengeance. When he finally revealed his identity, it was in words that could only have been spoken by one whose eyes had so often been washed with tears that now they saw clearly. "Now therefore be not grieved, nor angry with yourselves, that ye sold me hither: for God did send me before you to preserve life. So now it was not you that sent me hither, but God. . . ."[11] And a little later he reassured them with the unforgettable words, "But as for you, ye thought evil against me; but God meant it unto good. . . .[12]

Joseph was saying that his brothers had only *thought* that they were in control of the situation. As long as Joseph maintained his dependence on God, He was able to take all these evils that had befallen Joseph and weave them into His master plan. Thus an omnipotent God could make even "the wrath of man to praise Him". He can take any sins, any evil, any calamity—no matter where it originated—and make it "work together for good to them that love God". This practical omnipotence of God is the consistent cry of all of Scripture, written by a variety of men over a period of some thirteen hundred years.

It was also the viewpoint of Jesus. That black moment in the Garden under the olive trees when Judas betrayed his Master with a kiss appeared to be the opening scene in a drama written, staged, and directed by the powers of evil. It would seem to us that if ever the free will of wicked men—sundered from and at cross-purpose with the will of God—was in control, it was at the execution of Jesus Christ by crucifixion.

"Not so," was Jesus' assertion. Never for an instant during the acting out of that drama did God abdicate as sovereign ruler. Christ made this point over and over. In the Garden, when impetuous Peter whipped out his sword, Jesus ordered, "Put your sword back into its place. . . . Do you think I cannot appeal to my Father to furnish me at this moment with over twelve legions of angels?"[13]

To Pilate, as the Roman governor boasted to the Nazarene

of his power of life and death over Him, Christ retorted bluntly, "You would have no power over me, unless it had been granted you from above."[14]

The powers of darkness in control? It only appeared so. Long before Passion week, Jesus was explaining, "Therefore doth my Father love me, because I lay down my life, that I might take it again. *No man taketh it from me,* but I lay it down of myself."[15]

Thus even the events that swept Christ toward the cross had been woven into a plan for the greatest good of mankind.

Ever afterward there would be men who would glory in that cross "towering o'er the wrecks of time"—the wrecks that we always manage to make in every century. They would glory because the cross stands as the final symbol that no evil exists that God cannot turn into a blessing. He is the living Alchemist who can take the dregs from the slag-heaps of life —disappointment, frustration, sorrow, disease, death, economic loss, heartache—and transform the dregs into gold.

This is the hope and the promise that I claimed for myself that long-ago day and that I yearn to pass on to everyone whom life has hemmed in; to the would-be suicide, and to the merely discouraged who do not consider suicide but who also will not consider God.

So sure am I of this alchemy by which all things can be made to "work together for good to them that love God" that I would stake my life on it. This means that no sinner is hopeless; no situation is irretrievable. No case is past redeeming. That is why Jesus' insistence on our helplessness is the most hopeful note in Scripture. That is why every one of us— imperfect as we are—can take heart and thank God for the power of helplessness.

11: *The Prayer That Makes Dreams Come True*

ONE of the most provocative facts I know is that every man-made object, as well as every event in anyone's life, starts with an idea or a picture in the mind. It was my mother who first taught me this, as over and over she demonstrated to me the prayer that helps our dreams come true.

Mother always believed in action; she was certain that idle children—hers or anyone else's—were headed for trouble. It was she who suggested that my brother and sister and I make a collection of butterflies and moths, plant a wild-flower garden, build a treehouse in the cherry tree.

Mother also headed the Girl Scout programme for our West Virginia town—all six troops of us. She persuaded my good-natured father to go on camping expeditions (which he loathed), made him sleep on canvas cots in tents that often leaked, wade through mud, endure mosquitoes, warmed-over hot dogs and canned beans, and (what was worst of all to him) breathe the fumes of citronella. Father made endless jokes through it all.

Idle? Not a chance for any of us. Beyond all our family projects and the Scout programme, Mother devoted even more energy to her one-woman crusade for the individual and civic rehabilitation of Radical Hill.

This slum district was located in what should have been the town's most beautiful residential section on the side farthest removed from the railroad tracks. There unbelievable filth was surrounded by gently rolling hills and, beyond them, towering mountains.

Mother stood one day in the midst of it and envisioned what Radical Hill would be like with clean, newly painted houses, with tidy yards filled with flowers, with running water, plumbing, garbage disposal. And there would be a small white church. Her first move in the direction of her dream was to rename the district "Potomac Heights".

Next she started taking a personal census of the area. This involved calling on every shack. Some of the young people from our church helped. I have already described how awed we children were when Mother came back from her first afternoon of visiting and wept at what she had seen.

She and her young helpers found that, of some five hundred families in Potomac Heights, only eighty had even a nebulous connection with any church. So Mother and her group rented a building, cleaned it, painted it, crudely furnished it, and began holding a Sunday School on Sunday afternoons.

There mother met a boy, Raymond Thomas, who had no idea who his real parents were. He lived with foster parents in a small, clean house set in the midst of the dirt.

Dressed in working clothes and clodhoppers that seemed to reach up to his knees, Raymond came often to our home to talk with Mother. He was always clean, but he did not even own a suit of clothes. Despite a slight speech impediment that made him self-conscious, he would sit on the top step of our vine-shaded front porch on a summer afternoon talking . . . talking . . . while Mother sat in a wooden rocker shelling peas or stringing beans or darning socks. Mother soon saw that this boy had boundless energy and a fine mind.

During one of these talks there emerged one clear-cut idea—the dream of Raymond going to college. Once the dream was out in the open, standing there shimmering, poised in the air, Mother was delighted to see the wistfulness in Ray's brown eyes replaced by kindling hope.

"But how can I manage it?" the boy asked. "I've been working on the state roads, but I've been turning over my paycheck to my folks. I've nothing saved."

There was another obstacle, too: his foster parents had not gone to college; why should Ray? They thought the idea so foolish that they actively opposed it.

Mother quietly encouraged and prodded. "Raymond, whatever you need, God has a supply of it ready for you, provided you're ready to receive it. What seems impossible for you is entirely possible for God. Ours is still a land of opportunity, Ray. The sky is the limit! Money—what's money? Money should be the slave, not the master, of every dream that's right for you, every dream for which you're willing to work."

For a preacher's wife who had little enough herself, this was a doughty philosophy, but Mother believed it and had often proved it so. And these ideas took root in Raymond.

There came the day when Ray accepted Mother's philosophy so completely that she could lead him in the prayer that releases dreams to make them come true. On so many occasions in my own life has she prayed the dreaming prayer for me that I can easily imagine how it was for Ray: "Father, you've given Ray a fine mind. We believe You want that mind to be developed, sharpened, to know some of the wisdom of other men through the ages. You want Ray's potential to be used to help You lift and lighten some portion of our world. All resources are Yours. So will you please make it possible for Ray to receive what he needs for an education?

"And, Father, I believe that You have big plans for Ray. Unshackle him from all thoughts of lack. Let him know that there are no limitations to what You can do. Plant in his mind and heart the vivid pictures, the specific dreams that reflect Your plans for him. And, oh, give him joy in dreaming—great joy."

Raymond never forgot that prayer. A decade later he was recalling to me the fragrance of the clematis vines on the porch that afternoon, a fragrance that even now can recreate the moment for him. Long afterward he would be saying with awe in his voice, "To one woman I owe the key to life."

Even while Mother was praying the dreaming prayer with Ray, the name of a certain wealthy woman friend had slipped into her mind. So, without telling Ray, she wrote the friend about him and his yearning for more education: "All this boy needs is a chance. If it should seem right to you to help him, you will find that every dollar invested in his education will pay big dividends."

The reply came within a week. It would give her real pleasure to help a young man like this one. She agreed to underwrite a portion of Ray's expenses for the first year.

When Raymond read this letter, he stood speechless, looking at Mother, shaking his head. Finally he said, "Pinch me . . . I can't believe this is really happening to me."

When Ray's friends at our church heard what was going on, they wanted to have a part, too. A group of men bought him a suit and some other clothes. The women bought luggage and even packed for him. They thought of everything—even items like buttons, needles, thread. And Ray, his dream brighter than ever, climbed on a bus and went off to college at Davidson, North Carolina.

He insisted on repaying the woman who wanted to be his benefactress and who lived in the college community by mowing her lawn, scrubbing her floors, firing her furnace— anything she would let him do.

Soon Ray was sending Mother the schedule he had worked out. She was astonished at how he was budgeting his time as well as his money: a certain number of hours for study, for classes, for work, for church services, for recreation.

At Christmas he hitch-hiked home. His foster parents had softened and were glad to see him. The following summer he worked for the Celanese Corporation in Cumberland, Maryland. That enabled him to return to college in the fall with enough money saved for the first semester. From then on he made ends meet through some twelve jobs—waiting on tables, baby-sitting for the faculty, repairing typewriters, typing papers for other students. It was hard going sometimes, but Mother kept encouraging him with a letter a week. It was as proud a day for her as for Ray when he received his Bachelor of Science degree, *cum laude*.

Then during the second world war and afterward, I lost touch with Raymond. I had heard that his ship had been sunk under him in the South Pacific, and that in the explosion he had lost all but five per cent of his hearing. Some time after that Mother told me that he was living in Vienna.

In the summer of 1958, I was in Europe and wrote Raymond

that Vienna was on my itinerary. His response was immediate and enthusiastic.

In Rome, I found a glowing letter from him, listing for me the sights that I should see. Then when I checked into the hotel in Florence, the mail clerk handed me another letter from Ray:

When you see the high dome of the Duomo, remember that it took Brunelleschi fourteen years to build it. Last winter I climbed to the highest balcony right at the top of the dome and crawled all around it. . . .

The letters kept coming: Venice . . . "I've written to my friend at the Salviati Glass works and asked him to send a gondola for you. You must see the master glass-blowers at work. . . ."

Bad Gastein . . . "You'll find it rugged. I've skied quite a lot near there. . . ."

By now I was very curious. This man bore no resemblance to the under-privileged boy from Radical Hill. Obviously he knew Europe as few Americans do. And the drive and indefatigable zeal in his letters intrigued me.

Ray met me at the airport, a bouquet of flowers in hand. "Flowers and music are a part of Vienna," he explained. He had changed little, except that his hairline had receded. He was tall and spare and still had the trace of the speech impediment.

Later, over *Sachertorte* and coffee, I asked Ray about his life since graduating from college. He had absorbed European ways and would not be rushed. "After I learned from experience that what your mother had said was true—and had graduated from college, I knew that any right dream can be realised. Material resources *are* at the beck and call of the dream. There are no ceilings to dreaming."

Then he described his war experience. He was one of a handful of survivors of a torpedoed destroyer. During convalescence he had dreamed up a plan for the rest of his life.

"At that time my dreams were three," he went on. "I wanted to be a world citizen. That meant travelling extensively. I put no limits on that. But I knew I couldn't be a world citizen without mastering several languages. Tied with that, I wanted to get my Ph.D. preferably from a fine European university. After all, why stop with a B.S.? Then out of gratitude for all that America means to me, I wanted to serve my country somehow in peacetime."

"I'm amazed that your dreams were that specific," I interposed.

He seemed lost in thought as he stared out the window at the lights of Vienna. "I've come to feel that this dreaming process won't work unless we are specific. That's because a big part of the power to make the dream come true arises from a mental picture. And for a mental image, you need specifics."

"Ray, you astonish me! From Radical Hill—excuse me, Potomac Heights—to Vienna. Who would have thought it? Now tell me how these three dreams have come out."

"Well, so far I've travelled in sixty countries. I still haven't got to Australia, New Zealand, South America, or the southern half of Africa. I'm working on that! Every vacation I strike out for some new spot."

"And your studies?"

"I got my Ph.D. in physics from the University of Vienna."

"But, Ray, how did you manage the lectures with your hearing problem?" I asked.

"I found a girl who would take the lectures down in shorthand. That meant that I had to learn shorthand, too. Work on the Ph.D. also meant mastering German. I can speak Spanish now, passable French, some Italian, Dutch and Swedish, a little Russian."

And the dream of serving his country was coming true through his job with the United States Atomic Energy Agency here in Europe. "Ray, what does your foster mother back in West Virginia think of all this?"

"She couldn't be more proud. To hear her brag you'd think it was all her idea. I manage to fly home to see her once a year."

"So now you've achieved all these dreams, what next?"

Ray laughed. "One of the pitfalls of middle age is that we stop dreaming—especially dreaming big. But I'm working on one—"

In the spring of 1946 a friend, Anita Ritter, asked me to join her for a few days' rest at a little inn in the Valley of Virginia. Her invitation came at a welcome time. Peter and I had then been living in the city of Washington for nine years. The upheaval of the second world war was over. Both in church life and in private life, we were feeling the need of rethinking our situation to chart a clear course.

I took with me to the inn a religious book which someone had sent me.[1] One section charted a procedure aimed at helping an individual discover himself and what he wanted out of life. I decided to take this programme seriously—a minimum of an hour a day at the task. I took along a notebook and a dozen pencils, ignoring no technique that the author suggested as too infantile.

One of the first suggestions was that the reader retrace his steps to childhood to remember what his ambitions were then. Of what did the child dream before the adult world muddied the waters with its false values?

Thinking back to my childhood immediately conjured up two pictures. The setting for both was the same West Virginia town in which Raymond had grown up. First, I saw a girl sitting with her back against an ancient locust tree, gazing dreamily out over a panorama of valley and mountains.

The grove of locust trees—grotesquely stark in the winter, fragrant with white blossoms in the spring—was at the back of our large manse yard. Out beyond the locusts were granite ledges which we children called "The Rocks". They formed a sheer drop of some two hundred feet from the back of our yard to a dirt road winding around the base of the cliff. Ferns and rare Scottish bluebells grew out of the rock crevices.

From atop The Rocks we could see for miles up the narrow green valley hemmed in on two sides by the rugged Appalachians. This world of far horizons fed imagination and spirit and was the scene for much of my adolescent daydreaming.

There I conceived the idea of being a writer, in fact made first attempts at putting ideas, conversations, and descriptions on paper.

The second remembered scene was that of a girl sitting at the kitchen table by a window. Sheets of paper were spread out all over the oilcloth cover. One day I was writing a story with the unimaginative title, "Virginia Dare and What Happened to Her". On another occasion I began a "novel". It never progressed beyond the second chapter.

So definitely did the flavour of those childhood moments return to me that I could recollect the exact form of the little-girl ambitions I had put alongside the writing. . . . I had wanted to be "a pretty lady with plenty of perfume—and also a writer"! At age—what? I've no idea. Remembering that the perfume had been just as important to me then as the writing, I laughed at myself. Still, deeply entrenched desires were there.

The self-analysis went on. There were areas other than the childhood one to search out. What capacities did I desire for myself? . . . A better sense of humour? The ability to speak in public? Social graces? . . . What things, what possessions, did I want? . . . What kinds of ideas interested me? . . . What persons in my life? What kinds of friends? Suddenly I realised how important friends could be as a part of this dreaming. Is not aloneness every man's problem? And what can any one of us achieve apart from other human beings?

It was suggested that in all of these areas, we make the wishing as specific as possible.

After the desires were down on paper, then they were to be submitted to a series of hurdles to test whether or not they were dreams true to one's own nature and therefore requests that one had a right to make in prayer. Would the dreams fulfil the particular talents, temperament, and emotional needs that God had planted in one's being?

These are not easy questions to answer. But they are so important that any degree of probing or length of time required to answer them is worth the effort.

In the beginning I had wondered why the author of the book had implied a connection between constructive daydreaming and prayer. Psychologists tell us that no creativity is possible unless the subconscious and the conscious are both brought into play and working together and that the subconscious responds only to suggestion through visualisation. Thinking along the same line, the author suggested that praying can take the form of visualisation—which is dreaming in specifics. Jesus often insisted that people not only ask but be definite about what they wanted. There was a blind man who kept calling after Jesus, "Have pity on me! Jesus, have pity on me!" The man's chief problem—blindness—must have been obvious to Christ. Yet He required the man make his request specific by asking the leading question, "What do you want me to do for you?"[2]

As I pondered it, it seemed to me that guided day dreaming also lays a solid base for prayer, because it is certainly the Creator's will that the desires and talents that He Himself has planted in us be realised. God is supremely concerned about the fulfilment and productivity of the potentially fine person He envisions in each of us.

How foolish it would have been for Fritz Kreisler to dream of becoming a world-known labour leader. What wasted effort for Einstein to have dreamed of being a movie star!

On the other hand, would not Fritz Kreisler actually be committing a "sin of omission" if his whole life were not a prayer aimed at making a contribution to the world through his music? Knowing that, he has the strongest foundation possible for answered prayer. His music, written into his being, is "the will of God" and he can pray with absolute confidence for the overcoming of every obstacle in the way of its fulfilment.

Since those days at the little inn thinking about the Dreaming Prayer, I have discovered that there are those who are wary of the prayer that makes dreams come true on two counts: they have doubts about the rightness of praying for material needs; and they are cautious—correctly—about trying to use God and spiritual principles for selfish ends.

Both are valid objections that need to be considered. As

for whether God means for us to include material needs in our petitions, one answer would be that Christ was interested in the bodies of men along with their souls. He was concerned about their health and their physical hunger.

Christianity acknowledges material things—bread and wine, water, good and bad soil, the lilies of the fields, the birds, men's bodies; it seeks to lift all these material objects to serve man's spirit and God's purposes. I believe that is why the Scriptures make no distinction between the secular and the sacred, the everyday and the religious. The ideal is that all of life, every vocation and profession, is to be used to glorify God.

As for the danger that our heart's desire may be our selfish human will rather than God's, there are ways by which we can test this. Only when a dream has passed these two tests (so that we are certain that our wish is also God's dream) can we pray the Dreaming Prayer with faith and thus with effectiveness.

The first hurdle is simply our recognition that God's laws are in operation in our universe. Does our dream involve taking anything or any person belonging to someone else? Would the fulfilment of it hurt any other human being? If so, then we can be sure that this particular dream is not God's will for us.

Are we willing to make all our relationships with other people right? If we hold resentments, grudges, bitterness—no matter how justified we think they are— these wrong emotions will cut us off from God, the source of creativity. After all, no dream can be achieved in a vacuum of human relationships. Even one such wrong relationship can cut the channel of power.

Do we want our dream with our whole heart? Dreams are not usually brought to fruition in divided personalities. Only the whole heart will be willing to do its part toward implementing the dream.

Are we willing to wait patiently for God's timing?

Are we dreaming big? The bigger the dream and the more persons it will benefit, the greater will be God's blessing on it.

If our heart's desire can pass this first series of tests, then we are ready for an even greater hurdle. My experience has been that the last necessary step in the Dreaming Prayer sequence is that we hand our dream over to God to fulfil or not, as He wishes, and then go off and leave it with Him. This is where the prayer that makes dreams come true must also include the Prayer of Relinquishment. With this final test available to us, we need have no fear of trying to use God for selfish ends. We are asking only that His will be fulfilled in us.

One day soon after I returned from Europe in 1958, a close friend and I were discussing Raymond's story. Tessie is an attractive, lively brunette whose husband, Phil, had died suddenly at thirty-two, leaving her with three small children. She had loved Phil with all her being and, so far as I could tell, there had been a fine relationship.

Tessie's widowhood and mine had drawn us together. We had formed the habit of eating dinner together regularly. One of Tessie's deepest desires, which she had confided to me, was for remarriage.

"You know," she said one evening, "it's funny how our society is about courtship and marriage—that is, as far as women are concerned. It's all right for men to be frank about what they want and go after it. But we women have to be hush-hush and hole-in-corner. We have to sit and wait.

"So here I am, lonely, needing help with my children, and needing love—physical love, too, why not admit it? What am I supposed to do? Go around keeping up the false front that all is well? Everyone says that if we women appear too eager, *that* drives men away. . . . Where and how do we meet eligible men, anyway?"

As we talked it over, the story of Raymond and my mother and Radical Hill prompted Tessie and me to try the Dreaming Prayer for her problem. I pledged myself to work with her on it for as long as necessary. As I considered my lively friend and her three children, it seemed highly probable to me that happiness and fulfilment through a second marriage were God's will for her. Yet neither of us dared assume that. The last word would have to be God's.

Tessie's first steps were practical ones toward self-improvement. In her grief over Phil's death and her battle to be both mother and father to her children with no household help, she had neglected her appearance. She heard of a Charm School and managed the money to enrol.

The results—psychological as well as physical—were well worth the effort. After that came some new clothes. Tessie joined an informal dance group that met once a week and consented to her first dates since Phil's death. Yet she found many of these men unexciting, some even boring. It seemed to be a constant effort for her.

After talking that over, she and I decided on several other steps. It was time for Tessie to begin thinking specifically about what she wanted in a husband and in a marriage. This did not mean that she must decide on a man over five-eight tall, a blond with blue eyes, between thirty-five and forty-five who did not wear glasses. It was rather a question of the character of her man and the values she wanted in marriage.

The second step was that Tessie decided to stop thinking of dates simply in terms of having fun herself. She began concentrating more on the art of *giving*, for instance working hard on an occasional home-cooked meal for a date rather than always expecting him to take her to an expensive glamour spot.

These efforts led Tessie to a deeper realisation. One evening she confronted me with a surprising confession: "Remarriage may be God's will for me, but I'm not sure it's Tessie's will for Tessie."

"What on earth do you mean?"

"I've wanted the icing on the cake—the romance, the ego-satisfaction of being sought after by men. But lately something inside me has been asking questions, and they're making me squirm. Such as, do I realise that love isn't getting but giving? And what do I have to give to some man with deep needs? What qualities can I contribute to a new marriage! And am I willing to pay the price of the adjustment that will be necessary? Or suppose a man with some handicap fell in love with me, or one without much of an income, or a widower with children of his own? . . . See what I mean about the questions being disturbing?"

I saw, all right. I also recognised in this incisive realism the Spirit of God hard at work on Tessie and her dream. "I suppose all those questions point to the fact that it's dangerous to have any inner division about your heart's desire," I commented. "You have to want your dream with your whole heart."

My friend had a rueful look on her face. "Right! So this is as far as I've got. I've admitted to God that I *am* divided. For instance, at the moment I don't feel a bit enthusiastic about taking on a widower with children. So since I am divided—what's the next step?"

She and I pondered that one for a while. "You're being honest, Tessie," I said finally. "That's a big step in itself. Why don't we try asking God to mend those inner cleavages, make you completely willing for His will."

And both of us were silent, startled by the revelation that we are the ones—not God—who have to be persuaded to be stretched enough to receive from Him the realisation of our dreams.

The next bit of progress did not come until three months later. It amounted to Tessie's realisation that falling in love is more than a spontaneous burst of sentiment, through happenstance. She finally saw that it would be her capacity for love that would draw love to her.

We spent many evenings trying to think through how one can develop this capacity to love. I wanted the answer for myself as well as for my friend. We concluded that the ability to love is not limited to sexual or romantic love. If one cannot be loving in all areas of life, he or she is not capable of enduring love for the opposite sex either. So there is nothing for it but the hard assignment of giving love and being lovable in every area of life with people of both sexes, of all ages, shapes and sizes.

We tried to think through some of the qualities wrapped

up in that word *lovableness*. This was a start on the list that
we made together:

Outgoingness
Interest in other people
Vitality—physical, intellectual, and spiritual
Joy and a sense of humour
Sex appeal (the kind that's unself-conscious, not artificial)
Femininity.

In the midst of this, Tessie and I were learning that the
Dreaming Prayer, like all serious prayer, can be a difficult
business, difficult in the sense that God can ask for many
changes in the one praying, and changes are never easy.

One year and four months after my friend and I had
embarked on the prayer-project, Tessie met a crisis. A married
man with four children fell in love with her. There was a
great physical pull between them, and some undesirable
circumstances in the man's marriage provided the rationale: he
suggested a quick Mexican divorce in order to marry Tessie.

This period was painful. Tessie felt cut off from God, "I
used to have a sense of adventure about this Dreaming Prayer,
the feel of getting somewhere, no matter how slowly," she
told me. "Now I've hit a dead spot." Then she was defensive.
"But I do love this man, and our love is a beautiful thing.
So—What's wrong?"

In the end, Tessie answered her own question. I had admiration for the courage of her conclusion that this friend was
not the answer for her, because the situation could not pass
one of the acid tests for any right dream: the fulfilment of
our heart's desire cannot take anything or anybody belonging
to someone else. In spite of the rapport and the physical
attraction between them, this man was an essential part of
someone else's life pattern—not Tessie's. So with anguish and
tears, Tessie sent him back to his wife to make a new beginning
in his own marriage.

For a while, my friend was disconsolate. Then she concluded that since she had been "a good girl" God would surely

reward her by sending her dream man quickly. It was a nice thought, only we found out that God does not work that way. We cannot bargain with God and buy His blessings by being good. Another year and a half passed, and Tessie was still a widow.

This dramatised for us the fact that the Dreaming Prayer can require patience. God's perfect timing oftener than not seems slow—slow—slow to us.

In the meantime, the changes in Tessie were more apparent to me than to her. After her relinquishment of the man who had wanted to marry her, the lovableness that she had wanted so much suddenly wrapped her round like a cloak. Perhaps the difficult experience had mellowed her. Undoubtedly untouched emotion potentials were now released. Whatever the reason, suddenly she seemed all woman, with a tenderness and an aliveness that had not been hers before. Looking at her, I knew that the fulfilment of her dream could not be far away.

As it turned out, only one more hurdle lay between her and her deepest wish. This was an important one, and it grew out of profound discouragement. More than three years had passed since that first evening when Tessie and I had discussed the Dreaming Prayer and had decided to try it for her problem. It had been three years of intense, sincere effort at self-evaluation, self-improvement, and co-operation with God. Yet the dream still remained unfulfilled. Was our joint effort at the prayer a failure, a mockery? For several weeks my friend thought so and went into a mental slump. She grew almost bitter as she talked about "prayer being just self-hypnosis anyway. Why do we bother? Why don't we just throw out the whole experiment as a bad job?"

Then one day we met over luncheon downtown, and I found Tessie's mood changed. In fact, she was impatient to get the ordering done so she could share what was on her mind.

"It's about six years now since I gave my life to God," she began. "Since then, He's had a stake in me. From His point of view, I'm His child—even though I'm inclined to forget it sometimes. I suppose there are certain lessons He must teach me."

The waitress came with our order, and Tessie was silent until we were alone again. "I've come to the reluctant conclusion that right now one of these lessons is that He wants me to stop running off in all directions, trying to force the fulfilment of my dream. I've tried Charm School, new clothes, the dance group, socialising, trying to be outgoing and thoughtful in dating, the art of listening—you know, a hundred things. Let's face it—these are all valuable, but they simply have not worked."

"So what's your idea of a solution?" I asked.

"Well—I think God is trying to tell me to relax and let Him take over now. If He wants me to remarry, somehow I think He's capable of arranging it."

"Tessie, you've just said 'if God wants me to remarry'. Does that mean that you're ready to let Him decide whether or not remarriage is in the picture for you?"

Tessie grimaced. "What alternative do I have? My best efforts have failed. At this point I feel defeated. So—either God does this for me, or it doesn't come off."

There it was again—relinquishment! When Tessie made that decision, a lot of tension drained out of her. There were some surprising psychological and social results. By some radar which I do not pretent to understand, Tessie's male friends sensed the new relaxation and inner freedom in her. Their response was immediate. Soon she was having a difficult time finding enough evenings.

Apparently when she had finally handed her problem over to God's management she had also relinquished that over-intensity that puts men on the defensive. The new contentment and poise that resulted seemed to disarm and attract them.

About three months after our luncheon talk, she met Van at a dinner party. He was a bachelor from Cleveland, in Washington on business. It turned out that six years before Van had been engaged to an Army nurse who had died of pneumonia while stationed in Germany. His reaction to Tessie was instantaneous, though he did not reveal it that night. But frequent long-distance calls from Cleveland were soon revealing a confident man who knew what he wanted and was going after it with every power he possessed.

Tessie had often commented to me that she was wary of all bachelors over thirty-five or so. "In my opinion," she had insisted, "they're usually warped in some way, else they'd be married. They're momma's boys or women-haters or something. Anyway, I can't imagine any bachelor having the courage to take on a ready-made family of three squirming youngsters."

Van turned out to be an exception on both counts. The idea of assuming greatly increased responsibilities not only did not deter him but his masculinity responded to it. His proposal of marriage came just three weeks after they had met. Later Tessie confided to me, "Of course, my immediate reaction to his proposal was a sputtering 'Why, Van, you've lost your marbles! I scarcely know you at all.'"

I laughed. "And of course, that was true. You'd only had—what was it—three dates?"

"Four," corrected Tessie. "Van made it clear that he expected no answer right then. He wanted me to know how *he* felt, that he was positive in his own mind and determined. Then he added that if, at that moment, I was certain that he couldn't be a part of my future, he needed to know, so that he wouldn't go on hoping."

"That certainly is the direct road to courtship," I marvelled.

"Yes, and what left me gasping," Tessie added, "was the way Van made himself so vulnerable, so naked to hurt. It was a kind of raw courage ready to risk the rejection of the life that he was offering me."

I saw that there were tears in Tessie's brown eyes. "After that I began to realise that here was a man with rare qualities. Then came the special moment when it seemed as if Christ was standing over our courtship saying, 'This is My gift. Take it with joy and My blessing.'"

Van and Tessie were married that April.

And with the fulfilment of Tessie's dream, I saw all over again what Mother had taught me so many years before:

when the dream in our heart is one that God has planted there, a strange happiness flows into us. At that moment all the spiritual resources of the universe are released to help us. Our praying is then at one with the will of God and becomes a channel for the Creator's always joyous, triumphant purposes for us and our world.

12: Ego-Slaying

I SHALL long remember a certain June day in 1955. It was spent with a group of thirteen Christian friends at a rustic lodge in the rolling Maryland countryside. This day in the woods was to be a time apart. The plan was to share portions of two books—C. S. Lewis's *Beyond Personality* and A. W. Tozer's *The Divine Conquest*. Then we would separate for some individual meditation on what had been read; after that lunch, more sharing, and some prayer. It was hoped that the day would end with some definite step forward toward Christian maturity.

Tozer's thoughts and Lewis's are now merged in my mind. But, as I remember, what we were studying could be summarised this way: A misconception that many church people have is the theory that with Christ's help we can become "nice people". This teaches that the good in man can be separated from the bad, and the good developed. It says that education is the answer to most problems. It admonishes us to self-effort, human endeavour. Our lives are to be "man's best with God's help".

The main trouble with the "nice people" theory is that when we try living by it, we find ourselves getting nowhere. What is more, it is not Christianity. Nowhere do the Scriptures tell us that, with God's help, we can sort out the good and the evil in ourselves and cultivate the good. Rather, these writers insist that ever since the first man and woman were tempted to pull away from their Creator, hoping that they would be "as gods", all men have been tainted with the same desire to bow the knee to no one but themselves. Our nature might be compared to an apple shot through with brown specks of imperfection. There is no way to cut out every brown speck and save the apple; the doom of decay is on the fruit.

Just so, each of us is tinctured with self-will; with self-ambitions; with the desire to be pampered, cushioned, and admired; with over-criticalness of everyone else and over-sentitiveness about ourselves; with a drive to enlarge the self with an accumulation of things. Thus, try as we may to separate these self-centred qualities from the unselfish ones, the self keeps cropping up again and again, tripping us every time.

What is Christ's solution to our dilemma? It is recorded for us in the eighth chapter of Mark. "Whosoever will save his life shall lose it," He says, "but whosoever shall lose his life for my sake ... shall save it."[1] To put it another way, there is no solution apart from the painful, all-out one of handing over to Him all of our natural self to be destroyed (the good parts of the apple along with the brown specks) so that Christ can give us a new self, one born from above, one in which He will live at the centre of our being.

If the idea of Christ living at the centre of life frightens us it may be because we fear that by handing over self-will we would then become spineless creatures, colourless carbon-copy personalities. We need not be afraid on either count. Actually, it's when selfishness and self-will progressively take over in our society that we become carbon copies of one another. When an adolescent is still unsure of his selfhood, he has a horror of being in any way different from his friends. When adults are not in the least concerned about pleasing God, they are desperately concerned about pleasing each other. When we have few inner resources, we hold up masks to hide our poverty. And all the masks seem to be turned out by the same factory—suburbia, the "organisation man", "the man in the grey flannel suit", all aided by mass advertising, extended by the media of mass communication.

Whenever we exchange self-will for God's will, we find greater strength, a finer quality of iron in the new will given us. And, by a strange paradox, we then become more indi-vidualistic, with more unique personalities than we would have thought possible. That is because we have exchanged the mask for the real self.

On that day of retreat, I remember being impressed with

how vividly C. S. Lewis expressed it. I copied several sentences in my notebook:

> Christ says, "Give me *all*. I don't want so much of your money and so much of your work—I want *you*. I have not come to torment your natural self, but to kill it. No half-measures are any good. I don't want to cut off a branch there, I want to have the whole tree down. I don't want to drill the tooth, or crown it, or stop it, but to have it out. Hand over the whole natural self, all the desires which you think innocent, as well as the ones you think wicked—the whole outfit. I will give you a new self instead. In fact I will give you myself, my own will shall become yours."[2]

To the Apostle Paul this matter of handing over the whole man to Christ to be annihilated was at the heart of Christianity. "For we know that our old self was crucified with Him [that is, with Christ] to do away with our sinful body, so that we might not be enslaved to sin any longer. . . ."[3]

To Paul the essence of sin lay in a man's life being ruled by "My will be done" rather than by God's will be done. There is, he was saying, a fundamental choice at the heart of life. It is simply "Who is going to be master?" And if we fail to make a conscious choice on this, then we make it by default. In that case, self will rule from the throne of our hearts.

As we sat in the living-room of the rustic retreat lodge that day, some of us on cushions on the floor, Sheldon Turner, the lawyer and lay leader who was guiding the discussion, pointed out that the relatively new science of psychology has—independently of theology—arrived at the same conclusion: there is no maturity or fulfilment of man's personality apart from the slaying of egocentricity. A psychiatrist put it this way:

> Egocentricity in any form . . . always leads to difficult experiences which we call crises. . . . The more we are egocentric, and therefore rigid, the less we are able to bear life's burdens. . . . [Increasing egocentricity destroys itself! He who tries to save his life kills himself.] This is as it should be, since the breakdown of the Ego—the collapse of the system of mistaken ideas which like a shell encase the

Self and limit the expression of its power—is one basic aim of human destiny. . . .[4]

Just before lunch that day, paper and pencils were handed around, and each of us tried putting down the characteristics of the self-centred person as opposed to the God-centred person. Combining the lists, they looked something like this:

THE EGOCENTRIC PERSONALITY	THE GOD-CENTRED PERSONALITY
"My will be done"	*"Thy will be done"*
Is intent on self-glory.	Has true humility.
Is concerned about other people's opinions of self; craves admiration and popularity.	Is increasingly free from the necessity for the approval or praise of others.
Is rigid, self-opinionated.	Is flexible.
Cannot stand criticism.	Handles criticism objectively; usually benefits from it.
Desires power over others; uses others for his own ends.	Is devoted to the common good.
Wants ease; is self-indulgent.	Ease given up when necessary; knows that many comforts precious to the self may have to go.
Holds self-preservation of supreme importance.	Is aware that you lose your life to find it.
Tries to be self-sufficient; has a practical atheism by which he feels he does not need God's help.	Is acutely aware of his need of God in everyday life.
Feels that life owes him certain things.	Realises that life owes him nothing; that goodness cannot earn him anything.

THE EGOCENTRIC PERSONALITY	THE GOD-CENTRED PERSONALITY
"My will be done"	*"Thy will be done"*
Is over-sensitive; feelings easily hurt; nourishes resentments.	Readily forgives others.
Springs back slowly, painfully from disappointments.	Has capacity to rise above disappointments and use them creatively.
Trusts in material possessions for security.	Knows that security is in relationship to God, not in things.
Indulges in self-pity when things go wrong.	Has objective resiliency when things go wrong.
Needs praise and publicity for his good deeds.	Works well with others; can take second place.
Is tolerant, of, even blind to, his own sins; appalled at the evil in others.	Understands the potential evil in himself and lays it before God; is not shocked at any evil possibility in self or others.
Is self-complacent; craves the peace of mind that relieves him of unwelcome responsibilities.	Knows that warfare between good and evil will not allow undisturbed peace.
Loves those who love him.	Can love the unlovely; has a feeling of oneness in God toward all humanity.

When the group gathered again after lunch, one girl asked immediately: "But *how* does one deal with the 'My will be done'? Who can ever get rid of self completely?"

"Perhaps not in this life," Sheldon said thoughfully. "But no human progress could have been made in any field had we followed the line that if we can't do everything perfectly, we won't try. Remember—Christ promises us a miracle with this ego-slaying, a much bigger portion of self slain in this life than we think possible."

The girl repeated her question, "All right, how do you go about it?"

Sheldon then quoted Paul's words: "For you died, and your life is hidden with Christ in God."[5]

It was pointed out that the "have died" is the past perfect tense; it looks back to a definite point in the past. Therefore this matter of getting rid of the old tyrant self is a deliberate step, exactly as entering into the Christian life is a definite step.

We worked out a plan for ego-slaying which goes something life this:

1. We see the limitation of self-centred living and the danger of it in every area.
2. We pass sentence on the natural self by telling God that we are willing to have Him slay it. Our statement of willingness is a definite act at a given time.
3. We accept by faith the fact that God has heard us; that the next action will be His. We reckon by faith that He has indeed undertaken the execution.
4. There will be a crisis or series of crises. We live through them step by step. This is the overt evidence that the slaying of the self has been undertaken.
5. Every day of our lives we shall still have to choose between selfishness and unselfishness. But the big decision to let Christ rather than self rule makes all the smaller decisions easier. This is the "taking up the cross day after day" of which Jesus spoke.[6]

Sheldon warned the group that we had better not tell God that we desired ego-slaying unless we meant it. For no one can predict what painful experiences God will allow in order to make the experience real. After all, each man's self-will takes a different form, and God is going to touch self-interest at its most vulnerable spot.

Then he went on to add wryly, "But I don't want to sound too grim. Maybe this will be some comfort to you. For you who have already embarked on the Christian life, this execution of self is something that has to happen sooner or later, here or in the next life. So you may as well get on with it—get it over with, so that you can break through to real happiness now."

He grinned at us, and his blue eyes held a special light. We had known this remarkable layman for a long time. Somewhere back in his past he had left self behind to a degree that scarcely seemed possible. Yet he had not only survived the experience, but became one of the most delightful personalities I know, successful in his profession, powerful in his way with other men.

What Sheldon called "the execution of self" is the great "crisis", or the series of smaller crises, of which the psychiatrist spoke in the quotation above. This is Paul's "old self" in the process of crucifixion—and it is only human to flee that. Christianity, most of us think, is fine up to a point, so long as we can make it serve us. So long as it gives us peace of mind, settles some of the dust of our conflicts, makes us more likeable people—well, fine! But of course this is peripheral stuff. This is interpreting Christianity as a rosewater philosophy to make a comfortable atmosphere for nice people. But nice people have no cutting edge. Nor have they any anwers for the problems that beset our world.

We begin to see that no man is worthy to rule until he has been ruled; no man can lead well until he has given himself to leadership greater than his own. Even Jesus Christ was no exception. Repeatedly He said that He was not carrying out His own will, but the will of the One who sent Him.

I found Sheldon Turner's thought disturbing: "The Christ of the cross isn't going to become real to you until you come to terms with this hard core of reality at the heart of Christianity. How could He be real to you when you—not He—are still at the centre of your life?"

As the woods around the lodge grew dark and the retreat drew to a close, we had much to think about. Those of us who decided to take the plunge did not do so lightly. In fact, we felt rather as if we were agreeing to a sort of spiritual Russian roulette.

Before parting and driving back to Washington, we agreed that we would check back with one another to find out what had happened to us following the retreat. In actual fact, how would God make real to us this slaying of self? Looking back now, I know that not one of us could have guessed.

It would take a book in itself to tell the details of what happened to the seven of us who said _yes_ to the risky adventure of ego-slaying. For what I can tell here, I have changed names and a few details in order not to embarrass the friends concerned.

One businessman, Ed, was touched at two points—his masculinity and his professional reputation. He was the sort of married man who enjoyed flirting with women up to a point, especially with women much younger than he. He had told himself that the flirting game was harmless fun, so long as he always stopped short of actual affairs. I do not think it had occurred to him that in feeding his masculine ego with the adoration and flattery of young secretaries, he ran the risk of their falling in love with him and getting hurt.

It seems that for weeks he had been driving Isobel, the youngest girl in the office, home from work each afternoon. The attention of an older man, especially the boss, had been flattering. In her room at night, Isobel built dream-castles, romanticised every gesture, every remembered sentence. She even wrote the boss a series of love letters. She had no intention of mailing them, kept them locked in a leather jewellery case in her dressing-table drawer.

One night she forgot to lock the case.

In the process of cleaning her daughter's room the following day, Isobel's mother found the letters. From them she concluded that her daughter was having an affair with her boss. Incensed at the idea of an older man seducing an innocent girl, she decided on a course of action.

Soon Ed received an anonymous letter. It accused him of

adultery and threatened to reveal the matter to his wife and to his board of directors. At first he regarded the letter as a joke. He was not guilty of adultery! No doubt the letter had been written by some crackpot. Contemptuously, he tore it into small bits and tossed the pieces in the waste basket.

But by the time the second, the third and the fourth letters arrived, each more violent than the last, and now threatening blackmail, Ed was in a fine state of nerves. The reiterated threat of the anonymous writer to go to his wife made him decide to tell her about it himself. In addition, he went to the District of Columbia Chief of Police with the letters in hand and told him the story.

Using the United States mails for attempted blackmail is a penal offence, so the officers went into action. Through clever detective work, the mother was apprehended. When the Chief of Police telephoned Ed to tell him that the anonymous writer was Isobel's mother, he was horrified. How could just driving a girl home from work a few times result in such serious misunderstanding?

Then he had a clear-eyed look at himself and his old habit of using women for what he had regarded as harmless ego-satisfactions. With a new humility, he paid a call on Isobel and her terrified family. It must have been quite a scene in their family living-room that evening. Ed said afterward that during those hours he became a man.

He assumed full responsibility for what had happened. He assured the girl's parents that there was no affair. Gently he tried to spell out to Isobel how much he loved his wife and valued his marriage, and he asked her forgiveness for what she had interpreted as unspoken promises.

Isobel's mother would actually have received a prison sentence had not Ed personally gone to court and pleaded for leniency. He knew the judge, having played golf with him at the Burning Tree Club. Realising by now the connection between the sequence of events and the ego-slaying he had pledged, Ed felt that—pride or not—there was nothing for him to do but tell the whole story to the judge in his chambers. Surely, he told the judge, this woman had learned her lesson and would never repeat such an offence. It would be devastating to the family to have the mother taken away. And Isobel and her two younger brothers might never live down the stigma of their mother being sentenced to prison.

So, after a stern lecture to the mother, the judge suspended sentence and paroled her. But the detectives who had worked so hard to apprehend her at Ed's request felt that justice had not been done and made no attempt to hide their anger at Ed and his "softness". This was hard on his pride, too.

Thus the crisis ended. It had come only two weeks after Ed's decision at the retreat. Though the seven of us had known one another for a long time, we marvelled that Ed wanted to share so intimate an experience with us. He insisted on doing so. "Telling it to this one group of close friends is part of the therapy, I guess. Besides it will make it harder for me ever to repeat such immature nonsense. Sheldon warned us all that this process would be painful. It sure was! Yet I'm grateful, ever so grateful, that it happened to me."

Out of Ed's experience, and those of others, we began to see some of the characteristic ways God handles the slaying of the old self. In one sense, the crisis is not sent by God—that is, imposed from above. In each instance, the emergency is the direct result of weakness, the rigidity, the lack of wisdom of one's own self-centred actions. However, the timing of the various crises in the weeks following the retreat seemed remarkable.

Another feature common to all the emergencies was that they never got so completely out of hand that permanent damage resulted to the individual involved or to other people. The dagger thrusts were against the false values, against the evil masquerading as good. The real self emerged unhurt, indeed stronger than ever, with a fresh ability to stand up to life's problems. As in Ed's experience, God seemed to keep His finger on the situation, directing it, stopping it short of disaster.

This seemed to us awe-inspiring proof of God's love for the individual—that Divine love that combines in such an inimitable way tenderness and the iron of discipline. Ed told us that he thought he understood now what the writer of Hebrews had meant when he wrote: "The Lord disciplines the man he loves. . . . God is treating you as sons. . . . Discipline always seems for the time to be a thing of pain, not of joy; but those who are trained by it reap the fruit of it afterwards. . . ."[7]

Included in the group of seven was one minister. Roger had an impelling personality and had been born with a gift for preaching. Some thirteen years out of seminary, he was then the popular pastor of a thriving Lutheran church in northern Virginia.

Roger's crisis was merely uncomfortable compared to the pain Ed suffered, probably because Roger had already dealt more forcibly with the old self-centred tendencies than the rest of us.

"In the last few years," Roger explained to us, "I've had several overtures from other churches about becoming their pastor. Some have been important churches in our Lutheran conference. It's quite flattering to be waited upon by a pulpit committee, to be asked to preach a trial sermon to a congregation in some distant city, to be dined and fêted and wooed, to be offered all sorts of inducements to accept their call.

"I'd been telling myself that I had no way of knowing what God wanted me to do with each of these offers unless I investigated them. Sometimes that resulted in carrying the negotiations quite far. So the pulpit committees would be most hopeful that I would come. In the interim, my own church would plead with me not to go, sometimes offer inducements for me to stay. Then in the end I would know that I had to turn down the offer of the pulpit committee."

"But wasn't that a sort of ecclesiastical flirting?" someone asked.

Roger smiled. "I know that now. It was similar to the flirting Ed has told us about, and for the same reason. My ego got well fed every time by the process."

"What was the crisis?" I asked.

"Shortly after the retreat I received an overture from a church in Denver, Colorado. My wife and I went out there at the church's expense. Delightful trip!

"There were flowers in the hotel suite, corsages for Betty. There were newspaper stories with pictures of Betty and me. Headlines like VISITING PASTOR LIKES HOSPITALITY OF DENVER or VIRGINIA MINISTER TO PREACH AT 11 A.M. SERVICE TOMORROW; POSSIBLE SUCCESSOR TO DR —.

"We found the church divided down the middle theologically. Their previous minister had been an arch-conservative who had split hairs about the second coming of Christ. It was unfortunate for me that my visit got newspaper publicity. Two days after we got home, I received a letter saying that the pulpit committee had recommended that the congregation call me, but that the congregational meeting had voted 608 to 462 not to. They didn't think me doctrinally sound—or something.

"I know this may seem trivial to the rest of you, but my pride smarted for days. Betty laughed and said it was good for me. She's right, of course! But that newspaper publicity! Especially the headline that read: DENVER CHURCH WON'T CALL PASTOR; VIEWS ON CHRIST GIVEN AS REASON. My views on Christ weren't the reason at all. That hurt, because Christ is everything to me. Don't think the whole story didn't filter back to Virginia, too! Well, as a result I've had to face up to the fact that trifling with the feelings of groups of people— like churches—just won't do. And I've been probing for my motives in what you've called my 'ecclesiastical flirting'.

"Mixed up in it is always the temptation to run away from problems in my own church. Then there's the flattery of being wanted by two congregations. But the worst part of it has been lack of strict honesty with myself and with everyone else. From now on," Roger concluded, "I've got to be honest, completely honest in the most transparent sort of way."

I lived through Beverley's crisis with her, since she and I were the closest of friends. We had the intimacy that comes through sharing the deeps of life together. At first, we had been drawn together because we were both widows with sons to rear. Beverley had two boys, Kenneth, a teen-ager, and his younger brother, Sam. Her husband had been lost in World War II in the New Guinea jungle. At first he had been declared missing in action. But as the months melted into years, Bev's initial hope died and was replaced by a conviction that Jim would never come back. Nor did he; his body was never found. All of this she had shared with me—and much more.

During one of the recesses at the retreat, Bev and I had been sitting out under the trees. "I certainly needed this retreat," she confided. "I've been so mixed up recently. There's a barrier between me and the boys, especially Kenneth. Can't seem to get through to him at all. No zest in my work. I don't even get my fun out of recreation these days. The other night a friend took me to the Blue Room of the Shoreham. Suddenly, right in the midst of dinner, it was as if some part of me had detached itself and was standing off to one side watching objectively."

"And what did you see?" I asked.

Bev leaned her brown curly hair back against the tree trunk. "Oh, a lot of people, including me, determinedly working at trying to have fun. There was pretence at the heart of our play. You know—a sort of attitude of 'this evening is costing me plenty. I've paid for it, so I'm going to have fun, if it kills me.' "

We both laughed. "I know what you mean."

"Well, anyway," Bev continued, "already today I've found out what's wrong with me."

My friend toyed with a piece of grass reflectively. "Right after Jim went away, I did ask God to take over my life, rule it. But self has crept back and has been doing a lot of ruling in God's place."

"Looking on from the outside, it doesn't strike me that way," I objected.

"It's true, though. I've been compromising in the matter of drinking, for instance, and that can't be best for my boys. I find myself taking a cocktail sometimes when I don't want one at all, just so folks won't think I'm different. That's caring far too much about other people's opinions of me and not enough about my own.

"Then there's the matter of selfish use of time. I haven't been putting myself out for the boys. Some of their interests, like baseball, I find beastly boring. But I'm not making enough effort to identify with them. There's more, too."

We were called back to the lodge then, but with this much new insight into herself, Bev, was one of the seven who decided to take the plunge in ego-slaying.

Her crisis began on a certain Monday morning which was to hold heartache and drama for her. At seven-thirty the telephone rang. It was Detective C— of the Sixth Precinct, Juvenile Squad. His voice was gentle. He well knew that what he was about to tell this young widow would be a blow. Her Kenneth and three other boys had got into trouble on Saturday night. They had taken some property from their school—two axes and a fire extinguisher—and had broken the headlights of two school buses. Bev told me later that she began trembling so violently that she could scarcely hold the telephone.

"You and your son will have to appear at the Sixth Precinct Station at three-thirty this afternoon," Detective C— concluded.

Bev hung up and immediately dialled me. I was shocked for her but asked no questions over the phone. "I'll be over as soon as I can get dressed," I told her.

Her voice was quivering. "How on earth could Kenneth do something like that? I just don't understand?" She started crying, and we both hung up.

When I got to Bev's home, I found Kenneth with her in the den. She had kept him home from school, so that we could talk with him before the three-thirty hearing.

The boy was fourteen, tall, in the gawky stage. His face was alternatively flushed and pale that morning, his features pinched beneath a reddish shock of hair. His mother kept insisting, "Kenneth, you've got to tell us everything. It would be awful if anything else were sprung on us this afternoon.

It's time for honesty now—real honesty. Otherwise, how can we help you?"

But Kenneth had little to say, plead and probe as we would. He claimed that we knew everything there was to know. The barrier between him and his mother was there, all right.

Then the school principal telephoned. He wanted to see Kenneth later that morning. After the boy had gone, Bev and I prayed together. It was one of those real prayers—when two people mean business and get down to cases. Both of us wept.

That afternoon we spent three hours at the Precinct Station. Two men from the Juvenile Board were an hour and forty-five minutes late arriving. We waited with the other parents in the front room, watching the hands of the clock move with maddening slowness. I remember one father in particular—a man with black hair peppered with grey and large luminous brown eyes. He was wearing clothes that didn't match and tennis shoes in the middle of winter. And the sad shocked face of another father, his eyes with the look of a hurt animal's.

One mother with a lined, seamed face had brought along the little family dog. She held the little terrier close to her with a leash made from her son's tie. The parents of one boy were abroad and in their place had come a relative who was a psychiatrist, young and prematurely grey. I could almost see his trained mind wrestling with the question of what had happened to these boys from good families.

Finally the two officials arrived, and we were asked to go into a back room. Though it was informal, there was, nevertheless, a courtroom atmosphere. The Juvenile Board sat behind the one long table. There were several benches for the boys and their parents. I looked at Bev and knew that her head was throbbing, and that tears were close to the surface.

While we waited for the hearing to begin, one of the boys, the son of the man with the shocked, hurt eyes, put his head down on the table and began sobbing. He cried softly, not wanting to attract attention, trying to smother the sound with his arms. Later we found out that since early childhood the boy had wanted to go to West Point. If this incident went

down on a police record, he would never achieve his heart's
desire.

Through it all Kenneth seemed to have a permanent blush.
He kept chewing on his fingernails long after there was no
bit of surplus nail to chew. It came out in the questioning that
he was the one who had bought beer for the other boys.
How much had the beer been responsible for their conduct?
Who could tell? I knew that Bev would be connecting her
recent leniency on drinking with her son's buying the beer.

Kenneth stood straight and said, "Sir." I looked at him and
suddenly felt sure that this boy would turn out all right. But
that didn't lessen the agony I felt for Bev and Kenneth.

The men on the Juvenile Squad could not have been more
compassionate and understanding in their handling of the
situation. No word appeared in the Washington newspapers.
Wisely, they strung the matter out enough so that Kenneth
was badly frightened. A week after the first hearing, he and
Bev had to go down to the Juvenile Court again. Of course,
they were required to pay for the property damage. But in the
end, convinced that these boys had learned their lesson, the
Board dismissed their cases with no record against them.

Once again God had permitted circumstances to go only
so far as severe discipline would dictate but not to permanent
hurt.

A week later Bev was saying to me, "I didn't know a
mother's pride of ownership in her children could make her
so vulnerable. *My* sons . . . the fear that *my* reputation would
be hurt . . . the possible reflection on *my* dead husband's good
name . . . all self-pride!

"I know that my insistence on owning my children was the
crux of my problem with Kenneth. Kenneth is an individual
in his own right. He belongs to God, not to me; he's just
been loaned to me for a few years.

"Since then I've been talking to my son, person-to-person.
I've admitted some of my mistakes and fears and weaknesses,
where I need his help. Catherine, this one week I've watched
a miracle unfolding."

Bev's face glowed with her discovery. "That wall between

us has come crashing down like the walls of Jericho." Once again quick tears swam in her eyes—this time tears of happiness, relief, gratitude.

One cannot live through experiences like the seven of us had and retain any doubts about the thrust of a living Lord into contemporary life. We learned much in a short time. The literalness of His standing outside the door of our hearts and never intruding until we invite Him in . . . The immediacy of His invasion of our lives when we do open the door. His overweening concern that we call a halt to our trifling with life and move on toward maturity and effectiveness. His incisive knowledge of the most vulnerable weaknesses in each of us. Who but Christ could know so unerringly that point of mutiny, so covertly hidden even from ourselves?

All this left us wondering, awestruck. Worship Him? Of course? How can we help it? For He is the only One worthy of worship, supremely worthy! And yet the first step in the direction of that great love must always be ours.

13: The Gospel of Healing

OUR Sunday-school teacher was telling us the story of the man born blind who had received sight from Jesus. We were impressionable twelve-year-olds. I can remember hugging delightedly to myself the thought of the big commotion the healing must have caused. Surely everyone in the man's home village would have talked of little else. I imagined the conversation something like this:

"Isn't he the beggar, the one who's been blind all his life?"

"It looks like him!"

"It isn't possible. Who could cure a man who was *born* blind?"

"Let's ask his parents. They'll know. . . ."

And so they sought out the man's father and mother, who were non-commital: "We don't know what happened. Why don't you ask our son about it?"

While people wrangled and talked excitedly, there stood the man saying over and over, "All I know is that I used to be blind; now I can see. Isn't it wonderful?"

"But what did he do to you—how did he make you see?" his questioners had persisted.

Then the man had grown impatient. "I've told you before. He put a paste on my eyes; I washed it off, just as He told me to, in the Pool of Siloam. Now I can see. Don't you understand? I can *see*!"

But the elders of the church had not thought it wonderful at all, because the healing had upset their intellectual fruit-cart, and the fruit was rolling helter-skelter in all directions.

A certain exuberant quality in the story appealed to the rebel in me. I wondered if Jesus had enjoyed the ruckus too. . . .

Then, a few Sundays later, I heard a sermon that seemed to contradict the wonderful story that we had heard in Sunday school. I cannot remember the precise words of the man in the pulpit, but the gist of it went something like this:

"We should not expect miracles in our day like those recorded in the Bible. After all, the New Testament miracles were for a particular time. They were a special dispensation from God needed to authenticate the fact Jesus had really been sent from God. Also they were needed to get the Christian movement started. Gradually the miraculous element in Christianity died out, because it was not needed any more, indeed might have been dangerous. Today God answers our prayers in other ways, through drugs and the skill of modern physicians and men of science. . . ."

I felt let down and indignant. If the preacher was right, then why had they bothered to tell us the story of the blind man in Sunday school? At the time I had not enough knowledge of the New Testament to know what the holes in this man's position were. Later I discovered that he was reflecting the popular eighteenth- and nineteenth-century Protestant position regarding miracles. To these men it seemed a safe middle position, because it effectively preserved the inspiration of the Scriptures, yet did not put the theologians in conflict with the new discoveries of science.

For the next fifteen years I was not at all concerned with whether healing came about through miracles or science. I took health for granted. College, romance, marriage, the birth of a son filled my days to the crowding point. The question of whether those New Testament stories of supernatural cures have relevance for our time touched my life not at all—until . . .

Until that afternoon in May 1943, when the illness I have already mentioned stalked into my life. Over in Baltimore, where I had gone for a physical check-up, Dr Thomas Sprunt told me as gently as he could that I had an early case of tuberculosis in both lungs. I would have to go to bed full-time. It might take a long while to get well.

It did take a long while—three weary, endless years. Most of this time I spent in the big front bedroom of the manse with its five windows and five Peter Marshall seascapes on the walls. I travelled every tiny design in the pale yellow wallpaper with my eyes hundreds of times. I even remember two stains on the ceiling over my bed where Peter had swatted mosquitos the summer before.

How tired the muscles of one's back can become from too much lying in bed! What is there to fill the hours, the days, the weeks that stretch on and on? I could still work out the week's menus and make marketing lists. But as time went on, the kitchen seemed farther and farther away and food became of little interest. I would lie there, longing to know what was going on downstairs, hearing the hum of voices in the living-room. If only I could listen in on the conversations and take an active part in something!

At the beginning of my illness, Peter John was three years old. I could tell him an occasional story and help him with a wooden puzzle, if he would perch on a stool by the bed. I had the late afternoon to look forward to, when Peter would come back from the church office. Through him, I could get glimpses of the world beyond the bedroom walls.

But there was never much for me to tell him. All too often he came home to my discouragement, even my tears of weariness and rebellion. He was patient with me, loving, wise. But not even Peter could answer my pleading questions: "Why— oh, why do I have to lie here month after month? Why can't the doctors do something?"

As it became increasingly apparent that they could not, my need sent me back to the New Testament in eager search for an answer to the question that had so troubled my child's mind: did Jesus mean for healing by faith to be limited to His days on earth?

I made an honest search. Neither self-deception nor wishful thinking about what the gospel narratives meant would help me. The shadows on the X-rays of the lungs plus the weakness that chained me in bed were real enough. I was in search of truth as clearly as I could perceive it.

The results of several months of reading and pondering might be summarised like this: Jesus said that He had come to earth to reveal His Father's nature and will to man. Then what was God's attitude towards sickness and disease as reflected in Jesus? I found that He placed any deviation from health in the same category as sin: He saw both as the work of an evil force, both as intruders in his Father's world. Jesus consistently "rebuked" disease precisely as He did demons.[1] At the beginning of His ministry, He declared an all-out offensive against sin, disease, and death.[2] Practically speaking, that meant that Jesus' attitude toward sickness was exactly that of any doctor today: He fought it all the way.

Nowhere in the gospel could I discover any hint of retreat or compromise with this position against disease. Jesus never refused to heal anyone who came to Him for help. He reproved every question of His unwillingness or His inability to heal.[3] Never once did He say, as we so often do, "If it is God's will to heal. . . ." For Him there were no *ifs* about His Father's will for wholeness of body as well as of spirit and mind. In fact, roughly one-third of Christ's public ministry was taken up with the healing of men's bodies.

He seems never to have suggested that any individual was unworthy of healing. Worthiness or unworthiness were not the condition of receiving God's gifts. The criterion was rather the most practical one imaginable—the individual's need. He "cured those who needed to be healed."[4]

I could find no record of Jesus implying that an individual's spiritual state or the Kingdom of God would be furthered by ill-health. Not once did He say that sickness is a blessing. I was impressed with the fact that there is no beatitude for the sick or for those who suffer physically, while there is a beatitude for those who suffer persecution.[5]

Clearly it was Jesus' desire that we be rid of disease. What was his plan for achieving this? He said that faith in His Father's willingness and ability to give children all good gifts is the key. In His eyes there was no evil that faith could not vanquish, no need that faith could not supply.

I had not gone far in my study before I discovered that there were some religious leaders in Jesus' day who tried to interpret His miracles exactly as had that preacher in my childhood: that God used the miracles to prove to us that Jesus was divine. This was what Jesus called wanting "a sign" and He had harsh words for it: "Only an evil generation would demand a sign. . . ."[6]

Jesus' chief motive in healing seems rather to have been nothing more or less than pure compassion. The word *compassion* is used over and over to describe His attitude toward the sick. That was why He often went out of His way to heal when the sufferer had neither asked for nor thought of His doing so.[7] He delighted in straightening a bent back.[8] He rejoiced in that moment when a man gleefully flings away his crutches. He was glad that He could break up a funeral and give a beloved son back to his mother.[9] It was a gratifying thing to Him to see the light of reason and sanity return to the eyes of a violent demoniac.[10] Jesus healed because the love of God, flowing irresistibly through Him in a torrent of good will, simply swept evil away as the debris that it is.

Before Christ's crucifixion He commissioned His apostles to carry on His healing work and sent them out on several test missions.[11] When they returned, after having healed successfully, He rejoiced with them, "I watched Satan falling from heaven like a flash of lightening."[12] As restrained and stripped as the narrative usually is, a lilting, triumphant quality breaks through here. The physician-apostle Luke says that Jesus "thrilled with joy at that hour", breathed a prayer of thanksgiving and then turned to his disciples, exulting, "All has been handed over to me by my Father . . ."[13]

But then the next question to which I sought an answer was this one: Did Jesus mean for his disciples to continue with their healing ministry after His ascension? I found no doubt that He assumed that they would. How else could we interpret the solemn words spoken on the night before his betrayal, "Truly, truly I tell you, he who believes in me will do the very deeds I do, and still greater deeds than these. . . ."

Moreover, after the resurrection, Jesus' commission to His followers for all ages contains the admonition: "Go ye into all the world, and preach the gospel to every creature . . . and these signs shall follow them that believe; . . . they shall lay hands on the sick, and they shall recover."[14]

Matthew's version of the same great commission stresses

the "teaching all nations . . . to observe all things whatsoever I have commanded you. . . ." The "all things" and the "whatsoever" are inclusive enough. Certainly Jesus meant that the whole gospel should be taught and practised, not an effete, watered-down version of it.

The Acts of the Apostles leaves no doubt that Peter and Paul and the other apostles interpreted the whole gospel to include healing. For these men proceeded to heal on many occasions.

Going back to my original question, "Did Jesus mean for healing by faith to be limited to His days on earth?" I found that the New Testament cries a consistent, unequivocal, resounding *"No!"*

For me those were days of engrossing discovery. The four walls of my bedroom no longer confined mind or spirit. I was off adventuring in another realm, and I felt like a discoverer who had stumbled into a hidden valley rich with deposits of gold. Something of the pristine intoxication of those first followers of "the Way" winged out of the ancient records into my heart.

Obviously the next step was to appropriate what I had learned. My faith was simple, perhaps even naïve. I reasoned that, had I been living in Jesus' day, I would have been among those who sought Him out for healing. I knew that the Scriptures insist that nothing has changed about His compassion or His power, that He is "always the same, yesterday, today, and for ever".[15] And we have His unequivocal promise, "Lo, I am with you alway, even unto the end of the world."[16]

Then since He was with me—though I could not see Him or even feel His Presence—I pictured how the scene might be. I saw myself bowed before Him, looking up into His eyes, "Lord, I need Your help. You made my body. You can heal it. Will You do for me what You have for so many others?" He would have smiled at me, I thought, and stretched out His hand to lay it on my head. Then I proceeded in the simplest way to ask for His healing.

After that I waited impatiently for the next routine chest X-rays.

Usually I received the doctor's telephone report several days after the X-rays. The moment finally came; I found picking up the telephone by my bed for this particular call something of a traumatic experience. During the pause while the nurse transferred the call to the doctor's inner office, my heart began to race, my throat went dry. Every sense had its antennae out to catch the mood and timbre of the doctor's first words.

My imagination toyed with what I would say to him when he told me of his amazement in finding my chest healed. Would I tell him the truth? But what if—no, I wouldn't even admit the thought. I had read somewhere that real faith entertains no doubts. By a process of will power that I found somewhat wearying, I clung resolutely, desperately to the thought of complete health.

Finally at the other end of the phone there was a click and the doctor's voice came on. He sounded casual, "We find no increased density in either lung. The shadows and infiltration are just about the same. No real change . . . the sedimentation rate has gone down one point. Just carry on! I'll see you in a few days."

Slowly I rested the telephone back on its cradle. The doctor's words had already pricked and burst the self-inflated balloon that I had thought was faith. For that day and the next I was too numb, too stunned even to try to reason out what had happened. Then came rebellious tears, followed by a period of feeling sorry for myself and by hours of black depression. Finally my mind began to function again.

I knew that I had come to the boundaries of my human reason. I stood on the edge and stared off into an abyss of despair. Since medical skill was not solving my problem and my spiritual efforts—so far as I could evaluate them—had got me nowhere, what now?

Was it possible that Jesus Christ and Christianity were myths *in toto*, a carefully wrought system of nonsense? Or if God did exist, was He so bound by the natural law that He Himself had created that He was helpless, too?

In that mood of near-despair, I went for a visit to my

parents' home on the Eastern Shore of Virginia. My doctors still did not want me out of bed for more than thirty minutes at a time. The trip was made possible by my taking a boat to Norfolk. I remember that Peter actually picked me up in his arms and carried me up the gangplank to the bunk in my stateroom.

A few nights after my arrival—on September 14, 1943, to be exact—something happened to me that defies analysis. I have re-lived it in my mind hundreds of times since that night. All I can do is to describe it exactly as it happened. . . .

I awakened about 3.30 A.M. There was blackness all around me, not a sound. I had no idea what had awakened me. Nor did I understand why I had emerged suddenly from deep sleep into alertness with no interim drowsiness.

Then it happened, I was aware of a Presence, a Power, a Personality in my room. My physical eyes saw nothing, yet a new way of seeing was instantly available. My body tingled as with a shock of electricity.

The new set of senses which I had suddenly been given enabled me to perceive the vivid Personality who stood at the right side of my bed. There was in Him a curious combination of kingliness and tenderness.

Through His tenderness shone the fact that He looked upon me as a child, quite a foolish child at times. And He had a sense of humour—and the light touch. With my new eyes I saw that He smiled at me. His attitude was, "Why do you take yourself and your problems so seriously? Relax! There's nothing here I can't take care of."

I realised too that He knew every detail of my life and household. And with my new ears I heard Him speak in contemporary language. There was never a "thee" or a "thou".

"Go and tell your mother," He said. And then He smiled again. "That's simple enough isn't it?"

My humanness immediately asserted itself. "Go and tell my mother—what?" I thought. I wanted to argue, "It's the middle of the night, what will mother think?"

But again, I was conscious of that note of mastery in the One who had just spoken. And I understood something else:

he was standing there waiting, leaving me entirely free to obey or to disobey. For an instant I wavered between my disinclination to obey and that compelling quality in Him, sensing that something terribly important—as important as my whole future—hung on my decision. Then resolution welled up in me. "I'll do it, if it kills me," I told Him as I threw off the bed covers.

And once again, He smiled at my intensity . . . and stood aside for me to pass.

Mother wakened immediately and sat up in bed. Father was still asleep. "What's happened?" There was alarm in her voice.

"Don't be frightened. Something wonderful has happened. I just want you to know that I'm going to be all right now. I'll tell you about it in the morning."

This was scarcely fair, since Mother must have been consumed with curiosity. Yet because she sensed the combination of excitement and restraint in me, she did not question me further.

A few minutes later when I returned to the bedroom, it was empty. I lay there wide awake until dawn marvelling at what had happened. Now I knew what the New Testament writers meant when they spoke of Jesus "speaking with authority". I had felt His kingliness. I could understand how it was that the sceptic Thomas could in the same Presence pass in an instant from unbelief to worship before this Christ, saying "My Lord and my God".

In the morning I wondered if I was healed. Would the next X-ray finally show healthy lung tissue? But something far more important even than healthy lungs and body tissue was now clear to me. I knew that Christianity is no myth. I could understand why no intimidation, not even the threat of death, could shake Peter and James and John and the other apostles from their insistence that Jesus Christ was alive!

How was His resurrection possible? I had no idea. But suddenly all theological controversy as to *how* it had happened seemed unimportant in the face of the fact that it was so.

As for my health, I dared not assume that Christ had healed me. He had made no such statement!

As it turned out, this experience was the turning point in my illness. For the first time the next X-ray showed progress, as did every X-ray thereafter. Even so, months were to pass before I was pronounced well.

Why did it take so long? The tardiness was not God's will. Of that I am sure. Rather it was due to two deficiencies of mine. The first was an inner difficulty. As time went on, I began to realise that the psychologically penetrating question Jesus had once put to a man at the Pool of Bethesda—a man who had been ill for thirty-eight years—also applied to me: "Do you want your health restored?"[17]

This seems a ridiculous question. Who wouldn't want to get well? Yet many doctors today believe that one of the root causes of much illness is a deep-seated retreat from life. Psychosomatic medicine has much to say about the will to live and its converse, the subconscious death-wish. Apparently any interior division about this, any chronic state of indecision about facing some necessary adjustments to life, can directly contribute to illness.

So I had to ask myself, "Am I willing to go back into life ready to assume full responsibilities? Am I willing to make adult adjustments to whatever life hands me? Can I accept such robust health at Christ's hands that no one need ever feel sorry for me again, that I shall never again be able to use poor health as an excuse for avoiding some responsibility?" This had to be a clear-cut decision of my will. I was aware of Christ standing aside for me to make it, even as He had stood aside that night of September fourteenth while I decided whether or not I would obey Him.

But the second reason for the delay in my convalescence was not so easily resolved. It was my inability to grasp an inviolable spiritual principle—one that is seen everywhere in the New Testament—that faith must always be in the present tense. The most succinct statement of the principle is in Mark: "So I tell you, whatever you pray for and ask, believe you have got it, and you shall have it."[18]

I puzzled for months over this one verse. The verb tenses seem contradictory. How can one believe that he already possesses health, for instance, at the same moment that he is being promised health in the future? Yet I wondered if that was not exactly what Christ had been asking me to believe that night of September fourteenth: that, X-rays and medical reports notwithstanding, I was healed right then.

Every time that Jesus forgave sins or healed, he demonstrated this principle. One could pick examples almost at random. Though Zacchaeus had spent a lifetime in sin, Jesus told him, "This day is salvation come to this house."[19] The woman in the synagogue who had been bowed over [with arthritis probably] for eighteen years was told, "Woman, you are released from your weakness"[20]—right now, at this moment.

About this time, I came across Hannah Whitall Smith's statement that God's inevitable order is Fact, then Faith, and last, Feeling. In relation to health, this order would mean that health would precede one's faith for it; that feeling well, the disappearance of symptoms, and the clinical proof of health would come last of all. This too substantiates the formula that Jesus gave us.

I came to realise that our mortality, which forces us to divide time into past, present and future is probably the simplest key to the seeming contradiction in the verb tenses in the verse in question. In the world of spirit, there is only the eternal Now. But Jesus was trying to explain the principle to men still in the flesh. Even with this much understanding, the most my faith could grasp was that my healing was *in the process* of coming. I felt that this was scarcely good enough. No wonder my recovery was so slow.

There are those who are able to grip this principle of present-moment faith more firmly than I did, enough to act on it. In such cases, the healing process is accelerated accordingly. This was dramatised for me by what had happened to another tubercular patient. Her story was to be a decisive factor in my own recovery.

One afternoon in the late spring of 1945, during a period when my progress toward health seemed especially slow, a former college friend came to call. I had not seen her in years. Apart from her news of our classmates, one thing seemed uppermost in her mind—the story of Rosa Bell Montgomery. "She's just had a remarkable recovery from TB," the friend told me. "Her case was much worse than yours! In fact she was in a sanatorium in New Mexico and not expected to live out the month. Hers was a case of spiritual healing, pure and simple. She's fine now. In fact, she's getting married next month."

As I sat in bed propped up against pillows listening to this, I kept questioning, probing for more details.

My friend saw my eagerness. "I'll tell you what. I'll write Rosa and tell her about you. I think she'd be happy to write you herself and give you the story first hand. Would you like that?"

Would I like it!

The promised letter, however, was slow in coming. When if finally arrived, I could understand why. It was a lengthy letter for a girl to write in long hand on her honeymoon. It was postmarked New York.

How sorry I am to have waited so long to write to you. My only excuse or reason for this delay is that the letter telling me about you reached me in Los Angeles just a few days after I was married, and I have been on a lovely but hectic honeymoon ever since. . . . Now that we are in New York, far from the sweet attentions of friends and family, I can chat with you undisturbed. . . .

It has been more than three years now since I turned my case over to the Lord and He really did a good piece of work on me. No one talked me into it—in fact no one talked to me about it at all—and I didn't read anything that influenced me. This is how it happened, and I shall be as brief as possible. . . .

Rosa had been a bed patient in a sanatorium in Albuquerque for almost ten months, a cavity in the left lung, fluid on the right, losing weight steadily. There came the night when Rosa took a long look at herself spiritually. She felt that her heart had been wayward and proud. In her mind she went over all the things that she had been hugging to herself. Suppose God should want her to give up these things? For example, her deep desire to find a husband. Perhaps marriage wasn't in God's plan for her because of her health problem. But how could she bear the thought of never marrying?

Then suddenly, none of these things seemed to matter any more. She decided that she wanted Christ more than she wanted anything else. Lying on her hospital bed, watching the shadows from the desert moonlight on the ceiling, her will bowed itself before Christ and called Him Master. Immediately there was a feeling of peace.

The next day she had the same keen desire I had to search the Scriptures on the subject of healing. Rosa had grown up in a physician's home. She had been taught all her life that God uses doctors and medicine to heal today. But she also knew that medicine still had no real cure for tuberculosis. The doctors could co-operate with nature to achieve an arrested case —and that was all. So she determined to drop all previous ideas and to find out for herself what the Scriptures had to say on the subject.

Her conclusions were just what mine had been from the same sort of search. So she turned her case over to God.

Jesus had talked about the agreement of like-minded people as being one prerequisite for answered prayer. "If two of you agree on earth about anything you pray for, it will be done for you by my Father in Heaven. For where two or three have gathered in My Name, I am there amongst them."[21]

So one March afternoon, a few friends met Rosa in the sanctuary of a local church. Rosa was too ill to get dressed, so she went in her bathrobe. There, before the altar, the group gathered around her and prayed. It was simple and direct. Yet when they prayed nothing dramatic happened. Rosa felt no different, except for an inner assurance that the answer was on the way.

That being so, she no longer asked for healing but began thanking God for it. Here Rosa was demonstrating that principle that had so puzzled me, "Believe you have got it and you shall have it." She decided that she would begin acting her faith by getting up and walking about, so far as her strength would permit.

The fact that faith has to be in the present then led her to a daring decision: she would permit no more pneumothorax treatments.

Rosa's doctor at the sanatorium was appalled. Dr Werner cajoled and threatened. Once the lungs were collapsed, it was suicide to stop the pneumothorax before healing was complete! But his warnings were to no avail; Rosa quietly stood her ground. She knew how foolhardy her decision seemed to the medical men. Nor was she implying that others should act in so drastic a manner. But this, she felt, was what Jesus was telling *her* to do. She must obey. It was as simple as that. God would take care of the results.

Rosa found all the pressure harder to withstand than she would admit. Many symptoms of her disease were still bothering her—fever, a cough, the fluid in her left lung. Yet she knew that she had to keep her attention fixed on Christ, not on her symptoms; that she had to listen for His directions, not those of others, however well-meaning and loving they were.

Her doctor made one last desperate try. He asked that Roas's father, Dr Nelson Bell, in Montreat, North Carolina,[22] be appraised of the situation. "But I don't think it would do for me to talk to him just now," Dr Werner told Rosa. "I'm too upset about this." So a friend at the sanatorium put the telephone call through.

Dr Bell did some sharp questioning. When he had satisfied himself that Rosa was firm in her decision, and that she would agree to stay in the sanatorium where the doctors could keep an eye on her, he gave her his blessing.

After that, Dr Werner battled with Rosa no more, only watched her more closely than ever. By April she had begun to gain weight. Her pulse had gone down to normal. The afternoon fever was decreasing.

By June, Rosa was out of bed most of the time. By July she had formed the habit of walking sixteen blocks down the hill for an afternoon milk shake, then sixteen blocks back up the hill. In October she pleaded for and got a position in the institution's laboratory.

The following February—not quite a year since the little

group of friends had gathered in her room for prayer—the leading radiologist of New Mexico compared a new set of X-ray plates with the old ones. He was dumbfounded at the change.

In April the same technician found the cavity of her right lung "completely obliterated". At that time he also wrote Dr Bell that Rosa's "explanation of her healing is the only adequate one".

Then Don Montgomery walked into her life, and God gave her the one joy she had thought He might ask her to relinquish —love and marriage.

I am still in touch with Rosa. She has never had any recurrence of her old trouble. Nor has health required her to live in the south-west. She is no fanatic on the subject of healing, but her experience has made her relationship with Christ an intensely personal one.

In all her letters to me she stressed Christ's individualised treatment of each case. "You must listen for His orders, not copy mine," she warned.

The first hint of my directions came in an odd way. I dreamed that the lung specialist said to me, "There are people who don't get well until they get up and go about their business. Of course, as a doctor I couldn't take the responsibility for telling you that, but—" and I woke up.

I mentioned the dream to my mother. "That's queer," she answered as a startled look crossed her face. "The same thought has been coming to me over and over."

Still I was cautious about acting on this. After all, perhaps the dream had been nothing more than wishful thinking in my sleep. But in time, my orders did come in an inner conviction that did not fade with the passing of days: *As you give strength to others, strength will be given to you. Stay under the doctor's care, but start getting out of bed.* And that is just what I did.

I began with a small chore, tidying up the linen closet once a week; I could sit down to do that. Then I assumed the responsibility and fun of dressing Peter John each morning. After that came a short afternoon walk with Jeffrey, our cocker. First, a half a block. Then to the corner. After a few weeks, we were circling the block. I was inching my way, but little by little vitality was flowing back to me.

Then came the day when the doctor's nurse telephoned to report that the sedimentation rate had returned to the normal range. This meant that there was no longer evidence of infection in the blood stream. So far, so good. But the X-ray pictures still showed trouble.

By now X-rays were being taken three months apart. Two months after the good laboratory report, I went down to add the next routine chest film to the doctor's fat file. It was on a Tuesday morning that I was to telephone to hear the result.

The first time I called, the doctor was in the midst of a consultation. Would I please try again in about an hour?

During the hour, some of my old fears of those telephone reports came creeping back. *What if*—I thought—*No, "what ifs" are always silly, because they borrow trouble.* Nevertheless, when I dialled the number again it was with an unsteady hand.

The doctor's voice was as calm as always. "The appearance is that of perfectly healed lesions—"

"Perfectly healed!" I almost shouted at him. "You mean I'm well?"

There was a smile in his voice. "That's what I mean. But wouldn't you like to hear the remainder of the report?"

I listened impatiently to the droning technical language. How could he be so maddeningly placid about it? He was reading it as if this were a weather report! The first minute I could hang up, I dropped the telephone and rushed downstairs shouting the great news.

In a few hours when I could be calmer about it, gratitude of a deeper kind welled up. I was grateful not only because I was well again, but because of my personal encounter with Christ, which had settled certain questions for ever. Inestimable blessings had come out of a difficult experience. I had discovered myself and what I wanted out of life. The woman who rose from bed and went out to meet life was a different woman.

After such an experience, I of all people should have been

convinced for all time of God's power to heal. But there was still an area that continued to trouble me. I now had no doubt that an individual can open himself to the healing love of God. But can that love be sent winging to someone else? Can prayers affect another person's illness?

In the intervening years I have had this question answered for me again and again. The answer is definitely *Yes!*

I have chosen to use Karen Emmott's story out of many, because the medical facts are indisputable. Not only is the man who initiated the prayers for her a surgeon, but her father, too, is a doctor. Karen is the eldest daughter of Dr Ralph Emmott, a specialist in urology in Oklahoma City.

Her physical problem began soon after her fifteenth birthday in the spring of 1960. It was nothing serious—just an abscess which required a minor operation, incision, and drainage. Twenty-four hours in the hospital (the one where her father practices) seemed to clear everything up.

Karen plunged into a busy summer. Before me as I write this is a small picture of her as she was then. Yes, she was a charmer: short curly hair, sparkling eyes, a piquant quality about her. At the close of the school year she had been voted drum-majorette. Her five younger brothers and sisters were proud of her. She seemed to be following in the footsteps of their mother, who had been a campus beauty queen in Canada.

On July first, Karen noticed that another abscess was forming. Again her doctor recommended the minor operation and drainage. The operation was set for 1 P.M. on July fifth. It was such a routine matter that Karen's father went on to his regular afternoon clinic in the urology department.

As Karen was placed on the operating-room cart, she gave her mother a puckish kiss. It was to be her last volitional act for many months.

The first indication that Karen's father had that tragedy had struck came when the Operating Room Supervisor—a friend of the Emmott family—summoned him from the clinic. Hastening to the operating floor, he learned that toward the close of the ten-minute operation there had been sudden cardiac arrest. The chest had been incised. The heart had been massaged. Now it was beating again.

But during the emergency, no one in the operating room had paused to look at the clock. How long had it been from the cessation of heartbeat until circulation had been restored? Four minutes? Five? It was a question that was to haunt everyone concerned with Karen's case. For with cardiac arrest, time is of the essence. The sensitive brain tissues are damaged almost immediately when the constant supply of oxygen is cut off.

Karen's mother shut herself in her husband's office and tried to pray. In the recovery room, two doors away, everything that science knew was being done for Karen—a hypothemia blanket to keep body temperature at thirty-one degrees and prevent further swelling of the brain; a tracheotomy to help the paralysed lungs to breathe.

Kneeling by a leather chair, Mrs Emmott groped for a way to pray. "Oh God, let me have Karen back again. These fifteen years are so brief and unfinished. . . ." Then her thoughts would wander off. *Such a fine thread between this world and the life beyond. How can we be so indifferent to God when things are going well?* "God, will You take care of our girl? Oh, God. . . ." *This can't be real. . . . Karen will wake up soon and this scare will be in the past.*

But by nine o'clock that night, it was apparent that Karen was not going to wake up.

Except for the beating of her heart, Karen was dead. On the morning of July sixth, those watching beside her bed saw one eyelid flicker. Weeks went by and there was no other sign of life. Then the convulsions began. Sudden seizures with bloody froth on her lips and soaring temperature alternated with deep coma.

By mid-August the convulsions were under control. But the consensus of all the specialists on the case was that the outlook was hopeless, the brain damage beyond repair.

Every body function had to be artificially maintained. The girl's mother could scarcely bear the sight . . . a tube in Karen's chest; cutdowns in her leg veins for some limited nutrition;

the tracheotomy tube; a catheter, even needle electrodes stuck in her scalp and legs to monitor her heartbeat.

At last the doctors spoke the brutal truth. "Your daughter will always remain in a vegetative state," they told the Emmotts. "Alive, but unknowing. It is possible that we will be able to keep her alive for years. But we advise you to put her out of your minds and your lives. Forget she ever lived."

Forget? A mother and father forget part of their own hearts? Their lovely intelligent Karen alive, and yet not alive; dead and yet not dead. For Isabel and Ralph Emmott, horror closed in. There is no blackness like the eternal night of no hope. Isabel had long since stopped praying. Surely there could be no God of mercy, else He would not allow this to happen. Death could have no sting compared to this.

On August 16 to free a hospital bed for a patient whom the doctors could help, the girl was moved to a Children's Convalescent Home. A month passed. There was no change in her vegetative existence except a steady loss of weight.

On Thursday, September 28, Isabel Emmott was invited by a friend to hear a talk at a local church. She went only because the speaker was to be Dr William Reed, Consulting Surgeon at Samaritan Hospital, Bay City, Michigan. Mrs Emmott was mildly curious as to why a physician would be speaking in a church.

Dr Reed was a tall, earnest young man in his late thirties. He told about the sequence of events by which he had learned that medicine plus prayer can bring about cures otherwise impossible.

"Science, mathematics and physics, as a result of Einsteinian thought, have left the realm of the material and have in certain ways become mystical sciences. There is a sense in which medicine too must go beyond the material. The whole man must be treated. I am now convinced that neither medicine nor surgery can achieve maximum effectiveness—especially for the case which is beyond the scope of the physician to cure —so long as the body is treated to the exclusion of the spirit."

It was not the usual religious talk. Isabel Emmott was

fascinated. In all her years of churchgoing she never heard anyone mention healing through prayer. Nor had she heard of a doctor who prayed in the presence of the operating room personnel before he began each operation. Mrs Emmott smiled to herself as she thought of how he had put it. "I used to bow my head and pray silently. But then I thought the nurses might just think I had a headache. Now if I hesitate about the prayer, they remind me." And this was a doctor, not a minister!

At the conclusion of the talk, her friend told her, "I've done something without asking you. Hope you won't mind. I've already told Dr Reed about Karen. If you'd like it, he has agreed to ride out with us to the Convalescent Home this afternoon." Her eyes searched Isabel's face.

Light sprang into the black eyes. "Like it? Of course!"

That afternoon at the door of the Convalescent Home Karen Emmott's father was waiting. Dr Reed judged him to be about his own age. As the piercing brown eyes of the girl's father looked him over, the thought crossed his mind that probably Dr Emmott had already looked him up in the American Medical Association's directory.

In dispassionate medical terms, Karen's father told Dr Reed the history of her case. As the words of hopelessness poured out on him, Bill Reed was thinking, "Lord, you've handed me a tough one this time." He had never tried praying for such a difficult case. Yet he could not dislodge from his mind the words, "With God all things are possible ... all things. ..." Obviously his first task was to give hope back to Karen's parents. This would not be easy when one of them was a knowledgeable doctor.

Dr Emmott's face was a study in scepticism. "I'd advise you not to form any opinion until after you've seen Karen," he said, "Come on in, my wife is waiting for us in the room." The first glance was shocking. A once-beautiful girl, now emaciated, spastic, her black eyes—so like her mother's—wildly staring, without recognition. Constantly there were aimless thrashing movements. The sides to her bed were high to keep her from falling out. Dr Emmott was watching his face.

Cautiously Dr Reed told how it had been shown by some

men working in the field of hypnotism that the subconscious mind of a patient under anaesthesia is aware of what goes on in the operating room. "And I believe that it may also be true in coma," he added.

Dr Emmott seemed mildly interested in the thesis. As for Isabel Emmott, a faint light of hope flickered in her tired eyes.

"Now what I suggest," Dr Reed said, "is that we begin to treat Karen as if she were spiritually awake and spiritually perceptive. Do you think you could do it?" Both parents nodded. They had nothing to lose. "Then shall we begin right now?"

So Bill Reed placed his hands on Karen's head and prayed, not about her, but with her, taking her situation to God, thanking Him for His loving care. Nothing happened. The violent jerking and twisting did not even momentarily subside.

"I haven't the least idea how God will answer this prayer," he admitted. "But we've got to keep reminding ourselves that, in His eyes, there are no hopeless cases. Now let me explain what I think your role will be in getting Karen well again—"

Getting Karen well again? Mrs Emmott could scarcely believe what she was hearing. In all the long months since the tragedy, no one—no one at all—had even mentioned the possibility of Karen getting well. And here was this stranger . . .

Dr Reed outlined several steps: (1) Prayer continuous and confident; (2) Daily conversations with Karen, always assuring her of complete recovery; no negative words or even thoughts in her presence; (3) as soon as possible discontinuance of all artificial aids—sedation, catheter, breathing-tube, intravenous feeding, etc.

The following morning Mrs Emmott drove to the Nursing Home and sat down beside her daughter. Karen was showing the same thrashing movements as before. Gently she placed her hand on Karen's forehead. "Karen," she said softly, "you are going to get well. Your friends have been asking about you. They're missing you at school and at majorette practice."

Did she imagine it? Were the movements a little less violent? Day after day Mrs Emmott talked to Karen—about family activities, about Karen's friends, about what was happening at school. Always she would come back to the same persistent theme: "You are going to get well, Karen. God loves you, Karen. We love you. Won't it be wonderful to be well again?"

After the first day there was a definite change; Karen's spastic contortions were less violent. Two days later her mother and the nurses were able to put her in a wheelchair and take her into the sunshine for the first time in three months. But still she showed no sign of awareness.

The next step—taken in faith—was the removal of the catheter. With that, the severe urinary infection began to subside.

Then came the matter of food. Isabel Emmott decided to try letting Karen eat in the normal way. Three friends took turns helping her. At first, chewing was impossible for Karen; even swallowing was hard. But gradually she learned to eat baby foods and mashed potatoes.

Slowly the miracle unfolded. One evening in mid-November Karen's father put a ball-point pen in her hand. She punched the release button and began to scribble on the blanket cover.

Almost frantic with joy, her parents began handing her other familiar objects—a stick of gum, a Chapstick, sunglasses. She put the sunglasses on upside down, then righted them.

That night they went home jubilant. Now they set themselves a new goal, to have Karen home for part of Christmas Day. And it happened as they pictured it: on Christmas afternoon the whole family was together. Around the table at Christmas dinner every one of her brothers and sisters thanked God that Karen could be with them for a few hours.

Back at the Convalescent Home, Karen began rebelling. She hated the tube feedings that still had to be used to supplement the baby foods. Unless her hands were tied, she would pull the tube out. Then she began refusing the baby foods, too.

Her mother had an inspiration. She would prepare a tuna-fish sandwich. In the old days that had been one of Karen's favourites. She asked a group of friends to meet and pray for the little venture.

Karen gobbled the sandwich down with better co-ordination

in chewing and swallowing than anyone had thought possible. In the next few days ice cream, French fries and hamburgers met equal enthusiasm. Soon there were no more tube feedings, and Karen's weight at last started up.

Isabel and Ralph Emmott were learning. They would take a step at a time, each launched by hope, taken in faith. After this, they recognised rebellion in Karen as her readiness for another step.

December was drawing to a close. Still Karen had not spoken. Getting rid of the tracheotomy tube was next. During a ten-day period, successively smaller tubes were placed in the wound. On the tenth day, the tube was withdrawn entirely. The girl breathed normally but still seemed incapable of speech.

But with the tube out, now Karen could be brought home to stay. January fourth was a gala day for the Emmott family. Isabel could scarcely hold back tears of gladness over Karen's homecoming.

And then a few days later the girl began to whisper. Her first sentences in a low voice and with precise enunciation were a series of revelations. Her mother wrote them down, "I want to live my life in the old natural normal way." . . . "If heaven and hell are worlds, then I want to go to the heaven-world." . . . "I want to meet and greet the man Jesus." . . . "Please assure me that my life has been a successful thing. I need the reassurance if it has been."

Each evening as she tucked Karen in, Isabel would repeat the Lord's Prayer and the 23rd Psalm. On Easter Sunday, 1961, Karen repeated the Lord's Prayer by herself—with a few flourishes of her own: "Who art in heaven—way up in that world we call heaven. . . ."

Progress is slow, but progress there is. Karen now feeds herself, reads, walks unassisted. Last June she developed a new rebellion. Unless she is watched, she will slip out of the house and try to drive the family car.

Whenever Isabel Emmott needs more prayer-stamina and physical stamina for the long road ahead she gets down on her knees and thanks God for the long way Karen has already come from her vegetative state. Hopeless! No! The Emmotts know now that Bill Reed was right: in God's view there is no such term as *hopeless*.

Surely the preacher in my childhood was mistaken in thinking that the miraculous element in Christianity has died out because it is not needed any more. Not needed? When always there are so many—like Karen—for whom the doctors have no answer?

No, it is not the absence of need that has caused the sharp decline of the miraculous element in Christianity. Something has chilled and contracted our faith in God's love and in His freedom to stoop to our need and to heal our bodies. Healings through prayer are still the exception rather than the rule. Yet it takes just as much power to forgive sin or to release men and women from enslaving habits as it does to heal. And the truth is that these other miracles are just as rare in our day as are healings.

Still spiritual progress is being made, for in the last two decades there has been a groundswell of interest in spiritual healing among all religious denominations. The National Council of Churches recently surveyed a number of Protestant ministers to find out what they thought about healing through prayer. Thirty-four per cent of the clergymen answering the questionnaire said that they had attempted spiritual healing, in many cases with success astonishing even to them.

The new collaboration between ministers and physicians is also a sign that there is no longer an imagined conflict between religion and medicine. On the religious front, all those I know who are interested in healing believe that divine healing should always be undertaken in co-operation with doctors, never in competition with them.

On the side of medicine, every adequately trained modern doctor recognises the connection between his patient's mind and spirit and the tissues of his body. Many hospitals (like St Luke's in New York City) have full-time chaplains on their staffs.

Meanwhile, psychologists like Adler, Jung and Fritz Künkel

have steadily closed the lag in our understanding of how mind and spirit affect body. They are also bringing us closer and closer to Jesus' teaching that man's being is a whole, that he can in no way be separated into compartments.

Practically speaking, we shall have taken our greatest step forward in the realm of spiritual healing when the average Christian becomes as sure of God's will for health as he is of his doctor's. Only those who have settled this in their own minds can press forward in the adventure of spiritual research. And press forward we must, for Christ has commanded us to do so.

Of course, we shall not always succeed; neither do the doctors. Jesus Himself had some failures in His home town of Nazareth "because of their unbelief".[23]

But above all, let us not be stopped by a particularly subtle roadblock. "Isn't it a dangerous thing to ask for healing through prayer?" this argument goes. "Suppose you pray for health and fail. . . . Mightn't you then lose your faith in God altogether?"

One minister who has had a healing service every week for twelve years answers this by saying, "In twelve years I have never had anyone come to me and say, 'I followed your suggestions. I went all out. It hasn't worked. I will have nothing more to do with religion and the church.' But I have had marvellous experiences with people who have received answers that are even better than what they asked for."

In my own case, it was precisely while my prayer was still unanswered that I received the most vivid assurances of God's reality.

What this comes down to is the simple but powerful truth that God can be trusted in this regard as in all others. Hope is always of God; hopelessness is always of evil. Faith is always right; fear and despair are always wrong.

We can rest on the love of God, knowing that His love for us boundlessly surpasses our own. Nothing can ever separate us from that love except our own blind unwillingness to receive.

14: Journey into Joy

SOME time during the second year after my entering-in experience, I found myself with a lively curiosity about what seemed an odd subject—the Holy Spirit. Like most people, I had thought of the Holy Spirit as a theological abstraction, a sort of ecclesiastical garnish for christenings, weddings, benedictions, and the like. As for the term *the Holy Ghost*—that I regarded as archaic, if not downright eerie.

However odd the subject seemed, the fact remained that this was no passing curiosity. As is often the case when something is brought sharply to one's attention, everywhere I turned during those months, I seemed to hear or read something about the Holy Spirit.

During our vacation at Cape Cod, the church that Peter and I attended with Peter John included a talk for children as part of its regular Sunday service. The first Sunday we were there, the guest preacher gave as his sermonette an object-lesson talk on the Holy Spirit as related to the Trinity.

Three glass containers had been placed on a table before the young preacher. One was filled with water, the second with ice, the third with what appeared to be steam, probably dry ice.

"Children," he began, "perhaps you've heard of 'The Trinity'. *Trinity* means 'three'. When we speak of the Trinity, we mean the three Persons that go to make up God: God, the Father; Jesus Christ the Son; and the Holy Spirit.

"Now look at these three jars. This one has water. This one has ice, and that one, steam. They all look different, don't they?

"Yet you know that ice is only frozen water. And that when your mother boils water in a pan on the stove, steam rises from it.

"That means that water, ice and steam are really the same thing.

"Now, the same thing is true of the Trinity . . . Jesus Christ, the water of Life, is different from the Father—yet the same too. The Holy Spirit, like the powerful steam that can drive an engine, is different from Christ and the Father, yet the same."

I listened, as interested as any of the children. What the young minister said that morning gave me a new concept and provided a background for approaching the subject that continued to occupy my mind.

Then about two months later something happened which took this interest out of the realm of theory and placed it on a personal basis. It was in the early fall of that year that my friends Tay and Fern told me of the experience of guidance that they had had in Florida the previous winter (pp. 138 ff.).

I had known Tay for a long time. Often she had inner nudges and proddings of the kind that had sent her out to help her friend Grace at a time of desperate emergency. Curiously I asked her, "How do you explain these intuitions—this—well, Voice on the inside?"

"Some people call them intuitions," Tay answered promptly. "But I would prefer to call the help I got at Delray Beach that morning the direction of the Holy Spirit."

So there it was again!

Tay was looking at me curiously. "What does the Holy Spirit mean to you?" she asked.

I remembered the sermonette at the Cape Cod church. "Oh —one of the three Persons of the Godhead—the third Person of the Trinity."

"But I sense something in the offhand way you say that—" she looked at me sharply. "Let me guess that in your mind the Spirit has an insignificant and unnecessary place. Isn't that right?"

I nodded. "That's right."

"But I know from personal experiences that the Holy Spirit is just as great, just as needed as the other two Persons of the Trinity. Anyway you still haven't answered my original question, what is He to *you*?"

Tay's intensity seemed to demand a candid reply. "I've

got to be truthful, Tay," I replied. "He's nothing to me. I've had no contact with Him and could get along quite well without Him."

Although at the time I believed my own statement, I was soon to find out that it was not so. As a matter of fact, I could not get along at all well without the Holy Spirit. Some searching in the Bible told me why.

Using a concordance and a notebook, I began methodically looking up all the references I could find on the third Person of the Trinity. Gradually I worked the findings into a logical outline in the notebook.

I learned that the Holy Spirit is not "an influence" but a Person; not "a thing", an "it", but "He". In a sense, He is both the most basic and the most modest member of the Trinity, for His work is to reflect Christ and to glorify Him.

The obvious meaning of the word *glorify* is "to give homage to, as in worship". But there is a deeper meaning. Dr Leslie Weatherhead, in a 1952 Lenten sermon in the City Temple, London, brought out this richer meaning: "I would define glory as that expression of the nature of a person or thing which, of itself, evokes our praise."

Then the "glory" of a sunrise must be in the beauty of its delicate pinks and oranges reflected in the sky just before the sun itself appears over the hills. In this sense the glory is in the qualities or characteristics of the sunrise which we can perceive.

The "glory" of Jesus Christ lies in the characteristics of His nature that make us want to adore Him. These traits are not kingly trappings or the halo placed around His head by medieval painters. Far from it! Men saw His glory in His humanity—His instant compassion, tenderness, understanding, fearlessness, incisiveness, His refusal to compromise with evil, His selflessness which culminated in His ultimate self-giving on the cross.

The Apostle John puts it in unforgettable words: "And the Word was made flesh, and dwelt among us (and we beheld his glory, the glory as of the only begotten of the Father) full of grace and truth."[1]

But then I found the New Testament declaring that these qualities of Jesus' nature are not apparent to us any more than a sunrise is apparent to a blind man. That is why we need the Holy Spirit to make Christ's glory perceptible to us. It is as if the Spirit gives us a new way of seeing, with which we can perceive spiritual truth where all has been darkness before.

I found that Jesus had his own preferred names for the Spirit. Christ spoke in Aramaic, the tongue of His own people. This was the dialect of the bazaars and the seaside, replete with colourful idioms, metaphors and probably picturesque humour. There is good reason to believe that the tone of Jesus' speech was quite unlike the English of the King James' Version of the early seventeenth century. The King James' translators often rendered the Holy Spirit the "Holy Ghost". But Jesus liked to call Him "the Helper", "the Spirit of Truth", "the Teacher", "the Comforter", "the Counsellor".

The gospel of John was especially helpful in giving me more understanding about the Holy Spirit. In His last talk with the eleven (Judas had already left the group), Christ made it clear that they were to experience Him through the Spirit. On that last night, He had important things to say to His apostles, most of them concerning the Comforter.

The disciples knew that their Master was in imminent danger. They were frightened, sorrowful men.

"Do not be frightened about my leaving you," Jesus told them, in effect. "It is actually to your advantage that I go away."

Then He outlined His plan:

When He could no longer be with them physically, Another would take His place. This One—the Helper—would be the continuation and extension of His [Christ's] life on earth.[2] All the wonders that the disciples had witnessed of teaching, preaching, forgiving, cleansing, healing would go right on. But even greater accomplishments would be possible through the Helper, ones that had not been possible during Jesus' earthly ministry.[3]

This had to be so, because there was more truth, much more, to be discovered. And it would be the Spirit of Truth that would lead men into these undreamed of areas of exploration.[4]

This is the only plan by which men in all centuries could have fellowship with the risen Christ. Without the Spirit transmitting His continuing presence to us, we would have no more than the memory and recorded words and deeds of any good man, such as St Francis of Assisi or Lincoln or Gandhi.

Jesus made a surprising statement that last night to His apostles: the plan was that this Spirit would dwell in men's bodies. We were being offered the privilege of presenting our bodies to the Helper, so that He could not only be with us, but *in* us. This would be God the Father coming closer to men than He had ever been before. This is expressed in a variety of ways in Scripture. It is "God tabernacling with men". Paul was later to cry: "I live; yet not I, but Christ liveth in me."[5] And, "Do you not know that your body is the temple of the Holy Spirit within you—the Spirit you have received from God?"[6]

Christ promised His disciples that, if they would thus offer their bodies as an abiding place for the Helper, the Father's power and wisdom, as well as His [Christ's] would be theirs.[7]

He also warned that people in the world would think all of this odd, and could not possibly see or recognise the Spirit until they too had experienced Him.[8]

Then He instructed the eleven what to do in order to receive the Spirit.[9] And He admonished each of them not even to try to be His witness until *after* the Spirit had come to him.[10]

Probably the apostles understood little of this at the time. Even so, it must have been obvious to them that Jesus was putting maximum value on the Helper. And this brought me back full circle to my own statement to my friend Tay that I could "get along quite well" without the Holy Spirit. On the contrary, I found that according to the New Testament if we are without the Spirit, then we are without:

Joy
The awareness of God's love for us
The conviction of who Christ is

The ability to communicate the gospel in a life-changing way
The conviction of sin
Guidance
Healing
An intercessor with the Father
The gifts of the Spirit
The fruits of the Spirit
The pledge (or inner proof) of eternal life.

For anyone who has the least desire to be a Christian, this seems like an extensive list of blessings to forgo. Even from my incomplete examination, it was obvious that Jesus saw the presence of the Helper as the one gift encompassing all other gifts.

Having learned this much, my next question was "How does one go about receiving the Holy Spirit?" From the stories in the Acts, telling how different men received Him, it is obvious that there are many ways and no set techniques. Thus the outline I culled from Scripture at that time cannot be taken as final or rigid:

1. We have to be convinced that the Scriptures teach the indwelling of Christ in our bodies through the Holy Spirit, and we have to want His presence for ourselves.
2. We have to go to Christ and ask for the gift.
3. We then reckon that the Spirit has taken possession of our bodies and is dwelling in us.
4. We receive proof of this, what some have called "the manifestation" of the Spirit.
5. We keep His Presence through obedience to the Inner Voice.

Next I proceeded to ask for the Holy Spirit for myself. Nothing dramatic happened to me—no rushing wind or ecstasy or "speaking in tongues" as happened to the disciples at Pentecost. To this day I have experienced only a modicum of all that there is to know about the Helper. This is still a growing point for me, where further adventure awaits. But the little I have already learned about the Comforter I am eager to share, because it is exactly at this point that Christianity has become for me most practical and most provocative.

My first discovery was that there is nothing ethereal, no trace of the sanctimonious humbug that most people expect to find in the Holy Spirit. Nor is there any saccharine sentimentality. Quite the contrary; there is a down-to-earth quality of personality about the Holy Spirit so marked that I still would not believe it had I not experienced it.

The Spirit delights in mediating Christ to us in the everydayness of life. For instance: About two years after Peter Marshall had his first heart attack, one morning I was plagued by the insistent thought that I should learn to drive the family car. I mentioned the idea to my husband. He was not wildly enthusiastic; he knew that two drivers for one car could result in complications.

Over a matter of months the idea kept coming back, so persistently that I concluded that this was the Helper insisting. Finally Peter agreed to my taking driving lessons.

At the time of Peter's sudden death, I had been driving just long enough to have confidence to carry on. But if I had had to learn during the period of emotional turmoil immediately following his death, I might never have attempted it. Later on I realised that being able to drive also had significance in helping me towards the independence necessary to begin my new life.

The effect this sort of loving concern has on one is indescribable. To me this seems proof, as only the Comforter can give it to us, that God exists, and that He cares about us. It is one way that we can know, finally and for ever, that we are loved and that this love can be expressed in simple, everyday ways straight from the unselfish heart of God.

Thus I discovered that no detail of life is too small for the Helper's concern. For years I had been hearing Christians discuss the question, "Have we any right to bother God with the small details of daily life?"

Those who thought not would argue, "After all, it would be a low grade of Christian who would treat God as if He were a celestial bellhop created to serve our petty needs. Besides,

since God has given us common sense, He expects us to use
it for these small matters."

Certainly we should be wary of any interpretation of religion
so self-centred that it continually seeks, "What can my faith
do for me today?" We should have a healthy fear of making
our God too small. They are right who see Him as the God of
history with far-flung designs for man's destiny.

Yet the fact remains that Jesus added for us another dimension to the nature of His Father. "By all means you *should*
bother the Father with details," Jesus seems to say in so many
places in the gospels. He was constantly "bothering the
Father" with the practicalities of life—with people's health
problems, with securing the money for Peter's temple tax, with
supper for a crowd of hungry listeners, with the wine running
out at a wedding reception.

And after Jesus' resurrection, what then? Would men then
have to revert to the God of the Old Testament—high and
lifted-up, majestic, remote? No, the heavenly plan was that the
Spirit would go on showing us this intimate side of the
omnipotent God exactly as Jesus had. For in all ways the Spirit
reflects Jesus.

Jesus cared about the everyday needs of men; so does the
Spirit. Jesus stirred men's hearts, turned casual inquirers into
passionate believers. Just so, the Spirit will recharge our
emotions today. Sometimes I think this is the most vital work
of the Spirit in the twentieth century. It has been said of our
civilisation that it deadens emotion. For millions of people in
our thing-surfeited Western world, life has become tasteless.
Nothing is as much fun as we thought it would be. Creative
thought and work wither, since there are not emotional springs
to nourish it. Strength and romance go out of love.

Society assumes a tepid state in which it admires detached
neutrality, shows mild contempt for strong feelings. We are
suspicious of anyone who becomes agitated about a principle
or an issue.

This kind of apathy places our nation itself in jeopardy.
Upon his retirement as Chief of Naval Operations in July
1961, Admiral Arleigh A. Burke sounded a note of warning:

"I wonder if the American people have such strong convictions as they used to? We don't seem to see the necessity of living by our convictions and dying for them, if need be. I am concerned about comfortable living in relation to the people's determination to stand firm for what America believes."

If part of our problem today be lack of great passions, intense beliefs, then how is the Holy Spirit an answer? Because of His power to revive man's emotional life. For in the first century or the twentieth, people have never been able to confront Jesus Christ face to face and remain coolly impassive. Something about Him kindles either a total devotion or provokes men to violent opposition. And Jesus Himself seems always to have preferred antagonism to apathy. For apathy is the symptom of a sick and dying spirit.

Strong emotions surge through the gospels. Virile men did not leave their businesses and their homes to follow Christ without intense convictions. Men did not risk persecution and death out of lukewarmness. Those who were healed, who had sight restored, their children given back to them, could not be phlegmatic about it. The exuberance of the men who experienced the Spirit at Pentecost was such that they were accused of being drunk with new wine. Emotion beyond embarrassment, beyond caring what other people thought, towards the release of bound personalities—all this is there for anyone to read.

I have watched the same process today in those whom the Holy Spirit touches. Feelings are sensitised. Life takes on relish. Joys are heightened. Here is the way one woman described her encounter with the Spirit:

. . . I saw no new thing, but I saw all the usual things in a miraculous new light. I saw for the first time how wildly beautiful and joyous, beyond any words of mine to describe, is the whole of life. Every human being . . . every sparrow that flew, every branch tossing in the wind, was caught up in and was a part of the whole mad ecstasy of loveliness, of joy, of importance, of intoxication of life. . . .[11]

In the experience of everyone to whom I have talked about the Spirit, the word *joy* stands out. In the rebirth of our emotional selves this seems to be the essential missing ingredient which the Holy Spirit supplies.

I have written earlier in this book of the joy of childhood. For me it was in the fragrance of mint and honeysuckle, the feel of bare feet on moss, ice-cold apples, the magnificent fury of a thunderstorm, the far horizons of blue Appalachians. And all my life I have felt that this early joy was trying to teach me something, that it was not just a sentiment restricted to childhood. It seemed to reveal something fundamental and basic about the nature of the universe itself.

Surely I was right; surely this is the way things are in God's world! But only now do I see how God intends for us to know this. It is the Holy Spirit who is to open our eyes to the joy which undergirds the universe.

It was the Holy Spirit who opened Marianne Brown's eyes. Mrs Brown is the wife of the Presbyterian minister in the small town of Parkesburg, Pennsylvania, mother of five children and mistress of an old-fashioned rambling eleven-room manse. The details of her story come directly from her.

Six years ago, if you had asked Marianne Brown what was the most basic truth about life, the last thing she would have answered would have been "joy"! She might have said "duty" or even, if she had been feeling brutally honest, "exhaustion".

Like many another minister's wife, Mrs Brown was trapped in a maelstrom of activity—church meetings, the presidency of the women's organisation, constant entertaining, a neighbourhood kindergarten, supervising the area recreation programme. She had a merciless conscience that drove her and a concern about other people's opinions that made her unable to say *no* to any request. Like most ministers' wives, she was not able to afford any household help.

Her one escape from exhaustion was to be ill at frequent intervals and go to bed for rest. This was not too difficult to manage, because the constantly overtired woman was an easy target for assorted viruses and disorders. Furthermore she had been born with a congenital heart defect, diagnosed by the doctors as mitrostenosis.

Marianne would lie in bed and brood. Why was her vitality so low? Why did black moods descend so often, periods of retreating within herself? Sometimes she would go for days, speaking grudgingly even to her family. She introduced every other thought with the words, "The trouble is—" It was indicative of her joyless outlook on life.

"Looking back now," she told me, "it seems to me that all my life had been a search for the joy that had been denied me. I remember once seeing a ragged child standing at the great wrought-iron gates of an estate, his hands clasping the bars. His eyes were glued wistfully on the winding walks among the great trees, the sweep of lawn in which he might have run and tumbled, the flower-beds, even a brook where a small boy might have gone wading and fishing . . .

"Well, I was like that little boy, hungrily staring at vistas of joy that seemed for ever closed to me. That is, until six years ago."

Then six years ago a new life began for Marianne—quietly enough. A neighbour dropped in one morning. Over a cup of coffee at the breakfast table, the harassed minister's wife poured out her troubles. The friend admitted that she had no answers for Marianne but suggested that they pray together.

They did. There was nothing unusual or dramatic about the prayer. Yet it seemed to relieve the pressures, so they prayed together again. Then, one by one, other friends joined them. Eventually there was a small group of husbands and wives who met in each other's homes each Saturday evening.

A family crisis overtook the Browns soon afterward. Their high-school-age daughter suffered a nervous breakdown. The group that met in prayer gave them important support through the crisis. And once again prayer brought startling results.

Their daughter's early recovery filled the Browns with gratitude to God and to the friends who had shouldered their problems with them. On a certain Saturday night, as the meeting was being closed with a circle of prayer, Marianne

found herself slipping to her knees as deep feelings of thanksgiving to God for His nearness and goodness bubbled up and
spilled over into words, words that came and kept coming in a
torrent.

Then suddenly—to Marianne Brown in Parkesburg, Pennsylvania in 1955—the Holy Spirit came. She had done no
studying or thinking about the Comforter, indeed, was
scarcely aware of Him at all. Let Marianne tell it:

*God's Spirit took over and seemed to immerse my whole being—
body, mind, and spirit. The Spirit came like tidal waves of "joy
unspeakable and full of glory" and inundated me. Torrents of
God's love swept over me for what seemed only a few minutes but
lasted a long time. More than once I wondered if my human body
could bear the ecstasy, and I both begged God to stop and feared
that He would!*

*That night my emotions found perfect expression. I know now
that my emotions had been starved. I had been only half-living,
because I had been only half-feeling.*

*In those minutes God revealed more to me than I had ever
learned in books. . . . I knew that for the remainder of my life
Jesus Himself would by my first love. In Him every desire I had
ever had was fulfilled. And I knew that such communion with God
is His will for every human being!*

Marianne's friends, even her husband, were stunned at
what they were witnessing. The Reverend Mr Brown had
preached about Pentecost, talked about the Holy Spirit, sometimes in knowing theological tones. But witnessing Him in
action—that was something else again! He and most of those
present had always been wary of emotionalism in religion.
We Presbyterians usually are! With the erudite John Calvin
of Geneva and starchy John Knox of Edinburgh as the fathers
of our church, this is only natural. And the educated clergy
upon which the Presbyterian church has always insisted usually
put inordinate emphasis on the mind, little emphasis on the
emotions.

So it was a confused and wondering group that at a late

hour reluctantly told one another good night and went back
to their respective homes. Though they were not yet ready to
admit it to each other, already something had happened to
each of them through Marianne's experience: they too wanted
the Holy Spirit and joy!

In the weeks that followed their wish was granted. It was
like a fire that had descended on Marianne and then leaped
from person to person, including her minister husband! As
the fire spread, the group was welded together in a way none
of them had ever known before.

There was no difficulty now in sharing with one another
thoughts, joys, fears, hopes, disappointments, problems,
triumphs. They lived in each other's lives, not just spiritually,
but in practical fashion, too. They were discovering *Koinonia*,
the fellowship of the Holy Spirit that the first-century infant
church had experienced following Pentecost. Eventually the
one group grew into a series of them throughout the local
church community.

As for Marianne herself, "Six years have passed since then,"
she told me, "I have not spent one day of them in bed. I find
myself able, without fatigue, to care for my big house and
the needs of my family, still without outside help. And there
is more entertaining than ever. Our home is open house to
friends from all over the world.

"The guidance of the Helper about my daily tasks is quite
specific. He has enabled me to say a sure 'No' to what He
does not want me to do. For what He directs me to undertake,
there is an unfailing supply of vitality. Sometimes I have
taught as many as five Bible classes a week."

Marianne Brown no longer searches for joy. She bubbles
over with it. Her voice lilts with it. Life itself is joy.

It is the same exuberant joy that we experience as children.
Christ said: "Except ye become as little children, ye shall not
enter into the kingdom of heaven."[12] It is the Spirit saying
yea to man's *can I*?

At the beginning of the book, I referred to the point, so often
made now, that the only hope for our world is a change in

human nature itself. Is it possible that the rising tide of interest in the Spirit all across the United States today is evidence that the Helper is undertaking this task?

One day last year two friends and I spent part of an afternoon in the apartment of Dr Henry Pitney Van Dusen, President of Union Theological Seminary, discussing this very possibility. Dr Van Dusen's book on the Holy Spirit, *Spirit, Son, and Father*, reflects his own increasing emphasis on the Spirit as the most effective agent in human life.

The conversation turned to what each of us there that afternoon had at one time discovered: that the Spirit repeatedly brings us back to Jesus' emphasis—that real faith is no otherworldly affair. I know that again and again in recent years He has plucked me out of the clouds of theoretical Christianity back to earth where I belonged.

For when we allow the Spirit to guide us He will concern Himself with how we use our time and spend our money; with honesty and moral integrity and Christlike quality of character; with what is happening to our children; with the health of our relationship with other people and with our God. And, if our need is severe enough, the Holy Spirit will turn our lives upside down.

For man's chief problem is still man. The search that begins at the point of our need—the longing for Something More—in the end brings us back full circle to the inner man. With the threat of thermonuclear war hanging over us, civilisation's problem is still unredeemed individuals. No summit meeting is held, no international conference convened, but that our quandary is dramatised for us.

How then, can human nature change? Men have demonstrated that they cannot change themselves. Nor can men change other men. We have seen that education does not necessarily achieve it, nor legislation, nor raising incomes, nor plying them with all the gadgets that money can buy. That brings us to the crown of the Holy Spirit's work among men. Only Christ can change human nature, and it is the Holy Spirit that makes Christ available to needy mankind.

That is what happened to Saul of Tarsus, to Augustine, to

Ignatius Loyola, to St Francis of Assisi, and to thousands through the centuries. It is still happening to men and women in our day.

How drastically and profoundly the Holy Spirit can turn a man's character upside down was demonstrated in the case of Starr Daily.

It was the year 1924. In the courtroom in the Mid-West, the judge's voice was grave as he looked down at the prisoner standing before him. "I am about to sentence you to a major prison for the third time. I know you are sick. And I know that more punishment is not the remedy. But your record leaves me powerless."

And so "hopeless criminal" was society's judgment of Starr Daily. The verdict seemed justified. At sixteen Starr's only ambition had been to build a reputation as a dangerous man. He dreamed of the time when the police would refer to him with a shudder.

He achieved his aim by becoming the leader of a gang of safe-crackers. There was no safe he could not open, no time lock he could not take apart. But finally liquor made him careless, and he was caught.

There followed fourteen years of penal farms, chain gangs, and two extended penitentiary sentences. Through all that time Starr's father never lost hope that his son might be redeemed from his life of crime. His best efforts failed. He lived to see his Starr re-enter prison for the third time. Starr never saw his father after that. The broken-hearted man died with a prayer for his son on his lips.

In prison Starr made two futile attempts to escape. Then he evolved a plan to instigate a prison riot. The deputy warden was to be seized and used as a shield and hostage. A stool-pigeon betrayed the plan, and Starr was sentenced to the dungeon.

Most strong men could not survive "the hole" for more than fifteen days. American prisons thirty-five years ago could be grim and brutal places. It was winter, and the walls of the dank cell seeped moisture. At six every morning, the prisoner would be given a piece of bread and a cup of water. Then he would be left hanging in handcuffs for twelve hours. At six in the evening, he would be let down for the night and given another piece of bread and another cup of water.

Starr survived fifteen days of this. By the last day in the cuffs, he could no longer stand on feet black with congealed blood. That morning "the Bull"—the keeper of the hole—had to lift the almost-unconscious man into the cuffs.

For weeks after that, the prisoner was allowed to lie on the icy stone floor—emaciated, unspeakably filthy, near death. He lost track of time. Mired in the lowest hell imaginable, only hate was keeping him alive—hate for the Bull, hate for the deputy warden who had vowed that he would force Starr to crawl to him like a dog, begging mercy.

Then there came a moment when the man on the floor was too weak to hate. Through that momentary opening crept a strange new thought: *All of my life I have been a dynamo of energy. What might have happened if I had used that energy for something good?*

Then the thought faded. *It's too late now; I'm dying.* There followed a half-waking, half-sleeping state of unconsciousness: moments of delirium, times of awareness.

This was followed by disconnected dreams, like mists floating across the brain. Time was no more. The prisoner was aware no longer of the frozen stone floor, of his filth, or of anyone who came or went.

Finally, the dreams began to take on meaning, to become rational in form and sequence. Suddenly Starr seemed to be in a garden. He knew that he had been in this same garden before—many times in childhood. It was in a shoe-shaped valley surrounded by gentle hills. At one end of the garden a great white-grey rock jutted out. Then Jesus Christ, the Man whom he had been trying to avoid all his life, was coming toward him. Now He stood face to face with Starr, looking deep into his eyes as if penetrating to the bottom of his soul. Love of a quality that he had never before felt was drawing the hate out of his heart, like extracting poison from an infected wound.

With a strange clarity, one part of Starr's mind thought

I am submerged in Reality, I'll never be the same again, now and through all eternity.

There followed another dream in which all the people Starr had ever injured passed before his eyes. One by one, he poured out his love to them.

Then all who had injured him appeared, and on them too he bestowed the love needed to restore and to heal. The love flowed from beyond him, poured through him in a torrent of caring and ecstatic gratitude.

When the prisoner returned to consciousness, the cell did not look the same. Its grim greyness was gone. For him it was illuminated with a warm light. His feelings, too, were different. The prison environment no longer had the power to give him pain, only joy.

The next thing Starr knew, the door opened and the Bull said in a tone of voice Starr had never before heard him use, "Are you hungry? I could steal a sandwich from the kitchen and bring it to you."

The prisoner stared in amazement. But he was even more startled at his own reply, "No, don't do that. Don't risk your neck by breaking a rule for me."

It was the Bull's turn to be astonished. He went off wonderingly, came back with the doctor, and Starr was carried to the prison hospital. Through a swift and surprising series of events, prison doors swung open for Starr Daily in March 1930, five years ahead of the time set for his release.

Was his experience on the cell floor a hallucination? No, not unless we would call what happened to Saul of Tarsus a hallucination. The proof was the change in the man. He who had been declared incorrigible by penologists was from that moment cured of all criminal tendencies.

Peter Marshall loved the man that Starr Daily became and delighted in telling his story from the pulpit of the New York Avenue Presbyterian Church in Washington. In 1954, when I was in Hollywood for script conferences on *A Man Called Peter*, I drove out to the Dailys' home in Van Nuys, California, for an overnight visit with Starr and his wife Marie.

A tall spare man, greying now, Starr's face bears the lines of the long hard years. But flashes of dry humour, spoken in a Mid-Western drawl, lit up the face.

From this man who had only a sixth-grade education have come eight books. He has lectured all over the nation. His knowledge of the criminal mind has contributed to valuable rethinking of prison techniques. He has personally been the Holy Spirit's vehicle for the reclamation of scores of criminals.

In speaking to me recently about the experience that changed his life, Starr Daily said, "The Holy Spirit came to me through the glorified Christ. He did not give me the gifts of the Spirit, rather the fruits of the Spirit to be worked out in a day-to-day discipline. Perhaps that was necessary in my case, so that the fruits could be integrated with the drastic character changes necessary. Anyway, you remember that St Paul said that this was 'the most excellent way' ".

Can we change human nature? No, but the Holy Spirit can. His all-encompassing love is Jesus' love for us, the extension of Jesus' life and power in our day. The Helper takes our needs as His own. Our dangers He enters into with us. Our perplexities He illumines. Our joyousness, He sanctifies.

The Spirit was with John Sherrill that day when he entered into Life by saying *Yes* to Christ. He was with Stuart Luhan that night when the Winecoff Hotel caught on fire.

The Counsellor helped my friend Beverley through the crisis with her boy, Kenneth. He enabled Raymond Thomas to dream of a better life than Radical Hill could bring him. He is with Betty Elliott and her small daughter, Valerie, in the South American jungle. And even now He is with Karen Emmott out in Oklahoma City—Karen of the piquant face, who still hopes to live her life in "the old natural normal way".

Do without Him? How could any of us who have embarked on the pilgrimage that is Christianity do without Him? For we who long for something more, for strength and hope and wisdom beyond our selves, discover to our joy that as the Comforter reveals Christ to us, in Him we have our heart's desire.

15: *Afterglow*

It was the afternoon of May first. I sat at the typewriter in my basement office. Through the picture window, I could see the first faint traces of green on the sweep of trees down the hill. Spring had come late to New York state this year.

Suddenly the telephone rang shrilly. Mother's voice leaped at me over the wires from Evergreen Farm in Virginia. Her voice sounded strange, I thought.

"Catherine, I have bad news," she said. Then there was a long pause. "Dad's gone—"

"Dad is gone—?"

She rushed breathlessly on. "Dr Oliver just came to tell me—"

"How? When?"

"About fifteen minutes ago. Dad left the house, saying he was going up to the store for the mail, that he'd be back right away. He never came back."

"You mean—?"

"He was sitting on a wooden chair in the store, talking and joking with Mr Janney and some other men. All at once he gave two faint sighs—and that was it."

I sat staring at my typewriter, trying to take this in.

"Dr Oliver tells me that when he got there, Dad was still sitting in the chair, his legs crossed, his hands on his lap. His head was bowed a little. There was a peaceful, happy expression on his face—"

"Oh, Mother—darling—" Desperately I tried to collect my thoughts. "It will be forty minutes or so before I can tell Len. He's on his way home from the New York office now. He will know about plane schedules to Washington. I'll get there just as soon as I can."

"Catherine, will you telephone Peter John at Yale—?"

"You know I will. Immediately."

As it turned out, Peter was in glee club rehearsal, where the group was working on numbers for the concert tour of South America scheduled for the summer. He did not get the news about his grandfather until early that evening.

How suddenly death interrupts life!

Yet two nights later, as the family gathered in the living-room at Evergreen, it was not so much grief that we felt, but gratitude. In seventy-six years, Dad had lived a rich, full life. Forty-six active years in the ministry, nearly five wonderful years on the farm.

He had lived to give his blessing to Leonard LeSourd and me by performing our wedding ceremony on November 14, 1959, in the little Presbyterian Church in Leesburg, Virginia. Though he had shared the service with Len's father and with Dr Norman Vincent Peale, it was he who had insisted on pronouncing the solemn words that launched us on our new life: "By the authority vested in me as a minister of the Church of Christ. . . ."

A lifetime dream had been fulfilled the preceding summer on a trip to Europe to see the Passion Play. And at Eastertime as if to round out his last year, every member of Dad's large family had been gathered around him, including the three new granchildren—Jeffrey, Chester and Linda LeSourd.

Then there had been the Golden Wedding Anniversary celebration. Just a year ago, the old farmhouse had glowed and shone and overflowed with friends, some of whom had driven long distances to share Mother's and Father's joy. Exactly a year later on this third of May, Mother had memories that blessed and burned. On this, the evening of their fifty-first anniversary, Mother could not bear the thought of leaving at the impersonal funeral parlour the earthly form that Dad had cast off. That was why the casket was close by now in the farmhouse where our family had gathered.

"But how wonderful it was," Mother said, "that John had all this last year."

We spoke of our gratitude, too, for the gracious small providences of the last hours. How hard it would have been for Mother if she had been alone with Dad at the end. And what if heart failure had occurred at the wheel of his car on the way to the store? He had been spared invalidism, too. How he would have hated giving up his projects! To the end he was busy with them. We began enumerating them. . . .

Only three days before he had finished building a wagon bed so sturdy that we wondered if the farm tractor could haul it.

Then, with as much delight as a small boy with a first wagon, he had painted it bright, shiny red. On the day of his death, he had been wondering about how many baby chickens to buy this year; how many new strawberry plants to set; how soon he and Earl Cook, our helper on the farm, could start work on the second terrace by the chicken house. Then of course, the base for the sundial had to be built—

My brother-in-law, Harlow Hoskins, said at that point, "But I thought Dad was planning on using the stump of the bee tree as a base for the sundial—"

"You mean," and there was a certain supercilious note in Peter John's voice, "the stump of that tree that Mother made for ever famous with her deathless prose."

"Make fun of it, if you will, young man," his grandmother retorted. "Believe it or not, lots of visitors have wanted to see the stump of that locust tree."

"I can give you some new material, Catherine," my brother Bob added teasingly. "This happened when I was a little boy. Did you know about the Christmas that Pop was standing at the top of a ladder, trying to plug strings of outdoor Christmas lights into the socket on the porch ceiling? His hand slipped and he stuck his thumb in the socket. He let out a roar, almost leaped off the ladder, and out came a word that was hardly— um—ministerial. Then he looked down at me sitting on the porch floor, staring up at him with my mouth hanging open.

" 'Just forget I said that, son,' he said in a gruff voice."

Bob chuckled, "What Pop didn't know was that suddenly I felt a new and close bond with him. We men had shared something rather special."

A childish shriek in the hall pierced our conversation. Mary, my sister-in-law, and Em both rushed for their respective children, who had been playing tag on the stairs. Voices in the hall quieted down immediately, and we resumed our conversation. But a few minutes later, seven-year-old Mary Margaret crept into the room.

"Bobby is sitting on the top step and won't play any more and won't come down," she reported in her soft voice.

"Never mind, Mary," Mother said. "I'll take care of this," Then we heard her voice. "Bobby, you misunderstood. Your mother wasn't shushing you because she thought you were being disrespectful of your grandfather. Why, Grandfather wouldn't want you children to be sad and long-faced. He's happy, and he wants you to be happy, too. Besides, he loved having you children around him. You know that—"

"Oh, thank you, Grandmother," we heard Bobby say. She started to speak but then her voice trailed off, smothered in a little boy's hug.

Peter John shook his head wonderingly. "And on the night before the funeral. What a woman!"

"I suppose my children come by their exuberance naturally," Bob grinned. "Remember the lard-can story, Em?"

"Remember it! How could I forget it?"

Then they both started talking at once.

I looked up at Peter Marshall's portrait. It was easy to imagine what he would be saying at that moment, "Same old family. . . . Haven't changed a bit!"

Peter John observed, "We need Grandfather's booming voice to referee."

"All right," Em conceded. "I'll pass. You tell it, Bob."

"Well, Father was always immaculately dressed before he went into the pulpit of a Sunday morning. If possible he liked to wear a flower in his buttonhole. On this particular Sunday morning, he was wearing a freshly pressed white suit and white shoes—the only pair of white ones he owned. Just before leaving for the church, he headed for the back garden where he knew some Ragged Robins were in bloom.

"What he didn't know was that Em and I had booby-trapped the garden. We had begged empty lard cans from

Mother—big ones—fifteen-pound tins. Then we'd sunk the cans in the earth, filled them with water, and neatly laid twigs and tufts of grass across the top to camouflage them."

"It was a dirty trick," Em muttered.

"Anyway, Father walked right into one of the traps set in the middle of the garden path. Em and I heard him bellow like a wounded bull and we ducked for hiding places. But he was in a fine fury and promptly rooted us out. One of his pant legs was wet halfway up and, of course, his shoe was sopping. I'm afraid Em and I didn't further his spiritual state that Sunday."

Sister Em picked up the conversation. "I was lying awake last night, remembering a lot of things too. Len, you've never heard this one. . . ."

Then she related an incident from Father's West Virginia pastorate. One day he had been seeking out a newcomer in town who worked in the Round House at the Baltimore and Ohio railroad yards. When Father finally located the man, he found him repairing an engine.

"Sorry, I can't shake hands with you, Preacher," the man said, holding up hands black with coal dust and engine grease.

Impulsively, my father stooped over and rubbed his hands in the soot that lay an inch thick on the floor. "Now there's no difference between us," he said. "You see, sir, I *want* to shake your hand."

"That man," Em added, "was Father's friend for life."

"I can believe that story," Len said. "I've never known a man who loved people so much—all kinds of people. In Europe last summer, while Catherine and her mother would be looking at monuments or museums or paintings, Dad would be carrying on lively conversations with a bellhop, a guard, a policeman, or assorted shopkeepers."

Len was right about Father's love for people. How whole-heartedly people responded was dramatised for us by this incident, among many. Frank Scott and others from Dad's Eastern Shore Church drove all night to get to the funeral. Mr Scott is a farmer and a man of few words. "I loved Mr Wood," he said simply as he gripped my hand. "I had to come."

The funeral service was anything but sombre. David Crawford, the minister, had told me earlier, "Your father and I had
a fine relationship. In fact, so good that he could tease me
almost constantly. I couldn't possibly be long-faced in any
service for him. If you don't mind, I'd like to make this a
model of what I long for every funeral service to be."

So there was congregational singing. We sang Martin
Luther's triumphant hymn

> A mighty fortress is our God,
> A bulwark never failing. . . .

I looked round and saw Earl Cook standing in the back of the
church, cap in hand, his dusky face glowing, singing more
lustily than any of us.

Mr Crawford stood in front of the almost-full church. His
head was lifted high, a look of exaltation on his face. He had
picked passages of Scripture with the same ringing note in
them. One sentence from the 121st Psalm leaped out at me:

> The Lord shall preserve thy going out and thy
> coming in from this time forth, and even for
> evermore.

Not a member of our family could escape the feeling that
for Dad the Lord had fulfilled that promise exactly. Sitting
there in the little church, my thoughts went back to the final
afternoon of his life. . . .

"I'm going out for the mail," he had said. "I'll be right
back."

*The love of God had tenderly overshadowed him as he went.
The end must not come at the little single-land bridge abutment.
No—not there. Nor at the sharp bend in the road by the Quaker
Meeting House. No, he must have friends near, like Mr Janney
who owns the store—Mr Janney, so much a part of the tiny
community, the great-great-great-grandson of Hannah Janney.
Why, as Father was driving to the store, he passed the spot where
Hannah is buried. . . . I like to remember Hannah. About the time*

another Quaker family was building Evergreen, she had been busy having twelve children. But she still had time to be the leader of the Meeting and the arbiter for the community to the end of her ninety-three years. . . . Yes, somehow it was fitting that it was Mr Janney who had been with Dad at the end. . . .

So if the Lord had preserved Dad's going out in that minute way, we were sure that He had preserved his coming in to his new life as well. That was why we could not be gloomy during the fifty-mile ride to the cemetery.

The procession travelled over the new George Washington Memorial parkway where the first glimpse of Washington is the spires of Georgetown. . . . Across the Memorial Bridge where the gold Italian statues glitter in the spring sunlight . . . Circle the Lincoln Memorial and let the eyes rest on its white symmetry. Surely the most beautiful building in Washington. . . . The cherry trees around the Tidal Basin are fading now.

Down Constitution Avenue—so familiar, so familiar. How many times I have travelled it. And on into the Maryland countryside to Fort Lincoln Cemetery . . . Peter Marshall had preached so many sunrise Easter services there. Now Father will lie close to him. . . .

On the day after the funeral, Mother and I were going through Father's desk. From one drawer, I pulled out a letter that I recognised. It was a love letter I had spontaneously dashed off to Dad several months before.

"I'm surprised that he kept it," I commented.

"He read it over and over," Mother said. "You'll never know how much it meant to him."

I had forgotten what I said. Curiously I opened it:

I knew you were not feeling well when I told you goodbye at the airport. I've been thinking about you ever since then. This is being written on an impulse. Sometimes it's good to follow these spot impulses, speak what's in the heart. . . .

You and Mother gave me the most gorgeous childhood any little girl ever had, because you gave me so much of yourself. Remember all the things you built for me? That set of doll furniture . . . The little cupboard with the glass doors . . . And the dresser with its swinging mirror and the tiny glass knobs. I can see it yet.

Then there was the house in the cherry tree you made for me. And the croquet court with lights strung overhead. These were the myriad ways you entered so deeply into the lives of us children.

But of course, the greatest thing that you and Mother did for us was to bequeath us the sure knowledge of the love and goodness of God abroad in the world.

Am I getting too sentimental? What I really want to say is, you're very dear to me. . . .

Slowly I returned the letter to its envelope and put it back in the drawer. I was glad that I had followed my heart and written it.

Then I picked up Dad's final bank statement. I could scarcely believe what I was seeing. His balance was sixty-five cents.

It is true that you can't take it with you. But who ever heard of anyone coming out *that* even at the end of life?

How typical of Dad! He never did have any money. The salaries of preachers in small towns are notoriously small. Yet always he had been supplied with every need—even to a college education for each of his children and Evergreen Farm for his retirement. His sixty-five-cent statement somehow seemed right.

Father's life had taught me the one thing that really matters—human relationships. The bonds that unite families and friends are not forged for a little while, they are for eternity. They stretch across every boundary of space and time. They twine and interwine from one generation to another, weave and interweave, priceless beyond measure. They are something to be cherished, to be fought for, to be kept intact at all cost. People—with their fears and their foibles and their dreams. People—with their struggles toward faith, with the pain and the exaltation of their pilgrimage. People—with personalities that live on and on, growing, loving, lending helping hands to others. *People*—that is what life is all about.

Mother broke in on my soaring thoughts. Her mind was

darting ahead in several directions: "Probably the baby calf will be born in a few days. . . . Oh, and, Catherine, we must let Mrs Ten Wolde in the Netherlands and Ray in Vienna know, as soon as possible, about Dad's death. . . . Oh, and I've been thinking. There are some fine young people down at the orphanage in the Valley of Virginia. You know, it might mean a lot to one of those high school boys to live and work on the farm this summer—"

In her eyes I saw the promise of the future.

Notes

CHAPTER 1 *Something More*

1. *Life* (November 28, 1960), p. 101
2. The material that follows is from a speech made by Major William Meyer, Army Medical Corps, in San Francisco in 1958. This material has now been declassified by the Department of Defence.
3. Russell W. Davenport, *The Dignity of Man* (New York: Harper & Brothers, 1955), p. 25

CHAPTER 2 *The Unselfishness of God*

1. Deuteronomy 33:27
2. Taken from Romans 8:35-39
3. Romans 8:28
4. This and what follows is detailed beginning on page 219 of Hannah W. Smith's *My Spiritual Autobiography, Or How I Discovered the Unselfishness of God* (New York: Fleming H. Revell Company, 1903)
5. Psalm 145:9
6. John 6:38 (Moffatt)
7. John 14:9 (Moffatt)
8. Luke 15:11-32
9. Matthew 7:9-11 (Moffatt)
10. D. S. Cairns, *The Faith That Rebels* (London: S.C.M. Press Ltd., 1929)
11. II Timothy 1:12 (Moffatt)

CHAPTER 3 *How to Enter In*

1. Luke 6:46
2. Matthew 12:43-45 (Moffatt)

CHAPTER 4 *The Secret of the Will*

1. Revelation 3:20
2. This and the quotes that follow are from Oursler's *Why I Know There Is a God* (London: The World's Work (1913) Ltd., 1952)
3. Phillippians 2:13

CHAPTER 5   *Dare to Trust God*

1. Luke 7:50
2. Matthew 9:29
3. Mark 9:23
4. Matthew 21:22 (Moffatt)
5. Psalm 34:8
6. John 16:24 (Moffatt)
7. Matthew 7:11 (Moffatt)
8. Matthew 6:33
9. Psalm 81:10
10. Luke 12:33 (Moffatt)
11. James 2:17 (Moffatt)
12. I John 5:10 (Moffatt)

CHAPTER 6   *The Prayer of Relinquishment*

1. I Corinthians 1:25 (Moffatt)
2. Matthew 27:11-24; John 19:9-12
3. J. B. Phillips, *The Gospels Translated into Modern English* (London: Geoffrey Bles Ltd., 1952)

CHAPTER 7   *Forgive Us Our Sins . . .*

1. John 1:9
2. John 6:37
3. Isaiah 1:18
4. Psalm 86:5
5. John 15:3
6. I John 5:19, 3:19 (Moffatt)
7. C. G. Jung, *Modern Man in Search of a Soul* (London: Routledge & Kegan Paul Ltd., 1933)
8. From Peter Marshall's sermon "Letters in the Sand," *A Man Called Peter* (London: Peter Davies Ltd., 1951)

CHAPTER 8   *. . . As We Forgive Those Who Sin Against Us*

1. Matthew 6:14, 15
2. Matthew 5:23, 24
3. Ephesians 4:32
4. Matthew 6:15

CHAPTER 9   *How to Find God's Guidance*

1. Proverbs 3:6
2. John 10:3, 6
3. James 1:5
4. John 16:13
5. Hannah Whitall Smith, *My Spiritual Autobiography*, pp. 70-72
6. Romans 8:14 (Moffatt)

CHAPTER 10   *The Power of Helplessness*

1. Psalm 4:1 (Moffatt)
2. Romans 8:28
3. Fritz Künkel and Roy E. Dickerson, *How Character Develops* (New York: Charles Scribner's Sons, 1947), pp. 131-32
4. John 15:5 (Moffatt)
5. *The Interpreter's Bible* (Edinburgh: Thomas Nelson & Sons Ltd., 1953-54)
6. John 6:44 (Moffatt)
7. John 6:15-16
8. Ephesians 2:8, 9
9. John 5:30
10. A. B. Simpson, *The Gospel of Healing* (London: Marshall, Morgan & Scott Ltd., 1940)
11. Genesis 45:5, 8
12. Genesis 50:20
13. Matthew 26:52 (Moffatt)
14. John 19:11 (Moffatt)
15. John 10:17, 18

CHAPTER 11   *The Prayer That Makes Dreams Come True*

1. Glenn Clark's *I Will Lift Up Mine Eyes* (London: Arthur James Ltd., 1953)
2. Mark 10:47, 51 (Moffatt)

CHAPTER 12   *Ego-Slaying*

1. Mark 8:35
2. C. S. Lewis, *Beyond Personality* (London: Geoffrey Bles Ltd., 1944)
3. Romans 6:1-11
4. Künkel and Dickerson, *How Character Develops*, pp. 105, 114
5. Colossians 3:3 (Moffatt)
6. Luke 9:23
7. Hebrews 12:6, 7, 11 (Moffatt)

CHAPTER 13   *The Gospel of Healing*

1. Luke 4:39
2. Luke 4:18
3. Luke 5:12; Mark 9:23, 24
4. Luke 9:11 (Moffatt)
5. Matthew 5:10
6. Matthew 16:1-4
7. Luke 6:8-10
8. Luke 13:10-13
9. Luke 7:11-16

10. Luke 8:27-35
11. Luke 10:1-16
12. Luke 10:18
13. Luke 10:21, 22
14. Mark 16:15, 18
15. Hebrews 13:8 (Moffatt)
16. Matthew 28:20
17. John 5:6 (Moffatt)
18. Mark 11:4 (Moffatt
19. Luke 19:9
20. Luke 13:12 (Moffatt)
21. Matthew 18:19 (Moffatt)
22. Another daughter of Dr Bell, Ruth, is Mrs Billy Graham
23. Matthew 13:58

CHAPTER 14 *Journey into Joy*

1. John 1:14
2. John 7:39, 16:14
3. John 14:12
4. John 16:12, 13
5. Galatians 2:20
6. I Corinthians 6:19
7. John 16:13-15
8. John 14:17; I Corinthians 2:14
9. John 1:33: Luke 11:13; John 14:16
10. Luke 24:49; Acts 1:4, 5, 8
11. Margaret Prescott Montague, "Twenty Minutes of Reality," *Atlantic Monthly* (November 1916)
12. Matthew 18:3

MEETING GOD AT EVERY TURN

Meeting God
at Every Turn

A Personal Family Story

Catherine Marshall

Hodder & Stoughton

LONDON SYDNEY AUCKLAND

To
The Family – yours and mine,
God's loving gift
to mankind

Acknowledgments

I wish to express my appreciation for the loving, faithful help of my secretary, Jeanne Sevigny, and of Alice Watkins, who have patiently typed and retyped their way through so many revisions of this manuscript; to Gordon Carlson for his copy editing.

My gratitude to my husband, Leonard Le Sourd, who did yeoman service in the sorting, selecting, and editing of much of this material; to Elizabeth Sherrill for her fine, sensitive critique; to Marilyn Connell of *Guideposts* magazine for her ideas and suggestions; to my long time friend Gordon Cosby, pastor of the Church of the Saviour, Washington, D.C., for his permission to relate the incident in Chapter Nine.

And how deeply obligated I am to the members of our family, all the way from my mother, age 89, to David Christopher Marshall, age two months, for their tolerance of glass-house living with me; especially for their willingness to share with so many others the inside story of God's gracious dealings with our family.

Catherine Marshall
Boynton Beach, Florida
November 14, 1980

Contents

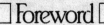

Foreword

For us, 1980 will always be our "family summer" when we had two weddings and a birth. In two months three new members were added to the family—Susan Scott, who became our son Chester's wife; Philip Lader, who married our daughter Linda; David Christopher, born to Edith and Peter Marshall.

Susan and Chester's wedding was in Chattanooga, Tennessee on August 9, with Susan, blonde and lovely; six bridesmaids; Peter Jonathan Marshall, age six, proudly carrying the rings on a satin pillow as he marched down the aisle beside the petite flower girl; Len as Chester's best man; Jeffrey standing beside him as head groomsman. After that, we took a deep, collective breath and plunged into preparations for the second big event.

In the crowded days preceding Linda's wedding in Washington on September 21, she asked one day for some special time alone with me.

Our talk took place in the upstairs bedroom—Len's and my retreat spot at Evergreen Farm—I, relaxed in one of the two blue lounge chairs, Linda sitting in the low slipper chair, hugging her knees.

Looking at her, I liked what I saw: a slender, lovely woman of thirty-one, her face alive, her blue eyes under her dark lashes full of love. So different from the chunky ten-year-old I had first seen, all knees and elbows, regarding her "new Mommie" with a degree of suspicion. What a long and often tortuous road this daughter and I had traveled. Yet how gloriously God had answered Len's and my prayers for her.

Linda must have been having some of the same thoughts. "Mom, first I'd like you to know how much I appreciate your hanging in there with me all these years. I know I made life hard for you sometimes. Thanks for not giving up on me."

We were silent for a moment, letting the serenity of the room with its pale blue walls, and the green of the rolling pastureland seen through the wide windows make its own oasis for us in the midst of the bustling turbulence of wedding preparations.

"And now I have a request," Linda plunged on. "Do you have any advice for Phil and me? You and Dad haven't had it easy. After over twenty years together, I know you've learned a lot. Is there any way you can summarize all that, give Phil and me some perspective on it?"

"Linda, you astound me," I laughed. "Sum up what your father and I have learned...?" I spread my hands wide, trying to express how unattainable this seemed.

"I know you've written about some of this—various books and articles—things like that, and we've talked before. But you see, Mom, Phil's new to a lot of this, and he's so eager to be a part of this family. He'd like to hear it in a straight line."

I groaned. How could I do what Linda was asking?

Nonetheless, even as the wedding preparations went forward, some part of my mind was pondering Linda's request. One word she had spoken kept playing back to me—*perspective*. Perspective—the vantage point of the years.

Slowly, the conviction surfaced and would not be put down .... Yes, I did have something to share with Linda and Phil, with Susan and Chester, and with others like them. I saw that the road of life I had traveled was no straight line as it so often appears from the wedding altar; rather it had had many a turn and twist and bump and detour. More significantly, I realized that even Christians do not arrive at any goodness or maturity all at once; our life is always a walk. Even on the straight stretches, for me there had often been such heavy fog that I had had to go forward by faith alone that Jesus *was* with me leading the way.

And every time where I had met God had not been on the easy straightaways but on the turns when I had least expected the revelation of His presence.

So after a very memorable wedding was over and the couple had departed on their honeymoon to see the Passion Play in Oberammergau, Germany, then on to England for Phil to introduce his bride to his old haunts at Oxford University, at last there was time to dig in and see what I had to share with Linda and the others.

In my quiet writing workroom I spread out books, letters, scrapbooks, files of magazine articles I had written. Last, I pulled off the bookshelves my Journals, one for each year, dating back to 1934. Such a variety of types of notebooks and bindings! I had begun with a five-year diary allowing four lines per day. No good. The author in me needed more space than that. Then had come a series of dark-green, bound books provided by an insurance company. One page per day. Better. On to larger bound books for the Journals—red, brown, blue.

As I picked up any one of these and dipped in at any page, memories thronged. Inserted between the pages of one was the first love letter Peter had written me after we were engaged. In another, a carefully kept temperature chart from the first weeks of my illness in June 1943. On other pages were the first, awkwardly askew, printed letters of Peter John, four. Often there were my own personal written-down prayers; clippings pasted in; lists; thoughts set down—so many of them. How could I have written so much over the years!

As I browsed through this mass of material at random, to my amazement fresh insights began presenting themselves, kept springing up even out of experiences I have shared in previous books.

In searching for God's purpose—the reasons behind events—I saw that whenever I had come to Jesus stripped of pretensions, with a needy spirit, ready to listen to Him and to receive what He had for me, He had met me at my point of need. *He can make the difference in every human situation.*

The word "impossible" melts away with Him. He knows no defeat; can turn every failure and frustration into unexpected victory. He can reverse a doctor's grim prognosis. With Him a seemingly dark and desolate future becomes a joyous new life.

I know all this to be true because I have lived it. I have met God at moments when the straight road turns … and He has picked me up, wiped away my tears, and set me back on the path of life.

Catherine Marshall
October 26, 1980

A Word to My Readers

Over the years a recurring theme in letters from the readers of my books has been, "Dear Catherine: Forgive me for calling you by your first name, but through your books I feel that I know you, that you are my friend."

I could receive no greater compliment. So here is a personal message to all these special friends.

In *Meeting God at Every Turn*, I have selected twelve periods in my life where an encounter with the Lord has come at a turning point or during a moment of crisis.

Some of these experiences will be familiar to you. A number I have already written about in books, others in magazine articles; some are told here for the first time. Most of the material from my Journals has never been shared. Those episodes which have been set down previously are retold here because His living Presence along with the passing of time, continues to bring fresh perspective and insight.

Judging from your letters, there has rarely been a time of such desperation and lostness in all parts of the world, in every strata of society. If you are one of those with seemingly inescapable needs in your life, then this book is for you. It is the true story of how God has met me and is still meeting me at every turn. It is the assurance that if He would deal so lovingly with someone like me, then you too can meet Him in a person-to-Person encounter, feel His love for you, and know that He is the answer to every cry of your heart.

C. M.

John Ambrose Wood

I

Our Father Who Art On Earth

❦

For this reason, then,
I kneel before the Father
from whom every family
in heaven and on earth
derives its name and nature....

Ephesians 3:14-15

Our Father
Who Art On Earth

My early childhood was a crazy mixture of exuberant joy interspersed with moments of fear. It was a mystery to me, and certainly must have been to those around me, why I was so shy and fearful.

Assorted odd things alarmed me, such as the dark, mice, spiders, snakes, the nuns in their flowing black habits in the Catholic school across the street, the patched snowman-shaped hole cut by a burglar in the back porch screening, the page in the *Book of Knowledge* picturing Joan d'Arc being burned at the stake. Yet as soon as my father was near, my world was invulnerable.

My dad, the young preacher, John Wood, was tall and very slim, with black hair always neatly combed and soft brown eyes with a glint of mischief in them. And very handsome, I thought. He was gregarious, full of good humor, a father fond of teasing and of practical jokes. Some of the most memorable moments of my early childhood revolve around him.

Until I was seven, I was the only child. Then came my brother, Bob, and 14 months later, my sister, Emmy. Because Dad was a Presbyterian preacher and chose to have his office at home rather than at the church, I saw more of my father than most children do.

Often I would creep into his home office unbidden, but he was never too busy for me. Invariably, he would smile and hold out his arms to receive me. "Girlie—my girlie," he would say.

Even when Father had a guest, he would allow me to sit quietly, silently on his lap while he carried on a leisurely conversation with some church officer or visitor or the young Catholic priest who lived on the next street and often dropped by. Dad's lap always seemed more commodious than Mother's, his arms more firm. For me, those arms were protection and reassurance, warmth, strength and nourishment. In some strange way, the love that flowed between us must have been nourishment for him too.

The setting for those earliest memories was a one-floor white frame home in Canton, a small mid-Mississippi town. This cottage-manse was dwarfed by the red-brick church sitting squarely beside it, overshadowed by huge old oak trees shading both yards. The giant oaks also lined Peace Street in front, creating a tunnel of green through which to walk or drive or bicycle, welcome respite from the cruel Mississippi sun.

My shyness might have led eventually to withdrawal and a feeling of inferiority, for I could not easily admit people to my inner self. Fortunately, this pervading reticence and tendency to hug childish secrets to myself was countered by the way my parents treated me. Since I had "discovered" Robert Louis Stevenson's *A Child's Garden of Verses* and enjoyed the sound of the rhythms and cadences slipping off my tongue, I was encouraged to memorize some of my favorite poems and to recite these to my family.

When Father wanted to chop down the wisteria vine, all but smothering the old coal house in our back yard, and I loudly protested, patiently he listened to my pleas, smiling at the ardor of my appeal. "If you feel that strongly about it..." he said, patting my hand, "I'll just give the wisteria a haircut." And I trotted away satisfied.

When I had progressed in my piano lessons far enough to play simple hymns, Father would sometimes allow me the fun of being the pianist in a small church parlor meeting.

Thus early I was given a sure sense of self-worth, the recognition of my individuality and the surety of being loved and cherished. These are securities that parents can give their children only through their actions.

The other side of such love and attention was that our parents were still the authority figures in our home. They let us children know that we were held responsible for our own conduct. Nor were we allowed to give up easily on tasks or lessons which we considered difficult. Their attitude was always, "We'll help you where help is really needed. Between us, *nothing* is too hard."

That included a regular Sunday afternoon session of memorizing the questions and answers of *The Catechism for Young Children*, followed by the misnamed *Shorter Catechism of the Westminster Assembly*. (Actually, the "Shorter" is considerably longer!) There would be a prize at the end of the long trek of memorization, but finished it must be.

A futile religious exercise? Not a bit of it! Couched in the chiseled English of another century, beautiful in its clarity and simplicity, this laid a very right base for those all-important questions about life and death, about God and our relationship to Him.

Q. What is God?

A. God is a Spirit, infinite, eternal and unchangeable, in His being, wisdom, power, holiness, justice, goodness and truth.

Q. What is the chief end of man?

A. Man's chief end is to glorify God, and to enjoy Him
   forever....

That last idea was startling to me. From some of the
pictures and tales in my Bible story books, the Jehovah of
the Old Testament seemed stern and unapproachable except for someone like Moses or Abraham. This God thundered from Sinai and asked for sacrifices. His fierce anger
destroyed large cities like Tyre and Nineveh, once flooded
the whole world and drowned everyone in it except for
Noah and his family.

Yet here was the Catechism telling me that God was not
to be feared but actually *enjoyed!* That I would have to
ponder long and deeply.

One day I asked my parents, "How can I love someone
I'm afraid of?"

"Because He loves you," came Dad's reply. "Remember
that Bible verse on your Sunday School folder just last
week, 'We love Him because He first loved us.' He loved
you before you even knew He was there."

"But I can't feel it, or hear any words, or see a face full
of love like I see your face, Dad."

"That's exactly why Jesus came down to earth, to tell
us and show us that the Father in heaven is all love, is
made of love. Jesus liked to say that even the best human
father couldn't be half as loving or kind or generous as the
heavenly Father."

Seeing doubt on my face, Dad added gently, "Sometimes I have to punish you or Bob or Em when you have
disobeyed or are clearly in the wrong. I'd be a poor father
to you if I *didn't* correct you. But that doesn't mean that
you're afraid of me, does it?"

Looking into those warm brown eyes, I saw only love
beyond measure and as always, that glint of humor. Certainly I could trust my earthly father. But God was still
vague, up in heaven somewhere. I still wasn't sure where
I stood with Him.

So I went my blithe way reveling in the freedom to roam in an outdoor world of never-ending delights. In the midst of this, the fact that our family had little money mattered to me not at all. We had each other, and we had fun together. And so many years later, I have only to turn my memory loose, instantly to recapture the feel of a small child's fresh, sharp joy of sight and sound and touch and smell.

To others the yard around our cottage-manse where I played with the boys next door and with my friends Tay and Laurie-Bodie, may have seemed ordinary enough; to me, it was my very own Eden fresh from the heavenly Father's hand. How could there be anywhere a more delicious fragrance than the southern honeysuckle that rioted over all the fences? And not only fragrance, but taste. Pick a blossom, delicately bite off the stem end of it, suck out the delicious honey. No wonder the bees loved it! What bliss in the spring to hunt for the first white bells of snowdrops amongst the green foliage and to bury my nose in the first hyacinths. How could my eyes absorb enough of the beauty of the purple wisteria vine I had persuaded Father to save? Had anyone before me ever really felt the enchantment of bare feet on the thick carpet of moss under the oaks? Or of perching high in the leafy bower of the fig tree, feeling as free as the birds that darted and wheeled and sang all around me? Did grownups really know the succulent deliciousness on the tongue of plump, juicy figs picked from the tree and eaten in that leafy fairyland?

Years later I would read the Genesis account of how the Creator looked with approval upon each day's handiwork after He had flung the galaxies of stars and planets into space. Then He created the creatures, the fish and fowl, the trees and herbs—and always He *"saw that it was good."* And reading it was like an echo out of my own deep spirit. Of course it was good—every flower, every fragrance, every fluffy, drifting cloud and singing bird. Not only "good" but glorious. My child's heart had known it all along.

But my private Eden also bore the unmistakable mark of my earthly father. It was Dad who constructed an out-sized sandbox for me where my playmates and I spent endless hours building elaborate sand castles.

It was he who built a see-saw, sturdier and longer than any to be found in any store. We children always marveled that everything Dad built was big and heavy, meant to last a lifetime.

And the swing! Quickly we learned to stand and "pump": begin slowly, bend the knees in rhythm with the swinging. Make it go higher, higher, up and down. Now again, swishing through the air, until finally the jerk of the chains told us that the swing had gone as high as it could. Then "let the cat die."

There were joys awaiting me inside our home too. As in many older, deep-South homes, the 10-foot wide, cool, center hall ran the length of our house with the rooms on either side opening off it. This gallery-corridor was the favorite site for games. All of these revolved around my father. What was pure gold were the hours he spent with us children playing *Parcheesi*, caroms, checkers, dominos, *Rook*, *Old Maid*, jackstraws, jacks or putting together countless jigsaw puzzles. For some reason, Mother could never get the hang of games, so she would mend or sew or read while Dad and I and anyone else we could pull in, battled tenaciously to win. Father was a sharp competitor, and he never gave us children any quarter because we were small. We liked it that way, for when we won, the taste of victory was all the sweeter.

Often I would walk to the grocery store with Dad for some needed item that Mother had forgotten to put on the grocery list. Sometimes of an afternoon when he was going "calling," Father would take me along, and I would ride proudly beside him in the front seat of the old Dodge touring car which we were able to afford only in the latter part of my childhood. In these situations however, there was the discipline of having to wait out each call alone in the car.

I enjoyed standing or sitting on the floor beside my father, talking to him as I watched him making repairs around the house. He was a good carpenter and painter, even bricklayer and stonemason, with an adequate knowledge of plumbing and electricity. I, and my brother and sister after me, were the recipients of our father's varied skills in a procession of bookcases for our bedrooms, wagons, clubhouses, croquet and basketball courts lighted for night use, goldfish ponds, doll houses and furniture.

It must have been the security of Dad's presence that made his office the most lived-in room in successive manse-homes in Mississippi, the eastern panhandle of West Virginia, and the eastern shore of Virginia. The study was always lined with open bookshelves floor to ceiling. A comfortable leather Morris chair with wide arms sat in the corner just within arm's reach of *The Book of Knowledge*, a beautiful set of Stoddard's *Lectures* on travel, *The Book House*, *The Harvard Classics*, McLaren's *Commentaries on the Scriptures*, along with novels, reference books and innumerable theological books.

Everywhere we moved—from Greenville, Tennessee, to Umatilla, Florida, to Canton, Mississippi, to Keyser, West Virginia—Father's capacious roll-top desk came along, always with a typewriter on a stand beside it. There would be two or three ample rockers in the room, ferns on stands, and in the winter, narcissi and hyacinth bulbs sitting in a sunny window in bowls of water and pebbles to produce a succession of blossoms and fragrance during the snowy months. A canary in its cage and frequently, pans of Mother's feather-light rolls rising on the hot air register completed the coziness of the room.

It was here that the family always gathered after the evening meal while we children worked on our school lessons. Sitting in the Morris chair or at one of the pull-out leaves of Father's desk or sprawled on the floor, we were surrounded by plenty of study helps. Dad subscribed to several magazines, and he always had catalogues from which we children could order books, for our town rarely had a bookstore. All our *National Geographics* were saved for school work, and a cupboard was crammed full of past issues. We were free to cut and paste them as illustrative material for school papers or exhibits.

Dad was never too busy to stop and answer some question about our school work or to help us assemble the material for a product map for a geography lesson, or to hold the book and listen while we recited some memory work for next day's lesson.

My father, of course, had his weaknesses. He could be stubborn. A case in point: the episode of the flamethrower. Fond of tools and gadgets, he was often tempted to spend too much of his meager salary on such things. Since the West Virginia house had a large yard with much lawn, he had treated himself to a power mower. Then soon after that he saw a flamethrower advertised and conceived the idea that a flamethrower was just what he needed. Apparently the War Department had overbought on flamethrowers and was anxious to unload a few.

Mother was annoyed at the idea. "What on God's green earth do you want such a thing for? You know perfectly well we haven't any money to spend on silly things like that."

Father looked wounded. He always looked wounded when anyone of us questioned his judgment about buying gadgets.

"The flamethrower is *exactly* what I need for getting rid of the tall weeds in fence corners," he retorted, "and I *am* going to buy it." With that he stalked off.

Buy it he did. We still have the flamethrower in the family. We also still have weeds.

Then there was his volatile temper. How vividly we remember the time my brother Bob was helping Dad string the Christmas lights over the front door when father's thumb accidentally slipped into the live socket.

Out came the thumb and out of Dad's mouth poured forth some startling, unclergymanlike words. Then Dad glared down from the ladder.

"Son," he said solemnly, "forget that I said that."

Bob never did, of course. Not only that, in later years he told me, "From that moment, I loved and respected Dad more than ever. He was not too 'good' to be human."

Nor could any of us forget the Sunday morning when Bob and Em mischievously created a minor crisis.

During the week before this Sunday, the two children made the rounds of the neighborhood begging empty 15-pound lard cans. Carefully, they neglected to report to our parents how the empty cans were to be used.

Sunday morning our preacher-father was all dressed for church—black hair slicked down, white suit, white shoes—his only pair of shoes not at the repair shop. Since he enjoyed wearing a flower in his buttonhole, Father went out to the garden to select one.

A half minute later we heard a howl. Then red-faced, he stomped into the house with a switch broken off the privet hedge to punish the culprits. It seemed that Bob and Em had filled several lard cans with water and sunk them in strategic places in the flower garden. Over these homemade booby traps they had neatly laid twigs, then a few tufts of grass. Father had walked into one of the traps set in the middle of the garden path. That Sunday Father preached with a wet left foot while two of his children listened with smarting legs.

But Dad was always fair in administering punishment. We knew he loved us even while he was chastizing us. There was no inconsistency with what he preached from the pulpit and the way he dealt with us as the head of the house.

It wasn't that my father was eloquent in the pulpit. He was an average preacher with only a mild interest in theology. His forte was people. He loved them and enjoyed mixing with them, friends and strangers alike. He was easy to be with and had a knack for finding a just-right conversational meeting ground with all manner of folk.

One of my favorite stories is about how Dad went down into the railroad yards near our home in Keyser, West Virginia, to seek out a new member of his congregation. Although our town was close to coalmining territory, Keyser's only industry was the Baltimore and Ohio Railroad's roundhouse and shops. It was in one of the B & O's enormous roundhouses that the Reverend Wood found his man at work.

"Can't shake hands with you," said the man apologetically. "They're too grimy."

John Wood reached down to the ground and rubbed his hands in coal soot. "How about it now?" he said, offering an equalized hand.

And so at an early age I knew I could trust my earthly father. But I resisted the sermons that urged us to surrender our lives to a faraway God. What did that mean? The idea of spending all my time praying, reading the Bible, and talking about God did not appeal to me at all.

When the evangelist Gypsy Smith, Jr., came to hold services in our town, I went with curiosity, but little more. A large tent was pitched on a vacant lot near the town limits. It did not prove large enough to hold the crowds that flocked there. On a platform of raw wood from which the resin still oozed, sat the massed choirs gathered from all the churches. Their favorite anthem was the spirited "Awakening Chorus":

> The Lord Jehovah reigns, and sin is backward hurled!
> Rejoice! Rejoice! Rejoice!

The "rejoicings" vibrated so shrilly that they raised goosebumps along my spine. As the congregation sang, the waving arms of the music director beat out the rhythms of hymns like:

> Stan-ding on the prom-i-ses of Christ my king...

or:

> Sing them o-ver a-gain to me, Won-der-ful words of
> life...

Each time we collectively took a breath, the pianist
would run in scales, chords and flourishes marvelous to
my childish ears.

Then came the preaching—so dynamic that decades
later Gypsy Smith's thundering sermon on Samson still
reverberates in my ears. The word-pictures were vivid:
Samson, blessed of God with great strength through his
hair, succumbed to fleshly temptations and was delivered
into the hands of his enemy, the Philistines. His hair was
cut, his strength gone, his eyes cruelly blinded.

Gypsy Smith would lean far over the crude pulpit, pausing from time to time to whip out a handkerchief and wipe
his flushed, perspiring face or to take a drink of water.

Then that final scene in Samson's drama where a re-
pentant Samson, his hair growing back, his strength returning, faced 3,000 Philistines gathered in the great hall
to make sport of him.

It was not to be. With his right hand on one of the two
key pillars supporting the house, his left hand on the
other, Samson bowed himself with all his might, and the
house fell, crushing himself and all his enemies who had
come to taunt him.

> "... So the dead which he slew at his death were more
> than they which he slew in his life."

The emotion in Gypsy's preaching, steadily mounting, had
transferred itself to the congregation. What did Samson's
story have to do with those of us who were listening?
Selfishness and sensuality brought only destruction, the
evangelist thundered. It would always be so. But each of
us had to decide which road we would travel.

Finally a hush would fall over the tent as the choir sang almost in a whisper,

"Softly and tenderly Jesus is calling, Calling for you and me..."

"Believe on the Lord Jesus Christ and thou shalt be saved," the evangelist urged.

Soon at the far edge of the tent someone would rise and slowly make his way down the aisle toward the front. Then another person... and another... and another... and another.

The repeated demands of the preacher did not impress me as much as the faces of the people who went forward. There was radiance and joy on those faces. Most of them seemed eager to get to the front where they knelt and wept and prayed and "gave themselves."

At home I asked my parents about the people who had made this act of commitment to God.

"Does this mean that they joined the church?" I asked. I had no problem with this. All kinds of people were joining the church for all kinds of reasons. As far as I could see, it did not seem to affect them much or demand a great deal. I wondered too, had not some of them "gone forward" out of the emotionalism of the moment or even out of fear? Could either be the right motivation?

Dad understood my wonderings behind the questions. Wisely, he answered, "Sure, most of them will join a church. You too will want to do that at the right time. But Catherine, joining the church is only part of it. The important act is the giving of your life to God so that He can use it for good."

I pondered that statement many times during those pre-teen years. What did it mean to give my life to God? Something deep inside me rebelled against any phony gift. Dad sensed that in me.

"Catherine, you should not join the church until it really means something," he told me one day. "It must mean the gift of yourself to Him."

Later on came that Sunday morning when I sat in church beside my mother (my brother and sister were in Sunday School classes) and watched my father as he conducted the service. My heart was full of love for him in a special way. I could never remember many things he said from the pulpit, but I felt the way God's love was flowing through him for all of us in the congregation.

At the end of the service, rather spontaneously as I recall, Dad issued an invitation for those to come forward who wanted to accept Jesus as the Lord of their life and to be a part of the church fellowship.

And suddenly I felt a stirring inside me. Very gentle. There was no voice or words, just a feeling of great warmth. I loved my father dearly. And I trusted him with all my heart. I loved him so much that I could feel tears forming behind my eyes.

And then came the assurance. All along God had meant for the love of my earthly father to be a pattern of my heavenly Father and to show me the way to make connection with Him.

Following this inner conviction came the sudden urge to act and the will to do it. To my surprise and Mother's, I rose from the pew and walked down the aisle to the front, joining a half dozen or so others.

At first Dad did not see me as the group lined up in a semicircle around the altar. He spoke to us briefly about the step we were taking and was about to pray when he noticed me.

Full recognition flashed into his brown eyes; he knew instantly that my being there was significant. I was presenting the gift of myself, a first step in faith. The resistance to surrender had been broken.

I shall never forget the look on my father's face. Surprise ... joy... sudden vulnerability. He stood there for a long moment in front of the altar, looking at me with eyes swimming in tears behind his spectacles. Then he pulled himself together and had us kneel as he prayed.

It was my first encounter with the living God and my heavenly Father. The catechism had said that He had loved me first. So had my earthly father. He must have loved me even before birth while I was in my mother's body.

Not only that, since I could love and trust my earthly father, how much more could I love and trust my Father in heaven—and then, without fear, place my future in His hands.

What joyous reassurance there was in that bedrock fact!

Leonora Whitaker Wood

II

Mother Never Thought We Were Poor

Give, and it shall
be given unto you....
make for yourselves purses
which do not wear out,
and a treasure in heaven that
does not run short....

Luke 6:38; 12:33—ASB

Mother Never Thought We Were Poor

~~~

While my father was the one to present God to me as a heavenly Father who tenderly cared about each one of His children, it was my mother who showed me how a relationship with Him could change everyday situations. The lessons God had taught her were indigenous to the poverty of the first eighteen years of her life. Either she had to settle down to lack, or find God's way out of it. The creative approach He gave her has been of help to countless numbers of people.

Leonora Haseltine Whitaker was born in 1891 and reared on North Carolina farms, first in Weaverville, later in Barnardsville. When she was eighteen she volunteered to join Dr. Edward O. Guerrant's mission in the Great Smoky Mountains of East Tennesse as a schoolteacher. Her experiences there with the mountain people in the Cove, buried in the mountains seven miles back of Del Rio, Tennessee, later would form the basis of my novel *Christy*.

Mother was taller than average and—judging from family album pictures—the Gibson-girl shirtwaist dresses made her seem even taller. She had extremely large, expressive blue eyes and an aquiline nose with a piquant tilt at the end. Her chestnut-colored hair was so long that she could sit on it, though she usually wore it pinned up on the top of her head. At a later period she began braiding it, then winding the braids twice around her head in a lovely natural coronet.

Soon after Leonora Whitaker got to the Cove, the mission was in dire straits for funds to meet basic needs. Mother thought and prayed about this, then an idea dropped into her head. Since she had received invitations to speak in nearby Knoxville to the Tennessee University Club and to the women of one of the churches, she felt there was a good chance these organizations would help her meet the mission's emergency. In addition, she planned to call on a Knoxville businessman with a reputation for philanthropy. What followed was an object lesson in how faith and creativity can blend effectively.

For these engagements she was determined not to look like a dowdy mountain missionary who needed to beg for herself as well as for the mountaineers. Since this was the Lord's work, she wanted her appearance to say, "I'm having fun being a missionary. Wouldn't you like to have a part in this adventure too?"

A visit to a beauty parlor was her first step. She emerged with an elaborate hairdo, curls on top, a figure-eight in the back.

Next, in one of the city's best stores, Mother found an enormous black hat with sweeping ostrich plumes. It would be perfect, she decided, with her one good garment—a black broadcloth suit. But the hat was priced at $25—every penny of her salary for one month. She pondered a long time. Should the $25 go directly into the mission fund? Or would buying the hat actually be an investment in the work? Mother bought the hat.

Her blue eyes sparkling with the fun of this feminine adventure, later that day Mother swept into the downtown offices of Mr. Rush Hazen, a wholesale grocer and philanthropist. Heads at rows of desks turned to stare. Even Mr. Hazen stared. In fact, he all but whistled. "You—a missionary! I don't believe it. Why hasn't somebody thought of sending out missionaries like you before? What can I do for you?"

Mr. Hazen did a great deal. Triumphantly, Mother went back to the mission with enough food and money to keep boarding students all winter, with the promise of more money for the future. She also went back more secure than ever in the conviction that God would supply our every need if we but ask Him to show the way.

It was at this mission that Leonora Whitaker met John Wood who had just graduated from Union Theological Seminary in Richmond, Virginia. They were married in Asheville, North Carolina when mother was nineteen.

My parents spent the next forty years serving Presbyterian congregations in small communities and living frugally. Yet that did not dampen Mother's creativity a whit. I remember vividly an especially harsh period—the early 1930s. By that time our family was living in Keyser, West Virginia. Because his church people were suffering so much financially, Dad had voluntarily taken three successive cuts in salary. That meant that our family of five barely scraped along.

Dad received his portion of what had been in the church collection plates on Sunday night, and it never lasted the week. Therefore, the Friday or Saturday grocery shopping had to include an element of acute embarrassment to us children. Even now I wince at the remembrance of standing beside my father, pretending not to notice, while he sought out our friend, the grocer, leaned over the counter, and said in a lowered voice, "If you will let us have this list of groceries, I'll drop by on Monday to pay you."

During these lean years our family had no car. We children walked or bicycled. Our parents walked, walked everywhere—for all shopping, to church, to call on parishioners.

Bob and Em and I could joke about Father sometimes receiving a fee of fifty cents for marrying a couple. And we did not mind the fact that we had to go regularly to a neighbor's to read the Sunday funnies since one of our economies was cutting out the Sunday paper. What we *did* mind were some of the clothes we had to wear. I've never forgotten one brown velvet dress Mother made for me out of someone's hand-me-down. The velvet was worn in places, and the chocolate brown was wrong for a young girl. I suffered in silence every time I wore it. And my sister was mortified, she tells me, by never having proper girl's snow togs of her own, always being forced to wear an old pair of her brother's pants as a snowsuit.

We children certainly did not enjoy those depression years, yet no tinge of fear about lack of money ever clouded our home. It never seemed even to have entered Mother's head that we were living through a period of poverty. She went through each difficult day of the depression as though she had some secret bank account to draw from when we were in need—and in a sense she did. But her real secret was an utterly confident inner attitude: always before her was the picture of a healthy, fulfilled family.

Though we did without many things, Mother always provided us with a feeling of well-being. One way she did this was the unique manner in which she contrived to give to others. Out of our meager pantry she would send a sick neighbor a supper tray of something delicious she had prepared—velvety-smooth, boiled custard; feather-light, homemade rolls—served up on our best china and always with a dainty bouquet from our garden.

While Mother always tried to provide her family a balanced diet with plenty of fruit and vegetables, often we went without meat and I cannot recall any luxury foods. The main course for many an evening meal would be french fries and hot biscuits with honey or jam, or salmon croquettes, or fried mush. But we children didn't mind the mush at all—not the way Mother made it: sliced thin, browned crisp, and served with maple syrup.

Mother could also turn fried mush into an occasion by even giving some of *that* away. This happened when she discovered that Mr. Edwards, our wealthy neighbor, was fond of mush. Since his wife never served him such lowly fare, from time to time he would be the grateful recipient of our hot, golden-fried mush. "Poor Mister Edwards," we would intone in mock sympathy to tease Mother.

Only unconsciously were we aware of it, but Mother was providing us constantly with an object lesson in giving. The message: no matter how little you have, you can always give some of it away. And when you can do that, you can't feel sorry for yourself, and you can scarcely consider yourself poor.

But there was even more to it than that. For Mother, giving was an act of faith, and the spiritual principle of giving out of scarcity came as easily to her as if she had invented it. Whenever we saw an old-fashioned pump in a farmyard, we knew what she would tell us: "If you drink the cup of water that's waiting there, you can slake your own thirst. But if you pour it in the pump and work the handle, you'll start enough water flowing to satisfy all our thirsts."

She likened the principle of priming the pump to God's law of abundance: we give, and He opens the windows of heaven and gives to us. It was a law of life, she explained to us children, and as certain to work as that the sun would rise tomorrow.

Mother had not been in Keyser long before she had a dream of helping the destitute of Mineral County, particularly those who lived in one section called Radical Hill, where people lived in tin-roofed shacks along rutted roads strewn with debris.

This was an unusual slum district because it was not on the wrong side of the tracks. It was located in what should have been the town's most beautiful residential district, far away from the railroad. There unbelievable filth was surrounded by gently rolling hills and towering mountains. The "nice" citizens of the town gave the area a wide berth. Yet the children who lived there, often unwashed and with lice in their hair, sat alongside the "nice" children in the public schools.

Mother's first step was to enlist the help of some of the young people of our church to go with her to visit each home and to take a survey of the district. Of some 500 Radical Hill families, she found that only 80 had any connection with any church.

At that juncture Mother offered her services to the county welfare board and to our surprise (but definitely not hers!) was given a job to help improve conditions in any way she could. Day after day, she would send us off to school in our hand-me-downs and our artfully patched clothing, and then she would go off to help what she called "the poor people."

The first thing Mother managed to do was to get the name of that area changed from Radical Hill to Potomac Heights—a new name for a new start, something to renew and lift the spirits. Then an old abandoned hotel was remodeled—partitions torn out, repaired, painted; bathrooms and a kitchen put in. This was for meetings of all kinds, a Sunday school and a weekday nursery school. A health clinic, craft classes, and Mother's own classes in child care and Bible study for teenagers were started Soon the work was flourishing. Those who had been giving up hope began to take heart because someone cared.

Then one day Mother was told that county funds had run out and that her employment had to be terminated. For only a moment did she give in to discouragement. Then she approached the director of the welfare board. "May I go on working?" she asked.

"But we can't pay."

"I understand," Mother said. "But why should I do for money what I would be willing to do for the love of God and humanity?"

The man stared at her. "What do you mean?"

"I mean," she said resolutely, "that the work must go on, salary or not. Shutting down now would be disastrous."

The director looked incredulous. Then, impressed by Mother's determination, suddenly his tone changed. Standing up, admiration and enthusiasm written on his face, he thrust out his hand. "All right then, of course, go right on working. I'll do something—we'll *all* do something. Somehow we'll get the community behind us."

So day after day Mother would trudge on foot to Potomac Heights, receiving not a nickel for her work. And the work not only prospered, it zoomed as a large task force of enthusiastic teenagers rallied around Mother to help.

Years later I saw on television Kathryn Forbes' warm Swedish-American reminiscences called "*I Remember Mama.*" Her family of five was exactly like ours—one son and two daughters. The youngest daughter, Dagmar, reminded me of our youngest, Em. And like our family on Overton Place, the family on Castro Street knew the same kind of financial stringency. They too lived from weekly payday to weekly payday.

I sensed still another point of similarity. Kathryn Forbes' Mama had a bank account. Each Saturday night as the stacks of coins would be counted out for the landlord, the grocer, for half-soling shoes and school notebooks, there would be great relief when Mama finally smiled. "Is good," she would say. "We do not have to go to the bank."

Mama's bank account was considered to be only for the direst emergencies. By hard work and much cooperation, the family made it through year after year; just knowing that Mama's bank account was there gave them a warm, secure feeling.

Twenty years later when daughter Kathryn Forbes sold her first story, she proudly took the check to Mama. "For you—to put in your bank account."

Then—finally—the truth came out. There never had been a bank account. Mama had hit upon this device because, she explained, "Is not good for little ones to be afraid—not to feel secure."

Suddenly in a blazing revelation it occured to me that my own mother also had a bank account that kept us— her children—from being afraid. Her bank account too was real—as real as the mountain air we breathed and the nourishing bread she baked, as solid as the gold in Fort Knox. Mother's family bank account was her faith in the Lord, her absolute trust that the promise of "give and it shall be given unto you" was as eternal as the mountains around us.

Even by age twelve I had begun to realize that the secret of Mother's strength was directly related to her daily prayer-conversations with God. I watched her go off alone to talk with Him and wondered what it was like to have a real conversation with God. Could you hear His voice? Was His presence and His love something you could actually feel? I had to find out.

At fourteen I was a thin and somewhat awkward-looking girl with too long a neck. I had naturally curly brown hair, usually unruly hair, with very large blue eyes set in pale face. I was a teenager with a head full of question marks, exclamation points, and some ridiculous and implausible dreams. For how could one live with Leonora Wood and settle down to limited horizons?

"You are the beloved children of the King," she never tired of admonishing us. "Each of you is very special to Him, and He has important work for you to do in the world. It's up to you to find His dream for your life. And take warning, our King doesn't fool around with petty stuff. The sky is the limit!"

By the time I entered high school, I had focused down on three major dreams. The first, born in early adolescence, I hugged to myself: Was there any chance that someday I could write books, be a real author?

Then when I was 15 there came a golden moment when two more dreams came into view. It happened early one spring at the home of Mrs. William MacDonald with whom I would sometimes spend the night when her husband had to be away on law cases.

The MacDonald's daughter, Janet, had gone to a college called Agnes Scott—glamorous and far away in Decatur, Georgia, on the outskirts of Atlanta. "Mrs. Mac" talked about how special the college was, how much it had meant in molding Janet's life.

The MacDonald home seemed luxurious to me: real mahogany furniture, a tall grandfather clock whose musical chimes marked the quarter hour...current books, lovely books of history and travel lying about; and they even received the *New York Times* every Sunday.

When I stayed with Mrs. Mac, it was her custom to serve us ice cream at bedtime—more ice cream than I could eat. Then she would tuck me in under an eiderdown in a bed with tall pineapple posts.

How well I remember one particular night when for me, time paused and stood still. "Good night, my sweet," she said as she turned to leave the room.

Then at the door she stopped, half turned, looked at me. "You make quite a picture lying there. One of these days a wonderful man, just the right man for you, is going to come and carry you away. Just you wait!"

Her words, shockingly daring to me, yet standing straight and tall, marched across the room and found permanent lodgement in my mind and heart. At that moment two dreams were planted inside me: to go to Agnes Scott College and to get ready for that wonderful man who would come from far away to marry me.

I did not realize it at the time, but now that I had given my life to God, He was using that perfect time—impressionable adolescence—to reach down and plant in the fertile soil of my girlish heart His big, pure, wonderful dreams. The fulfillment of them would be His work, not mine, but I was to learn that none of those gloriously impossible dreams could come true without the pain of self-realization and growth.

By the time I graduated from high school, the depression was daily dealing our town devastating blows: businesses failing, banks closing, bankruptcies, suicides, almost everyone living on credit. With our family's hand-to-mouth existence, how could there possibly be any money for college?

Already I had been accepted at Agnes Scott. Even though I had saved some money from debating prizes and had the promise of a work scholarship, we were still hundreds of dollars short of what was needed.

One evening Mother found me lying across my bed, face down, sobbing. She sat down beside me. "You and I are going to deal with this right now," she said quietly.

At this point Mother took me into the guest room, and together we knelt beside the old-fashioned, golden oak bed, the one that Mother and Father had bought for their first home. "Catherine, I know it's right for you to go to college," Mother said. "Every problem has a solution. Let's ask God to tell us how to bring this dream to reality."

As we knelt there together, instinctively I knew that this was an important moment, one to be recorded in heaven. We were about to meet God in a more intimate way than at bedtime prayers or during grace before a meal, or in family prayers together in Dad's study, or even as in most of the prayers in church. Mother was admitting me to the inner sanctum of her prayer closet.

In the silence, I quickly reviewed my relationship with this God with whom we were seeking an audience. At the age of nine I had given Him my life. Attendance at Sunday school and church had been regular ever since, little enough to do as the daughter of a preacher, I thought uneasily.

I had prayed many times since that encounter with Him years before, but how real had these prayers been? The truth then struck me—most had been for selfish purposes. I had given so little of myself to Him. I had not really taken much part in Mother's work to transform Radical Hill to Potomac Heights. And with a sinking heart, I remembered all the times I had seen members of the church coming up the front walk only to flee up the back stairs to my room where I could be alone to read and not have to give myself to others in the sharing of their problems.

Scene after scene flashed across my mind's eye of the times I had resented my brother and sister. Whenever they had interfered with what I wanted to do, I had scolded them, avoided them, rejected them. As I thought of the many occasions when my parents had gone without something they needed so that we children could have new clothing, piano lessons, books or sports equipment, I felt more unworthy than ever. And my going to college would call for yet more sacrifices from my parents.

I stole a look at Mother. She was praying intensely but soundlessly, with her lips moving. Then closing my eyes, silently I prayed the most honest prayer of my life to that point. "Lord, I've been selfish. I've taken everything from You, from Your Church and from my parents and given little of myself in return. Forgive me for this, Lord. Perhaps I don't deserve to go to a college like Agnes Scott."

A sob deep in my throat made me pause. I knew what I now had to do. "And Lord, I turn this dream over to

You. I give it up. It's in Your hands. You decide." Now the tears did come!

Those quiet moments in the bedroom were the most honest I had ever spent with God up to that point. I was learning that the price of a relationship with Him is a dropping of all our masks and pretense. We must come to Him with stark honesty "as we are"—or not at all. My honesty brought me relief; it washed away the guilt; it strengthened my faith.

Several days later Dad and Mother decided that by faith, I should go ahead and make preparations for Agnes Scott. They felt strongly that this was right and that the Lord would soon confirm it. I was not so sure. God had convicted me of my selfishness. Perhaps He wanted me to give up college and serve Him in some other way.

Days passed, then weeks. Then one day Mother opened a letter and gave a whoop of joy. "Here it is! Here's the answer to our prayers."

The letter contained an offer from a special project of the federal government for Mother to write the history of the county. With what I already had, her salary would be more than enough for my college expenses.

Once again, Mother's very real bank account had provided the necessary provision at a time of need. From those hours each day spent alone with Him had come her supreme confidence that He would always provide out of His limitless supply. How often she had told us children, "And don't forget, He will never, never let us outgive Him."

Out of this solid wealth, this certainty, Mother could always afford to give to others, not just material things, but showering sparks of imagination, the gleam of hope, a thrust of courage—qualities that provided more substance than the coin of any realm and which opened the door for fulfillment in many a life she touched.

Catherine at 16

III

My God Was Too Small

O Lord, You have searched me
and have known me....
Your (infinite) knowledge
is too wonderful for me;
it is high above me,
I cannot reach it....

Psalm 139:1,6—Amplified

My God Was Too Small

Travel from West Virginia to Atlanta, Georgia, for my first semester at Agnes Scott was overnight by train. There was not enough money for a Pullman berth, so I sat up all night in the day coach. But I discovered a way to avoid these sleepless, uncomfortable nights to and from college—make a friend of the conductor. If there was still an empty berth at midnight, he would let a passenger have it for a few dollars.

This need for careful husbanding of money dominated my four years of college during the depression years of the 1930s. My parents stretched their resources to the limit to keep me there with each semester's payment of tuition a cliff-hanger of suspense for me. Any delay of payment brought a summons from Mr. Tart, the college treasurer (aptly named, I always thought), with a resultant surge of panic inside me.

Upon arrival on the campus, I was immediately at home with the ancient magnolia trees, as in my Mississippi childhood, and was soon reveling in the mysterious beauty of

Georgia nights when a soft breeze blew from the south. I discovered grits again and southern accents and Atlanta's Peachtree Street. College life turned out to be a kaleidoscope of bull sessions and truth sessions, hard studying, often a set or two of tennis of an afternoon as a change of pace from long hours in the library, fire drills, endless hair washings and waiting for letters and checks from home. There were dates (since greater Atlanta burgeoned with men's schools), writing and typing papers, the constant jangling of dorm telephones and memorable after-lights-out feasts with boxes from southern homes—fried chicken, potato chips, beaten biscuits, salted pecans, spice cake.

As freshmen we were quickly plunged into "Rat Week." This involved wearing a dress backwards, shoes which did not match, six curlers in our hair and a dab of cold cream on each cheek in the shape of an "F." It also involved crawling whenever we encountered a sophomore.

I found that Agnes Scott girls liked to call themselves "Hottentots" and that the school song, when accompanied by a solemn, full-robed and hooded academic procession, could give me girlish goose pimples.

I discovered the spot on the quadrangle, somehow connected with the college heating plant, which always spouted steam. And I saw that at any evening of the year, the setting sun could turn the ivy on the ancient walls of Main Building to glistening, shining magic.

Gradually, as the weeks passed, I became aware of campus personalities: Dr. J. R. McCain, the college president, who always had time to talk to any girl and whose first pride was Agnes Scott's rapidly rising star in the academic world. Yet he boasted that these high scholastic standards did not subtract from the femininity and marriageability of the women Agnes Scott turned out. Did not 80 percent of Hottentots get married? Was not this a higher percentage than any of the large women's colleges in the East could boast? From time to time Dr. McCain would announce the latest revised matrimonial figure to his girls.

This seemed to please him as much as the list of those who had just made Phi Beta Kappa.

Then there was Dr. Henry Robinson, head of the mathematics department—a math genius but almost equally interested in matchmaking and the then much-debated cause of Prohibition. Dr. Robinson was to play a key role in my dating life at Agnes Scott.

There was Miss Hopkins, the college dean—"Hoppy" we called her privately. She was incalculably patrician; her dress, her walk and her manner were reminiscent of a bygone century. She wore her gray hair in the pompadour style of the early 1900s.

Virginia was my blonde, beautiful roommate. She knew how to use make-up in a professional manner—pancake foundation, eye shadow, mascara, eyebrow pencil. I struggled hard not to envy her. The struggle capitulated and faded into wistfulness when I allowed myself to think of her year's supply of cosmetics—and in all the largest size bottles and jars too. To this day, a whiff of *Evening in Paris* perfume reminds me of Virginia.

Our closets were side by side. On my side, the clothes included a few carefully selected simple dresses and blouse and skirt combinations. Virginia's side held not only a complete school wardrobe, but a black beaver coat to set off her blonde loveliness, a stone marten scarf, many dinner and evening dresses. She always made the beauty section of the Agnes Scott Annual; wherever she went, masculine heads turned.

I watched from a distance; prodded myself with reminders that I was fortunate to be in college at all—wardrobe or no wardrobe; fed myself platitudes that girls could not live by bread (or stone marten scarves) alone, though I often kept wondering what they *did* live by.

Scarcely a week went by during these four years of college that I did not agonize over my finances. Every penny was important; seldom were there extra funds for entertainment or side trips. Once I needed $15 to participate in a college debate against the debating team of England's Oxford University. I did not have it, nor did my parents. My roommate might have loaned it to me, but I was too proud to ask. Having been selected as one of two out of the whole student body for this event, to have to decline because of sheer poverty seemed too humiliating to bear.

At the last minute my parents came through; how they raised the money I do not know to this day.

During the spring of my freshman year came an experience which turned out to be one of the hinges upon which life turns. The English professor, Dr. Emma May Laney, had given us a choice of several authors to research. One name in the list I had never heard of—Katherine Mansfield, the New Zealand short story writer. The assignment was to be a definitive term paper on "our" author. The paper would decide most of our second semester grade.

Curious about Katherine Mansfield, I chose her and chose better than I knew. After reading several volumes of her short stories, I came upon her *Journal.* Passage after passage spoke to something buried deep in me and awakened a response: the way Katherine Mansfield fingered life, rolled it on her tongue so that not one but a dozen taste buds savored it. She had been as a little girl seeing inside everything, from a gull lighting on the water, to a crushed violet in the grass, to the plop of a hard little pear falling from a tree at the bottom of the garden, to watching her playmate, Kezie, "make a river down the middle of her porridge" and then helping her "eat the banks away"; to a little bird sitting on the branch of a tree "sharpening a note"—seeing it all with guileless round eyes, saying to us, "See! New shoes!"

Preparing for the term paper was not work, it was the breath of life. I had discovered pure gold, and I reveled in it. Into a notebook I copied lines from her *Journal* that I especially liked:

Fairylike, the fire rose in two branched flames like the golden antlers of some enchanted stag.

And the day spent itself . . . The idle hours blew on it and it shed itself like seed.

She was the same through and through. You could go on cutting slice after slice and you knew you would never light upon a plum or a cherry or even a piece of peel. . .

The sun shone through the windows and winked on the brass knobs of the bed . . .

They slung talk at each other across the bus . . .[1]

When I turned in the term paper, I had a good feeling about it. Thus I was quite unprepared for what followed.

A week or so later, I was summoned to the professor's office. Miss Laney was a fine teacher, but upon occasion she could have an acid tongue. All of the acid was showing that day.

"This could not be your original work," she hurled at me, her pencil jabbing at the Katherine Mansfield paper before her on the desk. "This paper has Miss Mansfield's style all over it." With her eyes flashing fire and her mouth drawn into a straight line, Miss Laney delivered a definitive lecture on the dangers, horrors, and gross dishonesty of plagiarism.

I burst into tears, too distraught to do anything but stammer, "I didn't mean to copy her style. I just wrote what I felt."

"But the paper reads as if Miss Mansfield wrote it. It's excellent, but I don't see how you..." She stopped, not knowing quite how to tell me that it was too good to be the work of a college freshman.

Strange, but I have not the slightest recollection of what grade I was finally given for this paper. I had enjoyed writing it so much that the grade was no longer the point. Rather, the work had become an experience in self-discovery. I had stumbled upon my special spot. It felt right—where I belonged.

As I painfully mulled over the professor's accusation in the weeks and months that followed, several conclusions emerged. My term paper had been unusual enough for a college freshman to make Miss Laney suspicious. Did I then dare to hope that perhaps, just perhaps, those glimmering, girlhood dreams of someday being an author might be an authentic dream?

And if the charge of plagiarism had arisen because I was unusually sensitive to the style of the author I was reading, I would have to be careful about this in the future. Years later I would be making this point in writers' workshops: every writer must put himself under sharp discipline as to what he reads while writing original material. It won't do to read Hemingway while one's own book is in progress and end up with Hemingwayish copy!

It was in the spring of my freshman year that I first heard the name Peter Marshall mentioned. He was the pastor of Westminster Presbyterian Church there in Atlanta. "A really good preacher," one of the upperclassmen told us, "Scottish and very handsome." Some of my classmates were going regularly to hear him preach, but an hour's ride by streetcar into Atlanta meant time and money I was loathe to spend.

When I finally did go to hear this young Scotsman preach, I was enchanted. I found Peter Marshall to be a tall, well-built man with the broad shoulders of a football player (he would have said "soccer player") camouflaged by his Geneva gown. His hair, which had been very blond, was turning darker. It was curly, never slicked down as my father's had been. His face was handsome in a rugged sort of way.

He seemed thoroughly at home in a pulpit. While he preached, he frequently used gestures, but they were never strained or artificial. Most of his emphasis was made with his voice—an extraordinarily resonant speaking voice, more flexible and dramatic than my father's, with the added delight of a clear, precise British diction garnished with his Scottish burr. There was also a marked poetic streak in his prayers and his sermonizing. As Peter stood in the pulpit, I, and no doubt others like me, saw him against a composite backdrop of Edinburgh Castle, John Knox, skirling bagpipes, and the renowned 51st Division, all with a touch of heather thrown in.

But there was something even more appealing. Here was a man who knew his Lord, spoke of Him as his Friend, shared intimate experiences of His guidance and help. This was the first time I had heard preaching that brought us, Peter's congregation, into contact with a present-day Jesus. Every bit of it touched something deep in my spirit.

By the middle of my sophomore year I had begun filling notebooks with my reactions and observations about my life at Agnes Scott. This entry was significant:

> I am awfully blue this morning for some unexplainable reason. It must be that let-down feeling after all my exams. They were simply awful. I wonder if other people suffer as much as I do over them.
>
> I am tired all over. Mentally, physically, spiritually. I am lazy spiritually. I would like to know God really—not in the abstract. But I don't seem to want to badly enough to do anything much about it. I can't fathom myself. Perhaps someday—but it's always someday.

The next Sunday I went to hear Peter Marshall preach and wrote:

> Today was glorious. At breakfast it looked like rain, but then the sun came out. While we were waiting for

the streetcar in town, it sprinkled a few big drops. They were like pearls in the face of the sun.

I don't know what's the matter with me. Perhaps I'm simply in a romantic frame of mind these days, but that man Peter Marshall does something to me! I would give anything I own to meet him.

A month or so later I wrote this item in my Journal:

Went to Sunday school and church at Westminster. After Peter had made his talk, he said he didn't know everyone in the class and couldn't we have a social to get acquainted? He said he wanted to meet some of us before all of us had a chance to get married. And then the funny part of it was that he *actually* blushed!

I had the strange and giddy feeling today that it was this particular morning that Mr. Marshall really noticed me for the first time. I could tell by the way he looked and smiled at me. It must have been my new blue hat, which *was* very becoming. . .

Soon I began saving clippings about Peter Marshall that kept appearing in the Atlanta papers, for this young preacher, still in his early 30s, was already making his mark on Atlanta: "A young Scottish preacher with native jargon and impressive dramatic personality... If ever we saw greatness in a man, they are in Peter Marshall. Yet there's an odd boyish shyness about him too... A charming young Scot with a silver tongue... Gay, brilliant, witty."

But reading comments like this, I knew that the elements of "greatness" in this man were not in his wit or his dynamic personality. Rather, in the indisputable fact that under the impact of Peter's praying and preaching, God was becoming real to those who listened. While he led them in worship, God was no longer a remote, theological abstraction but a loving Father who was interested in each individual, who stooped to man's smallest need.

My girlish heart was not the only part of me affected by Peter Marshall. My hunger for excellence was stirred by the quality of his preaching. Even more important, he pricked my spiritual consciousness deeply. Several entries in my journals that spring reflected this:

> I have come to a crisis in my life. It's very easy for me to see how people can lose their so-called religion when they have gotten enough education to make them think at all, particularly if their religion is simply an inheritance or a habit. I'm afraid this is happening to me; I have had no real, vital religious experience. God does not seem real to me. I believe in God now mostly because of people I know—a very few people—like Peter to whom religion is a vital, living thing.
>
> I can't go on like this. I know there must be something to religion, else all of life would be meaningless. Sometimes it is to me. People hurry and bustle and strive, failing to see the beauty around them. Their eyes are on material consideration wholly. We die, and apparently it is all over. I wonder what I was born for after all. *I must know.*

Then a few weeks later, this entry:

> Spring is so beautiful. All the trees are out now, a tangy fresh green. On the way to Decatur I saw pink honeysuckle and lilacs and the air is filled with the fragrance of wisteria. The earth is brown and wet and springy, full of the promise of better things—the hope of life and eternity.
>
> Yet amid all this exquisite beauty, the world is also full of sordid, ugly things. My trip to the University of Georgia was so disheartening. The students there live what seems to me to be superficial and meaningless lives, drinking, always with cigarettes dangling from their lips, gossiping and saying nothing when they *do* talk. None of them ever seem to study. Why do they go to college anyway?
>
> There has got to be something more to life than this, some real purpose. What is *my* purpose? I don't think I've found it. I want my life to be so full. I want to be

able to love and laugh and live and help others to the depth of my capacity.

That summer, still unable to get Peter Marshall out of my thoughts, I put myself through a crash course on Scotland, Scottish history—everything Scottish. Perhaps then I could understand better this Britisher whose background appeared to be so different from mine and who was so much older. Through careful questioning of my parents, I found that all my ancestors had emigrated from the British Isles. I made a bibliography of 37 books on Scotland and pored over some like H. V. Morton's travel account *In Search of Scotland*, Ian MacLaren's sentimental *Beside the Bonny Briar Bush*, Sir Walter Scott's *Minstrelsy of the Scottish Border*, Boswell and Johnson's gutsy account of *A Journey to the Western Isles*. And as I read, many times that summer I marveled at how strong the call of the blood can be for us Americans whose roots are across the sea.

And yet—to what purpose all this reading? Preparation for—what? The end of that summer became a time of sober reassessment. In college I was seeking a base on which to build my life. My mind hungered to be stretched. Yet there were those who had warned me about this: "Watch it! A lot of young people lose all their religious faith in college."

True. And I was vulnerable, coming to college from a traditional Christian upbringing. My concept of God was well-defined and structurally circumscribed. Despite that, the idea world and the learning process were proving to be such an intoxicant that I knew I would have to guard against intellectual gluttony. My strengths and weaknesses were obvious to me: courses in mathematics and science would be agony; those in English, history, philosophy, the arts, speech, music, a joy—and would bring out all my effort and skills.

Then where was God in all this? To my surprise, He was everywhere. Not so much in Religion 101-102, or courses on Old Testament and New Testament. These I found dull, almost stultifying. Especially with the professor who, in his effort to seem liberal and broadminded to us college students, offered us outlandishly contorted, naturalistic explanations for Old Testament miracles. I had respect neither for the far-out theories nor for the prof's too-eager desire to please his students.

But I did see God in the intricate marvels of mathematics, in the inconceivable vastness and complexity of all His creation as I glimpsed it in the sciences, in His footprints through the history of empires and nations and the lives of the men and women who had made history—He was everywhere. Even Comparative Religion proved no threat. Truth was and is truth—indivisible. Bits and pieces of His truth, as much as mens' minds were open to receive, were in all religions of the world. I was learning to assess and to think, and then how to allow Him to help me sort out truth from error.

Already I knew that I need never be afraid of using my mind, for at every point of discovery God came running to meet me, always bigger than my mind, ever out ahead of the greatest scientist, the most eminent doctor, the finest historian. Yes, my God had been too small. Those who had warned me had been wrong. He had given me the mind; His desire was that I use every atom of it.

Thus, the goal of excellence was before me every day of my college life. In fact, it has been in all of my life before and since. Always I have been fascinated, ecstatic over sheer brilliance and quality in writing, in the arts, in scholarship. The question was always before me: How could I throw my ability so totally into a work at hand so as to reach the absolute limit of my capacity? At Agnes Scott I hoped to find the answer.

By the time I returned to college for my junior year, I had decided that allowing myself to be moonstruck over

Peter Marshall was pathetic immaturity. He had made God more real to me; that was all to the good. But I made a firm resolve to be more grown-up about the situation that fall. I would attend Westminster Church occasionally to hear Peter preach, but date men from Emory, Georgia Tech, Columbia Seminary and other nearby colleges. Most of all I would concentrate on my courses, pursue excellence. Maybe a teaching career would be right for me.

As for romance, that might have to wait—for a long time.

Peter Marshall

IV

Romance

Now the Lord God said,
It is not good
(sufficient, satisfactory)
that the man should be alone....
....for love (springs) from God
....for God is love.

Genesis 2:18,
I John 4:7,8— Amplified

Romance

❧

I returned to Agnes Scott College the fall of my junior year to find a report circulating that Peter Marshall was engaged to be married.

True or not, this reinforced the resolve I had made at the last of the summer: I would be friendly but altogether casual with Peter. There *was* something ridiculous about a soon-to-be 20-year-old college student fancying herself in love with a 32-year-old bachelor-preacher who had captured so many other female hearts in the Atlanta area and who was already becoming well-known for his marriage counseling.

But why does he single me out with his eyes so much when he preaches? I asked myself.

"A dozen other women probably think the same thing," my logical mind snapped back.

The thoughts retorted, *But then why all that special attention after church? Having his secretary, Ruby Coleman, intercept me to tell me that he wants to drive me back to Decatur?*

I had no answer to that. Better drop all such ruminations.

That October a young man from Emory began to date me. There was a strong physical attraction between us, and I began to wonder if I could be in love with Fred. But then one day I realized that there was neither spiritual nor intellectual rapport, or anything like oneness between us. I stopped dating Fred, tried to forget romance and concentrate on my studies.

But soon, inevitably, I was drawn back to Westminster Church and Peter because of an aching void in my life. This notation in my Journal is revealing:

> There are several reasons why I'm attracted to Peter. For one thing, he has so much poetry in his soul.
>
> There is such a kinship between poetry and religion. They both try to see into the heart of things.
>
> One of the reasons I could never fall in love with Fred is that he has no appreciation for the beautiful.
>
> But then added to that, Peter combines an inheritance of the best of the European tradition with an acquisition of the best of the American. He has such a capacity for affection and tenderness, such a luscious sense of humor sprinkled with an earthy roguishness.
>
> Why must the embodiment of all my ideal be 12 years older than I and as remote as the South Pole?

To my fellow students, I must have seemed on top of things. My grades were good, close to an "A" average. I had achieved success as an intercollegiate debater, in Poetry Club and in other class activities. Yet underneath it all, I was still churning:

> Tonight I feel compelled to write until my hand is tired and exhausted. I am restless and unhappy these days because I am neither right with myself nor with God. Why this dissatisfaction with myself? I am driven on and on by an overwhelming sense of some destiny, of some task to be done which I must do. I can never be peaceful and happy and enjoy life until I learn why I am here and where I am going.

It is as if my soul is frozen and hard, and when there comes some mellow influence which melts it, my soul strains against these walls like a turbulent mountain stream whose course has been newly freed from encumbering rubbish. And I don't think it too dramatic to say that my life is just as barren and dry as the rocky stream-bed, parched through being deprived of the life-giving water.

I am tired of knowing and not doing, tired of thinking and not being. I despise myself because I am simply lazy in my religion. It is easier not to bother. Yet I know that I can never find God by not bothering.

Throughout that winter and into the spring my Journal notes were peppered with references to Peter Marshall.

The more I hear him talk, the more I realize we have the same ideas and ideals—we like the same things... How I wish I could tell him all the sleep he has made me lose... Dreaming this way about Peter is the most foolish thing that has ever happened to me.

Reading through my journals of this period so many years later makes me aware as never before how tender God was with me, never intruding on my willful self-centeredness, but always there when the heart hungers inside me cried out. And how beautiful was his timing in the slow—agonizingly slow to me—way the relationship between Peter and me developed until I, so much younger, was mature enough to meet Peter where he was spiritually and intellectually.

The film version of *A Man Called Peter* indicated that the turning point in our relationship was May 3, 1935, the Prohibition Rally (turned into a Youth Rally in the movies) at which Peter and a student from Emory University and I spoke.

My Journal shows that this rally was an interesting but only an early step along the way. As we drove to the schoolhouse where the meeting was to take place, Peter focused his attention on me. Pointedly, he squelched the rumor that he was engaged by saying, "Don't believe everything you hear, my dear girl. I certainly am not even about to be married." He pronounced the word "mar-rr-ied" with a very broad "a" and a rolling of the "r's."

When the meeting began with the singing of some old revival hymns, Peter quickly entered into the spirit of the evening, his fine baritone voice ringing out above all others. One by one we were then elaborately introduced, listened to patiently, and given more applause than we deserved. Frankly, I can remember almost nothing about what we said.

On the return drive we were both in the back seat. Peter tucked his arm through mine and held my hand all the way home. He explained that he had been wanting to talk with me for a long time and had never before gotten a real chance. Before we said good-by Peter asked me if I ever went bowling and said that he would take me out some night.

Afterwards, I was ecstatic. My dream of two long years standing had at last been fulfilled—that of getting to know Peter better. I had never thought he would actually ask me for a date.

A week went by, then another, and still Peter did not call. There were two get-togethers at the church where he overflowed with warmth toward me. Each time he would go out of his way to drive me back to the college. On May 12 he asked to return for me at 3:30 that afternoon after which we were together until 11 o'clock that night—our first real date. Lingeringly, tenderly, he bade me goodnight, his last words, "I'll be in touch with you this week."

The days dragged by. No call. What was I to think?

When summer vacation came, I went home to West Virginia more frustrated than the year before. Why did he always seem so interested when I was with him, but then never followed up with a note or a telephone call?

He had promised to write—and did. The postmark on the letter was June 17, 1935. I tore it open eagerly. A typed letter was enfolded in a church bulletin. My face fell, my hopes plummeted as I read:

> Dear Catherine:
>
> Your card was most welcome. I am glad you thought of me. My summer's plans have now crystalized. I sail for Scotland from New York on July 5th and shall be gone until the end of August. They have given me a month's vacation and a month's leave of absence. I shall visit home and try to be with Mother more than I was last year. I'll be driving up to New York with a party of five others, which will make it rather difficult for me to detour and go through Keyser to see you as I had hoped.
>
> Since you left I have been kept quite as busy as ever. I had only eight Commencements in eight days, but they almost wore me out before I got through. I have been at Agnes Scott all of last week, teaching in our Synodical Conference, and this week I preach every night at Villa Rica. I'll be melted away before I get to Scotland. Hope you are well, resting, and having a good time.
>
> My best wishes and remembrances.
>
> Peter

It could scarcely have been a more casual, impersonal letter! Disappointed again, once more I went through the summer process of trying to eliminate any thoughts of romance about Peter Marshall. In August came an even more casual card from Troon, Ayshire...

> Having a grand time in Scotland. Spent a week in London and had so many fine trips. Hope you are having a fine summer. Regards,
>
> Peter Marshall

That did it! It was time to stop acting like a schoolgirl and get on with the business of life.

Yet in thinking back over those few short here-and-there hours I had spent with him, I discovered that there were little things which had become memories dear to me: the peculiar look he had given me as we were standing by his car after his Mother's Day sermon when I told him how his idealism about women had moved me; the moment later that evening when his hand covered mine as we were leaning over the bridge and watching the moonlight as it made a patch of silver on the water; the intensity of his eyes looking into mine as we were driving out to Agnes Scott when he was telling me of his coming trip to Scotland; that moment when he came up behind me at the bowling alley and put his hands on my shoulders; later, the way he stroked my hair and said, "Little Catherine."

The ache in my heart continued though the summer and into the fall. I returned to college for my senior year determined to stay away from Westminster Church, convinced once and for all that there was no hope for the one thing my heart yearned for more than anything else. I must forget Peter Marshall.

Meanwhile, three years of college had greatly enriched and broadened the naïve, small-town girl from the West Virginia mountains. Whatever I lacked in ability I made up in heartfelt desire and intensity, and in hard, slugging work. In any discussion on world issues such as the League of Nations, Nazism, or America's economic collapse, my comments were never deliberate and measured but passionate, often laced with blazing indignation, prompting classmates to dub me "Calamity Catherine." Their inevitable joshing would finally bring me back to earth to find again some balance and the return of a sense of humor.

I must have averaged three hours a day in the college library where I dug into the classics, enjoyed novels, browsed poetry, dived into history, always enchanted with personalities, life style, and human interest data on the men and women who had *made* history What delight to happen one day upon Thomas Carlyle's precise expression of this approach: "History is the essence of innumerable biographies."

My reading ranged widely—from John Calvin's *Institutes* to William Hazlitt's and Thomas Carlyle's *Essays*, to *The Writings of James Madison*, to Dorothy Wordworth's *Journal*, to Matthew Arnold's prose and poetry; I was fascinated with published letters such as those of Horace Walpole and John Keats, and with poets like Shelley, Wordsworth, A.E. Housman; and I fell in love with Edna St. Vincent Millay and Robert Frost, who visited our campus via the lecture platform.

At the start of my senior year, I decided to pour all my energies into my studies, debating, the Hiking Club and Poetry Club. For a time I fancied myself the complete tragic poet, wallowing in the shortness of life and equally gloomy and too-serious subjects. Though it turned out that I was never meant to be a poet, unwillingly I stumbled on an important technique in learning to write. In poetry one has to find the precise word. One's thoughts have to be placed in small compass—sharp as an arrow. And imagination has to come into play, or the poetry is just blah or worse—mushy.

Much of this effort was even in that demanding form, the Shakespearean sonnet. There indeed was discipline— ah, discipline! All of it fine training for writing.

My resolve to stay away from Westminster Church lasted only until October 20 when I made this entry:

> Went to church at Westminster, but got there after 11 a.m. and had to sit in the vestibule and listen to Peter through the loud speaker. I had planned not to speak to him afterwards, but suddenly changed my mind. He pumped my hand and commented that this was the first time I had been here this year. So he *had* noticed my absence! He promised to get in touch with me. I shan't hold my breath until he does.

Gossip continues about the different women Peter goes out with. I don't think he plays around, but being a tender and affectionate person, succumbs for the moment and gives women the wrong impression. The reason he has never gotten married is that none of us has ever really come up to his ideal....

I was invited to have dinner with Peter at the Robinsons, to which he was quite late. Right away he brought up the past spring. Had I remembered it? We ended up looking at his pictures of Scotland, drinking tea, talking. He said he would call me, but I am skeptical. And so Peter once more invades my smug and fortified existence.

The entries in my journals for the next four months continued the pattern. When he saw me Peter was all interest. He arranged to take me to meals at a friend's where we talked, sang, played games like *Monopoly*, *Yacht*, *Parcheesi*. Once I was back on campus however, he seldom if ever called or sought me out. It's clear to me now that Peter as a bachelor in his early 30s and a preacher of growing importance was reluctant to take the initiative in seeking out dates with a college girl so many years younger than he. He knew that to others this would seem improper. And he was right. At the time I could not see this—or have any feel for God's timing in the situation.

The crucial turning point in our relationship came on Sunday, May 3, 1936. I had been asked to review a book at the Sunday afternoon fellowship hour at Peter's church. I chose one entitled *Prayer* by the Norwegian theologian, Dr. O. Hallesby, a professor at the Independent Theological Seminary of Oslo. This was an unusual book for any professor-theologian because its content was not theory; what Dr. Hallesby had to say seemed so obviously directly from his own experience.

Such an assignment would have been a challenge to me at any time and place. Since this was to be at Peter's church, and the pastor himself was likely to be in the audience, I did an inordinate amount of preparation. An intuition told me that this was the time and place for something important to happen between Peter and me—if it was ever meant to happen. The depths of Peter's inner being had been revealed to me through his preaching. But there had been no comparable chance for him to catch a glimpse of my inner spirit. The book review just might provide such a window into the real Catherine whom Peter had not yet seen. Hence the period of preparation for my talk was bathed in prayer. The writings of this Scandinavian seminary professor saturated my being.

When I arrived at the church that Sunday afternoon, the fellowship hall was filled with people, including Peter Marshall. Just before I was to speak I was stricken, almost paralyzed by tension and nervousness. Did I have anything really worthwhile to say to these knowledgeable people?

I felt so young and unimportant and unknowing. In my agony of self-doubt I closed my eyes and beseeched the Lord to rescue me, to place His hand on my trembling body, to calm my tumultuous thoughts so that words would come out which not only made sense, but would move these people toward a prayer life as the book had moved me.

"We tend to be superficial in our prayers," I began with quavering voice. "Most of us think of God as a kind of Santa Claus who waits to hear our requests. What He really wants to hear are the hungers of our heart and our confessions of deception and dishonesty."

Confidence and strength surged through my body. Since Dr. Hallesby had opened my eyes to my own smugness in certain areas, I admitted this and depicted how I had begun to change my approach to prayer. I confessed my hunger to know God better, to feel the Presence of Jesus, to be able to talk to Jesus as a Friend. I described situations like the Katherine Mansfield paper where I had felt so helpless in the face of the biting words of my English professor.

"The author has something to say about such situations which really helped," I said. Then I read this passage by Hallesby:

> Listen, my friend! Your helplessness is your best prayer. It calls from your heart to the heart of God with greater effect than all your uttered pleas. He hears it from the very moment that you are seized with helplessness, and He becomes actively engaged at once in hearing and answering the prayer of your helplessness. He hears today as He heard the helpless and wordless prayer of the man sick with the palsy.[1]

Because the book had revealed to me my own inadequacies, I confessed how self-righteous I had been during my college years. Emotion poured through my words as I described how the book had revitalized my prayer life. I felt lifted up and carried forward by a Power beyond myself.

Though the audience was quiet and attentive, it was Peter's face that commanded my attention. He stared at me with such an intentness that my stomach began churning. There was a moment when I almost felt that only the two of us were in the room.

After my talk Peter was subdued as he closed the meeting. He turned to me, took my hand and squeezed it tightly, a look in his blue-gray eyes I could not fathom. Then we went into the evening service where I made the mistake of sitting within three pews of the front.

My turbulent feelings and the emotion of the previous few hours were too much. The stone pillars and the Good Shepherd window behind the pulpit began to swim alarmingly. I was too sick to be embarrassed when Peter mentioned my name from the pulpit in connection with the talk I had just given. By the time he began his sermon, I knew it would be disastrous to stay.

As I rose to begin the longest walk in my life, the voice from the pulpit trailed off, and there was dead silence, broken only by the staccato clicking of my heels on the stone floor. I could feel Peter's eyes boring into my back every step of the way up the long aisle. Not until I was well out into the foyer did the voice resume over the loud speakers.

The college infirmary received me that night and attempted to diagnose this strange stomach ailment. The head nurse, properly starched and equipped with a strong nose for sniffing out lovesick maidens, had her suspicions.

The next day Peter and Ruby Coleman, his secretary, were eating lunch at Martha's Tea Room next door to the church. As a rule, they used that time to talk about church business or sermons. On this particular day, I learned later, Peter was unusually quiet. Ruby noticed that he seemed tense and introspective.

Suddenly he said, "You know, every time I meet a nice girl, she leaves town."

Ruby knew what he meant. She had been watching the slow unfolding of our friendship. She knew that in less than a month I would be graduating and leaving Atlanta.

"Well, look," she asked in her quiet way, "can't you do something about it?"

For a long moment Peter did not reply. He appeared to be in deep thought. Carefully, he buttered a roll. Then, "Maybe I can."

He did do something about it—within the next hour.

In the early afternoon the infirmary telephone at Agnes Scott rang, and the solicitous voice on the other end had a familiar Scottish accent.

"I'm talking from Miss Hopkins' office," the voice said. "I have secured her permission to come over and see you. May I?"

I gasped. No mere man—unless armed with a medical diploma—had ever, in all the college's history, been allowed inside the infirmary. Male visitors were simply taboo. After all, the young ladies were not properly clothed! How Peter had prevailed on Miss Hopkins I couldn't even imagine.

"I—really don't think you'd better," I said hastily. "I'm well enough to dress and come over. I'll meet you in the colonnade in ten minutes."

I should not have stopped him. Ever afterwards Peter accused me of having thwarted his only chance for fame with future generations of Agnes Scotters. If I had not interfered, as the first male visitor in this off-limits haven, Peter some day might have rated a bronze plaque on the infirmary wall in commemoration of the occasion.

Almost every day after that my Journal records items about the two of us.

> Peter was terribly solicitous about my illness... I believe now he wants to be serious... I think Peter is in love with me!!... Tonight we went to a play. Afterwards on the front porch he kissed me again and again... Tonight we talked until three in the morning and he proposed . . .

He framed his proposal in gentle words, like the delicate embroidery surrounding the strong, simple words of an old sampler.

And then a surprising thing happened to me. I found I could not give him an answer just then.

How strange! That made no sense. For three years I had been hopelessly in love with Peter Marshall (foolishly in love, I thought), and now had come the biggest moment of my life—a proposal from the man of my dreams. And I hesitated. Why?

It was because at that moment I became aware in a new way of how God operates in human lives, and in that moment of awareness, I did a lot of growing up. Suddenly I saw how wrong it is to go after what *we* want, and then— with considerable audacity—later ask God to bless it.

When Peter finally did propose, I wanted more than anything else to know God's will with certainty. Nothing else would do. The awareness of my ever-present will and emotions in this relationship was precisely why I could not now say "yes" without the sure knowledge that this marriage was not just my will, or even Peter's, but primarily God's will also.

When I shyly suggested to Peter that both of us needed to submit this decision to God in prayer, eagerly and quickly he agreed. So we prayed together, asking God if our fused lives and joint purposes would be a greater asset to the kingdom of God on earth than if we went our separate ways.

Almost from our first meeting I had had a strange sense of a God-given destiny about Peter. That made it of prime importance to be certain that I was meant to be a part of that destiny.

There followed days of praying about this separately. As unskilled and immature as I was in prayer, God chose this time to teach me a great lesson. I learned that because God loves us so much, He often guides us by planting His own lovely dream in the barren soil of a human heart. When the dream has matured, and the time for its fulfillment is ripe, to our astonishment and delight, we find that God's will has become our will, and our will, God's.

At the turning point of one of life's most important decisions, the choice of a life partner, Peter and I met God Himself. Only God could have thought of a plan like that!

As I took my last college examinations and wandered about the campus in something of a daze, a benediction slowly settled upon my head. What seemed too good to be true was true: God was not only giving His approval to this marriage, He had been in Peter's and my relationship all along, slowly guiding it and maturing it. In retrospect I could see that through all my impatience and frustration God had been the Divine Orchestrator of this romance in a way that would probably confound modern day romantics.

There remained only the pleasant task of giving Peter my answer.

I chose a moment when we were driving from Decatur to Atlanta.

"There's something I must tell you..." I began.

In the semi-darkness I could see a strained look cross Peter's face.

"Good... or bad?" he asked tensely.

When I then accepted his proposal of marriage, he said simply and fervently, "Thank the Lord!"

For several moments he drove along without saying anything more. When finally he stopped the car beside the road, it was to bow his head and to pray an achingly beautiful prayer. God was in every part of his life, he was God's, and with God he wanted to share this supreme moment. Only then did he take me into his arms.

On my graduation night Peter and I walked through an almost-deserted campus. I was to leave the next day.

The ancient oaks cast heavy shadows on the driveway, and the moon shone on white magnolia blossoms heavy with perfume. Main Hall had seen thousands of girls come and go. The venerable red-brick, ivy-covered walls had stood sentinel over many a tender farewell.

"If anybody had told me three months ago," said Peter, "that I would be standing in front of Main Hall telling the girl I love good-by and not caring whether all Decatur was at my back and all Atlanta at my front or who saw me, I would have thought they were crazy."

The night watchman, standing somewhere in the shadows, discreetly looked the other way.

The Marshall family

V

Illness

....He maketh me
to lie down
in green pastures....

Psalm 23:2

Illness

Peter and I were married by my father in a simple church wedding on November 4, 1936 in Keyser, West Virginia. Later that same day my new husband and I traveled by train to Washington, D.C., and spent our honeymoon night at the Lee House Hotel. With considerable chagrin Peter had informed me several days before that he had agreed to meet the morning after the wedding with the pastoral committee of New York Avenue Presbyterian Church.

This prestigious old Washington church had literally grown up with the nation's capital. Located within two blocks of the White House, this was where Abraham Lincoln had attended midweek and Sunday services. The President had been scheduled to become a communicant member on April 19, 1865. But five days before, at a few minutes before ten at night, he was shot at close range, a bullet in his brain.

Ever the history enthusiast (with this subject as my major at Agnes Scott), I was awed by such historical ties and intimidated by the new role into which I was being so abruptly plunged. The morning after our marriage, Peter, still contrite about having to leave me alone in our bedroom at the Lee House Hotel, hastened out to meet the church committee already waiting for him in a room upstairs. "I'll telephone down when you're to come up, Catherine," were his parting words.

I dressed carefully, trying to calm my churning emotions. "Please, Lord," the terrified prayer went up, "don't let me embarrass Peter or fail him in any way."

The men and women of the committee, very kind to me and apologetic for interrupting our honeymoon, informed Peter, "We have hunted all over the country, and you are the man we want for the New York Avenue Church."

In the end, Peter turned down the call. There was still, he later wrote the committee, unfinished work for him in Atlanta. Nor did he feel ready for such a big assignment in Washington.

We settled into a cottage on Durand Drive in Atlanta which Peter, the romanticist, had himself selected during our engagement. The house with diamond-shaped, leaded windows sprawled over the top of a hill. The approach to our new home was by a rustic bridge over a brook winding its way around the base of the hill. Behind the house towered a grove of fragrant pine trees.

Having for a long time been a "boarder" in a friend's home, Peter's delight in having a home of his own knew no bounds. Enthusiastically he helped me select every item of furnishing (even in decorating he was not about to let any decision be a solely female one), and with equal zest planted spring bulbs all over the front hillside.

Yet the following year came a second call to the New York Avenue Church: "Since you turned us down, we have combed the country. You are *still* the man we want for this pastorate. Will you come?"

After much prayer, this time the answer had to be "yes." We had both learned during our courtship days that in relation to any specific prayer for guidance our preferences and wills have to be relinquished, laid on God's altar for Him to decide, before He will speak to us.

It was not Peter's personal preference to move to the nation's capital. He loved Atlanta. There he had found his footing, and the thought of leaving was agony. Yet our word was that God had some larger plan in the offing. Yes, we were to go.

So at only 23 the young girl who had fled up the back stairs to avoid involvement with people now had to be hostess to a steady stream of social functions in one of Washington's largest downtown churches. And our new home, the manse on Cathedral Avenue, was next door to "Woodley," the estate of Henry L. Stimson, soon to be Secretary of War.

Still in pursuit of excellence, I was all-out in my determination to succeed in this new role. Prayer for help brought exactly the needed friends to my side. Kind church women like Mrs. Frank Edgington and Isabella Stott filled me in on New York Avenue traditions established by the long string of pastors' wives before me dating back to 1803 and the Thomas Jefferson era. Friends outside the church such as Winifred Hanigan, with her know-how about clothing, took me firmly in hand. I could no longer look like a small-town girl lately come to the big city. Anita Ritter, the mistress of an impressive town house on Massachusetts Avenue, gave me a crash course on Washington protocol, the do's and don'ts of the social and political scene. Soon the intensity of my efforts on all fronts was pushing me past my physical boundaries.

On the snowy Sunday morning of January 21, 1940 I bore my husband a son. Shortly before nine that morning the obstetrician gave Peter and my mother the news, "Congratulations, Dr. Marshall. It's a boy—a fine son."

The new father was ecstatic, almost awestruck. "A *son!* We have a son! How wonderful!"

What to name him? My husband wanted to keep the "Peter" since this had already been in the Marshall family for two generations. Finally, it was decided: the baby's name would be Peter John.

Now our happiness was complete.

Peter had often commented that trouble sends us no telegraphed warnings. So we discovered. Three years after Peter John's birth, I was to find out that even our greatest human desire and all-out effort are never enough.

Suddenly illness struck me down. Having almost fainted at a church meeting, I went to *Johns Hopkins* in Baltimore for a complete physical check-up.

After days of tests and X-rays, Dr. Thomas Sprunt's summary of my medical situation was devastating. The diagnosis was tuberculosis, with me ordered to bed full time. "Since tests have uncovered no infection-spreading bacilli," the doctor explained, "you can stay at home. But you should not, must not, do any housework or, in fact, work of any kind."

"But—but I can't go to bed," I stammered out. "I have a three-year-old son. He needs me."

"Mrs. Marshall," the voice was stern, "total bed rest is mandatory. You have no choice. There is no other cure. Just consider yourself fortunate that it's not a sanitarium."

"Then how long do you think it will take me to get well?" My voice was now almost a whisper.

Dr. Sprunt hesitated a long moment. "Oh, possibly three or four months." Then seeing my stricken face, "Mrs. Marshall, don't feel so badly about it. People *do* recover from tuberculosis."

When I later rushed sobbing into 'Peter's arms to blurt out the news, he was as stunned as I. For once, this most articulate of men was without words and mutely tried to comfort me with touch and caresses.

Dr. Sprunt turned my case over to a Washington lung specialist. A trained nurse was necessary because I was not allowed even to feed myself. Any arm motion might interfere with healing of the chest. Miss Mildred Beall, an RN from our church, volunteered for the emergency.

The specialist's orders: between-meal eggnogs to put weight on me; temperature to be taken six times a day and recorded; one chest X-ray per month; I could get out of bed only to go to the nearby bathroom.

But who would take care of Peter John? And how would any of us explain what was happening to a desolate three-year-old who needed his mother?

Our son was given a tuberculin skin test. Results: negative. So he was allowed to trot in and out of the bedroom. Years later, an indelible picture rises to meet me... Peter John, tall for his age at three, standing with his back to one of the windows, the light behind him making an aureole of his blond curls, staring at me lying there flat in bed, his big round blue eyes sad, hurt, and questioning.

It took all the will power I had to keep from jumping out of bed and running to him to hug him close.

There was no way. There stood the nurse watchfully, with sympathetic eyes.

"You can sit on the bed, and I'll tell you a story," I told Peter John limply. "Maybe later on we can play games together."

Sorry substitutes. I knew full well that such makeshift gestures could not provide the security our son needed. My mother came to take care of him and stayed as long as she could. There followed a long string of maids, nursemaids and assorted government girls. Help of any kind was very scarce, for we were now two years into World War II.

And so one interminable month dragged by after another.

On an especially low day Peter would often stand in the bedroom looking down at me propped up on the pillows, and turn prophet. "Cath'rine, someday you will look back with gratitude on these bleak days as some of the richest of your life." Then, seeing my incredulous inability to receive his words: "Besides, Cath'rine, you know perfectly well, *all* discouragement is of Satan."

I just wanted to throw a book at my Scottish prophet. Whereupon he would grin and pat my cheek and kiss me, turn on his heel and depart for the church office.

Yet looking back, I know that Peter was right. For me those two years in bed were a continuation in depth of the voyage of self-discovery and God-discovery begun in college.

The unforgettable truth of David's Psalm 23 came alive in my experience: "He *maketh* me to lie down in green pastures..." thus sometimes using illness to get our full attention. For me this became a period of equipping—of spiritual preparation—for a tumultuous life of changes, of great, high moments to follow and plunging low points. From the vantage point of the years, I can see now that my being forced to lie down in the green pastures beside very still waters indeed—the isolation of our bedroom— was a time of training. Day by day God was the Teacher and I, the pupil.

I was led through four areas of instruction in the "Green Pasture" classroom. The first had to do with becoming personally acquainted with my Lord, His character, His personality, and how He deals with us humans. And my first assignment in achieving that objective was a big one. I was to read and become knowledgeable about His Book in a new way. For Scripture is the ongoing story of how He has dealt with other men and women living through every conceivable experience; further, in it we discover what His will is for us humans and what it is not.

But there was more to this new way (new for me) of reading Scripture. I was to expect Jesus Himself to speak to me through the messages of His Book as I lay so helpless in bed, then to go further and also communicate to me through the "still, small Voice" in my spirit. After only a few days of this, I felt the necessity of writing down in my Journal the thoughts and insights He was giving.

One of my initial, joyous discoveries about Jesus' will is that having Himself created these awesomely constructed bodies of ours, of *course* He wants us to be well. All over the gospels is Jesus' positive zest for healing the diseased or the handicapped or the blind. In fact, he drew vicious criticism from the religious authorities because He could not wait even 24 hours to heal certain sufferers, thus unabashedly proceeding to break the Jewish Sabbath law, since in Jewish law, healing was "work."

And Scripture makes it plain that Jesus is "the same yesterday, today, and forever," projecting into future ages the same power He had while on earth in the flesh, and specifically passing on that power to future disciples who accept His full Lordship.

Then I had to conclude that my father and many another preacher had been mistaken. For in so many of their seminaries they had been taught that the gospel miracles were extended into the first century for a short time just to get the Church started and were never meant for now or for any future dispensation.

Since this very different message from Scripture was living water for my thirsty spirit and needy body, I received it with overwhelming eagerness. As I shared every bit of it with Peter, he himself dived into the subject of Christian healing. Soon it was spilling over into a series of sermons on this subject.

But then with the over-simplified presumption of the

typical new pupil, I expected Peter's and my joint prayers for my healing to bring quick results.

Not only that, enthusiastically I shared this wonderful discovery with other sufferers. Kenneth Gray, the Scottish groundskeeper on the Stimson estate next door, was dying of a brain tumor. And we had just received word that Gertrude, a dear woman in our church, was also dangerously ill with cancer. Surely, they too could claim for themselves those wondrous promises all through the Bible:

> .... I will put none of those diseases upon thee, which I have brought upon the Egyptians: for *I am the Lord that healeth thee* (italics added).[1]

> Surely he (Jesus on His Cross) *hath* borne our griefs and carried our sorrows.... and with his stripes we are healed.[2]

> Is any sick among you? let him call for the elders of the church; and let them pray over him, anointing him with oil in the name of the Lord: And the prayer of faith shall save the sick, and the Lord shall raise him up[3]...

And had not God promised us that His word "would *never* return unto Him void"?[4] Then surely our claiming with faith any one of these promises for ourselves was the way to healing.

Yet it did not work the way I expected. As test after test followed, my high sedimentation rate was not coming down, and the chest X-rays remained unchanged.

Still I had gained weight, and the trained nurse had long since departed. By June, 1944 I could be up for several periods each day of thirty minutes or so. I would help Peter John dress for school and sometimes eat dinner with the family at night.

But Dr. Sprunt had said three or four months; this was not much progress for fourteen months. What was wrong?

How had I misinterpreted? My Teacher had yet to show me the difference between the presumption that masquerades as faith and real faith. The dividing line between the two lies at the point of one's motive.

When eventually both cancer victims died, I was shown that without realizing it, I had fallen into the trap of presumption in praying for Kenneth Gray and Gertrude Wiber. In effect, like this: "Here's Your Word about healing, Lord, right here. You said it. I believe it and claim it in faith. Now You prove it by doing it."

Later on the truth hit me: Our sovereign, omnipotent God has no need to "prove" anything to any one of us, His creatures. Who are we to ask for *that!*

Then I realized that Jesus' third wilderness temptation had been precisely this one—to substitute presumption for faith. For Satan had led Him into Jerusalem to the highest pinnacle of the temple, and there had taunted Him:

> .... If thou be the Son of God, cast thyself down from hence....[5]

Whereupon Satan, himself knowing Scripture very well, went on to quote one of God's rich promises about angelic protection.

> .... He shall give his angels charge over thee, to keep thee....[6]

Instantly Jesus resisted with the rebuke:

> Thou shalt not tempt the Lord thy God.[7]

Then what *was* the way to real faith? Subsequently I would be shown the difference between the *logos*, one of the two Greek nouns used for God's written word in Scripture, and the *rhēma*. The latter is that part of the logos to which the Holy Spirit points us personally, which He illuminates and brings to life for us in our particular situation.

For instance, out of all the Old Testament *logos*, the Spirit had pointed out to me and emblazoned into my consciousness, nine words from the second verse of Psalm 23: *He maketh me to lie down in green pastures*. Those nine words were His rhēma spoken directly by the Lord Himself to me.

The point is that Jesus will not allow us to use Scripture as only an historical document or as a set of automatic rules. To do so is to ignore the risen, living Lord standing there just beside us at any given moment, as He promised He would, as well as the Holy Spirit in us to interpret, teach and to guide us into Truth (John 16:13). So our Lord stands sentinel over His Book to show us that we can use His word in Scripture with real power only as He Himself energizes it and speaks to us personally through it.

Was not this precisely what He was teaching us when He said,

> You search the scriptures, because you think that in them you have eternal life; and it is they that bear witness to me; *yet you refuse to come to me* that you may have life (italics added).[8]

We cannot do without our study of the logos, for that will ever be the treasure-pool out of which the rhēma is lifted. But only the rhēma has the power-thrust to cope with Satan's onslaught on our spirits, relationships or bodies.

It was increasingly obvious that my courses in the green pastures classroom had scarcely begun.

Gently, the Lord then led me to the second area of instruction: honesty and complete openness and transparency before Him. He is always Light, so I too must walk

in the light. All closet doors, every shuttered room in me must be thrown open. So began months of soul searching.
One Journal entry was deeply revealing.

> This morning came a disturbing thought. For years I have yearned for a free time away from household duties for a quiet time—alone, undisturbed. I was never able to obtain it—until I went to bed sick last March. *Could I have wanted to be rid of the burdens of daily living so much that I had a deep unconscious desire for illness as an escape—once I had made the difficult adjustment to bed rest—from them?* In this sense therefore, my illness has been satisfying. I have had all the time I wanted for quiet communication with the Lord, and others have carried my burdens for me.
>
> The Lord has asked me the direct question, "Do you really want to be well?" In other words, "Are you ready to face up to life, to assume the responsibilites of a normal person?"
>
> I can see that He wants me to be well. He wants to cure me. He wants my answer to be "yes." Therefore, to say "no" would be to frustrate His will.
>
> One part of me wants to be well, but another part of me is still hugging the bed, still exceedingly loath to part with it. I have given Him my will in the matter though, and asked Him to heal this schism in me, to make me want His will totally and to give me joy in it.

Disturbing thoughts! Pondering them, I even sensed that there was significance in the fact that one symptom of my lung disease was breathlessness: ever since moving to Washington I had been literally panting to carry the load I had insisted upon assuming.

Of course from the very beginning of my illness, Peter and I had regularly prayed together for my healing. Thus it was a shock to discover that a split-off part of me could have been voiding these prayers.

What else did I need to uncover so that a healing could take place?

I knew that anything unloving in me, any resentment, unforgiveness or impurity would shut out God, just as a muddy windowpane obscures the sunlight. Painfully, in agony of mind and spirit, I began thinking back over my life, recalling all too vividly all my transgressions and omissions.

There grew in me a desire for total honesty, born of desperation. I began to see that my wholeness was more than the search for physical health. That would come only as inner cleavages were healed, as I was more closely joined to the Source of my being.

In my prayer time I stood before my Maker starkly, stripped of pretenses. My unworthiness shrieked at me. My tendency to overcriticalness, to harsh, hasty judgments. My little jealousies, the self-centeredness that had made me a poor one for teamwork of any kind.

Lying in bed I summoned up the dishonesties of my past. Once in high school I had cheated on an algebra test. Another time when I had been treasurer of a school organization, I had "borrowed" some money from the fund and then paid it back ten days later.

There were dishonesties of a different sort: I had not always been candid with my husband. That same secretiveness I had been aware of as a little girl had surfaced in marriage as a tendency to bar Peter from a corner of my mind and heart. I well knew that this was no way to build a solid marriage.

Through agonizing days I made methodical notes on these ignoble traits and deeds. Then I asked Peter to hear me out on the ones that affected him. He listened, looking pained, not so much at what I was confessing as at the spiritual anguish he saw in me.

Surely now I had done all that was needed to receive a healing. My prayer went like this, "Lord, I have asked You to cleanse me of the dark spots in my life. I claim Your healing right now for my lungs. I ask that this healing be shown on the next tests.'

Eagerly I sought new tests. They were made and the report came back: no change in my lung condition.

Despair settled in. My prayers must still be inadequate. After more than a year in bed, where was I? My husband and four-year-old son needed me more than ever. As I tried to supervise the running of our home from my bed, our household situation was becoming more difficult with every month that passed.

The summer of 1944 came, and we went to our Cape Cod cottage for two and a half months. I got there through the special arrangements of a compartment on the train and an ambulance to meet me at the station.

At the Cape the Lord led me into the third phase of His teaching. First, I had made progress in getting to know Him better. Second, being ruthlessly honest about myself had given me an openness to receive more of His love and riches. Then one morning I found myself with a sudden and intense interest in the Holy Spirit. Questions nagged and would not be silenced. What was so significant about this ghostly-sounding term? Why had the Church clung tenaciously to something seemingly so archaic? In short, what was this Holy Spirit all about?

Obviously, God Himself had carefully planted the curiosity in me, for it was no passing whim. It did not go away, and it had ample emotional, intellectual, and volitional energy fueling it to keep me at a summer-long quest for answers to my questions.

I decided to go to the one place I could count on for final authoritative truth—the Bible. Scripture had never yet deceived me or led me astray. From long experience I knew that the well-worn words from the Westminster Shorter Catechism which I had memorized as a child in Mississippi, had it exactly right: the Bible still is "the only infallible rule of faith and practice."

At the same time I also knew that the search in Scripture could be no random dipping in; it had to be thorough and all-inclusive. A Bible, a Cruden's *Concordance*, a loose-leaf notebook, pen and colored pencils were essential tools.

All summer I gave a minimum of an hour a day to this. Using the various terms referring to the third Person of the Trinity, I looked up every reference in the concordance, Old and New Testament. Morning by morning revealed new truths—new to me at least. Such as that in Old Testament times only certain prophets, priests, and kings were given the Spirit. Even then, the Spirit was given them only "by measure"—that is, a partial giving. So that was why Joel's prophecy, fulfilled at Pentecost, was such startling news: in that great day the Spirit for the first time in history became available to *all* flesh, no longer "by measure" but in His fullness![9]

The messages kept piling up. Though not a one of us can recognize Jesus as who He really is until the Spirit reveals this to us, nonetheless the *fullness* of the Holy Spirit is *not* something that happens automatically at conversion. His coming to us and living within us is a gift, the best gift the Father can give us. But the Father always waits on our volition. Jesus told us that we have to desire this gift of gifts, ask for it—ask for Him.

Something else shimmered through too. It's the Spirit who is the Miracle-Worker. When our churches ignore Him, no wonder they are so devoid of answered prayer. No wonder they have rationalized and developed an unscriptural position: the belief that miracles were only for the beginning years of the faith to get the Church started!

Rather, the truth is that Scripture assumes miracles. And the Helper (one of the names Jesus gave the Holy Spirit) always brings miracles in His wake, moves in the climate of the miraculous, not antithetical to "natural" law, simply superseding it.

By now I was excited. I was also increasingly incredulous about the silence of the churches on this subject. How was it that I could not recall ever hearing a sermon on the Holy Spirit? Why was this not taught in Sunday School?

As the summer wore on I got out of bed more and more for brief periods. One morning I stood at the bedroom window looking out at the garden Peter had so lovingly planted... roses and white hollyhocks, yellow day-lilies, zinnias, all a riot of color... A blue sky above, the sea just over the brow of the hill.

Suddenly I knew that He was calling me to a new step of faith. The subject of obedience was to be the fourth stage of my training. It was a natural follow-up to what I had been learning about His nature, about honesty and about the Holy Spirit. I took a deep breath.

"Lord, from this moment I promise that I'll try to do whatever You tell me in order to get well, insofar as You'll make clear to me what Your wishes are. I'm weak, and many times I'll probably want to renege on this. But Lord, You'll have to help me with that, too."

I was trembling. I knew that this was a more all-out commitment to the Lord than that initial step at age nine when my father had given an altar call, and I had gone forward.

Yet nothing seemed different. The hollyhock faces still nodded at the window. Fluffy clouds still floated in the blue, blue sky. I turned and noted in my journal the date and the hour of the promise I had just made. There would be moments in the future when this pledge would not seem real to me. But it was real, and writing it down would help to remind me.

The proof of the reality of the pledge I had made began coming in the weeks that followed. My physical condition *was* improving. Each morning I would lie in the yard, soaking up sunshine. Next I began regularly joining the family for dinner. Then I began taking short walks some afternoons with Jeffrey, our cocker spaniel, trotting beside me.

It was a joy to stand at the top of the rise in the road and see the sea again, feel the tangy salt air on my cheeks, laugh at the sea wind blowing back Jeffrey's floppy ears as he stood poised, watching the circling gulls. It was even good to feel sand in my shoes.

But this stage too began with a setback. The many months of invalidism had eroded my self-worth as a mother and wife. My son needed me, but I still could not romp with him in the yard, or run with him along the beach, or go for long walks with him to hunt for shells, or to pick blueberries or beachplums. Peter John loved the out-of-doors, and I had to stay mostly inside. In the evenings I could read to him, but I could tell that he was becoming a lonely, wistful child, especially when his father had to be away for preaching or speaking engagements.

My husband was always understanding, loving, sympathetic, but he too resented my confinement indoors. When I heard his throaty, infectious laugh as he visited with the neighbors next door or quickly separated his Scottish brogue from other voices in a neighborhood discussion, my heart ached, and then I would have to battle self-pity.

At this point the imp with the pitchfork could wedge into my thoughts. *Peter is bored with you. He is tired of waiting on you. He likes healthy people around him. Fascinating women are always attracted to him.*

My Journal had this notation:

> There is fear in me that someone else will usurp my place in Peter's heart. I have often tried to make myself believe that it is fear for Peter, his reputation, his ministry and his spiritual welfare. But is it really? Isn't it simply fear for myself? I have prayed about this over and over and get temporary peace, but then soon the

same old fears engulf me again. Today I prayed that God would show me *how* to pray about it, that He would show me the lever by which I could lift it up to Him.

Within a matter of minutes this verse clearly came to me: "Resist not evil." In other words, the way to win out when I feel evil at work in my life and the lives of those I love is not to fight it in the ordinary sense, but to give over those I love completely into the Father's hands, knowing that I am helpless to cope with evil, but that "He is able."

I am to let my loved ones walk on into the lion's den; let evil come on in any guise it chooses—God will shut the lions' mouths. God will surround the one given over to Him with a league of His angels. If I think no evil thoughts, God will not let me be hurt, because I am willing to trust him.

This answer was of enormous help to me. Then in the days that followed God gave me further instructions:

Don't let your whole horizon be filled with Peter. Invite Mac and Polly for games some night.

I did as instructed. It was an evening of fun which Peter thoroughly enjoyed. The next instruction was even more surprising:

Get a new robe—a pretty feminine one.

Peter went with me to help me pick it out. Eagerly, I awaited the next message. It was in the same light vein:

Take an interest in the house again. Try doing your part to make it a home—not just a sleeping place.

As of old I began taking an interest in the garden and kitchen, surprised that strength somehow came to do each little task. I arranged flowers each day for the house. I asked members of the household to gather beach plums so that I could make jelly.

The summer ended, and our family had to return to Washington. With new confidence I went for the usual X-ray check-up of my lungs, only to get the report: "No perceptible change."

And I had thought that I was well on my way out of this morass of illness! Now I plummeted into real despair.

At this new crisis-point Peter John and I went to the eastern shore of Virginia to spend two weeks with my parents who were then living at Seaview. There I tried to reassess the lengthy road I had traveled. For two years I had given my all to learn of the Lord and to try to obey Him. Seemingly, I had tried everything, followed every lead, gone down every path. Yet here I was, still in bed for most of every day.

Only one way was left. Perhaps I had held back one heart's desire. So after many days of struggling, I handed over to God every last vestige of self-will, even my intense desire for complete health. Finally I was able to pray, "Lord, I understand no part of this, but if You want me to be an invalid for the rest of my life—well, it's up to You. I place myself in Your hands, for better or for worse. I ask only to serve You."

In the middle of that night I was awakened. The room was in total darkness. Instantly sensing something alive, electric in the room, I sat bolt upright in bed. Past all credible belief, suddenly, unaccountably, Christ was there, in Person, standing by the right side of my bed. I could see nothing but a deep, velvety blackness around me, but the bedroom was filled with an intensity of power, as if the Dynamo of the universe were there. Every nerve in my body tingled with it, as with a shock of electricity. I knew that Jesus was smiling at me tenderly, lovingly, whimsically—as though a trifle amused at my too-intense seriousness about myself. His attitude seemed to say, "Relax! There's not a thing wrong here that I can't take care of."

His personality held an amazing meld I had never before met in any one person: warm-hearted compassion and the light touch, yet unmistakable authority and kingliness. Instantly, my heart wanted to bow before Him in abject adoration.

Would He speak to me? I waited in awe for Him to say something momentous, to give me my marching orders.

"Go," He said in reply to my unspoken question, "Go, and tell your mother. That's easy enough, isn't it?"

I faltered, thoughts flicking through my mind. "Tell her"—*what* exactly? Jesus' words had an enigmatic quality.

Then came the next thought. *What will Mother think? It's the middle of the night. She'll think I've suddenly gone crazy.*

Jesus said nothing more. He had told me what to do. At that moment I understood as never before the totality of His respect for the free will He has given us and the fact that He will *never* violate it. His attitude said, "The decision is entirely yours."

But I also learned at that moment the life-and-death importance of obedience. There was the feeling that my future hung on my decision. So brushing aside any inconsequential thoughts of Mother's reaction, with resolution I told Him, "I'll do it if it kills me"—and swung my legs over the side of the bed.

How was it that though I could "see" nothing with the retina of my own eyes, I was yet aware of the gentle humor in His eyes as He quietly stood aside to let me pass?

I groped my way into the dark hall to the bedroom directly across from mine and spoke softly to Mother and Dad. Startled, Mother sat bolt upright in bed. "Catherine, is anything wrong? What—what on earth has happened?"

"It's all right," I reassured them. "I just want to tell you that I'll be all right now. It seemed important to tell you tonight. I'll give you the details tomorrow."

When I returned to the bedroom, that vivid Presence was gone. I found myself more excited than I have ever been before or since and more wide awake. It was not until the first streaks of dawn appeared in the eastern sky that I slept again.

The next day that extraordinary visitation was as vivid as it had been during the night hours. Yet there remained the ambiguity of the message I had been told to give Mother. Had Jesus meant that I was as of now totally healed? Or could this be a modern example of the way He had steadily used in the Biblical accounts, "according to your faith be it unto you?"

After breakfast I related the complete story to my parents. Next I wrote Peter a long letter describing every detail of this experience. Peter was never a letter-saver. Yet years later after his death, I found my letter written that day carefully stored among his important papers.

After my return to Washington, we awaited the next chest X-rays with special eagerness. For the first time there was marked improvement. And from then on, steady progress. In six months the doctors pronounced me completely well.

The years bring ever-fresh insights to what remains to this day the most real and vivid experience of my life. For it appeared that Jesus had not come to give an instantaneous healing, but to continue His teaching. There was also the total assurance that He loved me and had been with me all the way.

That night also gave me an understanding of Jesus' resurrection body and of the spiritual bodies we shall have after death. For in the bedroom at Seaview there was no vision as seen with the retinas of my eyes, no voice as heard with my human eardrums. No such crude equipment was needed to "see" Him, to "hear" every word He spoke, to catch every nuance of that compellingly vivid Personality.

Just so shall it be in the next life. Our spiritual bodies will have every faculty of our earthly tabernacles, only with heightened sensitivity and wonderful new freedom. We shall remember and know ourselves to be ourselves and recognize each other. We shall bask in His joyous, loving, delightful companionship.

Most important of all, He had shown me through more than two years of illness that I would always need Him every day for the rest of my life and more, throughout eternity.

At last I had the answer to my child's question about "enjoying Him forever!"

VI

Grief

....and whoever lives
and believes in Me
shall never die.
Do you believe this?

John 11:26— RSV

Grief

At 8:25 that morning the telephone rang. It was a call from the George Washington University Hospital with the message that my husband had died of a heart attack a few minutes before. My mind could not comprehend it. How could *Peter* be dead? Surely God would somehow yet intervene.

"Don't move him. Don't touch him until I get there," was my instinctive reply.

After I arrived at the hospital, the young doctor who walked with me to the door of Peter's room was solicitous. His eyes searching my face, he asked quietly, "Are you *sure* you want to go in there alone?"

"Oh, *yes*," I told him.

Saying nothing more, he withdrew.

As I opened the door and stepped inside the small room, there was the instantaneous awareness that I was not alone. Yet the man I loved was not in the still form on the bed. Though I did not understand it then and cannot explain it now, I knew that Peter was near and alive. And beside him was another Presence of transcendent glory, the Lord he had served through long years—years stretching back to his young manhood in Scotland.

Having already experienced that glory, how could I ever again doubt the fact of immortality? In a deep and intuitive way, beyond argument or intellectual process, deeper than tears, transcending words, came the knowledge that human life does not end in six feet of earth.

Yet the realization of the splendor was not to last. In that still hospital room, at a precise moment, the two vivid presences withdrew. Suddenly I saw Death stripped bare, in all its ugliness. With very human eyes I saw it: the fact of the man so dear to me. *There's nothing pretty about death. Those who sentimentalize it, lie. Carbon dioxide escaping from the sagging jaw. The limp hands. The coldness and white, white pallor of the flesh.*

Shivering, I rose to leave the room. I knew that this would be the last time on this earth that I would look upon my husband's face. So there in the hospital room, I said my last *au revoir*.

Now there was nothing to do but walk out. I sensed that out beyond the door, out beyond the chilly hospital corridor, a new life awaited me. That was the last thing in the world I wanted. But then Peter had not wanted a new life either—not yet anyway—not at just 46. And already he was embarked on that other adventure.

Two paces from the door, I was stopped as by an invisible hand. As I paused, a message was spoken with emphasis and clarity, not audibly, but with that peculiar authority I had come to recognize as the Lord's own voice: *Surely, goodness and mercy shall follow you all the days of your life.*

It was His personal pledge to me and to a son who would now sorely miss his father.

Looking back, I could see that God had been preparing

me for the shock of Peter's death during my two-year illness. The "green pastures" classroom had taught me my helplessness and the how of depending on Him as my only strength and resource.

During the funeral preparations and all the myriad decisions to be made, it was as though I were taken over and managed. In addition, a sort of protective shield was placed over my emotions. Somehow for those days I was lifted into a higher realm. Was *this*, I wondered, what it felt like actually to be living in the kingdom of God on earth?

The series of detailed instructions that issued from my mouth were straight from Him. The seeming maturity I was showing to Peter John, to my family, and to the members of our grieving congregation was the gift of His pure grace.

Then about eight days after Peter's death, suddenly that higher realm in which I had been so lovingly enveloped was gone, and I plummeted to earth to stand again on feet of clay in the valley where salt tears and loneliness and the fear of coping alone with the problems of everyday life are all too real.

My Lord was nearby of course, ready to help me all the way. Yet I sensed that another painful but necessary growth process stretched ahead.

At this point, the first need of the bereaved person is for comfort. God has pledged us that as part of our rightful inheritance as children of the King:

> For thus saith the Lord... As one whom his mother comforteth, so will I comfort you....[1]

This comfort had certainly been given me in the hospital room just after Peter's death. And it had continued during the days of shock and numbness right afterwards, granted,

I'm sure, by a loving Father who recognized my desperate need of knowing that He had not deserted me.

Then I found that some of the loveliest words of Scripture are for the longer-term soreness of heart that follows:

> I will not leave you comfortless....[2]

> ... he hath sent me to bind up the brokenhearted... to appoint unto them that mourn in Zion, to give unto them beauty for ashes, the oil of joy for mourning, the garment of praise for the spirit of heaviness...[3]

I was surprised to find that a great number of promises in the Bible are directed specifically to widows and to children who have had to part with one or both parents:

> The Lord will destroy the house of the proud; but he will establish the border of the widow.[4]

> Yet leave to me your orphans, I will save them; let your widows trust to me.[5]

And some of the most beautiful assurances of all are contained in that extraordinary 54th chapter of Isaiah addressed to us women, a chapter to be read over and over in its entirety by the deserted or bereaved until absorbed into one's bloodstream:

> Fear not . . . (thou) shalt not remember the reproach of thy widowhood any more . . . For the Lord hath called thee as a woman forsaken and grieved in spirit . . . with great mercies will I gather thee....

> And all thy children shall be taught of the Lord; and great shall be the peace of thy children.[6]

Yet there is another side to God's comfort for His ways are never man's ways. His is not the feather-cushion kind or a pat on the cheek, "There, there, dear child." It does not tiptoe into the chamber of grief with its shuttered windows: it marches in. There is steel at its backbone. It is a bugle call for reinforcements. It makes us remember that the word "comfort" is derived from the word *fortis*—which means "strength" or "strong."

God comforts us with strength by adding resources. His way is not to whittle down the problem but to build up our ability to cope with it...

> Fear not; (there is nothing to fear) for I am with you; do not look around you in terror and be dismayed, for I am your God. I will strengthen you and harden you (to difficulties); yes, I will help you; yes, I will hold you up and retain you with My victorious right hand of rightness and justice."[7]

It should not surprise us that a mainstay of God's comfort-resources are His people, the fellowship of believers. In the healing of my grief a first important step He asked me to take was to open my heart wide to other people.

When a deep injury to the spirit has been sustained—and grief *is* a real wound in the spirit and the emotions—the tendency of the sorrowing is to shut the heart and bar the door lest hurt be heaped upon hurt. Therefore, His insistence that we not give in to this will seem stringent indeed at the time.

When my own private crisis came, certainly I knew nothing about the way out of grief. I had never heard that psychologists and psychiatrists consider the matter of establishing new patterns of interaction with other human beings one of the most important laws for recovery. Or that from the standpoint of the experienced Christian counselor, the sorrowing one who almost involuntarily shuts his heart against his friends and lets bitterness creep in is, in a tragic way, insulating himself against that re-energizing love of God.

Part of the miracle of God's direction to me was His enabling me immediately after my husband's death to open my heart wider than ever before. I knew that it had to be God's doing because something broke through that deep reserve and thirst for privacy I had known since childhood.

The Sunday after Peter's death I was able to return to the New York Avenue Church and to sit with Peter John in our usual place in the pastor's pew. It would be excruciatingly hard, that I knew. For it would dramatize for me as nothing else could the fact that Peter Marshall would never again stand in that pulpit.

At points in the service I was unable to stop the flow of tears. Yet somehow, in thus facing reality, they became healing tears. God granted me the immediate gift of a warm-hearted Chinese woman who reached out to cover my hand with hers. I knew that she was sitting there ministering to me through prayer during the entire service.

The next day one couple who had been particularly fond of Peter came by the manse and sought me out in my bedroom. I remember that the young wife, her cheeks wet with tears, threw her arms around my neck. "Darling," she cried, "I love you so. We're going to have to stick awfully close together now."

My split-second choice at that moment was made by instinct—not in my conscious mind at all. It was a choice of whether or not I would merely politely tolerate such an overflowing exuberance of love—or really accept it. In yielding to it, I found a oneness with all human beings, a kinship with all suffering in the world—an authentic glimpse of the kingdom of God actually at work in a given community.

And so I opened wide the door of the manse. People came with warm handclasps and tear-filled eyes. They brought what they knew best how to make—soup, chicken salad, baked ham, angel food cake, custard, chess pie. The love that flowed like a great tidal wave through the Christian community of our church family blessed us all.

Those who helped me most were the few who understood about the stringent side of God's way of comforting and avoided the soft and gentle commiserating words which carry the unspoken message, "I feel sorry for you." Our response to that is usually self-pity. And self-pity is one of the worst of all stumbling blocks to the healing of grief.

Understanding what deadly poison the "poor-me" attitude is, how much I have come to value those tough-minded friends who dealt with me incisively when I was ill or grief-stricken.

One such friend was Anita, a tall, stately woman with the gift of rare discernment. I recalled one occasion during my illness when she had come to the manse to call.

On this particular afternoon, Anita had not walked into my bedroom—she had marched in. She had not even bothered to sit down.

Standing in the middle of the big room, she had cleared her throat as for a speech. Her eyes were sparking as much light as the star sapphire on her right hand. "Catherine, you've been on my mind for days. I've been tempted to feel sorry for you. Well, I'll be damned if I'll feel sorry for you. Forgive the language, but I feel just that vehemently about it.

"Pity wouldn't help you a bit. Besides, why should I pity you? You have all you need—the strength and guidance of God Himself."

Her words had been flung at me like ice water striking my face. I might have resented them, but I had not. In fact, when I had recovered from the first shock of the ice water, I had felt exhilarated, even as Anita had hoped I would.

Enough of this weakness and secluded life, had been my immediate reaction. I'm going to get out of here. And courage and the will to fight weakness and disease had mounted in me like mercury rising in a thermometer in the sun.

That day Anita had taught me an unforgettable lesson about the efficacy of following God's way in seeking to comfort one another. During those years, I had had hundreds of sickroom calls. Yet that one visit of Anita's towered like a mountain top above the others. Even remembering it helped because this was the kind of friend I came to value especially in the slough of grief.

Still another part of the down-to-earth quality of God's comfort was my discovery during those days after Peter's death that Scripture bathes the subject of death and immortality in the sunlight of normalcy, lifts it out of the realm of the dark and sinister unknown.

One of the reasons Jesus deliberately left the realm of glory to take on the limitations of human flesh for 33 years was so that

> . . . He might deliver and completely set free all those who through the (haunting) fear of death were held in bondage throughout the whole course of their lives.[8]

Part of the process of setting us free is reassurance piled upon reassurance in Scripture that at the death of the physical body, the real person inside lives on without interruption. The Bible tells us that the next life is not only a fully conscious one with every intellectual and spiritual faculty intact but that these faculties are heightened...

> For now we see through a glass, darkly; but then face to face: now I know in part; but then shall I know even as also I am known.[9]

This is the assurance that our loved one will be able to remember, to think, to will, to love, to worship, and to understand so much more on the other side of the barrier of death. Thus our new life will be no sleeping unconscious or unfeeling existence.

In Christ's parable of the rich man and Lazarus, He pictures both men as having a fully conscious life after death, of recollecting earthly life with no break in memory.

Then there are Christ's words from the cross:

> And he (one of the thieves who was being crucified)
> said unto Jesus, 'Lord, remember me when thou comest
> into thy kingdom.'
> And Jesus said unto him 'Verily, I say unto thee,
> Today shalt thou be with me in paradise.'[10]

Christ's promise to the dying thief would have been nonsense had He not meant that after death on that very day, both He and the thief would know themselves to be themselves, would remember that they had suffered together, would recognize each other.

That memorable night at Seaview when the risen Lord had come to me, I had learned first-hand about our spiritual bodies. Now I found the verification in Scripture.

"There is a natural body, and there is a spiritual body," the Apostle Paul tells us. Then he goes on to more detail. This spiritual body will give us much the same recognizable appearance that we have had on earth, except that if imperfect, deformed or diseased, all will be made perfect:

> It (the body) is sown in corruption; it is raised in
> incorruption: It is sown in dishonor; it is raised in glory:
> it is sown in weakness; it is raised in power....[11]

Once again, the illness experience had been such perfect preparation for the Valley of the Shadow. How gracious God was to have granted me that fleeting experience of first-hand, practical knowledge about the spiritual body. I knew now how real it is, how vivid are the physical faculties of sight, hearing, speech, thinking, smell, touch— only somehow transferred to the spiritual realm about which we know so little. More, how beautiful will be the casting off of the limitations of flesh and of earth's hampering framework of time and space.

Most of the sorrowing find it necessary to deal with the "what if" stage. I was no exception. Almost always this period of sharp questioning and self-reproach with some guilt mixed in, comes after the first numbness has worn off.

I remember that it was my mother who helped me through this as she sat in the little needlepoint rocker near me and with rare wisdom, simply listened. She offered no advise or pat words of sympathy. It was enough that she was there mourning with me, mixing her tears with mine. Unflinchingly, she allowed me to pour over her the broadside of negative, sometimes bitter thoughts.

After Peter's first so-sudden heart attack in late March 1946, had I done everything possible to save my husband? Had it really been God's will that Peter die? Or was this just another failure on my part?

Then I remembered that I had been annoyed with my husband and childishly petulant on the last Sunday of his life. On the way home from church, we had turned on the radio. Just as Peter had brought the car to a halt before our front door, the announcer had mentioned the approaching Saint Valentine's Day.

Peter had reached across for my hand. "Will you be my valentine, Catherine?" he had asked gaily.

And I had withdrawn my hand and ruthlessly crushed his small moment of gaiety by replying sarcastically, "Oh, sure! I'll be your valentine, having a gay time all by myself here in Washington while you're making a speech in Des Moines. I hear you decided to accept that invitation, too."

For a passing moment a look of pain had crossed his face. The remembrance of that look hurt me now.

Between sobs I told Mother of that episode and verbally whipped myself. "How could I have been like that? What on earth got into me? I'm supposed to be a woman—not a child. How could I have been so immature, so disgustingly petty?"

Grief fanned into flame my resentment against all those who had known of Peter's heart condition and yet had persisted in heaping demands on him. These demands had proliferated from 1947 on, after he had become Chaplain of the United States Senate.

"How often I've stood by," I said to Mother, "and heard someone say to Peter in one moment, 'Dr. Marshall, please don't overdo. You just must take care of yourself.' And then in the very next moment, plead with him to speak to their pet group. *Their* organization was always different; their group should always be the exception. How selfish can human beings be?"

Then, having struck out at people, I lashed out again at God. "Why? Why did it have to end this way?" I asked bitterly. "Were Peter and I duped? Has everything that Peter preached been just pious nonsense? If God is a God of love and has the power to help us, why didn't He do something about Peter's heart?"

Sorely troubled, Mother knew any words she might speak would make little difference at the moment. Every bitter thought—against myself and other people and God—had to come up and out.

She understood my need for an answer to the agonizing question every sorrowing person asks, "Where is the God of love who cares about the individual in what has happened?" She also recognized that if I was not allowed to ask this question, get it all out, there could be no healing of my bruised heart; that without this emptying of the bitterness and negativity, I would not later be able to receive the balm of Christ's healing oil. I would either flee life or live it on a busy-busy level, dragging an anesthetized spirit after me.

"In God's own time," she told me quietly, "you will get God's answers."

Mother knew so well that God alone can finally heal the brokenhearted. Grief is a mutilation, a gaping hole in the human spirit. After all, the ties that bind parents to children, brothers to sisters, and husbands to wives are the deepest of bonds, as real as love is real. Some beloved person has been wrested, torn bodily from one's life. The hurt is nonetheless factual even though the family physician cannot clinically prove it; Christ is still the greatest Physician to the spirit.

It was Rebecca Beard, a human doctor, who helped to put my sore heart into the hands of the Great Physician. Several years before, Rebecca had given up her medical practice to work full time in spiritual therapy. When I heard that she was passing through Washington briefly, I sought an appointment with her.

Soon I was pouring out my heart to her—all the hurt of it, the ineptness and the fear I felt about facing the future alone.

At first, as my mother had, this physician-friend just let me talk, saying little, offering no advice for the future. She was a motherly type of woman; sometimes there were tears in her warm eyes as she watched me.

Then finally, when the well of my emotion was dry, she said quietly, "As a doctor, I have only one remedy to offer for what ails you. Let's talk to Jesus about it."

Her prayer was a simple, heartfelt claiming of Christ's promise to bind up the brokenhearted. My heart had been broken and emptied. Now was the time to ask that He take it, make it whole again and fill it up with His love. When the two of us had finished talking to Him, she gathered me in her ample arms. That afternoon His gentle hand was laid on my heart.

And I knew that from that moment the healing had begun somewhere in the depths of my being.

Catherine at Samuel D. Engel's desk, Hollywood (1953)

VII

His
Call To Me

For we are fellow workers for God....
Each man's work will
become manifest; for the day will
disclose it, because it will
be revealed with fire, and the fire
will test what sort of work
each one has done.

I Corinthians 3:9,13—RSV

His Call To Me

The three men from the church were kind, eager to be helpful, but determined that I be realistic about my bleak financial situation. One of them, a knowledgeable insurance agent, had everything neatly worked out on a graph.

"I recommend that you spread Dr. Marshall's insurance over a reasonably long period of time. After all, it will be eight years before Peter John goes to college."

"How much income will we have each month?" I asked.

"One hundred and seventy-one dollars a month for the first eight years. Then the monthly income will take a drop."

"You must be clear-eyed about this, Catherine," chimed in the other businessman. "That won't be enough to maintain your car. You should probably sell it."

"And you're scarcely strong enough yet to hold down a real job," the other friend added. "It's only been two years since you regained health. By the way, what *could* you do job-wise?"

I began to have a suffocating feeling. "I—I don't quite know. I married right out of college—have only a bachelor of arts degree—not even teacher training. I couldn't be a secretary, I don't know shorthand."

The three men had all been Peter's close friends and were genuinely fond of me. Yet they considered me a poor prospect indeed for a bread-earning widow. I could see it in their eyes, feel it in the way they were approaching the subject of finances.

"I don't think you realize how desperate your situation is," one friend insisted, trying to drive home his point. "One hundred and seventy-one dollars a month in Washington won't even cover the bare necessities."

"The Cape Cod cottage is a tangible asset," another added. "I think you should sell it quickly."

The three men left that night distressed because I did not seem fearful enough. They suspected that they had failed to convince me that I was facing a severe financial crisis. They were right. It was not so much a stubborn refusal to accept their gloomy forecasts—financial or otherwise. Rather that even as a protective shield had been thrown over my emotions at the time of Peter's death and for a few days afterward, now I felt that same shield covering my faith regarding the future. It was not my doing; Someone else was sheltering me. Their fear-darts, however well meaning, had simply hit the protective covering and bounced off.

Yet I had not argued with these solicitous friends because facts and figures had substantiated all they had said. There the facts were (as the workaday world sees facts), all down on paper in neat columns and graphs. How could figures lie? Yet somehow I felt that they did lie. Something was missing.

Alone in my room I stared out the window into the moonlight shining on swaying treetops. In so many areas I was naïve, unknowledgeable. At thirty-five I had never in my life figured out an income tax blank, had a car inspected, consulted a lawyer or tried to read an insurance policy. Railroad timetables were an enigma to me. It was a rare occasion indeed when my household checking account balanced. I had never invested any money or braved a trip to the city of New York by myself.

The moonlight outside was almost white. One brilliant star above the treetops winked like a solitaire. Suddenly, standing there at the window, I knew what the missing factor was. My three friends who had meant to be so kind, who saw my many inadequacies, had reckoned without God.

I remembered how often Peter had faced this same attitude with his church officers. He would come home from a trustees' meeting looking sad and grim. "Cath'rine, no matter what's presented for their approval, their litany is always the same, 'But Dr. Marshall, where is the money coming from?' Where's their faith in God?"

But either God was there—I Am That I Am—a fact more real than any figures or any graphs, or He was not. If He was there, then reckoning without Him was certainly not being "realistic"; in fact, it could actually be the most hazardous miscalculation of all.

God had met me in Peter's hospital room that morning only an hour or so after his death. I had felt His Presence, known He was there. And the words He had spoken so clearly to me even as I had been about to leave the room were emblazoned on my consciousness: *Goodness and mercy shall follow you all the days of your life.*

It was His personal pledge to me. In the days ahead and indeed, during all the years to follow, I would hug that promise close to me.

So now I was facing one of those crises—a crossroad of life. I had to walk on into that new life, but which road should I take?

One decision I could make immediately: I would refuse to be destitute. The thrust of Mother's teaching in this regard had gone deep, so deep. Why should any child of the King consent to poverty?

So I claimed for Peter John and for me that great promise that stirs the imagination and sends creativity whirring into action...

> And we know that all things work together for good
> to them that love God, to them who are the called
> according to His purpose.[1]

How often Peter, in quoting this promise, from the pulpit, had pointed out that God never meant for this "good" to be limited to spiritual blessing; that He knows perfectly well our need for rent money and clothes and food.

But now the Spirit was singling out of this promise, His *rhēma* for me at this moment—*to them who are the called according to His purpose.*

I felt a tingling at the top of my spine. Dared I entertain a hope that He could actually be calling me for a purpose of His own; was there some special work for *me* to do?

A sense of adventure crept in. It would be exciting to see what God wanted me to do with my new life. I sensed that when His grand design for me was revealed in its entirety, it would include so much more than provision for economic needs.

But I could never have imagined that His answer to the "why" of this new life would embody more than just seeing that Peter's ministry did not die with his mortal body; that He might want to extend that ministry above all that I could ask or think or dream, all the while giving me unimaginable joy in being a part of that.

But meanwhile there were other things I was learning which I would share in the years ahead with those who had lost a loved one through death, divorce, or separation. For one thing, no major decisions should be made in the weeks immediately following the crisis period. Almost always one experiences deep shock in such separation. Sufficient time must be allowed for recovery before it is possible to have a firm basis for making any decisions.

I was fortunate in not having to make an immediate selection of where my son and I were going to live. We were able to stay in the manse for almost ten months while the church searched for a new pastor. During those months familiar, beloved, and once-shared possessions helped to soothe my sore spirit, such as Peter's wildly turbulent seascapes on the walls of our home and the well-worn games in the game closet. Being able to walk our cocker spaniel Jeff, along the same familiar few blocks, was balm to my spirit rather than added hurt.

Next, I found that the mechanics connected with separation are actually helpful, though they may seem hard. In the very beginning one may feel that these practical activities are an intrusion into grief or despair. The wounded person looks out on the world with new eyes, marveling that other people on the streets and in the shops are going on about their business as if nothing has happened, as if everything were just the same.

How is it possible, one wonders at such a time, to force oneself to sort out dresser and desk drawers; to change living habits; to rearrange finances; to put one's mind to business and insurance details; to cope with the dozens of telephone calls and personal messages, and deal with the loving concern of friends and family?

The truth is that the empty heart needs work for the hands to do. I learned that there is a certain therapy in these necessary mechanics. Peter's church office had to be emptied of all his possessions. On the self-appointed day I climbed the stairs to the office and sat down at Peter's desk. Impulsively I opened the front middle drawer. There was Peter's date book open to the week of January 23. It was to have been a busy week. I sat there staring at it. *How precipitously death invades life.*

And inserted in the front of the date book was a newspaper clipping with the caption, "Would You Live a Longer Life If You Could?"

I glanced up, and there on the top of one of the bookcases was a carefully detailed model of John Knox's house in Edinburgh. Once Peter and I had walked hand in hand up those narrow steps into that queer little medieval house. "On, memories that bless and burn. . ."

There followed hours of taking Peter's books off the shelves, packing them into boxes. Pictures—a group of etchings, all seascapes, and a fine lithograph of the American flag—had to be taken down and packed, all drawers emptied. Yet as I worked that day there was a strange, sweet easing of my pain.

An entry in my Journal at this time charted my course of action:

> I must use part of my Quiet Time to hear what the Lord has for me to do. He has indicated that He does have a plan for my life. Could it be that my dream of being a writer is part of this plan? I must be open to everything that could lead to this: letters, invitations, counsel of friends.

Several days later a friend wrote to me: ". . . . the following matter is on my heart and a like sentiment has come my way from various people in the congregation. I, along with thousands, earnestly hope that you will see to it that Peter's sermons, his prayers in the Senate and from his pulpit, will be published."

Soon these requests for a book making some of Peter's sermons and prayers available to everyone were coming at me from all sides.

But I had no contacts in the publishing field. No doubt friends could have been my go-betweens, but I shrank from pushing for this. Therefore, my response was the prayer for a sure sign. "Lord, if this is *Your* plan, then *You* open the door for it. That way I'll *know.*"

Within six weeks of this prayer I received letters from three publishers asking the same question: Would I be interested in compiling and editing a book of Peter Marshall's sermons and prayers? It seemed that God's word was "go."

After checking out the publishing houses and conferring with several knowledgeable friends, of the three I chose the Fleming H. Revell Company in New York. A contract was worked out whereby I would edit a minimum of 12 of my husband's sermons for a book to be published in late fall, 1949. A small advance was provided which helped me with living expenses during the next six months.

Peter had left some 600 complete sermon manuscripts filed in three worn, black-and-white cardboard boxes. The proposed book could include at the most only 15 to 20. The problem was, on what basis should I go about trying to choose from the 600?

While the editors at Fleming Revell had caught a whiff of excitement about Peter's preaching, I know now that more deliberate reflection on their part, plus reactions from tough-minded salesmen, had quickly tempered their enthusiasm once I began work on the book. "Fond widow editing preacher's sermons for publication" did not exactly make them envision a best-seller.

A casual or hurried job on my part could have defeated the project or produced a volume with a modest sale at best. But as the editing job progressed, I began to experience the deep satisfaction and inner contentment known only to those who have found the right vocational spot for them.

It was not that my adjustment to bereavement was complete. In fact, it had scarcely begun. But in spite of the empty void inside me, it was as if I had finally come home to my natural habitat.

The work of editing; the virility of the sermon material itself; Peter's extraordinary handling of the English language—his intuitive use of the precise word; his humor;

the instinctive knowledge that people near and far would find these messages food for their hungry spirits; the flashing facets of Peter's personality that leapt from the typewritten pages; the feel of paper and pencil in my hands—every bit of it was pure joy. And gradually I began to see that many things done in the years gone by had been meant as preparation for this task.

During the long quiet days of work on the editing of the manuscripts while Peter John was in school, a scene out of the past came unbidden to my mind, that scene in that room I had loved so—father's study—with books lining the walls floor to ceiling on several sides of the room. In that setting a love for books—for reading them, handling them, collecting them, even the dream of someday writing them, had become a part of my life.

From girlhood, I had been haunted by the dream of writing. In college the desire to write was ever with me. Preparing term papers in English or history was not work, but joy.

Marriage to Peter had postponed the fulfillment of the dream but not erased it. The Christmas after our first trip to Scotland, I had presented Peter with a neatly typed *Journal of a Trip to Scotland*, bound in a handsome leather notebook. The writing had been a labor of love, meant for his eyes alone. Something in me decreed that I had to keep on writing. Whether or not any of it was ever published seemed almost incidental.

Then during the period of illness, a portion of my soul-searching to evaluate the meaning of human life and mine in particular, had been the need to find out whether my girlhood desire to be a writer had been truly a God-given dream:

> If I thought I wanted to be a writer, but what I really wanted was fame or money, or even that my name would not die after me, then this would be false desire. But such I do not believe to be the case.

I have always loved ideas. I've enjoyed trying to express them in as accurate and beautiful a way as possible since I was a little girl. It gives me real soul-satisfaction. . .

After pondering all this for many days, necessarily long quiet days, I had decided that this dream passed the most honest tests I could devise. And just about that time two verses in the New Testament had seemed written in fire:

And this is the confidence that we have in Him, that, if we ask anything according to His will, He heareth us:

And if we know that He hear us, whatsoever we ask, we know that we have the petitions that we desired of Him.[2]

If the wish to be a writer was God's will for me, He would hear me when I asked for the help with it I needed; and if He heard, then this wish would someday be granted. The timing would be up to Him. So I sent this particular dream wafting back toward heaven with the confident awareness that He had already heard.

Now five years later strange events had placed the pencil back in my hands. Deep within me the message came, "There is a fullness of time for all things. This is the fullness of time appointed for your girlhood dream of being an author. This editing and writing is now My call on your new life."

If this work assigned me was truly God's "call," then He would send me to the right persons at the right time to give a special quality to this book of sermons.

At that juncture I remembered something else, another of Peter Marshall's favorite promises, prized because it had been tested and tested again in the crucible of his experience, and never found wanting. . .

"But seek ye first the kingdom of God, and his righteousness; and *all these things* shall be added unto you" (italics added).[3]

For me this had to mean that if I obeyed God's call for a vocation, then "all these things," meaning provision, would follow, simply be "added unto us."

During the next five months I watched unfolding before my wondering eyes that very juxtaposition of ideas, persons, and events for which I had asked God. Then this meticulous intermeshing of so many factors must be what the Apostle Paul had meant by the "working together" for good in that great Romans' promise.

First, a group of young adults in our church wanted to help with the massive job of reading and screening Peter's 600 sermon manuscripts. Sitting around our dining room table, the entire room awash in papers, these were stimulating, sometimes hilarious work sessions.

Someone would break the silence with "You've just *got* to hear this. . .

> 'Church members in too many cases are like deep sea divers, encased in the suite designed for many fathoms deep, marching bravely to pull out plugs in bath-tubs.'"[4]

A few moments later someone else would begin chuckling...

> Modern politics appear to be related to the art of conjuring. . . The skeletons in the nation's cupboards are replaced by the rabbits that come out of the politicians' hats.[5]

How did Peter ever think of such metaphors and similes?

> It is the same old brass of willful disobedience coated with the chromium of the 20th century.[6]

And then one evening Tom Wharton, a member of the group, made a significant discovery. The text of the sermon pamphlets, which the church had for years been distributing and selling for 10 cents, had been printed in the usual prose style.

But when Tom compared a passage from one of these pamphlets with the comparable passage in the typed manuscript Peter had carried into the pulpit with him, Tom was startled at the difference. The words of the typed copy sprang alive on the page. One could all but hear the sound of Peter's voice. The reader caught the same emphasis of word and clause that the oral delivery had supplied. And the extra amount of white space (for in the typed sermons the copy looked rather like blank verse) made reading sermons a delight rather than a chore.

There followed days of testing this out by typing a number of passages both ways and then trying them out on a variety of people.

The pamphlet form looked like this:

> To know great art—the red of Titian, the sunsets of Turner, the seas of Winslow Homer; to have felt the spell of epic heroisms; to have swung to the rhythmic pulse of Homer; to have known the tenderness of Francis of Assisi; to engrave the prologue to the Gospel of John on the heart; and to march with the majestic affirmations of the Nicene Creed: It does something inside a man. It stretches him mentally, stirs him morally, inspires him spiritually....[7]

But the typed sermon looked so different, so alive:

To know great art—the reds of Titian. . .
    the sunsets of Turner. . .
   the seas of Winslow Homer. . .
To have felt the spell of epic heroisms. . .
   to have swung to the rhythmic pulse of Homer. . .
    to have known the tenderness of St. Francis of Assisi. . .

To engrave the prologue to the Gospel of John on the
   heart... to march with the majestic affirmations of
   the Nicene Creed:

It does something inside a man.
It stretches him mentally. . .
   stirs him morally. . .
      inspires him spiritually. . .

All our readers agreed: the stair-step device which Peter used only for his own delivery would make all the difference on the printed page. The unanimous decision was that the Creator-God was at this point leading us to something new in publishing.

But then I faced the question, how could I present such an innovative (and probably expensive) typesetting idea to an old, conservative publishing house? Still, if an Omnipotent God was guiding this, He would see to its acceptance.

He did. The Revell Company agreed to try it. I learned later that they almost immediately regretted their decision since the stair-step arrangement of the words demanded a great deal of thought about book design, compounded the copyreader's task of marking the manuscript for the printer, typesetting problems and so forth.

Meanwhile our efforts and prayers were stirring interest in the book throughout the country the way ripples spread out in a pond after a stone is dropped into the water. Attention to small details pays dividends. When each person involved in a project communicates to others, a chain-reaction effect results.

Catching wind of this, I was dismayed to find that a first printing of only 10,000 copies had been ordered for the book to be published under the title of *Mr. Jones, Meet the Master*. I protested to the head of the Revell Company that they should print at least 25,000.

Mr. Barbour, then elderly, had been a publisher for a long time. He was not a tall man. But as he drew himself up to his full height, he seemed to tower over me. *"Mrs. Marshall,"* his voice was scathing, *"everyone* in publishing knows that posthumus sermons never sell."

With that, he closed the subject.

One final decision remained. An Introduction to *Mr. Jones* was needed. Whom should we ask? The publisher felt that some national figure and a prominent friend of Peter's, like Senator Kenneth Wherry or Senator Arthur Vandenberg, should be invited to write it. I refused to believe that Peter's material needed a "name" to launch it.

Moreover, it seemed to me that an altogether different sort of Introduction was needed for Peter Marshall's sermons. The readers should have a thumbnail sketch of Peter's flavorsome personality, including his refusal to be stereotyped in Washington where political and power stereotype has long been the order of the day. And the sketch should include Peter's strong tastes and convictions, even his goofs and idiosyncrasies. I felt that I alone could write a prologue like that.

Next question: How to present *that* idea to the by-this-time somewhat weary executives of the Revell Company? I sensed that these publishers looked on me as a sentimental widow without either writing talent or experience, bitten with grandiose ideas about "her" book as she sought to idealize her dead husband.

So I approached them cautiously, "Would you be willing," I asked over the phone, "to let me put on paper the Introduction I have in mind? If you don't like it, then you can throw it in the wastebasket and go ahead with other plans."

There was an almost audible gasp of relief at the other end of the line. On these no-lose terms, Revell agreed to my attempting to set something on paper.

One night, sitting propped up in bed, with the floor awash in papers, I wrote a seven-page sketch of Peter Marshall, the man. I called it "Here Is Peter Marshall" and sent it off to New York.

Two days later the publisher telephoned me. There was undisguised surprise in his voice. "Three of us have read your Introduction. We didn't think you—that is, well, I mean, it couldn't be more perfect. Of course we want to use it.''

Those seven pages of original writing turned out to be my foot in the door of the publishing world.

The first printing of 10,000 copies of *Mr. Jones, Meet the Master* was sold out before Publication Day was over. For the next year the publisher enlisted help from several printers to meet the demands for the book. There was no point in any "I told you so." Rather, I knew that it was cause for rejoicing.

When informed that *Mr. Jones* was to make *The New York Times* best-seller list, I was not as impressed as I should have been. For me, the real success of the book was measured in an altogether different way—by the hundreds of letters that were pouring in trying to express to me what the messages of the sermons were meaning in the lives of men and women.

The success of *Mr. Jones, Meet the Master* led to Edward Aswell, then editor-in-chief at the McGraw-Hill Book Company, reaching out for me. He had in mind a second book of sermons. Instead, I suggested that the story of the man behind the sermons needed to be told.

Mr. Aswell responded favorably to that idea but following an editor's usual procedure, asked to see an outline of the book I had in mind, together with a chapter or two and/or sample segments of manuscript.

By then Peter John and I had settled into "Waverley", the Cape Cod cottage for the summer. For days I struggled with an outline, a chore in which I am not adept.

One evening after I had gone to bed, a thought pierced my mind like a stroke of lightning—the real significance of the last words Peter had spoken to me on this earth.

The scene vividly before me, I turned on the bedside light, grabbed a pencil and pad off the nightstand and began to write feverishly to transfer it to paper... The setting, the front hall in our Cathedral Avenue home in Washington; the time three a.m., January 25. Parked on the street outside, the ambulance waited to take Peter to the hospital. I longed to go with him, but could not since that would have left Peter John alone in the big house.

Peter had looked up at me from the stretcher which the orderlies had set down for a moment. He must have known more surely than I the import of this moment. All the love in his eyes reached out for me. "Cath'rine," the words were gentle, yet somehow triumphant, "see you, darling, see you in the morning."

Why had I never thought of this before? "See you in the *morning*. No, not just any dawning, no ordinary day. Within the strange providence of a loving Father (whose plan I still could not understand, only accept), I would see Peter again on that other bright Morning, beyond pain, beyond time.

I wrote it, only a page and a half, with tears streaming down my face, splashing onto the page.

The following day, with relief, I shifted mood altogether and wrote part of a humorous chapter about Peter's foibles and eccentricities, and some occasions when he had botched it up with some of the overly-conservative church ladies quite unable to understand the unsanctimonious exuberance of their young Scottish minister.

The two pieces of manuscript along with my defective outline were then mailed off to Edward Aswell.

The day came when I stood in the tiny West Harwich village postoffice and found a letter from Mr. Aswell. Eagerly, I tore it open. Two sentences in the second paragraph leapt off the typed page...

"We shall be proud to publish this book. I am going to send you a contract immediately."

That book was *A Man Called Peter*.

With the writing of this book God fulfilled my dream of becoming a full-fledged author. And once again, He blessed the book with sales beyond my wildest imagination. *A Man Called Peter* stayed on *The New York Times* bestseller list for more than 50 consecutive weeks, something of a record.

Over the years fifteen books have followed. Often I pause to marvel at the way He has led me: my joyous fulfillment in the writing itself; the fact that what is shared on paper is of help and inspiration to others, and the dividend of this work assigned me by God taking care of all economic needs. Who but God could even plan such an amalgam!

We did not sell the car until it was time to trade it in for another one. We kept *Waverley*, the Cape Cod cottage, and Peter John and I and our friends enjoyed it summer after summer.

After not quite two years in a cramped apartment in McLean Gardens, a large apartment complex in northwest Washington, we bought a modest home just off Wisconsin Avenue between Georgetown and Bethesda. We suffered no economic deprivation, never had to borrow money. Not a single one of the kind businessmen's gloomy forecasts ever came true. The monthly insurance checks were nice to have, a loving, reassuring gift from Peter to his family, but we never had to live on insurance income alone.

Reckon without God? To do so would be as nonsensical as ignoring the sun as we watch a shifting pattern of sunlight and shadow on the ground.

Reckon without God? We'd better not, not in any area of life, if we are serious about knowing reality and about achieving our full potential. For our God never considers our work as merely a way to earn a living—so much an hour, so much a year. He has given each of us the gift of life with a specific purpose in view. To Him work is a sacrament, even what we consider unimportant, mundane work. When done "as unto the Lord," it can have eternal significance.

It is therefore important to Him that we discover what our particular aptitudes and talents are; then that we use those talents to His glory and their maximum potential during our all-too-brief time on earth.

For each of us, He does have a plan. What joy to find it and even out of our helplessness, let Him guide us in its fulfillment.

Catherine and Peter John on the beach, Cape Cod

VIII

Single Parent

For the Lord your God....
executes justice for the
fatherless and widows....
Fear not, for you shall not
be ashamed; neither be confounded
and depressed....For your Maker
is your husband, the Lord of hosts
is His name....

Deuteronomy 10:17,18;
Isaiah 54:4,5—Amplified

Single Parent

Peter John had just turned nine when his father died. I can still see his stricken face when he heard the news and feel his trembling body as I knelt down to take him in my arms. There were just the two of us now—mother and son.

Still, after the first state of shock, young Peter seemed to be bearing the loss of a father so much better than I was taking the loss of a husband. He asked such boyish questions as, "Who will help me finish my train set?" "Where will we live now?" "Will I have to change schools?" "Can I still join the Boy Scouts?"

The questions seemed so normal that at the time I did not realize the noxious brew of anxiety, loneliness, desolation, even anger the questions were covering up. Few children can articulate the real issue underneath the anger, "If God loves me, then why did He take away my daddy?" With a very young child, there can also be an irrational juvenile reaction that would never occur to an adult: "If my daddy (mother) really loved me, then why would he (she) die and leave me?" In either instance this anger is stuffed down into the unconscious to emerge as rebellion and hostility toward authority at some future time.

In the years since, I have learned that in divorce situations there is often hidden anger against the parent who the child feels is most responsible for the break-up. Also, sometimes guilt in the child... *"Did I do something wrong to help to drive Mommy (or Daddy) away?"*

I sensed none of this happening to my son. Carefully, he was included in the planning arrangements and in every part of his father's funeral. Repeated attempts were made to explain death and immortality to Peter John. He seemed to understand. Here again, adults often assume a comprehension simply not there.

Too shy and fearful to bare the heart (I too had been like that in childhood), my son became quiet and indrawn. Pictures of him during this period show a sad, strained face. Obviously, I was not sufficiently aware of his inner desolation during these months of adjustments and thus failed him at this point.

How should a single parent handle such a situation? I know now that we should never give up easily in our efforts at dialogue with the child. At meals I would ask questions about Peter's activities at school or play and get one-word answers: "Fine." "Okay." "Good." Of course these were phony answers, an effort to head off deeper probing into painful areas.

As time went on during our limping dinner-table efforts at conversation, I would get the mental picture of a boy crouching behind a stone wall, peering over now and again, but afraid to come out.

Afraid of what? That he would be hurt further in honest confrontation? Afraid to stop crouching behind the wall and join the human race?

I sought the advice of counselor after counselor, had session after session, but we could neither find the way to bring down that wall, or to make Peter come out from what he regarded as his only protection.

At other times as when the two of us would be driving the five hundred plus miles to Cape Cod, always I struggled to find subjects of interest to my son. After receiving monosyllabic responses, I would give up and retreat into my own thought world, somewhat to the relief of Peter, I sensed.

Many times my son would then find a ball game on the car radio. To me these were interminably boring affairs. "Ball one, strike one. . ." "Ball two, strike two. . ." "Ball three. . ." "Ball four." Every now and then there would be a flurry of action, but the droning of balls and strikes and other unrelated information seemed to be nine-tenths of the verbage. *Who cares,* I would ask myself, *whether the pitcher first scratched his left ear, then his right thigh, then shifted his feet three times while he was winding up*? How could such repetitious commentary possibly interest a young boy?

In an effort to relate, I forced myself to go to baseball, football, and hockey games with my son. Baseball to me was always excruciatingly slow and boring, with the players constantly chasing after, throwing, or swinging a bat at a small, white ball. How was it that thousands upon thousands of people could get so worked up about it?

Football seemed to be in the category of bloody bullfights. Men throwing themselves ferociously at one another, sometimes even knocking each other unconscious. The idea that countless millions of people could go into a frenzy of shrieking excitment about the progress of a melon-sized, brown ball moving up and down the field was more than I could comprehend. My only consoling thought was, "*If this can serve the male as a substitute for war, then it would be worth all the national time and energy and millions of dollars expended*".

Ice hockey was more enjoyable. At least the speed and grace of the skaters was exhilerating to watch. But again the vicious body contact made me wince. My mistake was in not trying harder to get interested in these sports so that Peter and I could talk about them together. The key to this for me, I later discovered, was the human-interest side of sports, learning the names of the players, how good they were, how much money they made, something of their family life.

There were other ways open to me in helping my son grow up without a father. One was to bring him into contact with other men as much as I could. My dad spent many hours with young Peter, trying to teach him to handle tools and do odd jobs around the house. My brother Bob could talk Peter's sports language and the two of them worked on many a handicraft project together. One Christmas they made most of their gifts. I received a bird house replete with a television antenna and rambling roses painted over the birds' front door hole. The pièce de résistance went to the Hoskins girls, Peter's cousins—a marvelous toy chest decorated inside and out with fairytale castles and characters copied from Peter's books.

All of this was to the good, but there was never enough of it. It takes a great deal of masculine companionship to make up for missing a father's steady presence in the everydayness of life.

My experience in this regard would indicate that our church fellowships fail to pick up a God-ordained responsibility in relation to widows. The many references to widows in Scripture indicate that this ministry—spiritual, financial, and help in child rearing—is important to God. Apparently the early New Testament church took seriously this ministry to widows and to their children. For instance:

> Now in these days when the disciples were increasing in number, the Hellenists, murmured against the Hebrews because their widows were neglected in the daily distribution.[1]

> Religion that is pure and undefiled before God and the Father is this: to visit orphans and widows in their

affliction, and to keep oneself unstained from the world.[2]

How much it would mean to these bereft children today, each to become a part of some father's "bundle," as the Quakers say, as a sort of surrogate father!

The need is more and more urgent. Present estimates are that in the United States, forty-five percent of all children born in any given year will live with only one of their parents at some time before they are eighteen. In 1980 children of divorce (minors) numbered eleven million, with at least a million more added every year. One can scarcely imagine the discouragement and neediness of all these single parents, not to mention the confusion and bitterness of the children involved.

In my situation the best answers to the sense of helplessness and frustration came through my early morning Quiet Time when in prayer I would seek God's guidance for my son. One entry in my Journal read:

> I am to make a date with Peter John to go over finances. Through this he will begin to feel needed.

> I am to begin to praise him more. Try the power of praise for him a lot more often.

> Question: What is he to do on Friday and Saturday nights? There has to be real planning ahead on this.

On another occasion when I was feeling very low, I wrote down this guidance I felt God was giving me:

> Do not be afraid for young Peter. No harm will come to him. He also is My child. *I* love him more than you do!

But it was hard to overcome my fears for Peter John as he moved into the teen years. When I caught him smoking cigarettes at age fourteen, I was devastated. My anger erupted and he retreated into sullen silence. When I stormed heaven about my inadequacies as a mother, I wrote down this answer:

> You have still not completely released Peter to Me. Don't strain too much after it though. It will come gradually, if you let Me do it—even as a plant grows under My care, so a child grows.

That summer I was upset because Peter wanted to spend most of the summer visiting friends. An invitation to be with a friend at a seaside resort brought the issue to a head.

One morning in my Quiet Time, I had this answer:

> The business of why Peter doesn't want to go to camp is directly related to the fact that you do not want him to go visiting a friend for five days away from you. You fear the unknown quantity here, the part you can't control and keep your fingers on. In the same way Peter fears the unknown situations he would have to face in camp.

> My answer to you is that these five days when Peter is at the seaside resort will be good practice for you in really trusting Me. When I promise you specifically that I will take over a situation, *I take it over*. Moreover, I can be with Peter every minute, whereas you cannot.

> Remember that worry and trust just don't mix. When Peter leaves you, he will be in My hands and there must be no more worry.

One day while cleaning Peter's room I found a stack of sex-saturated paperback novels. How was I to deal with this? My first inclination was to let my anger boil over and explode. The inner voice said there was a better way.

Quietly that evening I asked him if there was any real reason why he felt it necessary to seek out this kind of reading. He shrugged. "All the kids at school are reading them," was his reply.

This led into a discussion of peer pressure which he picked up and talked about quite freely. He admitted that being accepted by others was far too important to him, that therefore he was inclined to be a follower of what the crowd did. At the end of our discussion, on his own volition, Peter threw the paperbacks into the trash.

But the problem of peer pressure at school began a new period of fear in me. Not sharp fear, more a spiritual unrest which would come to me upon occasion, vague and undefinable, like a splinter in one's soul. One night I asked God what this feeling was all about and what I should do about it. This is the message I got:

> You are fearful for Peter because of deep-hidden guilt concerning him. Fear usually comes from guilt. You feel instinctively—and rightly so—that where you fail to supply strong enough discipline, then I, Peter's heavenly Father, will have to permit those disciplines to be supplied by hard and difficult circumstances. Not enough parents face up to this.

> You must quietly get My mind and direction about Peter in these areas and then *act* upon My guidance. As you do act, your fear will leave. But let Me warn you about this. Don't let your time with Me or what I am telling you lull you into a sense of false security or be a substitute for action—or the fear will return in full force.

> Here are My instructions:

> 1. TV and movies: You are to keep a careful check on what he sees. Plan ahead. Be so well informed about films and TV programs that you will earn Peter's respect in this regard. Where there is no good movie on a Saturday, some other activity must be planned ahead. Often you have taken the line of least resistance because you haven't been prepared with adequate information.

> 2. Tidiness and taking care of his own clothes: Insist that he take responsibility here.

　　3. Money, allowance, etc.: You have not been han-
　　dling this properly. You must take time—over and
　　over—to come back to Me to think these matters
　　through.

For a period of months there was a big improvement in
Peter's and my relationship. Children thrive under structure, and I was being given daily guidance on how to plan
ahead and use consistent discipline.

Then came a major disappointment in connection with
my writing and for weeks I was bogged down in discouragement. Schedules slipped; there was a period of spiritual
drought.

Finally a breakthrough came with a decision made about
my next literary project. Now I could get my house back
in order. I remember the sense of inner elation I had looking forward to Monday morning when I could get up at
6:30 a.m. for a quiet hour with the Lord.

At 7:30 that morning the telephone rang. "This is Detective C of the Eighth Precinct, Juvenile Squad," he began
gently. "Your son, Peter John Marshall, and three other
boys got into trouble last Saturday night. They are being
accused of taking school property (two axes and a fire
extinguisher) and breaking the headlights of two school
buses."

I began trembling as he talked. When he told me that
I was to appear with Peter John at the Eighth Precinct
station at 3:30 that afternoon, my throat was almost too
dry to respond.

No members of my family were nearby, so I called several church friends for prayer support. I asked Peter to
stay home from school so that we could talk through what
had happened. He was defensive and communicated only
the bare details. He and some friends had been messing
around the school and a few back alleys nearby. They
hadn't meant to destroy any property. "Honest!"

Later as I prayed alone, I saw that I could be in danger
of being too pridefully concerned about what the publicity

might do to my reputation as a Christian. So many people had put my family and me on a pedestal. Would such publicity hurt Christ's cause?

I wept and then remembered Romans 8:28, *All things work together for good to those who love God, to those who are the called according to His purpose.* I would concentrate on this promise.

Peter and I were at Eighth Precinct station from 3:30 until 6:30. As we waited nervously for the two men from the juvenile board to arrive, I have a vivid remembrance of the scene... the dirt in the corners of the room; the man representing the school, whose name ironically enough was Peter, had large luminous brown eyes, black hair peppered with gray, was wearing tennis shoes on a winter's day, and his clothes didn't match; the sad, shocked face of the father of one of the other boys, his eyes like those of a hurt animal.

One of the boys (the son of the man whose eyes revealed so much) put his head down on the table and cried, very softly, trying not to attract attention. Since a very little boy, I learned later, he had wanted to get into West Point. If this went on his record, he would never get there... There was the lined, seamed face of the mother of another boy, holding the little family dog by one of her son's neckties—a strange leash indeed.

Peter's face was tense. Not in a long time had I heard him snap to and say, "Sir." His blond complexion seemed to have a permanent blush. He kept chewing on his fingernails long after there was no bit of surplus nail to chew. When the decision was finally made to let the boys off lightly because they were first offenders, he was relieved but deeply sober.

I was impressed with the way the District of Columbia handled these first offenders. Each boy, with his parents, had to appear before a judge. As I remember it, these were private sessions. When Peter and I appeared before a kindly judge for our talk, to my surprise the judge raised the issue I had considered too prideful. "Peter, your father stood for something in the greater Washington community. You have a proud heritage. Don't tarnish it. Son, I want you to think deeply about all this."

In the aftermath of this episode, I saw that the wall between young Peter and me was in part my doing. The wall remained because I had failed to share with Peter at the depth of spirit. Our whole relationship had been pitched too much on the level of daily schedules, material things—all the superficialities of life between a mother a her 16 year-old son.

Was it too late to change this? I would try. The inner Voice instructed me to open the deeps of my own life and feelings to Peter and share with him. How much he would understand, I could not know. My business was to *obey*. God would have to take care of the rest.

There were no more crises involving Peter during the rest of that school year. Still, I drove to Richmond, Virginia for a conference with a fine Christian educator. He was a man especially knowledgeable about teenage boys and about the best secondary schools. Having heard me out and prayed with me, his advice was that at age 16, Peter needed male authority figures in his life; that therefore, a Christian boys' school was probably indicated for his senior year in high school.

Back home I continued to pray for God's guidance on this.

During these days a friend told me bluntly, "Sons in their teens are always difficult for their mother. When it's time for them to leave home, that's it. You'll get no more than glimpses of them after that."

In my morning time I heard the same thing in a somewhat different way:

You have done all you can just now. The time has
come to relinquish your son. Others will take over the
role of parents in his life. You must accept this as natural
and trust Me.

So what God wanted seemed clear. After investigating
and visiting several schools recommended by the educator, in the end Peter and I settled on the one at the top of
the advisor's list—the Mount Hermon School in north-
western Massachusetts. Peter was happy with the choice.

Even so, my spirit was heavy as we packed the car that
September day for the drive to Massachusetts. Peter had
obtained his driver's license and insisted that he drive.
Now over six feet tall, he so towered over me that I felt
almost intimidated by his size.

As we drove there was little conversation between us.
As usual, he was listening to a baseball game on the radio.

My mind kept wandering from the battle between the
Braves and the Giants—or was it the Indians and the Yan-
kees? Much to Peter John's disgust, I could never keep
these intrepid warriors straight.

When that certain moment for a good-by was upon us
in our rooms in the inn the next day, I was not big enough
to take it alone. But I knew where to go for help. Besides,
don't all such moments need a benediction?

I tried to keep my heart from showing—not because I
was afraid of the heart, but because I didn't want to embarrass Peter John.

"We should be pushing off for school," I said. "But first,
would you indulge me in something? This is a significant
day for us both. Would you be willing for us to have a
prayer together and ask God's blessing on it?"

Peter nodded a little impatiently, so I made the prayer
brief. The moment hung in space—passed. But there was
the unmistakable feeling in the prayer that we were not
two, but three with "Big Peter" a part in this intercession

around the throne of God—united across barriers that were no barriers.

Silently, my son picked up his suitcases.

I was a little disappointed in the room at school—circa 1890, golden oak woodwork, the floors well worn by generations of boys' feet, battered furniture, two small windows almost covered with a summer's growth of ivy.

But Peter did not seem to mind. He had just met his roommate, Bruce, and liked him—as blond as he, also a senior. This room would be their digs—their very own. What did 19th century scuffed oak woodwork and worn floors matter?

When Bruce's parents arrived I noticed how his mother, all unconsciously, leaned on her husband's arm, smiling up into his face. *An intact family*, I thought. *How wonderful it must be.*

Next Bruce's mother opened one of his suitcases and carried new shoes and galoshes to the closet, then piles of underwear and pajamas to his chest of drawers.

"I sat up until two last night sewing on name tags," she told me. "Can you imagine these boys acually getting their own laundry together each week—and on time?"

"No—I can't. I suppose they'll learn."

She eyed the iron beds. "Bruce, can't I make your bed for you one last time? You never get it smooth."

"Never mind, Mom, I'll do it myself—later."

She was acting out what I was feeling... the apron strings almost severed but the hands aching to perform a last chore or two. Yet she had three other sons, and Bruce was not the oldest. She had been through this before.

Peter looked at me. He knew, too—knew beyond his years. He said with hesitant dismissal, as if uneasy to have me there longer, "I think you'd better go now, Mom."

So I shook hands with Bruce and his parents, stood on tiptoe to hug my tall son, and walked out—down the worn, uneven steps.

Another era was over. I had parted with my husband. In a very real sense, I had just parted with my son. This was the beginning of his life on his own.

As I drove away, I was thinking, *So to what do I return now? An empty house? Greater loneliness than ever?*

A sudden rainstorm came up, the car's jerky windshield wipers keeping pace with my jumbled, gloomy thoughts.

Ten minutes later that rain ceased as quickly as it had come. I was driving into the setting sun, and the sun had turned the droplets of rain on the windshield into glittering globules of light.

Then to my astonishment, a rainbow appeared, every gorgeous color of the spectrum in its wide perfect arc.

The rainbow of promise. After the great flood in the days of Noah, the writers of Scripture tell us that God first sent the rainbow as His pledge of an

> "everlasting covenant between God and every living creature of all flesh. . ."[3]

> His promise, His covenant: ". . .for lo, I am with you always. . ."

Then I could forget my fears of returning to an empty house, dump by the roadside all my "what ifs" about this new era. *He would be there.*

The rainbow of Promise shimmered and beckoned.

IX

Loneliness

....trust God....when temptation
comes, He will provide
the way out of it....

....The God who did not spare
His own Son but gave Him up
for us all, surely He will give us
everything besides!....What can
ever part us from Christ's love?

I Corinthians 10:13
Romans 8:32,35—Moffatt

Loneliness

The years immediately after young Peter went away to school, first to Mount Hermon then to Yale, were the most difficult of my widowhood. We had finally sold *Waverley*, the Cape Cod cottage, since it was now obvious that Peter would seldom be there. The idea of living alone however, did not frighten me. I have never resisted this. In fact, I prefer being alone for long stretches of the day, as when I am writing in the mornings. But there is a big difference between aloneness and loneliness.

Loneliness is the aching need inside one to share one's life with another. Yet there are other wholesome relationships for single people outside of marriage where the aching void inside oneself can be satisfied. My question now was, what kind of life did God want for me?

During the first years after Peter's death I was convinced that it would be impossible for me ever to marry again, that this would violate something very precious my husband and I had had together. But as the years passed, I began praying about this matter simply by asking questions, by telling God that I did not even know for what it was right to ask. In this way I could leave entirely up to Him the decision as to whether I should ever remarry.

But that seemed a sloppy way of praying. Surely I needed to know myself better than that, what my own deep desires were. Knowing those, then I could at least present them to Him for approval or disapproval.

My growing loneliness was brought into sharp focus the night of a mother-daughter banquet for which I had agreed to make an informal after-dinner talk. Before my part in the program, a young baritone rose to sing a group of semi-classical songs. The last in the group was "Drink to Me Only with Thine Eyes."

I had heard Ben Jonson's words sung many times. They held no special memories for me, nor had I ever felt in the least sentimental about this song....

> Drink to me only with thine eyes,
>   And I will pledge with mine;
> Or leave a kiss within the cup,
>   And I'll not ask for wine.
> The thirst that from the soul doth rise
>   Doth ask a drink divine....

But toward the end of the song, suddenly I felt myself tighten. I was aware that my hands, hidden under the edge of the tablecloth, were clutching the evening bag in my lap until my fingers ached.

This won't do, I thought. *I'll just have to stop listening and deliberately think about something less sentimental.* My eyes roamed over the scene before me—the mothers in their finery with their daughters sitting beside them at the round tables, all listening intently to the tall young singer. I noticed a red-headed teenager's hairdo. Deliberately I studied it, trying to decide how some beautician had created the sleek turned-under effect.

By the time the last notes of the song had died away, the tension in my hands had relaxed, the fullness in my throat had disappeared. I was able to get to my feet calmly and even put some humor into my talk.

But this experience had stirred something within me of which I had been only hauntingly aware. I saw myself standing before an altar being married again. And every shred of me protested. Would that not be a betrayal of the husband who had had all my heart's love—therefore, a betrayal of the love itself?

Suddenly I knew that such a thing would never be possible except by an act of God changing my thinking, changing something deep inside that was an integral part of my being.

Several days later I made this notation:

> I must realize that loneliness, that sense of dissatisfaction, that feeling of some happiness just eluding me, is in all human beings, and is put there by God to keep us searching after Him. Perhaps when I just "settle down" to this doubtful state of single blessedness, inner peace will come. We shall see.

Even five or six years after Peter's death I found that my journey through the valley was still a running battle with self-pity. Several of the couples on our street would often take a stroll in the early evening. Sometimes seeing them, I would think, *Were Peter still with me, he and I would be the youngest couple on this street. But no, our marriage is over.* Or at the theatre I would see a gray-haired man reach for his wife's hand, and I would wince with a passing pang of self-pity.

Or at a dinner party I would find myself the only single person there. Always I knew that my hostess had not meant to be thoughtless. It is hard for anyone who has known only an unbroken family to imagine how this particular situation makes the single person feel. Try as I might to overcome it, I would find that being in the presence of couples threw my aloneness into sharpest perspective.

What then is the solution? It must lie somewhere in the realm of relationship. As solitaries we can wither and die. We long to be needed; we yearn to be included; we thirst to know that we belong to someone. The question is—how can we achieve that sense of belonging?

There is a price to be paid. The first tribute exacted is a modicum of honesty with ourselves. On the one hand, do we want to be rid of loneliness so much that we will allow ourselves no more wallowing in the luxury of pity-parties? On the other hand, how badly do we want to make connection with other people? For let's admit it, there are pluses in having only oneself to think of.

In the light of honest answers to questions like these, I decided I need not be lonely unless I chose to be. The first step was recognizing the necessity for a new dimension and the decision to perform a freshening-up on myself. Having to make many public appearances forced me to review my clothes situation. I found a specialist who, after studying my present wardrobe, my figure and my features, skillfully advised me on clothes shopping, even on the right selection for a variety of situations such as certain platform and television appearances.

Then came some quiet reappraisal of certain restrictions my parents had placed upon me in my growing-up years. They had been so full of love for me that the taboos they had put on activities like ballroom dancing and bridge had mattered little to me—then.

But now as a widow in sophisticated Washington, I was embarrassed when someone asked me to dance. Or I had to decline an invitation to play bridge with friends.

The answer was to learn how—and I did. I enrolled for a series of lessons in ballroom dancing. Then three women friends and I set aside an evening a week to master bridge. We spread out teaching manuals on a second table beside us and learned the game together by playing it.

Seven years after Peter's death a change was taking place inside me without my being aware of it. While resigned to widowhood in my mind, emotionally I was preparing myself for a new kind of life. This entry appears in my Journal at about this time:

> God does want me to be happy. God does want Peter John to be well-adjusted and happy. God has made me the way I am, has made me for happiness and love; I do not believe that He means or wants me to stay by myself for the rest of my life.

Odd, how as soon as I opened the inner door, outer doors began swinging open too. Men began seeking me out for dates—a procession of them. Widowers—one a college president, one an insurance agent, older bachelors, a wealthy California citrus-grower, a Washington professor, a Texas investment broker. Then there was the businessman I met while giving a dinner talk to a university convention at the Mayflower Hotel in Washington. Tall, slim, distinguished-looking, I liked him immediately.

I learned that Howard was a widower with two teenage boys, his wife having died of cancer the previous year. He was from a wealthy, influential southern family and had political aspirations.

Howard invited me out for lunch, then dinner, then for a weekend at his large family estate in South Carolina where his sister was the hostess. I was impressed, and Howard and his two sons seemed to like me.

I confessed in my Journal:

> The revelation today is that there has to be someone else for me into whose life I can pour everything. Since this is what my whole being cries out for, it is as sure of fulfillment as that the tides of the ocean will come in again. Somewhere there is a man whose life needs this lavish giving, whose personality and career will bloom and blossom under it. Whether that man be Howard, only God knows at this point—though my heart says "yes."

If there were pangs inside me that my sudden interest in Howard was a betrayal of Peter's memory, they did not last long....

> Today God gave me a beautiful gift, namely, the assurance that remarriage is *His* idea not mine. *He* wants it for me even more than I want it. But a gift is not truly ours until we take it.

> So I accept it with greatest gratitude. This means that I no longer have to worry about whether it's right to marry again; all I do have to do is to give thanks to God that the matter is settled and relax until God's time comes to meet "the man."

> I see that only now—after almost seven years—am I finally ready really to accept Peter's death fully, really ready to shut the door on the past and go out into a new life. Obviously, remarriage couldn't happen until this step was taken on my part. No man wants to be part of my old life. It's incredible perhaps that it has taken me so long to come to this position.

Howard was appointed to a high position in Washington and moved into an office in the Pentagon. As we saw each other more often, I became aware of some unsettling qualities in him. He tended to avoid any discussions about Christianity. I sensed that any faith he had was a sort of inherited social grace with nothing personal about it. He seemed overly fond of the superficialities of life—eating, drinking, clothes, cars and so on. He was restless and ill at ease whenever other people paid attention to me in regard to my books. Yet his charm, dignity, and statesmanlike approach to issues appealed to me. And he did have a warm, affectionate nature.

Questions about Howard kept arising in my journals:

> My guidance is that I am to leave entirely up to him and God if or when he will read *A Man Called Peter*; that I am to make no hints about this or try to encourage him to read it.

God has big things in store for Howard. In the next year or two he will lose his frustrations as he loses himself in something bigger than himself. I have a vision for him; so does God.

Howard began to do a lot more traveling and I saw less and less of him. He would call and explain the heavy new responsibilites laid upon him. I made this comment in my Journal:

The real explanation of Howard's lack of initiative at the present time is that he is *afraid* of becoming involved with me. He's not ready for it; he senses that it is dynamite. God tells me to be patient under this and to try to understand it.

Short notes began coming periodically from Howard with foreign postmarks: Geneva, London, Rome, Bonn. I was reminded of the long periods of silence I suffered during my three years of courtship with Peter.

Then one day I ran into Howard unexpectedly in the corridor of the Pentagon. He was startled; so was I. I stammered out an explanation of why I was there, a trifle too defensively.

"It's really good to see you, Catherine." He seemed over-hearty. We talked a few minutes, then he went on to a meeting.

As he walked away I was annoyed at myself for being so thrown off balance. I doubted that even a meeting with the President himself would have rattled me to such an extent. And of course it had to be poise that Howard admired so much.

The next entry reflected all this:

I have felt more detached from Howard lately. Is my feeling for him just a bundle of infatuation? If his influential position were removed, if his wealth and his relative youth (about 50 I would judge) were all removed, would I then still fancy myself in love with the man himself?

Then I would get provoked with myself and lack of patience and pour out my feelings and any new insights:

> God is Sovereign in this whole situation. Howard's actions and decision—and mine—are truly in God's hands. I am God's and have given my life into His care and keeping. I am to accept Howard's silences and what has *not* happened in recent weeks as having come directly from God's hands.

> I am to offer God the sacrifice of thanksgiving by thanking Him for all these unwelcome circumstances. This is the proof, the acting out of my faith in His Omnipotence.

That June a letter came from Howard after a silence of several months. It was a short note. He wanted me to hear the news directly from him, rather than any other source, he wrote. He was to be married again. The woman was the daughter of a general, a widow with three small children.

When the letter came I thought I had already relinquished the whole matter. Apparently, not so. There was a surprising emotional backwash. I did no serious writing for weeks.

My secretary Peg came to me with a handful of speaking requests and my resentment boiled over. "I've written myself into a corner," I stormed. "People put me on a spiritual pedestal with a sign hanging on it, 'Don't touch.' Who enjoys pedestal-sitting? The public insists on seeing me one way when you and I know that what I really want out of life is very different. I feel trapped."

Peg was clear-eyed and unsympathetic. "You stand for something. They want to look up to you—and they want the spiritual help you can give them. What's wrong with that?"

But I found it almost impossible to get back to my work. The fact that I was in such demand as an author and a speaker seemed meaningless. I was a forty-two-year-old widow whom life was passing by.

Meanwhile my concern had shifted from myself to my son's need for a father figure. So I asked for a conference with Gordon Cosby, the young pastor of the Church of the Saviour in Washington where I had become active. He was the type of man in whom I found it easy to confide.

Having begun his ministry in World War II as chaplain of the 327th Glider Regiment of the now legendary 101st Airborne Division, Gordon had demonstrated his deeply-felt pacifism by insisting on going unarmed into battle with his men. In some of the hottest fighting of the War—D-Day on the Normandy beaches, thirty-three continuous days of fighting to capture Cherbourg, then the epic Christmas 1944 seige of McAuliffe's men at Bastogne—the chaplain simply alternated between the battlefield and the aid station, ministering to the wounded. There with the men of the 327th, were hammered out Gordon Cosby's convictions which later became the guiding principles of the new church.

He brought to that church, begun in Washinton in October, 1947 a deep understanding of human weakness and need, together with an unusual incisiveness. The church building itself was, and still is, as unusual as its pastor. A brownstone townhouse at 2025 Massachusetts Avenue close to Dupont Circle was turned into a combination of sanctuary, meeting rooms and offices.

That day in Gordon's office I confided the need I felt for men in my son's life. "Would you keep your eyes open," I asked Gordon, "for men who would see this as a real ministry for us women forced to rear sons alone? It could take the form of going with Peter to baseball or football or ice hockey games, or on hunting or fishing or camping trips—any such thing.''

Gordon was not only sympathetic but agreed to help in any way that he could. Within the week he had located a number of men attending his church who offered to befriend the children of single parents.

A few weeks went by. Then Gordon introduced my son to Jim. He was from Wyoming, a plastics manufacturer, married, with two young children, but he had to be in Washington frequently on business matters.

Jim was a virile-looking, warm-hearted man with a good sense of humor and a fine mind. He had dabbled some in Wyoming politics at local and state levels. However, essentially he was an outdoor man who reveled in hunting and sports.

I was delighted when he invited Peter John for a two-day hunting trip or spent long hours with him in target practice. The two males seemed to enjoy each other immensely.

Then Jim began dropping by our home, and since he was there to see Peter, it seemed natural to invite him to dinner.

As time went on, Jim began asking questions about my life and activities, and I found myself responding quite openly and honestly about how lonely the life of a so-called Christian celebrity could be. He, in turn, began sharing with me some difficulties in his marriage. In the beginning, Jim's marital problems had not sounded serious; now they seemed to worsen the more he talked about them.

This should have rung alarm bells for me since I well knew that any single, unattached person of the opposite sex is not the wise choice for a marriage counselor. Instead, I would listen sympathetically, uncertain how to handle this, lulled into a false sense of security by Jim's ability to laugh at himself. That seemed to indicate at least a degree of healthy objectivity.

I will help him see how important it is for him to work out these differences with his wife, I told myself. And I did talk to him almost sternly about how important it was to get back to Wyoming and his family as soon as possible.

Then one evening after Peter had gone to his room, Jim blurted out, "Catherine, I've fallen in love with you."

A kaleidoscope of feelings swept over me: surprise, dismay, concern, fear, and yes—longing. But I knew it had to be squelched—and quickly.

"I'm startled, Jim. And—well—grateful. But it can't be right."

"I think it could be right, Catherine. But not until I'm a free man. I intend to get a divorce."

I protested and he argued. When he left that evening, I could tell that he was a very determined man.

The next morning I knew what I had to do: set the alarm, get up at 6:30 and come penitently before my Lord. With some trepidation I did this, then waited. I felt such kindness and love pouring from Him that the tears came in a flood. I knew that I had to be honest with my feelings, ruthlessly so. I poured out the residue of pain about Howard, then took pen in hand to try to analyze how I felt about Jim:

> The moments we have been together have had a special flavor, a special character. Maybe that's what often happens when one *really* lives in the present. But the companionship has the quality of something one may not keep. It's like walking through a garden and catching the whiff of a fragrance one cannot quite capture nor identify because one doesn't belong in that particular garden and can't linger there. Or hearing in the distance the haunting refrain of a melody that speaks to the heart and to the senses—but the melody must remain in the distance.
>
> Jim's friendship has done something for me. I have felt more *alive* during these days than in a long time. It's as if his touch on my life has awakened my emo-

tions, the potential warmth of me, out of a long, long sleep.

But Jim will go back to his family. He must. His friendship and companionship, the whole relationship between us, is just a loan, though a very precious one for a little time. Not the least trace of possessiveness must creep into it. I must be "hands off" in my emotional attitude towards him.

On that lofty plane I left it. But then began an insistent inner gnawing telling me that the Jim situation was unfinished business. There was a step I needed to take—a letter that would write "finis" to the whole thing. I dreaded doing it, postponed it for days. Then I forced myself to write it, stating clearly that God would never honor any relationship between Jim and me that came at the expense of his wife and children.

When I mailed the letter, it was as if I had shed a twenty-pound weight from my shoulders. The next morning I felt a surge of creative vitality I had not experienced in months. Confession and restitution had freed my spirit and out poured a torrent of words on paper:

For the past year, I have felt defeated and frustrated. And this certainly is not as God wishes it.

Here are some of the ways I have allowed my loneliness to defeat me;

1. The salt, the savor has gone out of life. Nothing, not even the very great success of *A Man Called Peter* thrills me much now. "Success" has turned to ashes in my mouth. The zest has gone out of everyday life. This is wrong. It is the outlook of a dying creature—certainly not a "new creature in Christ Jesus."

2. There has been—over the past several years—a growing coldness in my heart towards other people rather than an increasing love and warmth. Visiting the sick has been a chore—no joy in it.

3. Along with the above, there has inevitably come an increasing preoccupation with self. Or perhaps the preoccupation with self is the real cause of the defeats.

4. I have sought satisfaction in material things and have not found anything here that lasts.

5. I have become more irritable in the daily grind of everyday life. Slow drivers, inept salesgirls, parking lot attendants, provoke me much more easily than they used to.

6. I have known that God wanted me to get up an hour earlier each morning for prayer and Bible reading, yet have not been consistent about this.

7. I have failed almost totally in small disciplines of appetite—small self-denials which, at the time, I knew were right.

8. I have often failed to have the inner strength to discipline or to say "no" to Peter John, when I knew I should have.

9. Along with all these failures, I have often had a feeling of superiority to other human beings—which makes no sense at all.

I knew that the answer to this non-victorious living could be traced back to self-will. It had never been enough to go to Jesus and talk to Him about my desires and plans so that He could stamp "approved" on them. Instead, objectively, I had to seek *His* will for me in that early-morning time each day. Indeed, seek it eagerly, realizing full well that He knew what was best for me better than I knew.

In the early morning Quiet Time in my bedroom I even went back to review the Howard relationship in my Journals. I saw that what I had written seldom contained any revelations from God about whether He felt we had been right for each other. Most of my notations had amounted to wishful thinking. Too impressed with the man's stature, his appearance, his wealth, I had decided this was the one. He was not right for me—and God would have told me, had I come to Him with will and heart wide open to His counsel. Months later, viewing the relationship from God's eyes, I could easily see how mismatched we had been spiritually and emotionally.

No wonder then, the course of events with Jim had become so tangled.

Jim was not at all satisfied with my letter. He had returned to Wyoming, but then in the early fall, flew east to Washington to see me, determined to continue our relationship.

But the morning times had strengthened me and returned clear-eyedness to me. Moreover, I was learning something about how to cope with the temptations that come to the lonely: *Admit you are not able to resist on your own strength. Then step aside and let Jesus handle the situation.*

When I did this, inner direction came: *Call Gordon Cosby and meet with him.*

When I got Gordon on the phone, I hesitated only a minute. Then I told him the whole story.

"Bring Jim down here and we'll pray about it—just the three of us," he replied.

What a tremendous answer to prayer! Jim agreed to go. So we made an appointment, and I met him at the Church of the Saviour.

The moment Jim and I were seated in Gordon's study, I felt the Presence there with us. Compassionate. Approving. I could almost hear Him saying, "This is the way to handle those emotional situations that get out of hand."

Gordon listened to us without comment or change of expression. Always a creative, loving man with a pastor's warm heart, Gordon, at the same time was never afraid to use the stringent word "sin." I remembered his comments in a recent sermon to the effect that unredeemed human nature is capable of anything; that the only difference between individuals is slight variations in type and extent of sin. Then he had topped that with "The most red-blooded sinner is only capable of baby stuff compared to the manhood Christ requires of us."

"It isn't necessary for me to preach a sermon to you," Gordon told Jim and me. "You've come here because each of you wants to do what God wants you to do. I honor you both for this. Jesus always has the answer to every one of our needs."

He leaned back in his chair, smiling and relaxed. "How grateful we Christians should be! Without Jesus' agony on that cross there would be no cleansing for the likes of any of us, no miracle of changing what's wrong on the inside of us to what's right. The blood shed on that cross literally saves our lives.

"That's what the sacrament of communion should mean to us. I suggest we bring all this to the foot of Jesus' cross through communion. How about it, Jim? Are you ready to lay there your desires in this matter, what you thought was your will?"

Jim nodded, his eyes moist.

Now Gordon looked at me. "Catherine?"

"Yes, I'd like that."

The bread and the wine were there waiting on a little altar-table in Gordon's office. Never had the words been so meaningful: "This is His body broken for you..." "This is the blood of the *new* covenant, shed for many for the remission of sins. Drink ye all of it..."

We felt the Presence of Jesus in that quiet room. At the conclusion of the little service, as we knelt, Gordon blessd us both.

"Jim and Catherine, you are good friends and want to stay that way—friends. God has endowed you both with special talents and has a plan for both your lives. Jim has responsibilities to his God, his family, and his business.

God has given Catherine a son to rear and a ministry through her writing. Both need to be protected. Go your separate ways—freely forgiven, restored, refreshed, into new usefulness and creativity."

Then Gordon lifted us to our feet and hugged us both.

Several months later I heard that Jim was back with his family.

The wedding toast

X

Second Marriage

But seek first of all His Kingdom
and His righteousness
(His way of doing and being right),
and then all these things
taken together will be given
you besides.

Matthew 6:33—Amplified

Second Marriage

A strange thing happened after Gordon Cosby's communion service: I stopped thinking about remarriage. Not that the desire for it was wiped out, just that it had become much less important to me. My perspective had changed. This was the Lord's doing, of course, and came about because I was able to give the whole matter over to Him to handle.

One morning I wrote this in my Journal:

> I am to "seek the Kingdom of God first" in regard to remarriage. Should this be God's will for me, then in any given man I am to seek *first* those inner qualities of mind and heart that belong to God's kingdom.

> But what about *me*? What inner qualities should I have to qualify to be a wife again?

The next day this is what I wrote:

> Going back to the question I asked yesterday—I would list femininity, warmth of personality, vitality, interest in other people, the desire to give. A big order!

> But I am being told this morning that since it is def-
> initely God's will that I have these qualities, I am not
> to plead for them, but to believe that the prayer is al-
> ready answered, that God is giving them to me in His
> own way and in His own time.

Shortly thereafter the president of a midwestern college telephoned and asked to see me during his forthcoming trip to Washington. I had stayed at his home several years before while giving the commencement speech. Upon hearing that his wife had died, I had written him a note of sympathy.

He telephoned me upon his arrival in Washington and invited me out to dinner. By now I knew men well enough to realize that they usually ask you out for lunch if it concerns business, for dinner if it is more personal.

The college president arrived in a rented Cadillac and held my hand an extra moment when we met at the door. He was a small man, perhaps an inch or two taller than I, about fifty-five, balding, a compulsive talker. During dinner at a fine restaurant I learned everything about his college: the two million debt, the growing enrollment, the championship baseball team, the new library, the prob-lems with some of the faculty members. But the rush of words covered up a rather surprising nervousness for a man in his position. He was obviously interested in me as a person and intended to express it before the evening was over.

He did just that, sitting in my living room later that evening. He proposed marriage. There was no attempt at any romantic buildup; it would be a marriage of conven-ience and mutual interest. He would supply me a home and security in return for which I would be the first lady of the college campus. I was touched and honored by his offer. But as graciously as I knew how, I refused. For me there could be no marriage without romance.

During that same year I declined two more proposals of marriage. What was happening? There could only be one answer. Relinquishment of the intense desire for re-marriage, seeking God first instead of a husband had relaxed me in a way that was now attracting men to me. I could not analyze how I was different except that I could now empathize more with the other person and be much less concerned with myself. And the Kingdom-of-God-first yardstick was enabling me to hear the Lord's word advising me about each person.

A telephone call came one day from Leonard LeSourd, the executive editor of *Guideposts* magazine, asking for a luncheon date to talk about an idea for a future article. It had no special significance for me. I had written before for *Guideposts* and had met Len briefly one evening when I had spoken to the young adult group of the Marble Collegiate Church in New York City.

Over lunch in a Georgetown restaurant our talk ranged over many subjects. In an easy-going, personal way, Len asked many questions about me, probing, I thought, for a new subject on which to base an article. We found one, finished lunch, and he drove me home. As he stopped that car in front of my house, out of the blue came an intriguing statement, "In my twelve years at *Guideposts* I've learned a lot about the Christian faith. One aspect of it seems both bewildering and challenging."

"What is that?"

"The Holy Spirit. No one talks much about it, especially preachers. There's a mystery here—power too. Sometime I want to cover it in the magazine."

"The Holy Spirit is a He, Len," I returned quietly.

He looked at me curiously. "You know Him, then?"

"Not as much as I'd like."

The conversation ended and Len helped me out of the car and to the door. Not once during the two hours we were together did it occur to me that there was anything but a professional motive behind his invitation to lunch.

But there was nothing of the professional editor about the letter I received from Len several months later in the summer of 1959. "I would like to know you better," he wrote. "How do you react to this idea? We'll choose a day, and then you write on your calendar three letters: F U N. I'll pick you up in the morning in my car and we'll just take off to the beach or the mountains or whatever."

The letter seemed deliberately couched to say, "If you're interested in pursuing this relationship, let's have a go at it. If not, then tell me so right now."

I liked that approach. We set a day in early August. Len telephoned the night before from a Washington motel to say that he would call for me at 10:30 the next morning. He was delighted when I suggested fixing a picnic lunch.

The next morning turned out to be a beautiful summer day, not too hot. When I met Len at my front door, I found myself slipping easily into the adventurous mood he had suggested. I asked no questions about where we were going; he offered no hints. As he helped me pack the lunch into a picnic basket, I could sense his curiosity about my living situation.

"Peter John and I have lived here for several years," I volunteered, "that is, when Peter's home from Yale. This has been a good home for us, but I'm building a new house in Bethesda that will give me a better working situation.

"What's wrong with this?"

"Not enough privacy. Peter's friends are in and out a lot in the summer. I enjoy them, but there are so many other interruptions here too, and not enough space for my secretary. Anyway, I've always wanted to build my own dream house. It's already about half built."

"I see." Len was reflective. "Since Peter is at Yale nine months of the year, your dream house could end up being quite lonely for you."

"Yes—it could."

Len put the picnic lunch into the trunk of his car and we climbed into the front seat. "What do you prefer," he asked casually, "ocean or mountains?"

"I would choose the mountains."

"Which direction?"

I aimed him west toward Skyline Drive. As we drove along, I studied this fortyish editor sitting beside me. He was of medium height; dark hair beginning to grey; lithe, athletic figure. His gray-blue eyes were direct, warm, the lids often crinkling with humor. He was a good conversationalist, probing but relaxed. I relaxed too. It was going to be a good day.

While driving out Route 193 toward Route 7, we came to a sign: *Great Falls Park.*

"What's this?" Len asked.

"A scenic spot on the Potomac for picnics and walking on the rocks."

"Let's try it."

We parked, got out, and walked along the water. Since it was rocky terrain, Len reached for my hand and continued to hold it. We had lemonade at the refreshment center and then continued our drive west.

By the time we were on Skyline Drive and heading south, it was time to look for a picnic spot. Len chose a grassy knoll under a large shade tree. He took a blanket from the trunk of his car and spread it out for us to sit on. Then as I began removing the food from the picnic basket, he returned to his car trunk for another item. A ukulele!

Out of the corner of my eye as I watched Len tuning it up, I hoped that I was not about to receive a country music concert. I have nothing against country rhythms. They're fun sometimes. But on the whole, I much prefer classical music.

"I was dancing... with my darling... to the Tennessee waltz..." Len's voice had a strong nasal quality. I winced a little in spite of my effort to keep an expressionless face.

After a few bars, Len put the ukulele aside and laughed self-consciously. "You're not a country music fan, are you, Catherine? I taught myself to play—poorly, I'm afraid. And I have no singing voice. Anyhow, I'd rather talk than sing."

I sighed with relief, making a mental note that Len was perceptive, or I was very transparent—or perhaps a little of both.

It was hard to believe that two people could talk continually for eleven hours, yet feel they had scarcely made a start on subjects of mutual interest. But when Len said good-by that night, I had no real indication he could be serious about me. True, I sensed that he was surprised at certain discoveries, especially that I was not the overly-sanctimonious, lofty creature some people had painted me. We also knew now that we were both seekers, strugglers, groping towards real growth as Christians. Both of us were reporters, always interested in how to capture on paper scenes, drama, personalities, new discoveries about men in relation to God. We had an open, honest communication at a deep level.

Len's home situation however, put me on guard. For years he had been trying to rear three small children alone; he was obviously interested in finding a wife who would be willing to share this load. There was no way I could see myself in this role.

Then began frequent telephone calls. When Len invited me to come for a weekend to his little town of Carmel, New York to meet his children, to my surprise I found myself accepting. *The least I could do,* I told myself, *is to be open-minded enough to take a look at this.*

On Friday afternoon Len met me at New York's La-Guardia Airport. During the drive out to Carmel, he told me that I would meet only his two sons, Chester, six, and Jeffrey, three, that weekend. Ten-year-old Linda was at camp. Mrs. Goutremont, the elderly housekeeper, would serve as our chaperone.

The *Guideposts* property in Carmel included the magazine's business office, formerly a girl's school, and a sprawling, eight-room white clapboard house, once the home of the school president. Len and his children were living in this house set in a spacious lawn.

A picnic table had been set up outdoors under a maple tree—apparently for our supper. Diminutive Jeffrey met me with a wide smile, impish blue eyes and a hug. Chester's big, sad brown eyes stared at me suspiciously, then he held out a tentative hand. During the less-than-gourmet meal of greasy, cold fried chicken, cole slaw, potato chips, and watermelon, Chester's suspicions of me seemed to increase.

Suddenly his hand knocked over a paper cup filled with milk. Quickly I moved to one side, barely avoiding a lapful.

When Len snapped a sharp rebuke at his son, Chester flounced from the table. With the order to come and sit back down, the small brown-eyed boy fell on the ground in a wild tantrum of crying and kicking.

With a quick move, Len swept his son up in his arms, threw him over his shoulder like a sack of potatoes and carried him into the house. In a few minutes the annoyed father was back, alone.

"Chester will stay in his room until he's ready to apologize," he explained. "He seems to resent outsiders until he gets to know them, especially all women."

Jeffrey had meanwhile snuggled up close to me, obviously hungry for love. "Well, I've made one conquest anyway," I said.

"Two," replied Len with a grin.

After dinner a neighboring couple joined us for several rubbers of bridge, and I struggled to cope with three skilled players. *I'm about as adept at bridge as Len is with his ukulele,* I thought to myself.

The neighbors left, the children were asleep, Mrs. Goutremont had retired to her room. Len suggested we go outside for a walk about the grounds. It was a still, moonlit night. Suddenly his flow of talk stopped as he abruptly leaned over and gently kissed me. Then he chuckled rather self-consciously.

"We're right under Mrs. Goutremont's window, and I'll bet she's looking down at us."

I darted a quick look up at the window. It was dark. "How can you tell?"

"I can't. But she's very, very curious about us."

"Why?"

He did not answer, but instead led me to the other side of the house by the porch. Two lawn chairs were positioned there side by side, and we sat down. "I'm sorry about the episode with Chester," he began.

"It worked out fine. Your son came downstairs while you were in the kitchen and apologized. I think we're friends now."

Len sighed. "That's good. Chester looks to me for almost total security. Anyone else who visits here seems to threaten him. That has to change."

He talked about his two sons and daughter with pride. "They're such good kids. Smart too. Being without a mother the past few years has been rough. Mrs. Goutremont is the sixth housekeeper we've had."

As Len talked about his children, I saw that he had a father's heart, and I liked what I saw. He was a caring man, affectionate, comfortable to be with, mature. He approached problems calmly, I decided, thought situations through carefully, acted deliberately.

After coming to these flattering conclusions about Len, he promptly blew apart my reasoning. As he was talking about his dreams for the future, suddenly I heard him say, "and I see the two of us together."

"How do you see us?" I asked, surprised.

Even in the moonlight I could see that Len looked startled too. "I hadn't meant to go this route." He paused, struggling. "I find myself wanting to say things that will probably seem very impulsive to you. Somehow I have to—I do see the two of us together, Catherine. There's something supernatural involved in all this that I'm not sure I understand."

He stopped again and shook his head with an almost dazed expression. "I was so miserable a few months ago.

I told God I didn't see how I was going to make it alone and cried out to Him for help. Immediately after that prayer, your name, Catherine, dropped into my mind. It had to be God's doing."

"Why would you conclude that?" I queried. "I mean, why necessarily?"

"Because on my own I would never have thought you were—well, my type."

"All you knew about me came through my book about Peter Marshall?"

Len nodded. "That's mostly true. What man wants to play second fiddle to a famous Scottish preacher? Surely you must realize that *A Man Called Peter* made yours one of the great love stories of our time."

He paused, struggling for the right words. "Frankly, I thought you were too ethereal and spiritual to be any earthly good. But the Lord seemed to be telling me that I was *assuming* this about you, that I'd never really know until I investigated. So I did. That first luncheon was really an effort to probe under that professional veneer of yours. I didn't get very far that day. It was only that brief conversation we had about the Holy Spirit just before I left that kept me from forgetting the whole thing."

He reached out for my hand to cradle it in his. "All my preconceptions were exploded that day we spent together on the Skyline Drive. When I drove back to New York the next day, I kept thanking the Lord all the way home. I'm convinced He brought us together and that we are right for each other."

There was a long pause. "But I certainly hadn't intended to tip my hand so soon," he went on. "I try to approach things carefully, not blurt out my intentions like this."

I said nothing for a moment. My mind was racing furiously. *This amounts to a proposal of marriage. By making himself so vulnerable, Len is risking deep hurt.*

Finally I found my voice. "Len, you astonish me. This is only the second date we've had. How can you be so sure so soon about us? Don't you realize that with what you've just said, you've walked out on the end of a limb? The limb could so easily be chopped off. Why would you deliberately put yourself in such a position?"

"I told you—I hadn't intended saying all this. Maybe it's a deep desire for full honesty with you."

"And I honor that and respond to it. But Len, it's too soon for me to know. You're going too fast for me."

Only later did I realize... by following the dictates of his heart rather than the usual sophisticated game-playing approach, unwittingly Len had found the most direct route to my love. I felt the stirring of tenderness for him.

A few days after my return to Washington Len was back on the phone. He wanted me to come with him to Christmas Cove, Maine, for the Labor Day weekend to meet his parents. Almost wondering what would come out, I opened my mouth to reply and heard myself saying, "Yes, I could do that."

Again I flew to New York's LaGuardia Airport where Len met me. As we began the six-hour drive to Maine, Len briefed me on his parents. His father had been a Methodist minister for seven years before he had turned to education. Now he was dean of the School of Communications at Boston University. His mother, while rearing Len and his sister, Patricia, had been very active in women's clubs, Kappa Phi, church organizations.

For some time Len's parents had been conducting a yearly tour abroad and summering in Maine. From Europe his mother would bring home interesting items to stock the "Santa Claus Shop" which she had opened years before. It was a big hit with summer visitors in the Christmas Cove area.

"Mother is impressed that I am bringing you to Maine. She will want you to meet a lot of people," Len said uneasily. "I told her that we wanted to be alone to talk."

Len would be an unusual male, I thought, if he could turn off a socially-conscious mother.

We arrived at the grey-shingled LeSourd cottage on the inlet at South Bristol, Maine. The invigorating salt air brought back nostalgic memories of *Waverley*, our Cape Cod cottage. Len's parents greeted me warmly. However, the confrontation between him and his mother took place almost immediately.

"I know you said you didn't want any parties, Leonard," she began soon after we had unpacked the car, "but Mrs. Stuart insisted on having us all for a lobster dinner tomorrow night. Leonard, there simply was no way I could refuse."

"Sorry you did that, Mother," Len replied quietly. "You'll have to tell Mrs. Stuart we had already made other plans. Tomorrow night Catherine and I are going over to Boothbay."

"But, Leonard, you can go to Boothbay Sunday night."

Len shook his head. "We're going to Boothbay tomorrow night, Mother. I'll explain to Mrs. Stuart if you like. And please—no more surprises."

Mrs. LeSourd protested a little more—to no avail. Then she swallowed her disappointment as graciously as she could and made no further attempts to tie us down socially.

Len continued to be firm—to my relief. The last thing I wanted was a mother-dominated male. He kept to his plans for the two of us to be alone, to relax in the sun and talk. We started one morning while sitting on the rocks at Pemaquid Point. At three o'clock in the afternoon we suddenly realized that we had forgotten about lunch and had been in the sun too long. My legs were lobster red from sunburn.

For the next three days the almost nonstop exchange went on in cooler places. Though Len appeared to be by nature an easy-going relaxed person, he could also be determined. "We're middle-aged adults, Catherine, who have reached a point of maturity where we can make decisions more quickly," he pressed on. "I feel the Lord has brought us together; He's given me a love for you that overwhelms me, and I am ready and eager to marry you as soon as possible."

"Len, you may have your word from God, but He hasn't spoken to me yet," was my answer. "I think I'm in love with you, but I'm not yet ready to make a decision about marriage. Be patient with me."

Back in Washington after Labor Day weekend, my emotions were in a turmoil. I was facing the ultimate question: Was I going to give the rest of my life solely to a writing career—or did it also include marriage?

If I married Len I would have to move to the New York area near his work. That would mean putting my unfinished dream house on the market. I would have to leave Washington, all my friends, family and more than twenty years of memories.

One morning that still, small Voice in my inner spirit asked me some searching questions:

> You are right to be counting the cost and taking a good look at the major readjustments necessary for another marriage.

> Are there not certain areas of your life where some rigidity is creeping in? Did you not realize that My way would be to send you a man not just to satisfy your own needs of love and romance, but because he has gigantic needs himself?

Pondering this, I realized that in a first marriage, romance usually suffuses and dominates everything. It is only later, deep into marriage, that commitment to one another and the responsibilities that go along with this become as important as romance. Otherwise, the marriage has no chance of success.

But in second marriages, when we are older, commitment is writ large even at the beginning.

The question was whether I was ready for that much commitment, not just to a husband, but to three children too? Part of me was excited and stirred; the other part wanted to flee. Now I began to pray almost desperately for help and guidance.

When Len came down to Washington to meet my family and friends, Peter greeted him suspiciously at first. But I could soon tell that Len's amazing knowledge about sports was making an impression.

Len and I had dinner with my sister Em, her husband Harlow, and their two daughters, Lynn and Winifred. We drove to Evergreen Farm to meet my parents. There we also met my brother Bob, his wife Mary, and their three children, Bobby, Mary Margaret and Johnny. It was a difficult time for Len because he was put under intense scrutiny. I liked the way he handled himself: no attempt to impress, no straining for acceptance.

There were several more trips back and forth... to meet Linda, Len's ten-year-old daughter, and to talk to Norman and Ruth Peale, old friends of mine, older friends of the LeSourd family. Len had been at *Guideposts*, which the Peales had founded, for many years. Norman and Ruth confirmed all that I had heard already about him: talented editor, devoted father, spiritual seeker.

The time had come and I knew it. D-day—"Decision Day."

I was flying back to Washington from New York. As I sat in the hot, stuffy plane waiting for take-off, flocks of birds darted and wheeled beyond the edge of the runway. *Just like my darting, confused thoughts*, I mused.

The pilot's voice came over the intercom: "Sorry for the delay, folks. Things are a little stacked up here at La-Guardia this morning. Only four planes ahead of us now; maybe about fifteen minutes more."

Fifteen minutes. I did not know it then, but imbedded in those next minutes of waiting would be one shining moment that would shape the rest of my life.

As I sat buckled into my seat, I realized something: I had thought I wanted love again. But now that love was staring me in the face, I was afraid. Why did I so want to flee? What was my heart trying to tell me? Could it be because this romance was not tailor-made to my dream specifications? Len was asking me to love not only him, but to begin all over again with child-rearing. Three young children. At my age!

"Lord, You always give it to me straight," I breathed. "What am I to do?"

As I listened for His word, my mind reviewed a list of qualities that I had dreamed of in the man I wanted to marry. Basic character qualities were crucially important; others less so, like height, color of hair or eyes, whether he would be interested in yard and garden work, or a Mr. Fix-it in the house, whether he preferred loud or muted colors, or liked my favorite authors or certain beloved symphonies or piano or violin concertos. Such things I had never dared stipulate. This man, like all men, would have defects and weaknesses, just as all of us women do. Surely it is because of those human imperfections that involvement—especially in the close bond of marriage—stretches and tests us even to the point of pain.

In the past these thoughts about a second marriage had been generalities. *Now, Lord, I must focus on the particular man who has asked me to marry him. Len is offering me love that promises an end to my loneliness. I must give him an answer.*

I thought with longing of the new house being built for me in Washington, almost finished. Adjoining my bedroom, cut off from the rest of the house, would be a stepdown room where I would write. It would be my sanctuary. I was most reluctant to give up all that. Still, I would live in that house alone except for those brief holiday times when my son, Peter John, would be coming back from Yale University.

Two roads stretched ahead, and I was at a crossroad. In that house being built I might produce many articles and books. There I would have a cushioned, sheltered life—yes, and probably a lonely one.

And if I chose the other road, I would plunge directly
back into a turbulent life. It meant being a mother to Jeffrey, that mischievous imp of three; to Chester, six, with
those enormous brown eyes and a passion for baseball; to
Linda, ten, close to adolescence, and I had had no experience in rearing a daughter. I would battle to find enough
time for my writing. Someone else would enjoy that beautiful, step-down room off the bedroom.

My thoughts turned again to Him: "Lord, aren't You
overdoing it? Awhile back I told You that I was ready to
plunge back into the mainstream of life, but does it have
to be quite *this much* life? And when I thought child-rearing
was over? I don't understand, don't understand at all..."

There was no immediate answer, only tumbling thoughts
and question marks.

And then I remembered a sermon Peter Marshall had
preached with the intriguing title "Praying Is Dangerous
Business." With a clarity I would not have thought possible, several sentences came back to me:

> Perhaps you have tried to imagine in what way pray-
> ing could be dangerous. Well, for one thing, it is dan-
> gerous to pray for something unless you really and truly
> mean it. God might call your bluff and take you up on
> it!

> Again, God may require something of the one who
> prays. The answer to our prayer may involve some real
> effort, maybe even some sacrifice. God's method in
> answering almost any prayer is the march-into-the-Red-
> Sea-and-it-divides method or march-right-up-to-the-
> walls-and-they-fall-down technique. You've got to have
> faith for that sort of venture and courage, too. That's
> why some prayers may be dangerous.

So I had prayed about remarriage, and it turned out to
be one of those dangerous prayers which Peter knew so
well. My bluff was indeed being called.

I took a deep breath, for there was a luminosity about this moment that I recognized. I had met it before. It had nothing to do with the other-worldly type of inspiration which many people associate with prayer and with God. It was no off-in-a-rosy-cloud vision. Actually, it was more like being slapped in the face with a wet washcloth. Or like being brought to earth with a thud and sharply bidden to stand on one's feet and behave with maturity.

Suddenly, the choice God was presenting to me was clear. To say "Yes" meant adjustment, involvement. Yet I saw that if I chose the other road, I would be turning away from the mainstream of life. That way would be comfortable, but it would take me farther and farther from contact with people. It could also mean the slow, softening deterioration of the real person inside, of the spirit God had been molding and shaping and chiseling, often so painfully.

The plane was moving now, gathering speed rapidly. We were lifting off the runway, climbing at a steep angle. The sun blazed off the silvery wings and was reflected back in pinpoints of brilliant lights.

At that instant I knew what I had to do, I would say "Yes," to life.

In deciding where we would live after our November wedding, Len and I narrowed our house-hunting down to the Chappaqua (Westchester County) area. Being considerably closer to *Guideposts'* New York editorial office than Carmel was, that would cut Len's daily commuting time.

Though these did not feature in our decision, this section held two additional pluses for me: I already had fond teen-age memories of the beautiful countryside dating back to nine weeks spent at the National Girl Scout Camp at nearby Briarcliff Manor. And Edward Kuhn, my editor at the McGraw-Hill Book Company (publisher of my books since the first one, *Mr. Jones, Meet the Master*) lived in Chappaqua. Since the relationship between author and editor is a close one (if one has the right editor), it would certainly enhance communication to be living in the same village.

With surprising ease a real estate agent helped us find the house ideally suited to our needs: a sprawling, white clapboard house with dark red shutters, three floors, 11 rooms, set in an enormous yard.

Since the house was built on a sloping lot, all of the back windows of the fully-finished ground floor looked out on the big back yard. There I would set up my hideaway workroom for writing.

As we stood hand-in-hand looking at this room, figuring out on which wall we would build bookcases, Len said, "Catherine, there are a couple of things, I—well—need to say to you. I believe that God gave you writing as your work in this world. So it's important that you keep on with that.

"And another thing—after so many years of being 'Catherine Marshall' to the public, it would be unwise and even silly for you to change your writing name at this point. I've been in the writing-editing world so long that I have no problem with it at all."

I looked at my husband-to-be, astonished and grateful. Len's face was serious, but there was a twinkle in his eyes. He meant it—and really did understand.

We were married on November 14, 1959 in the Presbyterian Church in Leesburg, Virginia, with my son, Peter, giving me away. Never have the bonds of matrimony been tied more completely by clergy: my father, a Presbyterian pastor; Len's father, a Methodist minister; and Dr. Norman Vincent Peale, a pastor to both of us, all three officiating at the ceremony, using the memorable wedding service Peter Marshall had always used, part of which he had written himself.

Linda was starry-eyed as she edged up to Peter John, her new six-foot-five brother. Chester had by now accepted me. Jeffrey, Len had decided, was too young to attend, but was eagerly waiting to see his "new mommie" again.

Early that evening after the reception at Evergreen Farm, Len and I would be flying to Los Angeles, then on to Hawaii for our honeymoon.

On our way from the church back to the farm, Len and I learned that Chester had missed seeing the ceremony. Seated beside his Grandmother LeSourd, at a moment when her attention was on the wedding service, he had slid his lithe body off the pew to the floor and mysteriously disappeared from his grandmother's grasp. Chester had spent the remainder of the service crawling under the pews from the front of the church to the back, slithering his way between the legs of the wedding guests, mopping up the floor with his best pants. At the time we laughed over the ludicrous antics of a small boy.

It should have been fair warning about what lay ahead.

Chester, Leonard, Jeffrey, Catherine, and Linda

XI

Second Family

God setteth the solitary
in families....
Beloved, let us love
one another: for love
is of God....

Psalm 68:6; I John 4:7

Second Family

In December, 1959 upon Len's and my return from our honeymoon, I found it deeply satisfying once again to assume the role of all-out homemaker. First, there was the task of combining our possessions, deciding what to use, what to eliminate, what gaps were left to fill. The decorating job of bringing together this amalgamation was challenging and fun.

The yard dared me to make it beautiful. An outcropping of New York granite in the front yard cried out for a rock garden. A stone wall across the entire front of the property demanded a perennial border. Soon I was poring over nursery catalogues and garden books.

The children watched all this with fascination, Linda enchanted with her own room and the chance to help decide colors and other details, the boys elated over their immediate discovery of playmates next door and of so much space outdoors in which to roam.

But it takes more than a house, no matter how attractive, and possessions, and even a wonderful yard to make a home. For what is a home but people, the individuals in it, and the interaction among them?

The scene of our first dinner together as a new family is forever etched in my memory. We were gathered around the dinner table with Len's three young children: Linda, Chester and Jeffrey. My son Peter was away at Yale University.

I had lovingly prepared food I thought the children would enjoy—meat loaf, scalloped potatoes, broccoli, a green salad. Len's face was alive with happiness as he blessed the food.

But then as Chester's big brown eyes regarded the food on his plate, he grimaced, suddenly bolted from the table and fled upstairs, slamming the bedroom door behind him.

"Let him go, Catherine," Len said. Then seeing my stricken face, he explained ruefully, "I'm afraid my children aren't used to much variety in food. Mostly I've just fed them hamburgers, hot dogs, or fried chicken from a take-out place."

Len then went upstairs to persuade Chester to come back to the table. He found the little boy in bed, covers over his head, rocking back and forth. When he tearfully refused to come back downstairs, my new husband sternly told his son to undress and go to bed. There would be no supper for him. I was devastated at the thought of Chester going to sleep hungry. The dinner was spoiled for all of us.

Had Len and I but known, that scene was a harbinger of what lay ahead. Linda's resistance towards her new stepmother surfaced that first night when she refused to wear slippers on the cold hardwood floors, insisting that she had always gone barefoot around the house. I understood only too well what it must have been like to be the only female in the family. Now suddenly she was vying with me for Len's time and affection.

The two boys wanted to room together, yet were forever tussling like bear cubs. When they started scrapping yet again after lights were out, Len summarily removed Jeff to another room. The little fellow sobbed himself to sleep.

That night as I was sitting propped up in bed reading, my attention kept wandering from the child psychology book to the problems at hand. "Sibling rivalry," the learned author tagged it. "Parents, remain calm and unperturbed," his advice ran. "It happens in every family. Just remember, this too will pass."

Oh, sure, went my rebellious ruminations. *It will pass by the time parents are weary basket-cases.* I could see it so clearly: the bespectacled child psychologist before his typewriter in his cubicle of an office, the door bolted against "siblings" of all ages, cheerfully clacking out his jocular words of wisdom for us beleagured parents in the thick of it.

Later on the same night, after Len and I, exhausted, had just fallen asleep, the shrill ringing of the telephone awoke us. It was Peter. "Mom, I got picked up for speeding on the Merritt Parkway. I'm at the police station."

We agreed to post bond for Peter's release.

Yet all these troubles were but surface symptoms, the top of the iceberg of difficulties. Flooding in on us day after day were problems relating to our extended family— Len's parents and mine, along with other relatives—together with the children's emotional trauma from six housekeepers in two years. Even Peter was still suffering from his loss, shock and loneliness following his father's death ten years before.

How do you put families broken by death or divorce back together again? How can a group of individuals of diverse backgrounds, life experiences and ages ever become a family at all? I did not have the answers, but I knew Someone who did.

So I began slipping out of the bedroom at dawn while the children were asleep for a quiet time of talking-things-over prayers, Bible reading and writing down thoughts in the ever-present Journal. For example:

> Our very first step in solving family problems is resolutely to view our particular difficulties as God's schoolroom for the truths He longs to teach us and the immense riches of His glory He wants to pour into our lives—if only we will let Him. He's going to have to be our Teacher all the way. What's required of us is the open-mindedness of the eager learner, plus taking the time day by day to submit practical questions to Him.

During those early morning times there dawned the realization of something I had not wanted to face: Len was one of those men who felt that his wife was more "spiritual" than he, somehow having more Christian know-how. Len liked to point out that I was more articulate in prayer. Therefore, he was assuming that I would take charge of spiritual matters in our home while he would handle disciplining the children, finances, and such things.

I already knew from my mail how many, many women there are who find it difficult to talk with their husbands about anything religious, much less pray with them. How could I make Len see that "spirituality" was as much his responsibility as mine? *Lord, what do I do about this one?* I hurled heavenward.

Somehow the answer was given me that nagging a male about this would not work. My directive was to go on morning by morning with my Quiet Time, saying nothing about it but otherwise refusing to accept the spiritual responsibility for the home. The assurance was given me that then God would work it out.

Meanwhile, how desperately I needed that early time with Him! I had been transplanted from metropolitan Washington to typical suburbia, USA. Chappaqua was and still is a sprawling Westchester County community nicknamed "the bedroom of New York City." Every weekday Len and most of the other Chappaqua men caught early morning trains to the city, arriving back in the evening at a weary 6:45—or later. During these long days, the women had to carry all family responsibilities, including seemingly endless chauffeuring of children.

A typical morning for me might go like this...A loud yelp from the boys' bedroom took me there on the run. Chester was rubbing his leg. "Jeff bit me," he grimaced. Sure enough, there were teeth marks on Chester's leg.

"You're going to be punished for this," I told Jeff sternly.

"But Chester kicked me first. Want to see where?"

I really didn't, but Jeff showed me anyway.

At that moment Linda appeared in the hallway in her night clothes, a dazed, sleepy look on her face, her feet bare. "Linda, the floor is cold. Put on your slippers."

"Can't, Mom. Can't get my feet in. The washing machine shrank them."

Obviously it was to be "one of those mornings." I went on to the kitchen to start breakfast and to fix Chester's school lunch. But I had not done my housework properly the night before: it was necessary to empty his lunch box before I could fill it. I extracted two packages of bubble gum, three rocks, a pack of well-thumbed baseball cards, and a teacher's note which he had forgotten to deliver.

The doorbell rang for a boy to hand in a special delivery letter. Then the telephone rang. Chester dripped jam on his freshly pressed school pants and had to change them. Peter, who was home between semesters at Yale, called out that he had a dental appointment in New York and that he couldn't find any clean undershorts. Linda and Chester dashed for the bus, banging the door behind them. Through the window, I saw that they *had* made it. I turned around to pour myself a second cup of coffee, and there on the kitchen counter was Chester's lunch he had forgotten to take. So-o-o, yet another errand.

I sank into the nearest chair, sorely needing that cup of coffee. As I sipped it, trying to get back some calmness and perspective, in my mind I was addressing the Almighty. *Lord, what is this about anyway? When You put people together in families, just what did You really have in mind?*

Despite myself, I could see some humor even in my previous early morning insight that God uses family problems as part of His schoolroom. "Lord, are You sure this family bit is not one of Your more sneaky tricks? I mean for hammering and chiseling and molding us into the characters You intend us to be? But You *never* give up on us, do You?"

My thoughts rambled on. Day by day I was beginning to catch glimpses of what the Creator must have had in mind by decreeing that we be born as helpless babies into the nurture of loving parents who in their turn, are required to give of themselves fully to their offspring. So the family is meant to be the training ground for life, a true microcosm for the world outside the home where person has to get along with person, pupils with each other and with teachers, employees with bosses, management with labor, nation with nation.

So how do we learn patience and tolerance and forgiveness of each other? How to stay calm and not get angry? How else except by living elbow-to-elbow in the family unit, even if there is some biting and kicking on the bedroom floor and considerable sandpapering of varying interests and personalities in the process.

I was also learning that most of us are not anything like as realistic as our God. *We* like to deal with high-flown theological abstractions. (After all, they can be kept at safe arm's length.) *He* deals with the lilies of the field, the yeast in the housewife's bread, patches on garments and curing Grandmother's arthritis. So of course the master design for us to advance toward our heavenly home via the nitty-gritty of family life would be just like Him.

Then I remembered that during His time on earth, He Himself had had to get along with at least six other children in a humble Nazareth household. What a comfort to know that He has experienced what families are up against, sympathizes, and stands waiting and available with the wisdom and help we need.

As the days went by, Len was becoming curious about why I was getting up so early. "What are you doing each morning?" he asked one day.

"Seeking God's answers for my day. I know He has them, but I have to ask Him, then give Him the chance to feed back to me His perspective and His practical helps. You see, if I don't take time for this as the kick-off of the day, He gets crowded out."

"That would be good for me, too," was Len's reaction. "After all, we're in this together. Why not set the alarm for 30 minutes earlier so that we could pray together before we start the day?"

Thus an experiment began that was to change our lives. The next day at a local hardware store I found an electric timer to plug into a small, four-cup coffee pot. That night I prepared the coffee tray at bedtime and carried it to the bedroom. The following morning we were wakened by the pleasant aroma of coffee rather than the shrill ringing of an alarm clock.

We drank our coffee, and I started to read at a spot in Philippians. But Len wanted to get on with the prayer. "You start, Catherine," he said sleepily.

"But *how* are we going to pray about this problem of Linda's lack of motivation to study?" I asked. A discussion began. It got so intense that time ran out before we got to actual prayer.

After a few mornings of this, Len agreed that we needed more time. Our wake-up hour went from 6:30 to 6 a.m. Discipline in the morning meant going to bed earlier. It became a matter of priorities. The morning time together soon changed from an experiment to a shared adventure in prayer.

By this time, Len, always methodical, had purchased himself a five-by-seven, brown loose-leaf notebook. He began jotting down the prayer requests, listing them by date. When the answers came, those too were recorded, also by date, together with how God had chosen to fill that particular need. Rapidly, the notebook was becoming a real prayer log.

Not only that, as husband and wife we had found a great way of communication. Bedtime, we had already learned, was a dangerous time to present controversial matters to one another. When we were fatigued from the wear and pressures of the day, disagreements could easily erupt.

Yet when we tackled these same topics the next morning in an atmosphere of prayer, simply asking God for His wisdom about them, controversy dissolved, with communication flowing easily between us.

Of the hundreds of entries in Len's brown notebook during this period, these were the most repeated:

1. That household help be found so that Catherine can continue the writing of her novel *Christy*.

2. That Peter will forget trying to be a playboy at Yale and find God's purpose for his life.

3. That Linda will stop rebelling against authority at home and at school.

4. That Chester will learn to control his temper and accept his new home situation.

5. That we can find the way to get Jeff out of diapers at night.

Morning by morning the requests from outside our home also piled up and up: a neighbor dying of cancer, a close friend involved in adultery, an associate with a drinking problem, parents we knew asking for advice about rebellious children, and on and on.

We were learning that specific prayer requests yield precise answers. So we did not simply ask for household help; we recorded a request for live-in help, a good cook, someone who loved children, who would be warm and comfortable to live with.

The day came when Len set down the answer to this in the brown notebook—middle-aged Lucy Arsenault. She was sent to us through Len's mother who had known her in Boston years before. Finding her enabled me actually to pick up work on *Christy* again.

I had tried to get help with Jeff's diaper problem from a highly trained pediatrician in nearby Mount Kisco. All that netted was: "Mrs. LeSourd," and the doctor's voice was tinged with sarcasm, "forget it! He'll get over it before he goes to college."

What was the point of reminding the pediatrician about the wasted time and added daily wash load of three to six diapers, plus sheets? Yet nothing we tried solved this puzzler.

That summer when we went to visit my parents at Evergreen Farm in Virginia, I felt an inner nudge to seek the homely advice of the local country practitioner. After he had heard me out, the doctor, his eyes sparkling, said, "I meet the bed-wetting problem often. I sympathize. But Catherine, you've made it too easy for Jeffrey. Nothing's wrong except that he's simply too lazy to get up and go to the bathroom, too well-padded with too many soft diapers.

"So here's the solution I suggest: waterproof the bed well. Take *all* diapers off. Steel yourself to let Jeff wallow in wet misery the rest of the night.

"But temper that with praise and reward. Put a monthly chart marked off into days on the wall by his bed. Each morning Jeff makes it dry through the night, paste a big gold star on the chart and praise him lavishly."

It worked. And we thanked God and the country doctor for his humor and common sense.

But unless we had been recording both the prayer requests and the answers with dates, we might have assumed these to be "coincidences" or just something that would have happened anyway. With those written notations marking the answers to prayer, we found our gratitude to God mounting. The prayer log was a marvelous stimulus to faith.

Len and I were certainly being taught about prayer as we submitted the practicalities of daily life to God. Yet not all prayers were answered the way we had anticipated. We found that prayer is not handing God a want-list and then having beautiful answers float down on rosy clouds. Also, His timing is certainly not ours; most answers came more slowly than we wished, and piecemeal.

Those answers were also presented to us not simply through some change in external circumstances, but just as often through inner guidance. That meant that what God had to say to us in our early morning times was even more important than what we presented to Him.

Out of His direction came some household rules:

1. Meals at regular hours and at least the evening meal eaten together as a family unit whenever possible. Dinner thus to be the focal point of each day.
(Each child soon learned to say a grace, was encouraged to articulate personal thoughts and needs, and to participate in the discussion of current events. At the end of the meal Len or I read something from the Bible and then closed with prayer, again with each child participating, if only one sentence.)

2. Regular bedtime, though later on weekends.

3. No television for children on school nights. TV and movies on weekends to be screened carefully.

4. Linda's endless telephone conversations with friends to be limited to one period, 3:30 to 6 each afternoon. No twosome dates until she is 16.

5. Time to be given to the children on weekends for family outings and/or home games. (We kept a bulging closet of games.)

6. On Sundays go as a family to church.

7. Len and I to share checking on children's school homework. Our full interest and participation in the Parent-Teacher Association and all school events pertaining to our three.
(Though we would listen carefully to our children's complaints and be fair, we stressed that the teacher's and principal's authority would always be upheld.)

8. Discipline always to be part of our life together; punishment to fit the disobedience; spankings (administered by Len) by no means ruled out.

The implementation of all this was never easy. In the seventh grade, Linda was bright and freckle-faced with all the instincts of a tragic actress. Like all her peers, she was trying to grow up too soon. Len and I became accustomed to the cry, "Oh, you just don't understand-d-d."

Naturally, the majority of our notations in the prayer log focused on our children during those early years. In rearing them, we were gradually learning that God was more interested in our learning the patience to wait for *His* answer to particular problems than in our painfully learning the hard way by rushing ahead of Him trying out schemes *we* had devised.

Patience? What could be better calculated to teach patience than trying to drum manners and tidiness into children? Before dinner on three nights out of five: "Boys, you call *those* hands clean? Back to the bathroom you go..." "Jeff, elbows off the table." "Chester, it's no good trying to hide the carrots under the lettuce leaf..." From Len, "Linda, are you trying to use your *hair* for dental floss? *Take your hair out of your mouth.*"

Or, "For the 687th time, who left towels on the bathroom floor this time?"..."Boys, this room is a mess. Get those clothes off the floor and hang them up."... "Linda, I've asked you over and over *not* to doodle on the wall while you're on the telephone...." Surely the writer of that Holy Writ, "Let patience have her perfect work" must have had parents in mind.

Or consider Jesus' admonition that we forgive seventy times seven. Perhaps Christ was not thinking specifically of the family unit when He spoke those words, or I think He might have trebled the figure.

How to get practice in forgiveness? There was the matter of Jeffrey repeatedly leaving ink cartridges in his pants pocket and in that way ruining an entire tub of laundry. Each time I put away the family wash, every white garment had the navy-blue measles. Forgiveness. Forgiveness!

Then there was Chester's habit of forgetting everything because his mind was floating around somewhere on cloud nine. He could not wear his P.F. Flyers because he had left them at the public tennis courts; his sweater was abandoned at Donn's house; it was impossible to do his assignment because he had left his book at school. As I would step on the accelerator for those time-consuming trips to the tennis courts and to Donn's house to collect possessions, I knew that I must find the way "not to let the sun go down on my wrath."

Or late one afternoon I glanced out one of the front windows and did a double-take at Linda kneeling in the newly planted rock garden. My mind refused to believe what my eyes were seeing. Carefully, methodically, she was dragging, first on one side, then the other, newly purchased white sneakers through the garden dirt. My indignant protest brought only a withering, "Mom, *everyone* wears dirty sneakers. I'd just look crazy if mine were all new and white."

And there was Jeffrey's strange fascination with, of all things, shoelaces. One morning in nursery school the teacher asked him to stand up and recite. Jeff tried hard to struggle to his feet, he really did. But how could a guy straighten up when he had tied the laces of his Keds securely to his belt?

Then there was the afternoon I put him down for a nap. In no time disconsolate crying was issuing from the bedroom. I found Jeff trapped under the bed, his shoelaces woven in and out of the bedsprings, knotted over and over.

Or after he had learned to read: "Jeff, no wonder you're so irritable this morning. You sneaked reading again last night, didn't you?"

"Well..." The look was downcast.

"No use denying it. I found *The Secret of Fiery Gorge* shoved under your bed.

But Jeff liked to fight with his back to the wall. "But Mom, how could I have read? Bet you didn't see my light on."

"No. But you read anyway. And I know how."

The blue eyes searched me suspiciously, only half believing. "How *could* you know?"

"Special radar."

This was too much. Now he must know. "How? Tell me how then."

"By lying on the floor by the door with the book tilted to catch the light from the hall, that's how."

Jeff looked at me, all his impishness showing. "Gee, Mom, I wish I had a *dumber* Mother!"

Through all this we learned that even though children resist discipline, all of them crave the security of firm structure and are confused and rudderless when parents give in to them out of fear of their own offsprings' displeasure. Years later our children would be admitting that secretly they had been relieved at the way we had stood our ground with them.

As an older girl, Linda would often comment, "I feel sorry for poor so-and-so. She can do anything she wants to do. I think her parents just don't *care*."

As time went on, an especially significant answer to prayer was unfolding before me, my plea that Len would assume his proper role as the spiritual head of our home.

His first insight was the realization that the two boys were going to pattern almost everything after him. This was so obvious with something like athletics. Len had begun teaching his sons to swing a baseball bat as soon as they could lift it. He pored over the newspaper sports pages each morning. As soon as Chester and Jeff could read, they too were studying the sports pages.

If the Christian faith was to become important to them, it would happen through their father. Otherwise the two boys would conclude that religion was for the womenfolk and ignore it. With this revelation, Len did an about-face on turning spiritual matters over to me; he became the one to call the family together for prayer around the table.

As the boys witnessed their father spontaneously praying and were called on to follow, they were soon responding, praying aloud with no self-consciousness.

One evening we went to dinner at a crowded restaurant. I had just picked up my fork when Chester quietly remarked, "In school today our teacher was talking about saying grace before meals. He said that we should not skip doing this even when we're eating out."

There was a pause during which Len and I looked at one another. Len nodded in agreement. "Your teacher was absolutely right, Chester. We should have done that all along."

Around the table we inclined our heads slightly. In a low-keyed voice Len thanked God for the food. Jeff's chatter started as soon as the soft "Amen" was out of his father's mouth. We thought that we had been exceptionally unobtrusive in the crowded dining room.

But when the meal was almost over a nice-looking young

man approached Len, leaned over, spoke several sentences for his ear alone, smiled, and left.

"What was that all about?" I asked curiously.

Len was looking bemused. "The man wanted me to know that he thought it was great for a family not to be ashamed to pray in public. I feel I've been given credit for something I don't deserve."

So part of the beautiful answer to this prayer, I sat there thinking, is that Len himself does not realize *how far* he's come. As he became the spiritual head of the household, I was given the freedom to play the supporting role as I had in my marriage to Peter. In no way did I consider this a secondary role. Len and I continued as a team, checking and sometimes correcting each other. Household help freed me to write in the mornings, leaving afternoons and evenings for family matters.

After five years in Chappaqua the cold New York winters were handing me frequent colds, all too often ending in protracted bouts of bronchitis. The doctors advised a warmer climate for me.

Len dispatched me to Florida to investigate rentals for the four-month winter season of 1964-65. We ended up buying a house in Boynton Beach and moving there in November, 1964 since Len discovered he could still handle his editorial responsibilites at *Guideposts* while commuting back and forth between Florida and New York City.

The two boys quickly adjusted to the change of location. Linda, however, was finding life more difficult as she entered a stage of adolescent rebellion against her parents. There were occasions when I felt close to this gifted but often troubled girl, more times when I felt like a rejected parent. I struggled with all of the negative stepmother images. Often I caught myself resenting this child and her attitudes. Since this was not my image of the "good mother," I tried to ignore or bury such emotions.

When we were still living in Chappaqua, I would seek God's help for this in my Quiet Times. He met me one Sunday in church. The winter sunlight was streaming in the tall arched windows laying long patterns of light across the white colonial sanctuary. I was sitting there thinking about Linda. Suddenly in my mind and heart His voice was speaking to me with particular clarity and intensity. *Unless you love her, you don't love Me.*

Lord, I know that's true. The thought stabbed me. *But how do we love certain persons when we hate some of the things they do? Please tell me how. And Lord, I have another problem. I can't manufacture love. Nobody can. How can I manage it unless You give me that love as a sheer gift?*

With the issues thus clearly drawn, I struggled on. Over and over I would take a fresh grip on my willingness to love Linda no matter what she did—all the way from minor infractions to slipping out of her bedroom window after midnight for a date with a senior football star five years older than she. Or an ostensible trip to the library being rather a rendezvous with a boy in the village. Since we did not want her to date until she was 16, she showed us how many devious ways there were around that rule.

As I willed to love, I asked God to take care of my emotions and make my love real. For a time it would work, and our home would know contentment and harmony. Then another crisis would develop and I would fall on my face.

The difficulties grew until Linda was finding life all but unmanageable. For years, schoolwork had been difficult. Here was a bright girl whose grades seesawed wildly between "A" and flunking. Almost every term report carried teachers' comments about "poor attitude and motivation" and "work not up to level of ability." Tutors and extra sessions and finally, a preparatory school brought no demonstrable results.

During these years, both in Chappaqua and in Florida, her father and I had tried everything we knew—guidance counselors, a child psychologist, counseling with Christian friends, group prayer, prayer at Linda's bedside while she was asleep—every type of prayer we could think of. There had been some breakthroughs, such as the times she came home from prep school and really participated in our family devotions. Even so, Len and I knew that the root problem remained. It seemed to be centered in her will; she appeared to be unable to want to be any different.

In college the trouble grew. To academic difficulties was now added the youth revolution of the late 1960s. Linda plunged wholeheartedly into it: life pattern, clothing styles, long straight hair, wire-rimmed spectacles, protest meetings, campus sit-ins, hitchhiking to peace marches and rallies, one of them all the way from the city of Delaware, Ohio to Washington, D.C.

Graduation from college came for our daughter in June, 1971. Linda's father, grandparents, and I arrived at the graduation scene to find a very unhappy girl on our hands. There was a thin veneer of normality, but flashes of irritation and anger kept breaking through to us. The strain in the relationship between Linda and me was obvious, her dissatisfactions deep.

Watching the academic procession walk by on sneakers or T-thong sandals, with mortarboard caps tilted on the heads at every possible angle, I wondered what the other graduates were feeling. Were most of them malcontents too, with life somehow out of kilter, values all a-jumble?

The scene left me with such heaviness of spirit that after our return home I spent one morning working on the release of all my resentments against Linda stretching back over the years to age ten. To my astonishment, I filled three pages.

Though I found it difficult to show this list to Len, I felt the need of such "walking in the light" as a step towards cleansing. Certainly Jesus had made it clear that our harboring any resentment is a sin needing the Father's forgiveness. Not only that, a sin carrying a dreadful penalty:

> And whenever you stand praying, forgive, if you have
> anything against any one; so that your Father also who
> is in heaven may forgive you your trespasses.[1]

With the list before us, Len and I prayed about this together. First, my confession of these resentments followed by the claiming of His glorious promise of immediate forgiveness.

Yet I well knew that resentments are emotions so deeply imbedded that we cannot shed them by a shrugged-off wishing them away. How great then to know that as we set the rudder of our wills to forgive and tell God so, *He* will undertake for us the task of untangling and cleansing at the emotional level.

At that point I got a fresh view of the meaning of the Cross. Our resurrected Lord stands before us, nail-pierced hands outstretched, saying, "Hand Me your resentments, your grudges, your anger. *All* of it. *That's* what I died for. As you decide in your will to hand Me all these negatives and tell Me so, I still, in the present, literally absorb these negatives into My own body. Even as the corruption of death was transmited into Life in My resurrection body, so in exchange for your sin I hand you My love—freely, abundantly enough to over-flow to the very one you have resented."

So, I thought wonderingly, then the exchange made possible by Jesus' Cross—His love and new life in return for my sins—was not just something that happened at a point in time, historically. That atoning work is still going on.

This shed new light on the Apostle Peter's words:

He personally bore our sins in His (own) body to the tree... that we might die... to sin and live to righteousness. By His wounds you have been healed.[2]

Neither Len nor I told Linda anything about our prayer of release. We did not have long to wait to see results.

Several weeks later on Cape Cod during that tumultuous summer of 1971 came the climax to our long years of struggle with this particular situation. When my grandchild, Amy Catherine Marshall, was born on July 22 with severe liver, kidney and brain damage—a group of us gathered on the Cape for concentrated prayer.[3] On an impulse I telephoned Linda, who was working in her grandmother's Santa Claus Shop in Maine. Would she care to join us?

There was a moment's silence. "Yes," she said, "I'd like to be there."

Afterward, Linda told me that she wanted to come because I was the one who had telephoned and invited her. What happened when she got there literally reversed the direction of Linda's life. As is usually the case, people other than her parents—Len and me—were used by God as the catalyst for our daughter. The turning point that followed is best told in her words...

> On the afternoon after my arrival at Cape Cod I was about to take a shower. A particular moment is crystallized forever for me. I had one foot on the bathroom rug, the other in the shower stall. At that instant, like a bolt, the realization hit me that one foot in, one foot out was an accurate representation of my life so far. Several times I'd gone through the motions of committing my life to God. Yet I did not have an obedient heart. I was living in outright rebellion against Him.
>
> I sensed that this was the moment to decide—for Him or against Him. There could no longer be any middle ground.
>
> Standing there, I carefully weighed what choosing the Lord's side would cost me. Obviously, some things

in my life would have to go. But I was tired of living in two worlds and not enjoying either. Desperately, I longed for His peace in my heart. I took a deep breath and said aloud, "I choose You, Lord." Then I got in the shower. That shower was my true baptism.

The following day came many hours of agonizingly honest dialogue with Len and me. Tears flowed. After that I understood why the direction given me in the Chappaqua church—*Unless you love her, you don't love Me*—had been so difficult for me.

"I thought I wanted a loving relationship with you when you married Dad," Linda told me. "But resentment crowded in. The reason was that at a gut level I thought you were taking Dad away from me. I would no longer be number one in his life."

During this long evening of honesty and confession among the three of us and then to God in prayer, many barriers came crashing down. For Linda it was the release of years of hostility and guilt. For us, it was a facing up to mistakes and fears and lack of understanding.

Following this, it was Linda herself who wanted to crown all these events with a "believer's baptism" in the ocean followed by a communion service on the beach.

That was not the finish of this particular episode. For God had some further work to do in me the morning after the communion service.

During the intervening hours, my mind must have flicked at some secret thoughts along the line, "All those years of agony she put her father and me through, then she's forgiven by God *instantly*. Isn't that too easy a forgiveness?" Ugly secret thoughts—except God knew.

The next morning I was awakened to the clear, incisive internal message, "Remember My story of the prodigal son? You're in grave danger of taking the place of that elder brother. That morning you didn't quite mean business about finally releasing all those 'aughts' against Linda, did you? I heard and answered anyway. *Now let them go*. For now, take the lowest seat at My banquet table, below Linda. And I want you to confess all this to Linda this morning.''

Thus I was properly zapped, as our boys would say. Humbly and a trifle haltingly, at breakfast I made my confession to Linda. She wept again, this time for joy, then ecstatically hugged me. It was a reconciliation written in heaven.

And so Len and I have grown over the years as parents, and our morning time together has set the tone and direction of over 21 years of marriage. That original coffee-timer (still operating, although with many new parts) is one of our most cherished possessions. We know that neither one of us, or both of us, without God have the wisdom to handle the problems which life hands us day by day. But as early morning prayer partners we have added assurance that "where two or three are gathered together" in His name, our all-loving and all-wise Saviour, Rescuer, and Lord is indeed with us.

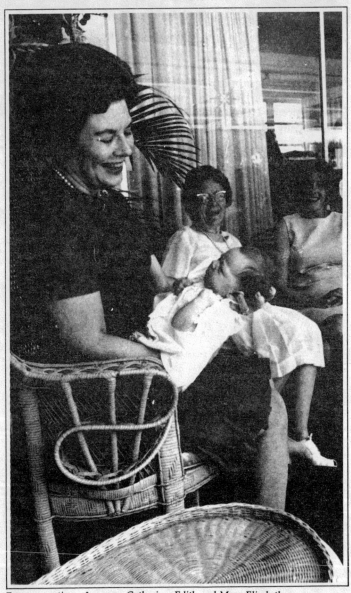

Four generations , Leonora , Catherine, Edith and Mary Elizabeth

XII

Grandmother

And all thy children
shall be taught of the Lord;
and great shall be the peace
of thy children....
The Lord shall bless thee....
(and) thou shalt see thy
children's children....

Isaiah 54:13; Psalm 128:5,6

Grandmother

A never-ending source of wonder to me is the way God continues to reveal new truth to His children, especially to those who reach an age when they think they know a few things about the Christian faith. As the years went on, I thought, *Surely now in my latter years I'll be able to put to good use what wisdom I have accumulated.* Instead, I have been going through one of the most intense learning periods of my life. Especially in connection with our children and grandchildren.

Peter John graduated from Yale in rebellion against a God who had taken his father away by death. During one of our morning prayer times, Len received the guidance that he was to encourage Peter to attend a conference of the Fellowship of Christian Athletes at Estes Park, Colorado. Peter surprised us by deciding to go. There he was challenged by his huddle leader, Donn Moomaw, a former all-American football player, now a Presbyterian pastor. When Donn bluntly told Peter that he was fleeing God and messing up his life, Peter was so convicted that by the end of the conference he had made a commitment to Jesus Christ. Len and I stood by almost as spectators and watched as amazing changes took place in Peter.

First, he enrolled at Princeton Theological Seminary within a month after his experience at Estes Park. There he began attending a prayer group composed of students who had experienced an infilling of the Holy Spirit. To the uneasiness of seminary authorities, the students were manifesting some of the gifts of the Spirit in these meetings. Healings were taking place, damaged relationships were being restored. A new movement of the Holy Spirit was moving among the seminarians.

When Peter next came home on vacation, he challenged Len and me about our openness to the Holy Spirit. Had we been baptized with the Spirit? If not, how could we really hope to make any progress in the Christian Life?

As he talked, I thought back, remembering that summer of 1944 when I had found myself with such intense curiosity about the Holy Sprit; how this had resulted in a careful study of the Old and New Testaments, ending with a quiet asking for this Gift of all gifts. But Peter was still not satisfied. Then why, he questioned, was I not manifesting some of the *particular* gifts of the Spirit?

Stunned by the 180-degree change of direction in my son, here is a notation I made at the time:

> When Peter graduated from Yale, he informed us that he might decide to be a beach boy at Virginia Beach for awhile. Now he is deep into the Holy Spirit movement. What is going on, Lord? We prayed that Peter would find You in his own way, and this has been gloriously answered. But now I must look deeply into this somewhat strange but exciting new contemporary activity.

Len and I had already become interested in this movement through our editorial relationship with John and Elizabeth Sherrill. While writing *The Cross and the Switchblade* with David Wilkerson, the Sherrills had had an experience with the Holy Spirit, resulting in some momentous changes in their lives. The impact of all this on Len and me was to bear lasting fruit in our lives.

Then Peter announced to us that he thought he had found *the* girl, a fellow-student at Princeton Seminary, the daughter of Dr. and Mrs. Calvin Wallis, medical missionaries to Guatemala. One weekend he brought her home to Chappaqua.

Edith Wallis was tall, blonde—a joyous creature—and a real answer to prayer.

Before Peter was in his teens I had begun praying for my son's future mate, wherever she might be. As I continued praying, I had asked myself, *What would be the characteristics of spirit and mind and heart of that "just right girl" for my son?* I was not so much concerned with whether she would be a blonde or brunette; surely the inner beauty would dictate the outer.

Being me, I took pencil in hand and committed to paper, item by item, the lineaments of my dream girl. Most important of all, this girl would have met Jesus Christ for herself and would have fallen in love with Him. She would have a good mind, with enough education for mutual, intellectual stimulation. She would have a lot of the joy of life in her, a sense of humor, a certain zing—and so on and on.

Then when the portrait seemed complete, one morning I placed the dream in God's keeping, asking Him to correct any flaws in it and bring it into fruition in Peter's life in His own time and His own way. I stuck the note about my dream girl between the pages of an old Bible and forgot about the paperwork on it.

Ten years later, as I was dusting and rearranging a shelf of books one morning, the slip of paper fell out of the old Bible. I read it, astonished. Here was a perfect description of Edith Wallis. God had thrown in a few extra goodies as dividends. She was tall like Peter, blonde like Peter, a wonderful cook—what man wouldn't like that! She was interested in gardening like Peter. And I loved her immediately and have never stopped thanking God for such a momentous answer to prayer.

Peter and Edith determined that their wedding must be in keeping with their Christian commitment. Three ministers would take part, which reminded Len and me of our wedding. There would be congregational singing and a sermon, features rarely included at that time. Moreover, the elders of the Rye Presbyterian Church, where the service was to be held, would administer the sacrament of the Lord's Supper not only to the bride and groom as the first act of their married life, but also to the entire congregation. As it turned out, this unusual wedding lasted one hour, twenty minutes.

Naturally there were some cautious comments afterward about the uniqueness of the wedding—all the way from, "Well, we've never seen a couple married so thoroughly," to "I've never been so touched by the sincerity of two young people," to "I couldn't help wondering what So-and-So thought about a *sermon* at a wedding!"

But Len and I noticed that to 16-year-old Linda especially, it was everything a wedding should be. She had glimpsed true romance, had seen it in front of the altar being dedicated to God. There were stars even in her still rebellious, nonreligious eyes. "It was the greatest wedding ever!" she exulted.

Fifteen years later we were to see the significance of Linda's reaction.

After graduation from Princeton Seminary, Peter's first

charge was as an assistant pastor in West Hartford, Connecticut.

Then in early May, 1967 Edith and Peter gave us the exciting news that they were expecting their first child.

Peter telephone me on December 3, 1967. "It's a boy, Mom." But his voice was not as excited as a man's should be over his first child. Then it came. "Something's wrong, Mom. 'Poor muscle tone,' the doctors say."

Lung congestion followed, the threat of pneumonia. That Sunday Peter crawled in under the oxygen tent to christen the baby Peter Christopher—"Christ-bearer."

I wanted to come at once, but the new parents urged me to wait. Days dragged by with the baby still in the hospital. Early one morning during a time of prayer, I was told that now the time had come to fly north. This was followed by the rather surprising instruction, "Go—and crown my prince with thanksgiving."

The next day I began the journey to West Hartford. During a seemingly interminable three-and-a-half hour wait at New York's Kennedy Airport, a heaviness of spirit alerted me. There must be some crisis involving the baby.

Later I found out. During my delay at Kennedy, Peter Christopher had stopped breathing, had turned blue, then stony white. The loving hands of friends had been laid on the baby in prayer and miraculously, he had begun to breathe again.

But not for long.

The first glimpse of my new grandson was of a pink and normal looking baby, his perfect round head promising blonde hair. Memories came flooding back. The baby looked exactly as his father had as a new-born.

I so yearned to cuddle my grandson. But I had my instructions, "Go—and crown my prince with thanksgiving."

It was easy—and hard. Easy because Peter Christopher was such a perfectly formed baby with a gentle spirit felt by all of us. Hard to crown God's little prince with *thanksgiving* if he was about to be taken from us.

With Peter and Edith standing by the crib and the doctor and some nurses looking on from a discreet distance, gently I laid my hands on the soft skin of that little head. "You gave him, Lord. He is Your prince, You told me. We hereby, according to Your instruction, crown Peter Christopher with thanksgiving, the golden crown of gratitude for this life You have given."

Thirty-five minutes later, the young doctor sadly informed us, "He is gone." It was almost as if that gentle spirit had been hanging on until I got there to bestow the blessing.

As all of us present tried to minister to Peter and Edith, I struggled with my own emotions. *Lord, I don't understand. When Peter Marshall died, Your sure word to me was that "goodness and mercy" would follow me all the days of my life. Lord, is this goodness and mercy?*

I looked at Edith, her face wet with tears. Edith, born to be a mother. *What about it, Lord? Is Edith then, not to know the joy of motherhood? And am I then not to be a grandmother?*

The Lord's answer to this questioning came two and a half years later with the birth of Mary Elizabeth Marshall, a healthy baby with perfect muscle tone. "Thank you, Lord. Forgive me for my doubts." In my rejoicing over this new life, I pushed down deep inside me the unresolved questions with which I had been wrestling.

I loved being a grandmother. Not since I was a small girl had I had so much fun. Not only that, I learned volumes about the delight of living in the Kingdom of God while still on this earth.

As a tiny girl Mary Elizabeth had large, round blue eyes and a piquant nose framed by blonde hair like her mother's. By the time she could walk, she had sturdy, well-formed legs that carried her into the most unlikely places, a disarming smile with a touch of coyness, and a way of pronouncing "Yes" and "Oh, no—no—*no*" that made her sound like a charter member of the Women's Liberation Movement.

When this child visited us what she did to our household was remarkable. My writing schedule was forgotten while Mary Elizabeth and I would enjoy a tea party using tiny blue cups which I had carted from Salzburg, Austria, in anticipation of such a golden moment. Our son Jeffrey had no objection to becoming a baby tender. He never walked Mary Elizabeth around the block in her stroller; he raced her while she chortled. And when she flirted with her grandfather, Len would become so entranced he would drop down on all fours, bray like a donkey and kick his heels in the air.

All of this added up to joy. We watched Mary Elizabeth awaken each morning to a world full of wonders. What had become commonplace to us jaded adults still had the freshness of surprise for her. The flying birds, the cloud formations, cows seen in a field, a flower, fragrances, food over which to smack the lips, the rhythm of nursery rhymes and poetry, music—all filled her with excitement.

And like any normal child, she had that wonderful God-given gift of living in the present and expressing what she felt immediately, exuberantly, without self-consciousness.

She shared this gift with us almost from the beginning. One such memory: On the patio of our home in Florida we were celebrating Mary Elizabeth's second birthday. The candles had been blown out on the cake gaily decorated with circus animals. The ice cream had been eaten. Finally, it was time to open the gifts. Adult hands helped Mary Elizabeth open a box almost as big as she was. The last bit of tissue paper was lifted off and out of the box came the little girl doll "Puddin'." Joy, glee, exultation chased themselves across my granddaughter's face. She clasped her hands, then reached for "Puddin'," hugged her to herself, chortled, cried for joy, gasped, shouted. No present ever hit the mark so surely. Every female atom in the little girl was focused on the doll with an intensity of awareness.

From that moment, "Puddin'" became Mary Elizabeth's love and has remained so through ten years, two new wigs, arm and leg replacements, and twenty other rival dolls of all sizes and types.

But the moment was also a gift for us who watched, the gift of a memory to enjoy over and over.

Through adventures like this with our granddaughter, the rest of us were reminded of Christ's extraordinary statement, "Except ye become as little children, ye shall not enter into the kingdom of heaven." We began to understand why Jesus was careful to specify the diminutive "little children." These very tiny ones are still fresh from the hand of their Maker, children who have not yet had time to absorb the prejudices, the resentments, the social distinctions and cruelties, the conflicts and repressions which we grown-ups mistakenly call "wisdom."

In my reading recently, I came across descriptions of how adults feel when they enter the Kingdom of God through what Jesus called "the new birth." Interestingly, what they experience is almost identical with what we watched in Mary Elizabeth. This is how one woman describes it:

> "I cannot say exactly what the mysterious change was. I saw no new thing, but I saw all the usual things in a miraculous new light, in what I believe is their true light.
>
> Every human being, every sparrow that flew, every branch tossing in the wind, was caught in and was a part of the whole mad ecstasy of loveliness, of joy, of importance, of intoxication of life..."[1]

It made me think of Mary Elizabeth's father at age five, standing with his nose pressed against the windowpane, laughing with glee at the fireworks of an autumn thunder storm. "Mommy," he told me, "the lightning looks like string beans dancing." They did indeed, but my prosaic adult mind would never have caught such an analogy.

Another aspect of this springtime of life—almost as if small children were back in the Garden of Eden—is that Mary Elizabeth felt the necessity of naming every living creature around her. She was not really at home during her first visit to our new Florida setting until she had decided upon names acceptable to her. Thus Mary, who helps us keep house, became "Yehh-yehh"—usually enunciated as lustily as if Mary Elizabeth were rooting for the Braves. Great-grandmother was tagged "Na-na." Len was "Popi." By Christmas time, Mary Elizabeth could manage "My-grandma," but "Jesus" was impossible, so He became the "Baby Zoohpff." I believe that He heartily approved.

Oddly this naming task was one of the first functions that God gave to the original man Adam: "... the Lord God formed every beast of the field and every bird of the air, and brought them to the man to see what he would call them..."[2]

I had often wondered why the writer of Genesis brought in this specific detail. Mary Elizabeth showed me why. God loves *all* of His creation. Whatever He made He saw that "it was good." So the name is just one indication of how special, how cherished all of us and the beautiful world in which He set man, are to Him. In the Kingdom of God, His love is all inclusive, from a bug crawling on the floor, to a butterfly floating over the flowers, to all animals, to each one of us.

And in the Kingdom of God the heart is tender. We grown-ups have only to watch little children to realize how calloused we have become. Among Mary Elizabeth's favorite books was one of the nursery rhymes set to music. The first time her mother sang to her

> "Rock-a-bye baby in the treetop
> When the wind blows the cradle will rock,
> When the bough breaks the cradle will fall
> And down will come baby, cradle and all"

Edith was startled to have her daughter burst into tears. Then she understood: Mary Elizabeth was crying because the baby had fallen down. Since the tears were genuine, Edith made up a story about how Daddy had come and picked up the baby, kissed her, and had found that the baby was not really hurt at all. That comforted Mary Elizabeth temporarily. But from that day on, whenever she came to that page in the book, there was a loud "No!" as she flipped over the page.

Watching all this, we could but conclude that the little child has no problem about belief in God. These small ones are still living on the borderline of two worlds. "Train up a child in the way he should go and when he is old, he will not depart from it" goes the old proverb. Since Jesus said, "*I* am the way," I am grateful that from the beginning our granddaughter was taught about Him. She did not feel comfortable about going to sleep at night until she had shut her eyes tightly, held hands with whoever was putting her to bed and said a happy good-night to the "Baby Zoohpff".

In November, 1967 Peter accepted a call to the First Wesleyan Community Church in East Dennis, Massachusetts. Then on July 22, 1971 a third child was born to Peter and Edith. It was apparent from her birth that Amy Catherine had suffered severe damage to internal organs. By now the doctors were calling it "genetic aberration cerebrohepato-renal syndrome.'' Medically speaking, they gave no hope. Of some forty-odd cases recorded, all had died within about six months.

Those of us on the scene felt called to pray in total faith, asking for a miraculous healing. We were joined by Peter's congregation, by ten close friends who flew to the Cape to join us for intensive prayer, and by many, many others. If ever a family went out on the end of a limb of faith, we did. As for me, not since Peter Marshall's first heart attack had I thrown everything I am and have, every resource of spirit and mind and will, into the battle for a human life.

Meanwhile, in the space of a few days those who had gathered on the Cape were seeing extraordinary answers to prayer: Jamie Buckingham, one of the group, prayed for a friend's granddaughter, eight-year-old Amy, on the same floor with Amy Catherine at Boston Children's Hospital. The little girl had cystic fibrosis. One lung had been removed, infection had set in, and Amy was dying. Later we found that the child's miraculous recovery had begun that day. Her grandmother later reported, "Amy is now in full health, attending school in Connecticut."

There were miracles of a different kind too. Our daughter Linda experienced a complete reordering of her life, lifting her out of darkness and confusion into a new beginning; a man's resentment against his father, festering since childhood, was healed; our friend Virginia Lively was given the key to her daughter's health, an answer she had been seeking for a long time; a floundering marriage was made right again. It was as if tiny Amy had become a divine catalyst, calling forth a concentration of God's power and love.

When our friends had to depart after three days, I moved to Children's Inn near the hospital in Boston, while Peter and Edith took turns keeping vigil over Amy and driving back and forth to Cape Cod to be with Mary Elizabeth. Day after day we sat beside the baby who was stretched out on a slanting "heat bed" under a big light. Was not the light, I wondered, agony for the sensitive eyes of a new-born? And Amy was hungry. She would open her mouth expectantly like a baby bird, yet was unable to suck; she had to be fed intravenously, the seemingly endless tubes sticking out in all directions.

She needs to feel loving arms, my heart kept telling me. Finally, the nurses assented and one morning they carefully placed her in my arms, tubes and all. She cuddled up, nuzzling me, seemed more alert. With this much encouraging response, we decided to increase our vigil to an around-the-clock one, so that Amy could have some cuddling even during the night. It was apparent that this baby's spirit was different from the gentleness we had felt in Peter Christopher. It was as if he had been a small angel who had briefly brushed life on earth, while Amy was a fighter who wanted to live.

Nonetheless, on the morning of September 4, as I was holding the baby, she began to have difficulty in breathing. A few minutes later Amy's heart stopped beating. Her time on earth had been but six weeks.

As it had at Peter Christopher's death, the agony returned to my spirit. The taking of Amy Catherine devastated me even more than that of Peter Christopher; it went deeper because now it had happened twice.

I wrote in my Journal

> My heart, my whole being has been acting out 'Rachel weeping for her children and would not be comforted because they were not.' (After Herod's slaughter of the innocents.)

> An unexpected revelation is how slight the difference is between the feelings of a mother and a grandmother. Scarcely a hair's breadth! I had not anticipated this. I could not have been more acutely sensitive to Amy and her plight had I borne her in my own body. . .

During the next few months I experienced the most intense misery I have ever known. Life went gray. Nor was it all psychological or spiritual. Events in the professional world began going against me. Such as: A major Hollywood studio purchased my novel *Christy*, then decided not to produce it. The fiction manuscript on which I had been working was presenting massive problems. Soon it was apparent that after pouring myself into it for three years, I was going to have to abandon this particular book.

Not only that, but outside, external inconveniences came on in waves: the dishwasher went out, the bathroom plumbing went awry; a truck driver backed into our mailbox and demolished it; the lawn developed chinch bugs; the car kept stopping cold on us. Petty discouragements, except that they kept piling up.

My rebellion extended for a period of six months. I see it now as a rebellion against God because I felt He had betrayed me. "What *can* we believe about healing through prayer?" I asked with seething anger and doubt just under the surface.

Almost everyone has gone through the same inner struggle over what seems like an unnecessary death. "How can God permit such things to happen?" is the cry of our hearts. "If He is a loving God, surely He would not want such evils to befall us." Here I was a grandmother, and still I had not come to terms with one of the basic problems of evil in all religious inquiry.

Years before I had met this same issue in Hannah Whitall Smith's *The Christian's Secret of a Happy Life*. I had been able to accept and profit from all the rest of Hannah's book, but my rebellion was violent against chapter twelve, "Is God in Everything?" I asked myself how God could be "in" the death of a three-year-old who wandered into the street in the path of a truck? Was God in war? In cancer? The answer that welled up inside me was a resounding "Certainly not!"

Further, I even considered such submissiveness wrong when Christians confronted with such tragedies, intoned, "Then it must have been God's will" and quoted old harassed Job, "The Lord gave, and the Lord taketh away; blessed be the name of the Lord." To me this seemed an especially cruel and offensive form of piosity.

But Hannah Smith asserted that for believers there could be but one basic response to the evil we encounter—the Scriptural admonition repeated over and over in the Old Testament and New: "In *everything* give thanks: for this is the will of God in Christ Jesus concerning you."[3] And "everything," she insisted, did mean everything—bad things as well as good.

Hannah warned that unless we do accept the fact that God is in everything, we can know no contentment. For how can we accept or give thanks for what is less than good if we do not believe that God's shielding Presence has deliberately stepped aside to allow those forces to reach us? Even more, that His purpose in stepping aside is for good—not evil?

I had decided that while Hannah Smith fully accepted this thesis, it was not for me. I had convinced myself I was hanging the matter on a hook for further consideration. Practically speaking, this was simply rejection.

I stood against Hannah Smith's thesis from 1945 until 1972. Twenty-seven years!

Amy Catherine's death brought me back face to face with it again. His voice did get through to me: *I, your God, am in everything. The baby died, but Amy is with Me. And while she lived, she ministered to everyone who prayed for her. Are you too stubborn, too arrogant to see it, Catherine? Are you going to continue to live in darkness month after month?*

I am grateful that at that juncture my husband Len and two close friends, Freddie Koch and Virginia Lively, were stern with me. "You're wallowing in self-pity, Catherine," they told me. "That can't be right. The self-pity, (wounded pride, perhaps?) the questioning God's love—all of it is standing between you and God."

Virginia Lively leaned forward, looked deep into my eyes. "Remember, Catherine, the word the Lord gave me during the Amy Catherine crisis?"

Yes, I remembered. With ringing authority, Virginia had delivered to Peter and Edith a prophecy: "The Lord wants me to assure you that any other child you have, you can have with perfect confidence."

Several of us there were inclined to be suspicious of prophecy, wary of false prophets. But Virginia was an old and trusted friend with a valid continuing relationship with Jesus Christ. Could we really put our weight down on this hope?

"That prophecy still stands, Catherine," Virginia went on. "You've got to trust Jesus for the future, that He always *restores*."

"But for now," Len's voice was very gentle, "if you'll only admit the self-pity and rebellion to Him, Catherine, He'll remove the cloud. I know He will."

They were right, of course. Finally on my knees, with a flood of tears, I made my confession. Then I saw that when life hands us situations which we cannot understand, we have one of two choices: we can wallow in misery, separated from God. Or we can tell Him, "I need You and Your presence in my life more than I need understanding. I choose You, Lord. I trust You to give me understanding and an answer to my 'Why?' if and when You choose."[4]

Sweet peace flowed into me, the first I had known in months. After that God took me back in my life to show me step by step how He had dealt with me through illness, death, lack of friends, loneliness. He *had* been with me in all of it.

Then I realized that it was Jesus Himself who in His timeless story of the Prodigal Son, gave us the best illustration of how eagerly He receives back any of us who have turned away from Him. Here was a son who had wandered far from his God-marked path.

With my rebellious spirit, I too had been adrift in a far country. But like the Prodigal, the minute I turned around and faced Home, I found God, my Father—more loving even than my earthly father—running down the road to meet me.

At that moment God's restoration work began.

When Edith and Peter told us two years later that they were expecting their fourth child, knowing the history of the two genetically-damaged babies, the obstetrician was unable to give Edith any medical prognosis. She was to find out later that the doctor himself had been on tenterhooks all during her pregnancy.

Fear kept rising unbidden to our minds despite Virginia Lively's reassuring prophecy. It was a difficult time for all of us, especially for Edith. Repeatedly she sought some assurance from the Lord, but no direct word was forthcoming.

Often during those days Edith found that she could identify with the agony of the Psalmist David as he too experienced the silence of Jehovah—God...

"How long, O Lord? Will you hide Yourself forever?[5]"

"Why," she wondered, "has God always required of His children periods of enduring His silence, His inscrutability? Is it simply that the limitations of our humanness can never finally penetrate or comprehend the infinite mind and purposes of God? Or are such periods—when 'the heavens being as brass'—a necessary part of teaching us to trust God even in the dark?"

At last the long wait was over. Labor pains began on the morning of May 4, 1974. A few hours later in the delivery room at Goddard Memorial Hospital in Stoughton, Massachusetts, as a baby boy was born to Edith and Peter, the obstetrician began chuckling, then laughing. "Nothing wrong with *this* baby, Edith. He's *plenty* vigorous. Superstar muscle tone!"

A few minutes later, as the doctor almost bounded out of the room, he paused at the head of the delivery table. Very tenderly, holding Edith's face between his hands, his voice alive with feeling, he told her elatedly, "It's moments like that that make this business worthwhile."

So Virginia's prophecy was right. Peter Jonathan—robust, with irrepressible vitality and an exceptionally happy disposition, was to be the first of God's joyful surprises.

Left Side: Jeffrey, Chester, Linda, Lucille (seated), Leonard, Catherine
Right Side: (clockwise) Peter, Edith, Mary Elizabeth,
and Peter Jonathan Marshall, Leonora (Christy) Wood, and Prince

The Road From Here

....you will know them
by their fruits.
....he shall see the fruit
of the travail of His soul
and be satisfied....

Matthew 7:20; Isaiah 53:11

The Road From Here

The evening of August 18, 1979 Len and I waited expectantly in our bedroom at Evergreen Farm in Virginia. I was wearing an evening dress, he, a formal summer coat. The knock on the door came at 6:40 p.m. Len opened the door. Outside stood our grandchildren—Mary Elizabeth, 10, in a long dress, and Peter Jonathan, 5, in his Sunday suit.

"We came to escort you to the drawing-room," they announced with giggles.

Peter Jonathan reached up for my arm, Len took Mary's and we descended the stairs. At the bottom flashcubes popped. There the members of our family greeted us. Slim, dark-haired Chester, our 26-year-old son, called for silence and announced from a long scroll

"Hear Ye, Hear Ye, Hear Ye
Sarah Catherine Wood Marshall LeSourd
and
Leonard Earle LeSourd
having been joined in holy matrimony, lo, these 20

years, it is only fitting and proper that this august occasion be set aside to honor your union and its subsequent fruits.

Heretofore, be it known that the undersigned do express their heartfelt gratitude and admiration, acknowledge their overwhelming debt, and pledge their loyalty, love and service.

Delivered this 18th day of August, 1979, by

Leonora Whitaker Wood	Leonard Chester LeSourd
Edith Wallis Marshall	Jeffrey Alan LeSourd
Peter John Marshall	Mary Elizabeth Marshall
Linda Ann LeSourd	Peter Jonathan Marshall"

Thus began one of those family evenings you would like to have on stop-action film so that you could rerun it over and over. The actual date of our 20th anniversary was November 14, 1979. Since the August date was when most of the family could be together, it was chosen as a time for something special—we were not told what.

Chester came from Chattanooga where he is an English teacher and tennis coach at McCallie School. Jeff, 22, flew in from Sikeston, Missouri, where he is a Bell Telephone supervisor. Linda, 30, drove out from Washington where she was working with young people for the National Prayer Breakfast movement. The Marshall family had been staying with us at the farm over the summer, bringing together four generations of our family ranging in ages from 5 to 87.

Secret preparations had begun early in the week. Brown sacks filled with edibles were brought in and furtively stashed away. The night before, two cars of family arrived after Len and I had gone to bed. We heard muffled laughter with many trips from the cars to the kitchen; lights were still on well after midnight.

The next morning Len and I were told to stay away from the refrigerator. No wonder! Odd, thumping noises were coming from it. And green stuff—could it be seaweed?—

kept oozing out. Chester seemed to be the keeper of whatever was in there, faintly drumming. Nervously, he kept returning again and again to the refrigerator, keeping anxious vigil.

During the day several rehearsals were called from which we were excluded. Our children and grandchildren made it clear that today they were taking complete control of the household.

After we had assembled in the living room, the first course was served—steamed clams in large bowls along with melted butter. We moved to the dining room for the second course—delicate green salad served on crystal plates. The table was set with the best linen, crystal, and silver. My mother had ordered pink roses for the centerpiece, set off by tall, pink tapers.

Next came the stellar entrée—live lobsters flown in from Maine, then boiled. So live lobsters had been the refrigerator-thumpers. And that explained the oozing seaweed and Chester's great derring-do to keep the lobsters alive for 24 hours. When corn on the cob and fresh asparagus with hollandaise sauce were served, it was obvious why questions about our favorite foods had been put to us weeks before. The meal-end fillip: Baked Alaska with raspberry sauce.

The evening's finale was another surprise. "Now we're ready to have the full story of how you met—and your courtship," Linda instructed us, as everyone around the table pushed their chairs back to find a comfortable position.

"We want a description of the first kiss, when you knew you were in love—every last detail," Jeff continued unabashedly.

A surprised look crossed Len's face, reflecting my reaction too. "You kids can't be serious! Why would you be interested in personal details like that?"

"Oh, but we *are!*" It was a chorus.

"Come on, Dad! Tell it all," Chester prodded. "Only *not* all those old stories about what brats we were—like my sliding spinach off my plate and tossing it behind the radiator in the kitchen."

"Oh, let's have those too," Mary Elizabeth bubbled.

"Also tell us," Edith suggested, "what you consider some of the most important lessons you've learned over the past twenty years."

As I sat there looking around the table, into my mind played back some words I had written in 1961 as part of the Foreword for my book *Beyond Our Selves*:

> Len's three children have joined Peter John in calling me "Mother"... Many experiences have tested me in my lifetime, but none more than this one. And none has made me happier. But writing about it must come later. *A man swimming a horse across a turbulent stream does not stop to take a picture of the experience. I'll get my colts across the stream, see them thoroughly dried off, well fed and on their way—then perhaps, the picture.*

Eighteen tempestuous, crowded, fulfilling years had passed since I had penned those words. Gratitude welled up in me as I thought of the One who had been with us all the way to see us safely across the rough crossing. And here the colts were, not only dried off and on their way, but for this evening, having taken charge of their parents with competent maturity.

And so for the rest of the evening Len and I covered the highlights of courtship and twenty years of marriage including many of the stories recounted in this book. It was an unforgettable evening of sharing between four generations of family...

A new experience in communal living had begun in November, 1977 when Peter had resigned from his church in East Dennis, Massachusetts, after ministering there for eleven years. He and his family had then moved temporarily into the house next to ours in Florida while Peter continued his nationwide preaching and teaching ministry, awaiting a new call from the Lord.

At that time the family stretched all the way from Peter Jonathan, age three, and Mary Elizabeth, almost eight, to my mother, their great-grandmother, 87. Our plan had been to retain the two smaller family units for breakfasts and lunches but have communal evening meals, alternating between the two homes.

As time went on the dinner hour remained the reporting and clearing center for the day's events and for the thoughts, insights, and problems we wanted to share. Most of the time the dilemma was getting in a word edgewise. This proved especially frustrating to Peter Jonathan, to whom we promised to set aside a chink of time so that even his "news" could be heard.

Typically, a ten-year-old Mary Elizabeth might report what she had learned in school that day about chlorophyll in leaves of plants and about the distributive property of multiplication. Her blue eyes would sparkle as she enthused over her horseback riding lesson... "I learned to post." And could one of us please help her wallpaper another room of her miniature dollhouse?

Len was doing what he loves most: nurturing and building a Christian work from a small beginning. First, it was *Guideposts;* now it was the Chosen Books Publishing Company.

Peter's book, written with David Manuel, *The Light and the Glory*, had sold 80,000 plus copies...

That day ten eager women had come to my mother's weekly, home Bible study on the epistles of John.

Recreation was an important lubricant for this extended family life. Such fun as Peter teaching Peter Jonathan how to throw a ball and swing a baseball bat; swimming lessons; handicrafts; Peter Jonathan and Mary Elizabeth learning correct tennis from their grandfather Len; family tennis doubles; Peter Jonathan and Mary Elizabeth cuddled up to Len, one on each side of him, listening spellbound to one of their grandfather's "Lucky stories."

Lucky stories are now a family tradition, first told to Chester and Jeffrey when they were small. Wild tales of suspense, always in exotic settings, with a man named "Lucky" as the hero, the story always containing a moral. Len spins out the plot as he goes along. He claims that this talent for instant story plots stems from having read shelf after shelf of every *Tom Swift*, *Rover Boy* type of series books while he was growing up.

Invariably today's chapter ends with Lucky in a tough spot, hanging by his fingertips over a pool of hungry crocodiles, or about to be trapped by thugs as Lucky plunges deeper and deeper into the shaft of an old mine.

Then too, games have always been a big part of family recreation: *Rook* and croquet and *Parcheesi* and bridge and, of course, *Geography*.

This is a favorite after-dinner game enjoyed by all four generations and any and all guests present. Paper and pencil are handed out; two teams choose up; a letter of the alphabet such as "P" is selected; take five minutes in which to write down any town, city, mountain, lake, river, etc. anywhere in the world beginning with "P."

Mary Elizabeth's paper is always studded with every hamlet and pond on Cape Cod. Mother's is invariably loaded with those outlandishly remote places from the Great Smoky "Christy country" she knows so well, like Persimmon Hill, Pebble Mountain, or Pigeon Roost Hollow. Len, who has played this game since he was a boy, usually comes out on top as the sophisticated *Geography* expert.

Scoring is simple. Each person reads his list aloud. With six people playing, if Mother, for instance, is the only one with "Pebble Mountain," then she gets six for that; if all

six have it, each scores only one. The winning team is the
one with the most points.

Geography is always highly competitive (heated discussions such as whether "Chesapeake" is a bay or a penin-
sula), educational and fun, often hilarious.

Then, as in all extended families, there are those special
affinities that develop person to person. What *is* that special bond between Peter Jonathan and his great-grandmother "Nana"? Who can tell! Is it that age has dropped
out a lot of false values and finally retains the imperish-
ables—a childlike imagination and faith?

Almost any afternoon about four o'clock would find
Peter Jonathan marching in the back door with favorite
books under his arm, after which he and Nana would sit
close together at one end of the davenport or in the lounge
chair in her bedroom. She has read her way through stacks
of juveniles, told her great-grandson the wonderful Old
Testament stories, and begun to help him memorize the
Catechism for Young Children.

Who but Peter Jonathan could have succeeded in turning
his great-grandmother into his helicopter co-pilot? Edith
walked in on them one evening to find her son sitting
squeezed in beside Nana in her armchair. A baseball bat
lay in front of them resting on both arms of the chair.
Nana, instructed to hold on tightly to the "safety bar" with
one hand, was looking a little sheepish.

"We're playing 'helicopter'," Peter told his mother. "I'm
the pilot, Nana's the co-pilot."

"Are you old enough to fly a helicopter?"

"Yes, we're both 158 years old, and Mommie..." the
five-year-old pointed out the picture window to the full
moon in the sky, "Nana told me about the man in the
moon. Somebody forgot and left him there. We're goin'
fly up there and bring him back."

There are many pluses and blessings for extended families such as ours has been for this three-and-a-half-year period. Among them, the obvious advantage of always having someone around for baby-sitting and child care; always someone to read or tell stories to the children or to play games; always someone for the mending and the darning, for the household baking or to prepare vegetables for dinner, to make special desserts, even perhaps a big freezer of homemade peach or strawberry ice cream.

When I was growing up, it was a usual thing for families to include a grandparent, an uncle or aunt, or an unmarried daughter or a bachelor son. Sociological facts verify this: In the 1920s 50 percent of the households in Massachusetts, for instance, included at least one adult other than both parents. Today that figure is only four percent.

The change in family life today is startling. Now not only is the extended family a rarity; even the intact nuclear family is becoming the exception. Divorce is so epidemic (one million divorces a year in the United States with the figure rising rapidly) that the number of children now living with only one parent approaches 40 percent. This one parent at home is usually the mother, and increasingly, she is not there either because she is working. One of the effects of "women's liberation" is that between 1947 and 1975 the number of working wives shot up 205 percent. Even for mothers with tiny children under three, one in three is now working. And judges in divorce courts are finding an increasing number of cases where neither parent wants custody of the children.

Behind all this is a rampant "me-first" philosophy. Endlessly, we are hearing about the "rights of the individual." The question then becomes, does solitary, self-centered living really enable one to find oneself? *Does* selfishness bring happiness and fulfillment?

Our experiment in communal living has shed much light on these crucial questions, for four generations cannot live together without rubbings. In that lovely verse from the

Psalms,[1] we are told that "God sets the solitary in families." Now we know why: He knows, if we do not, that every husband and every wife are "incompatible"; all parents are "incompatible" with all children. So what does that prove? Only that the Creator made each human being a distinctly unique individual.

That being so, in the first years of life, each of us needs the nuturing love and also the discipline of the smaller nuclear family unit before being plunged into the rough hurly-burly of community life. And so He has ordained the family as society's most important unit and as its finest proving ground and character training school for us to learn how to handle our uniqueness.

So we found it. The rubbing and scraping often produced a crisis. God's way is not to flee the crisis but to uncover the root of it and so a growing edge of the inner spirit. As we handled problems together in prayer, we surrendered yet another layer of selfishness and subsequently grew in maturity.

For instance, my mother frantically called to Edith one afternoon, "Quick! Get Peter Jonathan down. He's climbed almost to the top of the big mango tree."

Edith's response was calm. "Gram, it's all right for him to climb trees."

We were learning that the same "Christy" who, at 19, traveled alone into the wild Great Smokies, walked seven miles through the snow with the mailman to get to Cutter's Gap, was a daring horse-woman, and faced down moonshiners, now approaching 90—has many fears as she looks about her at our world.

That night at dinner the heart of the question was submitted: How many of my mother's fears were the wisdom of age and therefore legitimate? Or could we be in danger of passing on to children a fear-filled attitude to life?

The discussion grew heated. The woman who so many years before had swept majestically into Mr. Rush Hazen's office, flaunting her big-plumed hat, the same one who had stood off the roughest mountaineers, can still be fiery: she could not help her fears for the children's safety and thought them legitimate.

"But," Edith protested, "it isn't that I want any life-threatening danger for my child..."

"Isn't falling out of a high tree life-threatening?" Mother shot back, sparks in her eyes.

"I want my son to have the freedom to climb and run, to have some rough and tumble," Peter interjected. "Children, especially boys, can't be protected from all danger and hurt, Grandmother."

Almost always our give-and-take sessions end up in prayer for the wisdom of God's specific direction for the problem and for the right attitude in each of us. For throughout these years we have found prayer the best lubricant of all—in fact, indispensable.

As in all families, selfishness, jealousy, haughtiness, anger erupt at times. If it comes from a child, then there is correction; if from an adult, we gather together to pray it through, letting the Helper—the Holy Spirit—do the correcting. It is amazing how often He does, with gentle incisiveness.

Like most people I resist criticism; my defenses go up quickly when I see it coming even though I know it is essential to Christian growth. The reason I cannot slough off my wrongdoing is that the price of setting it right came so high—even to God Himself. Jesus went to the cross to make possible the Father's forgiveness for me, for everyone of us—past, present, and future.

But we Christians have heard these words so often that, like well-worn coins, they slip through our fingers. On a certain morning several years ago, God graciously made them shining and new for me.

It was during a period when an awareness of my own mistakes and wrong turnings had given me a sense of isolation from God. As I sat in a living room chair pondering this, there came to me a deep interior experience.

I did not fall asleep, so this was no dream. Nor was it an otherworldly "vision." It seemed real, as real as the fabric on the chair, or the Florida sunlight pouring through the windows or the trilling of a mockingbird in a ficus tree outside. Suddenly, I felt the presence of Jesus.

"We're going on a journey," He told me.

Soon we were in a long, long room, like a throne room. Crowds of people lined the walls on either side. As we walked the length of the room approaching One whom I knew to be God, the Father, I spotted in the crowd those I love who have gone on before: my father who died in 1961, Peter Marshall, and my grandson, Peter Christopher—now not a baby, but a tall, slim, thirteen-year-old. There was my granddaughter, Amy Catherine, a delightful little girl.

Then I looked down at myself: to my horror I was dressed in rags—torn, unwashed, filthy. How could I bear to stand before the Father, the Lord God Omnipotent, clothed so vilely? When we stopped before the throne, I could not even look up. I had never felt so unworthy.

In the same instant Jesus spread wide the voluminous robe He was wearing, completely covering me with it. (Interestingly, this was no kingly robe, rather the roughest homespun material. I understood that until all His children are brought to glory, He continues to wear the robe of His humanity.)

"Now," He told me, "My father does not see you at all—only Me. Not your sins but My righteousness. I cover for you."

Then I was aware again of the living room and the chair, only now feelings of joy and gratitude were washing over me. So that's what the Cross means! The theologians have a high-sounding phrase for it—"substitutionary atonement." Jesus in our place. Jesus our substitute. Jesus covering for us.

Even though I'm now a grandmother, I know more clearly than ever that I'm still as needy and dependent on the Lord's help as when I was a child, first hearing His voice. He has allowed me to go off on selfish tangents and wander down wrong paths, but always He meets me at every turn and brings me back to Him.

Two new members have been added to our family in the past year: Susan Scott, whom I described earlier as Chester's lovely new wife, and Philip Lader, now Linda's husband.

On the evening of September 19, 1980 at Linda's and Philip's rehearsal dinner in the dining room of Fellowship House in Washington, D. C., the cooks and waitresses were Linda's friends, part of a small Washington "fellowship family," as she called it. Among impromptu speech-toasts after dessert were those of Jim Hiskey, a professional golfer, a sort of chaplain to athletes, a man who has been training young people in Christian discipleship for over twenty years. He had been our daughter's first boss in Washington. Len and I listened, fascinated, as Jim described the Linda he had first seen and her subsequent development…"Chunky, long straight hair, granny glasses. I needed a secretary. I remember the first letter I tried to dictate to Linda." Jim paused and chuckled. "There must have been, oh, thirty-odd mistakes on the first typed page.

"But then I watched Jesus Christ slowly transform a girl, rub off the rough edges, develop the potential deep within her. I saw the unfolding of a lovely young woman, like a rosebud opening in the sunshine.

"Only that development made possible what we are celebrating here tonight. I knew that this new Linda was going to need a strong husband. Well, she's about to have one. Because Philip Lader is an achiever and an idealist if I ever saw one. He's earned his own way from the beginning—through Duke University, Harvard Law School,

Oxford University, a bachelor until 34. But I don't think he would have fallen for the first Linda we knew."

Jim's comments were dramatized for Len and me two days later during the wedding at the National Presbyterian Church. The setting—the jewel-colors of the tall, stained-glass windows complimented by the rose red of the brides-maids' dresses and the brilliant vestments of the two cler-gymen. The two grandmothers—Lucile LeSourd and my mother, Leonora Wood rolled down the long aisle in their wheelchairs; Phil's widowed mother, Mary Lader, and his aunt, Eleanor Tripoli, beaming from the other side of the aisle. They had been praying for Philip's future wife for many years, they had confided.

We kept catching echoes of Peter's and Edith's wedding 15 years before, since this too was not just a marriage ceremony, but a worship service as well. There was con-gregational singing, two portions of scripture read by friends of Linda's and Phil's, the bride and groom kneeling together, taking communion as the first act of their married life.

This service also included something new to most of us. Just prior to the traditional wedding vows, Linda and Phil faced one another, while each pledged to the other vows they themselves had written. There was an astonishing meld of a romantic idealism centered in the love of God along with a clear-eyed grasp of the responsibilities being assumed.

Phil's deeply resonant voice began,

> "Linda, after our first moments together, I prayed that you would one day be my wife. You caused me to understand that man's way to joy is a remarkable love. The 'I will' said today is not so much fact accom-plished, as responsibility assumed....
>
> "You and I are commissioned by this wedding to make God's love believable to the world.
>
> By His grace however, we have different gifts, and

these beg quarrels. When frustrated by your tenacity of opinion, I shall not waive my own,"—ripple of laughter over the congregation—"but shall honestly and patiently seek resolution....

"My acceptance of you and your freckles is unconditional. There will *never* be a price of admission to my heart.

"However poetic this view of marriage, I promise always to be an idealist. But an idealist without illusions. I ask you to challenge us to practice the presence of God.

"My marriage proposal in a tree house was to symbolize what little material security I can offer you. We shall not fear to risk our prosperity for the principles and dreams we share. I shall thereby shield you from the leprosy of boredom and convention....

"I shall heed the lilies of the field to make time for us amidst the clamor of events....To watch sunsets, to call dolphins. Let's laugh at ourselves and together strive for a riper, more delicious happiness than we have ever known....

"I commit to you that ours will be a death in love and not a death of love; that in the evening of our lives, the joy will have been worth the pain....

"That sun will all too quickly set on our lives. But even then as your husband and as a Christian, I shall—and here Phil's voice trembled and broke—*never* say good-by."

As Linda, looking radiantly beautiful, began to speak before the hushed church, Len and I found out later that we were having much the same thoughts. That first morning of our coffee-pot experiment 21 years before, we had struggled to find the right prayer for Linda. At that time the problem seemed to be how to get this talented girl moving in the direction God had for her.

In a special sense, what was unfolding before us that afternoon was as though God were placing in our hands the golden crown of Answered Prayer—indeed, of countless prayers melded in the furnace of His love.

As we watched Linda, her blue eyes looking deep into Phil's hazel eyes, pouring out the desires of her heart to him, we knew that never had a dream been so gloriously fulfilled.

> "Phil, I not only love you, I respect you. I'm honored to become your wife today. I desire always to be an encouragement to you, and I want to provide a haven and a resting place for you and for our children.

> "I promise to speak and live the truth in love with you to the best of my ability. At times that may be painful for one or both of us. Yet I, too, am committed to work through any differences that arise with love, understanding and resolution as our goal. And I promise to uphold and stand by you always....

> "I am excited about what lies ahead, a bit overwhelmed by the enormity and the irrevocability of the commitment we are making. But open-eyed, counting the cost and exulting in the assurance we both have of the rightness of this covenant, I will walk with you through the challenging and glorious future God has for us...".

Our eyes moved to Mary Elizabeth Marshall, the junior bridesmaid, standing with the group around the altar listening. Len and I saw much the same starry-eyed look on her face we had seen on Linda's at Peter's and Edith's wedding. Even so, He passes on His great love and His incredible idealism from generation to generation.

Edith could not be there to see her daughter, for she was in Florida expecting the addition of the next member of our family any moment.

Three days later, on September 24, David Christopher Marshall was born, a healthy beautiful baby. Because this was "natural" childbirth, Peter was there standing at the head of the delivery table to encourage and to help Edith, to cradle his son in his arms minutes after he was born.

And so once again, Virginia Lively's beautiful prophecy of healthy babies for the Marshalls was fulfilled—as indeed, all of our Father's promises are eventually worked out for us.

Goodness and mercy shall follow you all the days of your life. This had been His pledge to me on that dark day of Peter Marshall's death as I was about to leave the little hospital room with my life lying in shambles about me. "Goodness and mercy"...*His* goodness. *His* mercy. How bounteously He has honored His pledge to me.

Sometimes we have to lift our eyes to the hills to get His perspective, wait for what seems to us earthbound creatures a long time to see the fulfillment of His promises.

But this I have learned—we can trust Him.

Life Principles

Chapter one

We can trust the character and love of the
Father in heaven to surpass that of the best
earthly father we have ever known or
can imagine.

Chapter two

God still controls all the riches of earth and
heaven. As a child of the King, we are not to
think poverty. His promise to each of us: *if you
give of yourself, your time, your material resources
to others, I will open the windows of heaven and
pour down My blessing upon you.*

Chapter three

God wants us to use all our mind, along with
our emotions and will, to love and serve Him.
Therefore we need have no fear about where
Truth will lead us. He is still out ahead of the
greatest scholars or scientists or theologians.

Chapter four

It was God who thought up romance in the
first place. He alone, at the center of the man-
woman relationship, can give to physical
attraction the lustre, the idealism, the romance,
the durability of which we dream.

Chapter five

Jesus came to earth to show us the Father's
will. He who created the incredible human
body still heals today, but not as a divine
magician. We need to seek *His* way, His
timing, and the lessons He wants us to learn
along the way.

Chapter six

When life caves in, we are to seek God in our problem. God has a plan for every life by which He will bring good out of evil.

Chapter seven

We should never hesitate to try the impossible. God does have a special work for us to do in the world. Should this involve a big dream, we must believe that the bigger the dream, and the more loving and unselfish it is, the greater will be God's blessing on it.

Chapter eight

God has special promises and provision for all those single parents who must rear children alone. We are not to clutch our children to ourselves. What we hold too tightly, we can drive away or break. When we give our children up to God, He will eventually give them back to us.

Chapter nine

Since God made us for companionship, loneliness is not His plan for us. But there is a price to be paid in seeking God's remedy, not ours. This includes a decision to give up self-pity, the determination not to compromise honor and purity and idealism, and the willingness to let Him fill our heart's lonely places with His love which can then spill out into loving concern for others.

Chapter ten

God is forever in the repair and restoration business. When we are willing to be taught by Him and to make Him the center of the new home, He will produce love and harmony and joy as He fits together the pieces of two broken households.

Chapter eleven

Husbands and wives are basically incompatible. Parents are incompatible with their children. God made us all different. That's why the home is His classroom for moulding and shaping us into mature people.

Chapter twelve

God uses children and grandchildren to keep older people flexible. When anyone of us has a painful experience that our mind cannot equate with a loving God, there is this remedy: "I want You and Your presence, Lord, even more than I want understanding. I choose You." When we ask this, He then gives peace and illumination as His gift.

Notes

Chapter 1   Our Father Who Art on Earth

   1.   Judges 16:30

Chapter 3   My God Was Too Small

   1.   J. Middleton Murray, *Journal of Katherine Mansfield* (London: Constable, 1927). Used by permission of Alfred A. Knopf, Inc., and the Society of Authors as the Literary Representative of the late Miss Katherine Mansfield.

Chapter 4   Romance

   1.   O. Hallesby, *Prayer* (Translated by Clarence J. Carlsen) (Minneapolis, Minnesota: Augsburg Publishing House, 1931, 1960), p. 17. Used by permission.

Chapter 5   Illness

1. Exodus 15:26	4. Isaiah 55:11	7. Luke 4:12
2. Isaiah 53:4,5	5. Luke 4:9	8. John 5:39 *(RSV)*
3. James 5:14,15	6. Luke 4:10	9. Joel 2:28; Acts 2:17

Chapter 6   Grief

1. Isaiah 66:13	3. Isaiah 61:1,3
2. John 14:18	4. Proverbs 15:25

   5.   Jeremiah 49:11   James Moffatt, *The Bible, A New Translation* (New York: Harper & Row, 1935)

   6.   Isaiah 54:4,6,7,13
      An especially encouraging translation of verse 13 is worth noting here: "All your sons will be taught *by* the Lord, and great shall be your children's peace." *(New International Version)*, italics added.

7. Isaiah 41:10 *(The Amplified Bible)*	10. Luke 23:42,43
8. Hebrews 2:15 *(The Amplified Bible)*	11. I Corinthians 15:42-44
9. I Corinthians 13:12	

Chapter 7   His Call to Me

   1.   Romans 8:28   2.   I John 5:14,15   3.   Matthew 6:33

   4.   Originally from one of Peter Marshall's "Postscripts" in a church bulletin...Quoted also in: Peter Marshall, *Mr. Jones, Meet the Master* (Westwood, NJ: Fleming H. Revell Company, 1949), p. 34

   5.   Catherine Marshall, *To Live Again* (New York: McGraw-Hill Book Company, 1957), p. 54. (Lincoln, Va.: Chosen Books, 1979), p. 54.

   6.   Ibid, p. 53

Chapter 8   Single Parent

1. Acts 6:1	3. Genesis 9:16
2. James 1:27	4. Matthew 28:20

Chapter 11   Second Family

1.   Mark 11:25,26 *(Revised Standard Version)*

2.   I Peter 2:24 *(The Amplified Bible)*

3.   See the following chapter for the outcome.

Chapter 12   Grandmother

1.   Margaret Prescott Montague, *Twenty Minutes of Reality, The Atlantic Monthly* (November, 1916)

2.   Genesis 2:19   3.   I Thessalonians 5:18

4.   Here I was merely learning for myself the important lessons thousands of Christians before me have had to come to. Succinctly expressed by the seventeenth century Brother Lawrence:

> "....a sharp distinction should be drawn between acts of the understanding and those of the will—that the former were of small account and the latter, everything...."

Brother Lawrence, *The Practice of the Presence of God* (New York: Paulist Press, 1978), p. 72.

5.   Psalm 89:46 *(The Amplified Bible)*

Scripture references

Chapter 1

1.   Judges 16:30

Chapter 5

1.   Exodus 15:26

2.   Isaiah 53:4,5

3.   James 5:14-15

4.   Luke 4:9

5.   Luke 4:10

6.   Luke 4:12

7.   John 5:39-40 *(RSV)*

Chapter 6

1.   Isaiah 66:12-13

2.   John 14:18

3.   Isaiah 61:1,3

4.   Proverbs 15:25

5.   Jeremiah 49:11 *(Moffatt)*

6.   Isaiah 54:4,6,7,13

7.   Isaiah 41:10 *(Amplified)*

8.   Hebrews 2:15

9.   I Corinthians 13:12

10.   Luke 23:42-43

11.   I Corinthians 15:42-44

Chapter 7

1.   Romans 8:28

2.   I John 5:14-15

3.   Matthew 6:33

Chapter 8

1.   Acts 6:1 *(RSV)*

2.   James 1:27 *(RSV)*

3.   Genesis 9:16

4.   Matthew 28:20

Chapter 11

1.   Mark 11:25-26

2.   I Peter 2:24 *(Amplified)*

Chapter 12

1.   Genesis 2:19

2.   Psalm 89:46 *(Amplified)*

A CLOSER WALK

A Closer Walk

Catherine Marshall

Edited by Leonard E. LeSourd

Hodder & Stoughton
LONDON SYDNEY AUCKLAND

I am weak but Thou art strong
Jesus, keep me from all wrong;
I'll be satisfied as long
As I walk, dear Lord, close to Thee.

Just a little closer walk with Thee
Grant it, Jesus, if You please;
Daily walking close to Thee
Let it be, dear Lord, let it be.

Acknowledgments

Special thanks go to Jeanne Sevigny, Catherine's trusted secretary and close friend of fourteen years, who not only did the typing of Catherine's handwritten journal items, but served as advisor on the selection of material used in this book. Also to Regina Trollinger and Yvonne Burgan for their secretarial skills.

A big debt of gratitude to Elizabeth Sherrill, whose book expertise guided Catherine for twenty-two years through the writing of *Beyond Our Selves*, *Christy*, *Adventures in Prayer*, *Something More*, *Meeting God At Every Turn*, and *Julie*, and who edited the editor of this manuscript with her usual sensitivity and brilliance.

Contents

Using This Book . . . On Your Own Walk

For you – as it has for me – *A Closer Walk* can become not so much a book as a travelling companion, inviting us to share the rough places and the mountain tops with a fellow pilgrim, Catherine Marshall.

In personal journals kept during her most creative years as a writer, wife, and mother, Catherine recorded her encounters with such roadblocks as . . .

> Criticalness
> The Poverty Complex
> Resentment
> The Dry Period
> Chronic Worry
> Illness

Most importantly, she described also the 'way through', which she found in the Scriptures.

Throughout her journey, the Bible was the traveller's staff on which Catherine leaned. From every page shines her commitment to daily Bible reading – and her faithfulness in applying what she read to that day's need.

If you're like me, two things will happen as you make this pilgrimage with Catherine. Your own Bible reading will become more focused, more personal, infinitely more exciting. And you will be nudged to start your own 'travel diary'.

This was exactly the impact on Len LeSourd, after reading the first of these entries. Before he married Catherine, Len recalls today, he had never thought of

putting his own spiritual struggles down on paper –
certainly not *as* he was living through them.

Shortly after their marriage in 1959, however, a moving
van delivered Catherine's possessions to their first home.
Len watched in husbandly amusement as Catherine
hovered over one particular carton, clearly attaching
more value to it than to the clothes, dishes, and pieces of
furniture that arrived along with it.

'My journals,' Catherine explained.

When Len still looked blank, she drew from the box a
dark green volume, four inches by seven, with 'Year
Book 1934' stamped on the front. Catherine had filled the
book with reactions to campus life that sophomore year
at Agnes Scott College in Georgia. Three more green
journals in the box covered the years through 1937.

There was a five-year diary for 1938–42, recording
Catherine's soul-searching as she met and eventually
married Peter Marshall. Journals of various shapes and
colours detailed her years as Peter's wife: the birth of
their son, her own serious illness, the loss of her young
husband. As a widow in the 1950s, Catherine entered her
spiritual questing in a succession of spiral-bound notebooks.

In growing astonishment, Len helped Catherine store
the volumes on a shelf. What discipline and devotion
these thousands of pages represented! Where would a
person find the time?

Len soon found out. Early in the morning, Catherine
would take from a dresser drawer a bright red hardcover
Daily Reminder. No amount of fatigue from the previous
day spent coralling three small stepchildren, no pleas
from a sleepy husband, could keep her from this daily
appointment-in-writing with God.

When Catherine finally allowed Len to read some
current entries, he understood her commitment to the
discipline. These were more than simply prayer records,
more even than the joyful recording of answers. The act
of writing itself was part of Catherine's relationship with

God; it helped define her needs, focus her prayers, act out her trust.

Len soon joined her in this early morning time and began keeping a prayer record of his own. His approach was somewhat different from Catherine's. Each individual's format, style, and frequency will of course be unique. But right from the start Len discovered the secret that Catherine had known for years: *putting prayer issues on paper* eliminates the vagueness that so often diffuses personal devotions.

Her lively new family, Len confesses, sometimes made it difficult for Catherine to keep a set time of day for her journal. Before long she was making her entries at any and every moment when the dust settled.

But make them she did. For the next twenty-three years Catherine poured her hopes and dreams, questions asked of God and answers received from Him, into the growing collection of *Daily Reminders*. The current volume accompanied the LeSourds on trips, appeared in the laundry room and at the breakfast table. When Catherine's pen was stilled on March 18, 1983, these journals were her rich legacy to Len, with instructions to disclose the contents with wisdom and discretion.

A Closer Walk is the result.

It will remain only 'someone else's story', however, unless you and I come along.

Elizabeth Sherrill

A Woman Called Catherine

The first time I saw Catherine was on December 1, 1955, at a luncheon in the Waldorf Astoria ballroom, where she was to receive the Salvation Army's 1955 Award for her contributions to 'the spiritual life of her time'. A poll that year had listed her as one of the ten most admired women in America. As the dignitaries, mostly men, filed onto the stage, Catherine, overshadowed by their physical presence, looked small, fragile, a bit overwhelmed.

I stared at her more closely. What was the secret of her sudden propulsion onto the national stage? Writing a best-selling religious book like *A Man Called Peter* couldn't do it alone. Watching her animated gestures as she conversed with master of ceremonies Walter Hoving (president of prestigious Tiffany's), noting her trim figure and stylish grooming, I decided that she was a phenomenon – a devout preacher's wife who had also won the admiration of nonbelievers.

How had she done it?

I listened carefully to Catherine's speech that described the 'supernatural intervention of God' at Dunkirk during World War II. *Unlikely subject for a sophisticated New York City gathering*, I thought to myself. But she avoided religious clichés and held her audience. *A high voltage, spiritual woman, but with worldly wisdom*, I concluded.

Some months later Catherine was invited to speak at our Young Adult Group at the Marble Collegiate Church. There, I met her face to face for the first time, bathed for a short moment in her warm smile and controlled intensity. Yet, too, a shyness. In her speech I liked the practical way she applied biblical truths to her personal struggles.

As the editor of *Guideposts*, I wrote and asked her if she would write a piece for our small inspirational magazine, which had just reached a circulation of one hundred thousand. We talked over the phone about it. Her article 'How You Can Receive God's Guidance' sparked eager reader response.

In 1957 I was functioning in the role of single parent, trying to rear three small children in Carmel, New York, while commuting over a hundred miles each day to work in New York City. It was a lonely, difficult time for me. One night I poured out my agony to God and laid before Him my need for a wife. Then, remembering Catherine's article on guidance, I took out a yellow pad, prepared to write down the names of any possible mates He might suggest.

Catherine's name popped into my mind.

It seemed almost ludicrous to tie Catherine Marshall to my plea for a partner. 'That can't be your idea, Lord,' I said, dismissing the thought.

Then I recalled Catherine's book *To Live Again* and the chapter that had entranced me – 'They Walk in Wistfulness.' In it she had given a poignant answer to a doctor's question about her emotional well-being. I reread the chapter and came to these words:

> Do you really want to know what it feels like to be a widow? God made men and women for each other. Any other way of life is wrong; because it is abnormal. The last few months it's been like having a gnawing hunger, a haunting wistfulness at the centre of life. I can forget about it for short periods – ignore it some-times. But it's always there – always – and I'm afraid not even you can prescribe any pills that can cure it.

Elsewhere in that same chapter she wrote:

The need is to love and to be loved — that ultimate of life. Could I, and all those like me who walk the earth in wistfulness, find the way to trust God even for that?

Suddenly I knew that Catherine and I had something in common — loneliness. But so little else, it seemed. The whole idea was ridiculous.

I ticked off the reasons why.

First and foremost, who would want to follow the Peter and Catherine act? Their romance and marriage had entranced and stirred millions of people through her best-selling books; more millions had been captivated by the beautifully-done movie of *A Man Called Peter*.

Why would I want to marry a super-spiritual Christian celebrity? Who was almost five years older than I was?

Even more to the point, why would Catherine, at age forty-four, even supposing she should be attracted to me as an individual, want to marry a man who was rearing three small children?

Looked at logically, the idea of Catherine and me pairing up made little sense from any standpoint.

But . . . a voice deep inside reminded me, God is not bound by logic.

The least I could do was give it one good shot, I decided. If God was in it, I'd soon know. So I called Catherine, said *Guideposts* was looking for another article (true), and asked her if I could come to Washington and take her out for dinner. Requesting a dinner date should signal to her that I had more in mind than just an article.

She parried that proposal with the suggestion we make it lunch.

Strike one.

I took a plane from New York to Washington, rented a car, and drove to her town house just off Wisconsin Avenue. Catherine emerged, wearing a dark blue dress with white collar and cuffs; silver earrings and a diamond brooch added distinct feminine touches. A lovely woman. Something quickened inside me.

Lunch at a Georgetown restaurant, however, was a letdown. Catherine was friendly and full of ideas for an article. Yet she neatly sidestepped all probing into her personal life. She was the consummate professional.

Strike two.

I drove her back to her town house, prepared to say goodbye and dismiss once and for all any thoughts of a personal relationship. Just before opening the car door, I happened to ask her a question regarding the Holy Spirit. It was as if I had found the combination to a valuable safe. An excited conversation followed that lasted for another half hour. Our two spirits had touched, then been ignited.

I was still at bat.

A week or so later I wrote to Catherine, asking if I could see her on the way back from an upcoming trip to California. With my plans a bit uncertain, I listed two possible dates, told her I would telephone beforehand. There wasn't time before I left for the coast for her to reply.

I did call Catherine from California – several times – but got no answer. The morning I was to fly from Los Angeles to Washington I called again – still nobody there. Then I came to a conclusion.

This is ridiculous. Catherine has no interest in me personally. I'm being silly to pursue this. Besides, she's not even home.

I changed my reservation from Washington to New York, flew home, and decided to forget the inner nudging that I should seek a romance with Catherine.

Strike three?

No, not quite. A foul tip, perhaps, that the catcher dropped. Several days later I received a letter from Catherine. 'What happened to you?' she wrote. 'You asked me to hold two dates. I did, but you never appeared. Or called. Is anything wrong?'

I was startled. Then stimulated. Catherine was obviously annoyed with me. But that was not all bad. In fact, it was many moons better than indifference.

In a spirit of contrition, I started to call Catherine, then stopped. A new, more direct approach was needed. *Drop your editorial front, Len; don't be defensive. Approach her man to woman.* In this vein, I wrote her a letter.

In *Meeting God At Every Turn* Catherine describes how she reacted to this change of style in me:

There was nothing of the professional editor about the letter I received from Len several days later. 'I would like to know you better,' he wrote. 'How do you react to this idea? We'll choose a day, and then you write on your calendar three letters: F U N. I'll pick you up in the morning in my car and we'll just take off to the beach or the mountains or whatever.'

The letter seemed deliberately couched to say, 'If you're interested in pursuing this relationship, let's have a go at it. If not, then tell me so right now.'

I liked the approach. We set a day in early August. Len telephoned the night before from a Washington motel to say that he would call me at 10:30 the next morning. He was delighted when I suggested fixing a picnic lunch.

The next morning turned out to be a beautiful summer day, not too hot. When I met Len at my front door, I found myself slipping easily into the adventurous mood he had suggested. He put the picnic basket in the trunk of his car and we climbed into the front seat. 'What do you prefer,' he asked casually, 'ocean or mountains?'

'I would choose the mountains,' I replied.

'Which direction?'

I aimed him west toward Skyline Drive. As we drove along, I studied this fortyish editor sitting beside me. He was of medium height; dark hair beginning to grey; lithe, athletic figure. His grey-blue eyes were direct, warm, the lids often crinkling with humour. He was a good conversationalist, probing but relaxed. I relaxed, too. It was going to be a good day.

It was a good day, an amazing day. We talked for almost eleven hours straight. All my resistance to following the Peter Marshall romance, to her 'super spirituality' and to our age difference dissolved in my astonishment over Catherine's physical warmth, simplicity, and earthy good humour. I was overwhelmed by the idea that God had perceived all this beforehand and had brought us together. During that one astounding day I fell in love with Catherine and began to think ahead toward marriage.

Catherine was slower in coming to this conclusion. She had to face more obstacles than I did. Mine had been mostly ego problems. Hers were substantive: taking on three small children, turning at a right angle to the life that had seemed to stretch so comfortably and predictably ahead of her – for which her dream house was even then being built. This home in Bethesda, Maryland, was to be ready for occupancy within a few months; Catherine had personally designed it to meet her career-woman needs.

That she was able to overcome these obstacles had to be the Lord's doing. For weeks she prayed, probed the Scriptures. And it was during this time of her intense searching that I began to find answers to the question I asked myself at that Salvation Army luncheon: What was the special charisma in this woman that had captured both believers and nonbelievers?

First, a down-to-earth quality that shunned subterfuge and embraced candour and openness. Ever since the success of *A Man Called Peter*, people had tried to put her on a spiritual pedestal. She resisted, refused to play the role of guru, insisted that she was a struggler for truth like everyone else.

Second, the spirit of adventure. She saw her faith in this light. Jesus was bold, imaginative, unpredictable. God's plan for each life was unique, did not fit any set formula. Both the death of her first husband and the rebirth of love interest in her life were totally unexpected, yet within the illimitable providence of the God she knew.

Third, vulnerability. Catherine was honest about her flaws, admitting her inadequacies in such areas as child rearing and certain social situations. Result: she learned from her mistakes. This quality also made her open to editorial advice in every book she wrote but one, and that one had to be abandoned.

I learned a lot about Catherine during this period, but the deeper secret of her success eluded me. That first date, rambling along the Skyline Drive, was in early August; we were married three months later on November 14, 1959.

Catherine had huge adjustments to make. She sold her Washington dream house to move to Chappaqua, forty miles north of New York City, so that I could continue to commute to my job at *Guideposts* in the city. My children – Linda, ten; Chester, six; Jeffrey, three – had been through a deeply unsettling two years, adjusting to a variety of housekeepers. They had mixed feelings toward moving into a new house, and especially toward 'the new Mommie that Daddy's bringing home'.

Catherine's son, Peter John, nineteen, was going through a period of rebellion at Yale. It's hard enough for a young person to cope with one celebrity parent, but Peter's father and mother both were 'Christian personages'. Peter told us one day with a straight face that when he graduated he wanted to be a beach boy at Virginia Beach.

Catherine and I had so many things to pray about that we began to rise an hour early each morning to read the Bible and seek answers together. Her current journal lay open beside us in these pre-dawn prayer times, recording our changing needs, His unchanging faithfulness.

Our togetherness as an author-editor team was tested early in our marriage. Catherine had already been working over a year researching her novel *Christy* and had written some fifty or so pages. One day she handed me her manuscript. Outside of her typist, I would be the first to read it. I started in with much anticipation.

Two hours later I faced a dilemma. The manuscript was wordy, short on action – yes, a bit dull. Conversation between mountain people was almost undecipherable because of Catherine's attempt to spell out the dialect as she had heard it. On the plus side, the characters were truly believable. Should I tell her the whole truth, or just centre on the good things I saw in the manuscript?

Drawing a deep breath, I told her the truth as I saw it. She flinched for a moment, then stared at me with a new light in her eyes. 'You're right on all counts,' she admitted. 'I felt it was weak, but hoped somehow I was too close to it to see its strengths.' She sighed, 'Let's start with the mountain dialect.'

Thus did I pass the first crucial test of our professional relationship. If I had been less than honest, she would have eventually gotten the needed critique from Ed Kuhn, her McGraw-Hill editor. But she and I were full collaborators at work, now, as well as in the home.

As the years passed Catherine and I, as a writer-editor team, became more and more productive: between us we were responsible for nearly one hundred *Guideposts* articles and more than thirty published books. There were dozens of appearances as a speaking team; numerous courses conducted together on Christian subjects, highlighting the movement of the Holy Spirit.

I have one major regret about all this. We didn't take enough time to smell the flowers, to learn what it really means to take a vacation. We went from deadline to deadline, from crisis to crisis, dealing with what had to be done, forgetting too often to mark on our calendar those letters FUN. I feel deeply convicted about this, but the truth is that Catherine and I were workaholics.

During our twenty-three years of marriage I did discover the secrets behind her extraordinary gifts of communication. There were two. One came out through the dedication she showed in rearing my three young children – despite lungs that never operated at more than seventy-five percent normal capacity. It emerged as she struggled for the precise descriptive phrase in her writing, as she sought the exactly right colour for a living room chair, in her search for tonal perfection in stereo music. She tried to lift the sights of her family and friends by planting dreams in our hearts of achievements that appeared beyond us.

This reach toward excellence was a part of everything she did.

One example, I'll never forget. Catherine was preparing a dinner party for special friends. The day before, she asked me to drive her to Falls Church just outside of Washington – an hour's trip. 'Some errands,' she told me.

One errand, as it turned out. At a bakery, which sold a certain kind of macaroons. As we drove about Falls Church looking for this bakery in steamy weather, I fought off a growing irritation.

'Catherine, why are these macaroons so important to you?'

'I have a great recipe for grinding them into a wonderful sauce.'

'A sauce! For what?'

'For the fruit compote I'm planning for dessert.'

I turned and looked at her in amazement. 'We're taking three hours out of a day, in terrible heat, to drive through miserable traffic to buy a bag of macaroons so people can pour a little sauce on their dessert!'

'That's right,' she said. 'It's the sauce that makes the dessert.'

That was Catherine. She gave herself unreservedly to what she was doing, would settle for nothing but one hundred percent, was one-eyed in the scriptural sense whether it was writing, speaking, painting, decorating, preparing meals, building family life.

Her intensity spilled over into everything and I loved

to watch it erupt. One night during the late 1960s, she strode into our bedroom where I was reading and began to pace the floor, face furious. 'What's happened?' I asked in alarm.

She didn't answer right away, just stared at me with tears in her eyes. 'I'm so upset I can hardly speak,' she said.

'Over what?'

'Viet Nam! We shouldn't be fighting there. It's wrong . . . wrong . . . wrong. God will punish us for this.'

I looked at her in amazement, surprised again at the emotion she poured into her convictions that could focus one moment on a child's poor study habits, the next on a war ten thousand miles away.

But there's another more profound reason for Catherine's extraordinary accomplishments. Her love of Jesus, expressed through a love affair with Scripture.

Bibles were scattered throughout our house . . . all editions, plus reference books and concordances. We often went to bed, turned out the light, and listened to a chapter of Scripture on tape. If she could have found a way to spread Bible passages on a slice of bread, Catherine would have devoured it.

When upset or under spiritual assault or in physical pain, Catherine would go to her office, kneel by her chair, and open her Bible to the fifty-third chapter of Isaiah, or the ninety-first Psalm, or the second chapter of Acts, or the eighth chapter of Romans. She would read, then pray, then read, then pray some more. She liked to pray with the Bible clutched in her hands; it gave her strength. She would rest her case on its promises. Catherine didn't read the Bible for solace or inspiration, but to have an encounter with the Lord. Sometimes she emerged from these sessions contrite, sometimes at peace, sometimes still in turmoil. I think these were the most intense moments of her life.

All of Catherine's Bibles are marked with underlinings;

colour shadings make certain passages almost leap out at you. Question marks and exclamation points dot page after page. A long comment will be scribbled at the top or bottom or along the side. Sometimes 'Yes! Yes! Yes!' indicates Catherine's exuberant confirmation of a teaching.

Some of her happiest moments were when she was preparing a Bible study for one of our classes or for a writing project. She chose our king-size bed for this adventure, propping herself up with pillows, while Bibles, reference books, a thesaurus, a concordance, and yellow pads were spread all about her.

Catherine's passion for the Word permeated her whole life. It undergirded her writing. It formed a base for us as a married team in the making of family decisions. It provided substance to her counselling of people through the mail. I'm convinced it was also the basis for her inner vitality, her charisma, and the mantle of authority she wore with some reluctance.

Her grappling with the Word mostly took place in the early morning hours, as she fed her questions and discoveries into her journals. Material from these writings – her 'closer walk' with her Lord – provide the content for this book. They cover our struggles in bringing together two broken homes, learning to relate to children and stepchildren – and later, our relationship to their spouses and our grandchildren.

What shines through Catherine's words is that Christian growth and adventuring never stop. The search for more of the truth is endlessly absorbing: the promises God holds out are worth every moment of struggle, the 'walk' never arrives at some static, fixed point, but leads on into ever deeper intimacy with God.

A Closer Walk is the record of Catherine's encounters with the Lord of Scripture along the way, most appearing in print for the first time. The book is divided into six sections that move chronologically from our early life together as a family, through Christian creativity and growth, into spiritual warfare, to the final triumph of her death.

Years before Catherine died, we had talked about the probability that I would outlive her. Since I had worked so closely with her on every writing project, she knew we were in accord on one basic principle – no book of her writings would see print unless it measured up to her standard of excellence. The principal guardians of this standard were to be myself and her long-time friend and editorial advisor, Elizabeth Sherrill, whose talents we both admire so much and who has carefully gone over this manuscript.

May this book bless you who read it, and stimulate you to seek 'a closer walk' with Jesus.

Leonard E. LeSourd

Section One

The Home As His Classroom

Upon returning from our honeymoon in late 1959, Catherine and I confronted all the problems and adjustments involved in bringing together two broken homes. Catherine's greatest self-doubt centred around the responsibility for mothering three young stepchildren. (Her son, Peter John Marshall, was attending college.) Always a perfectionist, she felt she lacked the patient, accepting qualities of an ideal mother.

The early morning time when we sought answers together in the Bible became lifeblood for Catherine. Time and again from Scripture she drew insight and answers. Praying together in advance of the inevitable conflicts and confrontations solidified our marriage. It is hard to stay upset or angry at your mate when you are sitting up in bed side by side, holding hands, reading God's Word.

The setting for the following episodes was an eight-room home in Chappaqua, New York, a suburban community some forty miles north of New York City, where we lived for the first five years of our marriage.

LL

1

A New Way to See Jesus

As Len and I begin our new life together, I'm enjoying a new way to read the New Testament – undoubtedly a way known to many Christians through the centuries but new to me: during my early morning devotions I'm reading the words as if Jesus were speaking directly to me.

At the time of my discovery, I was going through the Gospels consecutively, desiring above all else to get a vivid portrait of Jesus. And a portrait emerged all right, not so much what He looked like, as the characteristics of His person. I discovered in Him one who is totally alive – physically stalwart, emotionally sensitive. Humour, I definitely found. And grief – not for Himself, but for others' hurts and the tragic havoc that sin brings. And love, an amazing love that pours out of Him with never any effort to hide it or dam it up. Yet it is a love with steel in it.

Over and over I have come upon this steel – a note of stringency in Jesus' conversation and His way of dealing with people that, for the most part, seems alien to the teaching in our churches today. Never have I found a trace of coddling or compromising or self-protectiveness in Him.

For example, there was the Pharisee who asked Jesus to lunch at his house. Jesus accepted. But if there was anything pleasant about the conversation around the table, we were not told so in Luke's account. Indeed, centuries later, the words all but blister the page:

But woe to you Pharisees! for you tithe mint and rue
and every herb, and neglect justice and the love of God
. . . you love the best seat in the synagogues and
salutations in the market places . . . you are like graves
which are not seen, and men walk over them without
knowing it.

Luke 11:42–44 rsv

It is clear that Christ chose to tell this particular man and
his guests the simple, straightforward truth rather than
keeping quiet or being socially correct. That takes
courage of a rare sort, and Jesus must have known full
well that it could lead only to a cross.

There is an unexpected dividend from reading the
New Testament as if Jesus were speaking to me: when I
look away from the problems in my new marriage to turn
my full attention to Jesus, He proves Himself alive by
concerning Himself with my life, family, and friends and
talking to me about these matters morning after morning.

Last week, for example, as I read the twelfth chapter of
Luke, it was as though Jesus were saying:

Beware of pretending before the family to be something you are not, or to have attained spiritual values
that you have not attained. This is hypocrisy. And
nothing is more futile than trying to keep anything
secret. There is nothing covered up among family
members that is not going to be uncovered.

Later in the same chapter He seemed to tell me:

You think that because members of your family believe
in Me, all should be peaceful and serene. Not so. My
presence is not going to bring sweet peace and an easy
time. On occasions, My thoughts and My way will
bring severe discord. Do not be surprised when this
happens. Realise that out of temporary disharmony – if
it includes honest facing-up – comes growth for each

member of the family and a further knitting together in Me.

This new way of letting Jesus speak to me may help me relate to a new neighbour too. She's asked me to assist in a community project in which I do not believe. I was puzzled as to how to handle the situation without hurting her feelings. In the eleventh chapter of Luke I heard:

> You think that you do not want to tell your neighbour the truth because you do not want to hurt her. The real reason is that you want to protect yourself from her displeasure, or antagonism. It is wrong to keep quiet because you care more about her friendship (or anyone else's) than you care about her growth in Me. That is just another way of putting yourself first.

What are the results of these meditations? Increased honesty in our family has already led to more openness toward God in the lives of two of our children. I find that I'm less threatened by family arguments. So far I have not found the way or the courage to be honest with my friend. I ducked out of the project through an excuse.

But this I can say – the resurrected Jesus is a continual reality in my life. How can I ever find words to express the joy of His presence?

2

Stepmothering

This morning I am pondering my bizarre dream of last night to see if the Lord is telling me something through it:

In my dream a small animal emerged from a swelling near my shoulder. Looking more closely, I saw that the animal was wounded. 'Those cuts will have to be sewn up,' I thought, and then I woke up.

As I listened for God's word about the dream, I recalled how both Len and I have referred to the two small boys as being like bear cubs the way they roll and romp about the family room. Yesterday they broke a vase doing this. I have to admit that sometimes the children 'get under my skin'. Obviously the Lord is pointing out that changes need to be made in my attitude.

Part of what Len and I have to resolve comes down to the proper order he places on his new wife and his children by a previous marriage. All the stepmother tales in fairy stories and folklore tell us that we are confronting something basic and difficult here.

Len's emotions toward his flesh and blood are *so* strong that perhaps it is against nature for him to try to put his wife first. In his mind, he's done this, but his instinctive emotion is to defend and protect his children. Yet not to put the wife first is to risk disaster in the marriage.

I turned to the nineteenth chapter of Matthew:

For this reason a man shall leave his father and mother and be joined to his wife, and the two shall become one.

Matthew 19:5 RSV

Fortunately, Len and I can pray together and can talk over these problems. I was able to tell him about my dream without fearing he would use it against me. We are learning to admit our weaknesses to each other.

3

Around the Dinner Table

After much experimentation, Len and I have settled on the evening meal as the ideal time and place for growing as a family. Mornings are too pressured, evenings too filled with school work, meetings, phone calls.

Being at the dinner table each night of the week is a command performance for Len and myself, Linda, Chester, and Jeff. No TV dinners in front of the tube. No dinners for our children at friends' houses except on weekends. A major effort by Len and me to keep our professional activities from interfering with this time.

The meal begins with grace, and the children do most of the praying, learning to overcome shyness until they can talk to God easily. Soon I hope we'll learn to say grace just as naturally when we eat as a family in restaurants.

Len and I try not to dominate the ensuing conversation, but draw out each child. 'What did you learn today in school, Chester? . . . Which teacher do you like the most, Linda? . . . Who is your best friend, Jeff?'

Criticism in this setting, we learned, quenches fragile spirits; it's better saved for one-on-one encounters. After dinner there's a reading from Scripture and family prayer around the table. One of our main objectives is to show Jesus as so engaging a Person that we would all enjoy it if He joined us at the table.

'Jesus had a sense of humour,' I mentioned once.

This seemed to surprise the children so the next night I came to the table armed with examples from Scripture. About the hypocrisy of the Pharisees He said, 'You blind guides, straining out a gnat and swallowing a camel' (Matthew 23:24 RSV).

This is the humour of exaggeration, I explained, pointing out that Jesus' humour was always for a purpose. Sometimes it was His bridge to an individual He would otherwise have had trouble reaching. Most often it was to illuminate a truth.

There was the occasion when Christ joshed His disciples about spiritual timidity: 'Is a lamp brought in to be put under a bushel, or under a bed?' (Mark 4:21 RSV). The point He was making: 'I need disciples who don't hide their light.'

When the apostles became too impressed with the crowds Jesus was drawing, knowing full well that crowds gather for many reasons, Jesus commented dryly, 'Wherever the carcass lies, there will the vultures gather' (Matthew 24:28 MOFFATT).

Once we reread the Gospels, watching for Christ's wit, we find it everywhere. 'Can one blind man be guide to another blind man? Surely they will both fall into the ditch' (Luke 6:39 PHILLIPS). Or the comment made about the rich man who valued his possessions too much. 'It is easier for a camel to go through the eye of a needle than for a rich man to enter the kingdom of God' (Luke 18:25 NEB).

To awaken people at every level of their being, Jesus used every weapon of language and communication to achieve His goals; most effective were the humorous thrust and banter about those who put on airs and think more highly of themselves than they should. Jesus sees all our incongruities and absurdities, and He laughs along with us.

As the result of these dinner table discussions, we're all finding that our spontaneity and fervour in worshipping Him increase. Our goal with the children: to help them see in Christ an incredible Man with that rare blend found nowhere else – purity, strength, compassion, and sparkling humour.

4

Loving the Unlovely

As I look out over the bright greenery of our backyard this morning, I realise how hard it is for me to love people, even members of my own family, when I disapprove of their behaviour. I know this is wrong, Lord Jesus, because You demonstrated time after time that it is possible, even necessary, to love people without judgment.

There was the woman taken in adultery and about to be stoned when You asked the mob surrounding her, 'If any one of you is without sin, let him be the first to throw a stone at her.' As You told her to go and sin no more, I could almost hear the caring quality of Your voice. Likewise with the woman You met at the well, the one who had had five husbands. Uncondemning love was in Your manner.

I have no trouble forgiving certain people, but recently I have seen that the forgiveness is not complete in Your eyes until I can love them too.

Ever since we moved here to Chappaqua, Marilyn[1] has been a thorn in my side. She's overbearing, overweight, and always overreacting. Her criticalness rubs me raw. Forgive her, sure. Love her, so hard for me. We can't manufacture love, can we? Until now I haven't even been willing for *You* to love Marilyn *through* me.

Queer about love . . . Is it a quality so of a piece that when we deliberately withhold it from any single human

---

[1] Not her real name.

being, we deny love itself and, in the end, are rendered incapable of loving?

So last night, down on my knees in Len's presence, I confessed all this. With Len and You as witnesses, I'm giving You permission to give me the gift of love for Marilyn.

But this morning I'm not willing to stop there; I would like to be able to love people the way You love them. In Your Word this morning I came across some verses that give me a handle on how.

In 2 Peter 1, the apostle rejoices in the 'precious and very great promises' by which we may be 'partakers of the divine nature.' Then he gives us a ladder of seven steps leading to this high goal:

1) To faith, add *virtue*. (v. 5)
2) To virtue, add *knowledge*. (v. 5)
3) To knowledge, add *self-control*. (v. 6)
4) To self-control, add *steadfastness*. (v. 6)
5) To steadfastness, add *godliness*. (v. 6)
6) To godliness, add *brotherly affection*. (v. 7)
7) To brotherly affection will then be added, *love*. (v. 7)

'For if these things are yours and abound,' Peter concludes, 'they keep you from being ineffective or unfruitful in the knowledge of our Lord Jesus Christ' (v. 8, RSV).

I want to climb that ladder, Lord, to be able to know You and love You more than ever before.

Seeking Excellence

I've been troubled about Linda's school work. Considering her high IQ she's not doing anything like her best. Last night at the dinner table I told her about one of my favourite Bible verses, which appears no less than three times in the Old Testament: He maketh my feet like hinds' feet, and setteth me upon my high places (Psalm 18:32–33, 2 Samuel 22:33–34, and Habakkuk 3:19 KJV).

'What in the world does that mean?' she asked, with a frown on her freckled face.

To answer, I told her about a friend of mine. . . .

When I was six years old, this family friend whom we called 'Auntie Chamberlain' purchased the book *Hiawatha* for me. But this was no ordinary copy. It had hand-cut paper, beautiful illustrations, a pronouncing vocabulary for difficult Indian names, even a section for handicraft projects.

She had searched all over town to find it. And this was so typical of Auntie Chamberlain – a woman who gave herself totally to life. Auntie Chamberlain taught me the importance of doing every task with my whole heart. Soon I discovered that family games – like Parcheesi – were the most fun when played with total enthusiasm and concentration. Piano lessons took on added lustre when I not only learned to read a piece of music, but also memorised it. School assignments were more fun when I did more than the minimum required.

I found that something more important than good

grades came from this approach: a deep inner satisfaction, a glow, a happiness. And conversely, I discovered that when I undertook any project halfheartedly, the result was usually half successful.

Later on, while living in Washington, I saw to my delight this 'Auntie Chamberlain quality' in another individual – Dr Lida Earhart. She, too, gave all of herself to whatever task she undertook and had been the first woman to attain the rank of full professor at Columbia University. After retiring, she came to Washington to live and regularly attended services at our New York Avenue Presbyterian Church.

One day someone asked Miss Earhart to give a talk on the Book of Job at the monthly meeting of the church women's association. This was probably a tossed-off invitation, with the usual kind of talk expected. But the talk turned out to be far from usual. For two months Miss Earhart had studied the Book of Job. She had researched the archaeological features of the time of Job and his contemporaries. She had read biblical scholars' analyses of the book. She had pondered deeply the book's theme: the problem of evil in our world. The result was one of the most memorable presentations I ever have heard.

Even more remarkable, she had done all that work for an ordinary church meeting. Nothing extraordinary had been asked or expected. Yet she knew *the secret of hinds' feet*.

'What is the secret?' Linda asked.

'The rear feet of the female red deer, known also as the *hind*,' I said, 'step in precisely the same spot where the front feet have just been. Every motion of the hind is followed through with this same single-focused consistency, making it the most sure-footed of all mountain animals.'

As the feet of the female deer are to the mountains, I told her, so is the mind of man to the heights of life. 'Ask yourself – how many things have I done with single-minded devotion, nothing held back?'

'Not many,' she admitted.

'It's not easy in our modern world,' I agreed, 'to make our lives like hinds' feet. Too much today is done with minimal effort. This attitude can begin with school work done sloppily – but there's no joy in halfhearted efforts.'

Linda listened with real interest to this biblical simile. Lord, make it come alive in her life!

6

The Contagion of Joy

As I absorb the Gospels this September morning, I'm seeing Jesus so clearly as a vital young Man who loved life and was filled with joy.

I'm influenced no doubt by my experience last month [August 1961] at a conference of The Fellowship of Christian Athletes in Estes Park, Colorado, where I spoke to the wives of the coaches and leaders. I never had seen so much muscle and maleness packed into one area. During the entire week there was a virile, vibrant atmosphere. And who was the central figure? Jesus Christ!

Of primary interest to me was the involvement of my son Peter, who had graduated from Yale the previous June. Peter admitted his purpose in coming to the conference was to get close to nationally known athletes. 'I'm not interested in hearing any Sunday school stories,' he told Len and me. During high school and college to my great dismay he had rejected his Christian heritage.

Instead of Sunday school stories, Peter heard some of the biggest names in sports unashamedly tell how they had found joy in the Christian faith. From the beginning my son was swept along in the excitement of young men singing, shouting, laughing, competing, and praying together. By the fourth day he was literally catapulted into making a personal commitment of his life to Jesus Christ as Saviour and Lord.

'It is an awesome thing when you meet Jesus for the first time,' he told me later. Gone was his bored, know-it-all attitude, in its place a new aliveness. A decision to enter Princeton Theological Seminary followed a few weeks later.

It makes me eager to take a fresh look at the qualities of the One who has such an attraction for young people – in His time and ours. The Gospel picture of Him is of a joyous man with a buoyant zest for life. The New Testament in one place describes Him as 'anointed . . . with the oil of gladness' (Hebrews 1:9 KJV).

As I read through the Gospels, I see that Jesus had quite a bit to say about joy. We are *not* invited to a relationship that will take away our fun but asked to 'enter into the joy of [our] Lord' (Matthew 25:21 KJV). The purpose of His coming to earth, Jesus said, was in order that our *joy might be full!* (John 15:11 KJV).

No wonder the young in the full tide of life adored Him and left everything to be with Him! And the young today still respond to the lure of adventure and the giving of their all to a cause. That is why the stringency and the sacrifice called for by movements like the Peace Corps have so much appeal.

I can see that Jesus drew men and women into the Kingdom by promising them two things: first, trouble – hardship, danger; and second, joy. But what curious alchemy is this that He can make even danger and hardship seem joyous? He understands things about human nature that we grasp only dimly: few of us are really challenged by the promise of soft living, by an emphasis on me-first, or by a life of easy compromise.

Christ still asks for one's total surrender and then promises His gift of full, overflowing joy. It was that Spirit of joy that I felt in the young people at Estes Park. It was this Spirit that captured my son and turned his life around.

Quenching a Child's Spirit

After three years of marriage, Len and I are groping for wisdom in relating to each of our children. Gradually we have become aware that family life is God's classroom for shaping us into the kind of people He wants us to be.

God often speaks to me through dreams. Last night, for example, I dreamed I was talking to Jeff, our irrepressible six-year-old. In my right hand was a bottle of what looked like baby aspirin. Jeff and I were having one of our typical confrontations. In the dream, however, I lost my temper and somehow the bottle hit one of his eyes. He cried and to my alarm I saw on my hand fluid from his eye.

The next scene was of Len carrying Jeff into our bedroom, where I was standing by the window. Sitting on his father's knee, Jeff took his forefinger and ran it around his eye socket. I looked and – to my horror – there was no eye there.

'Let's get him to an eye doctor fast!' I urged.

Len's stance was his usual patient tolerance, though now full of sadness. 'It's too late. There's no eye there.'

I was overcome with grief – then, to my great relief, I woke up.

This morning when I asked the Lord if He was telling me something through this dream, I was led to one of Jesus' teachings in the Sermon on the Mount.

The eye is the lamp of the body. So, if your eye is sound, your whole body will be full of light.

Matthew 6:22 RSV

Then came His gentle but firm correction to me. I had been putting out, quenching, some of Jeff's light by the way I had been treating him.

Convicted of my sin, I confessed immediately the specific ways I have been quenching the light in Jeff: (1) Through losing my temper (quite inexcusable); (2) dominating him because I'm bigger; (3) not demonstrating enough love for Jeff.

I asked for and received God's forgiveness for these sins. Then I sought out Jeff, hugged him, and asked his forgiveness.

'That's okay, Mom,' he said with a grin. Pause. 'Can I have Rodney over for lunch today?'

Several weeks later: I dreamed again last night about Jeff. This time he and Chester were tumbling about on the back porch. Suddenly Jeff lost his balance and fell down the steps, his head striking the pavement below.

The next picture was of Jeff being carried off on a stretcher covered with blankets neatly tucked in, with his head heavily bandaged. And in my dream, suddenly I realised how much *I loved this little guy*.

Malnutrition of the Spirit

The problems that arise in second marriages are more than I could ever have imagined. Being a new mother to three young children is exhausting, leaving little time for creative writing. There are times when life seems to go grey; I have no zest for anything.

When this happened last week I recognised my problem: *malnutrition of the spirit*.

It was Carol, my friend from California, who had made me aware months ago that spiritual undernourishment can be quite as real as physical starvation. When I first met Carol, it was obvious that she had problems, but not the usual ones. She had a happy marriage; no major troubles with her three children; everything fine economically; no health difficulties.

But she felt tired all the time from the daily routine. 'Nothing is much fun anymore,' she had said. 'I have so little energy that no undertaking seems worth attempting. What's wrong with me?'

An hour and much talk later, I had a sudden inspiration: could it be that Carol's inner spirit was starving to death?

Taking up my Bible, I turned to the Old Testament story of Daniel. I read to her about how Daniel was in exile in the king's palace. 'His windows being open in his chamber toward Jerusalem, he kneeled upon his knees three times a day, and prayed, and gave thanks before his God, as he did aforetime' (Daniel 6:10 KJV).

'We have three meals a day,' I suggested. 'Perhaps we need spiritual food three times a day too.'

'But what *is* spiritual food? And how do you take it?' Carol asked.

'Jesus said that His words are spirit and life indeed. He used metaphor upon metaphor to tell us that His Spirit is our life substance. He described himself as "living water" and "the bread of life". Meeting Him in Scripture is like an intravenous feeding from His Spirit to our spirit,' I replied.

'So,' I challenged Carol, 'would you be willing to try spiritual food in the form of life-giving Bible verses three times a day for one month?'

At a Christian bookstore Carol found an 'Inspiration Box' of paper capsules, each containing a verse of Scripture. They were to be taken daily as spiritual vitamins. (This word 'vitamin' means 'life substance'.)

Later, with another spiritually undernourished friend, we decided that an additional blessing came when we took the time ourselves to dig through Scripture and put together a homemade card file of spiritual vitamins.

So last week I produced a 'Vitamin Box' of dozens of favourite passages for my new family. I used a concordance and looked up words such as *strength*, *food*, *bread*, *water*, *hunger*, and *thirst*. Other cards were culled from Christ's own words. Now before blessing the food at each meal, we pass the box, and one of the children chooses a card to read aloud. The nourishment is most effective when the life-giving words of Scripture are memorised and so become the permanent possessions of mind and heart.

But they that wait upon the Lord shall renew their strength; they shall mount up with wings as eagles; they shall run, and not be weary; and they shall walk, and not faint.

Isaiah 40:31 KJV

For the Lord disciplines the man he loves. . . . So up with your listless hands! Strengthen your weak knees! And make straight paths for your feet.

Hebrews 12:6, 12–13, MOFFATT

Oh that men would praise the Lord for his goodness, and for his wonderful works to the children of men! For he satisfieth the longing soul, and filleth the hungry soul with goodness.

Psalm 107:8–9 KJV

. . . My grace is sufficient for thee: for my strength is made perfect in weakness.

2 Corinthians 12:9 KJV

By saturating my mind with these and other verses, I find that the greyness lifts, the spirit is infused with spiritual food, and I am ready to meet any difficulty that comes along.

9

Early Morning Time

Awake my soul, and with the sun
Thy daily stage of duty run;
Shake off dull sloth, and joyful rise
To pay the morning sacrifice!

Shine on me, Lord, new life impart,
Fresh ardours kindle in my heart;
One ray of Thine all-quickening light
Dispels the clouds and dark of night.
                    Thomas Ken (1637–1711)

As Len and I arise at 6:00 A.M. this morning, I find the above verses help move me from 'dull sloth' to 'fresh ardours'. Then in Psalm 5, I read:

Give ear to my words, O Lord, consider my meditation. Hearken unto the voice of my cry. . . . My voice
shalt thou hear in the morning, O Lord; in the morning
will I direct my prayer unto thee, and will look up.
                                    Psalm 5:1–3 KJV

God, who created heaven and earth, will hear *my* voice?
The King of the universe will consider *my* meditation?
Oh, thank You, Lord, for the undreamed-of opportunity
of this audience with the King! Anyone who has a favour
to ask of an earthly monarch has no chance of having
his request granted until he makes his wish known to

the king. That *could* be second-hand – generally is, in protocol-bound human societies. What a privilege to have an audience in person! Yet this is the status and the honour You allow each of us, Lord.

Even more privileged is he so in favour with the King that he is allowed as long as he wishes to be with the One he loves, listen to Him, watch Him, bask in His presence. In earthly courts, such a one would be considered favoured indeed, and the courts we're invited to enter are of an 'infinite majesty'. Just to say 'Thank You' seems inadequate. This morning I make it a welling, swelling gratitude!

10

Subject One to Another

This week I've been focusing my thoughts and prayers on the fifth chapter of Ephesians.

> Wives be subject – be submissive and adapt yourselves – to your own husbands as [a service] to the Lord. For the husband is head of the wife as Christ is the Head of the church. . . . As the church is subject to Christ, so let wives also be subject in everything to their husbands.
>
> Ephesians 5:22–24 AMPLIFIED

Like many women, I've struggled with conflicting emotions over the current emphasis on 'submission'. Especially when I hear of a case, as I did last week, of a husband who used this passage in Ephesians to intimidate his wife and force her to accept and condone his own adultery with another woman. An extreme situation, of course, but one of many instances where the basic truth of Scripture is violated or distorted when taken out of context.

For example, the admonition 'Wives, submit to your husbands' is coupled in Ephesians with, 'Husbands, love your wives, as Christ loved the church and gave Himself up for her' (v. 25). Yet this complementary verse is frequently overlooked.

This week's Bible focus was promoted by a letter:

'I am having a mighty struggle with my role as a

Christian wife,' the woman wrote. 'Something inside of me literally rebels at the words – obey, submit, subject! At times I have considered the apostle Paul to be a male chauvinist. Also, I can't believe that my loving heavenly Father, as I personally know Him, would want me to be as completely and blindly submissive as these Scriptures seem to indicate.

'I realise my resentment and selfishness is sin, yet when I try to submit to my husband, I end up feeling angry and hypocritical. Or like a spiritless dumb animal. How do I understand and accept this teaching?'

To answer this question, I've taken time to review my own relationship as a wife to Len, study the Ephesians chapter, then talk and pray some more with my husband.

When we were first married, Len suggested that I assume spiritual responsibility for our home. This seemed wrong to me. It went against a number of scriptural teachings. Also I doubted that Len's two sons would respond to this; they would perhaps see religion as 'a woman's thing'. In fact, Chester, the elder son, who is gifted in all sports, sees God the Father primarily through his own athletic father. Once Len and I began to search the Bible together in the early mornings, he saw for himself that he should take spiritual leadership of our home and did so.

But there's more. As we study Ephesians 5, we're beginning to believe that this may be one of the most misinterpreted chapters in the New Testament. Nor do we believe that St Paul was any kind of male chauvinist.

Much light is shed when we investigate the background against which Paul was teaching. He had come out of Judaism, a patriarchal system where women were considered their husbands' property. Still, Jewish women were better off than most. In the other countries around the Mediterranean basin of Paul's day, wives had no political or social status whatever, were allowed no education, no activity beyond the home. In the Greek world, for instance, groups of single young women were trained to provide the social and sex life of Greek husbands whose wives stayed at home, did the menial tasks, and cared for the children.

In Ephesians, chapters four to six, Paul is speaking out against this immoral system and is trying to teach new Ephesian Christians how they should relate to one another. It is only against this pagan backdrop that we can see how revolutionary Paul's 'Husbands, love your wives' was! Not only was Paul not against women, he, like his Master before him, was teaching that women are equally children of the Father and as such are to be respected and beloved. At that time this was a radically new approach to women.

In the end we're discovering that the hub upon which the Ephesian 'submission' passages turn is the statement that introduces them: 'Be subject to one another out of reverence for Christ' (Ephesians 5:21 AMPLIFIED). This is the irreducible minimum of Paul's instructions to all Christians – male or female.

What is coming out of Len's and my seeking prayers on this subject can be described as a triangle of authority more than a pecking order. God is at the apex of the triangle; the husband and wife are equally positioned at the lower corners. Thus both mates are equal in His sight, equally beloved by Him, equally committed to each other and to Him.

We're finding 'Be subject to one another out of reverence for Christ' to be intensely practical. It means a spirit of mutual respect, a willingness to listen. It means giving – and sometimes giving in – on the part of both of us, since sometimes God gives His direction through Len, at other times through me. Most importantly, at the peak of the triangle God Himself has to be acknowledged as the final Authority in the home.

In thinking further about the subject this morning, I realise that I want for our home everything in that Ephesians chapter. I want Len to be its spiritual head. I want him to be a husband whom I can love and trust and submit to in the biblical sense. I want him to love me as Jesus loves the Church, to love me as he would love his own body. I also want to 'respect, reverence, honour, love, and esteem him exceedingly'.

Section Two

Adventuresome Living

Travel is often called 'the door to adventure'. Catherine and I had our share of this kind of excitement. During the early years of our marriage we visited Uganda, Kenya, the Holy Land, drove through central Europe, painted with oils on the beaches of Bora Bora and Moorea in the South Pacific, shared stories with missionaries in such remote places as Tonga, Fiji, and Tahiti, ministered to groups in Samoa and Australia.

Yet the real adventure for us was always spiritual: testing scriptural truths, exploring different kinds of prayer, sharing in fellowship groups, teaching together from the Bible. The base for the first five years of our marriage was Chappaqua, New York. When Northern winters caused increasing congestion of Catherine's lungs, we moved to Boynton Beach, Florida, in November 1964.

The first of our children to marry was Peter who met Edith Wallis at Princeton Theological Seminary. They were married on May 29, 1966, and their daughter, Mary Elizabeth Marshall, was born on March 1, 1969.

During these years life was tumultuous, demanding, often exhausting. With God in charge of our lives, there was the never-ending suspense of wondering what He had in store for us next.

LL

1

The Prayer of Agreement

I am impressed this morning with the power in a
Scripture verse about prayer.

When my son Peter accepted an invitation to give a
speech in Kansas City, I had a telephone call from a
dentist in that city who was on the sponsoring committee. This man asked me to pray for the meeting and that
Peter's message would be God's topic for this particular
audience at this particular time.

The dentist and I decided to claim the promise of Jesus
in Matthew 18:19–20 rsv:

> 'If two of you agree on earth about anything they ask, it
> will be done for them by my Father in heaven. For
> where two or three are gathered in my name, there am
> I in the midst of them.'

In heartfelt accord, my caller and I asked God that His
word only be spoken at the upcoming gathering.

Peter's talk was in the newly decorated ballroom of the
largest hotel in Kansas City, with six hundred people in
attendance. The audience were both Christians and non-
Christians, a cross section of civic Kansas City.

Len and I learned later that just before Peter was to
speak a black man with a powerful voice sang 'There Is a
Balm in Gilead'. This got to everyone, especially Peter.

On the table beside him were the notes of the prepared
speech, which he had in fact planned to use. After
hearing the song, he shoved aside his papers, rose, and

picked up the theme of the song for his talk. For one hour and fifteen minutes he laid out before that Kansas City audience Jesus Christ as *the* 'balm in Gilead'.

The room was so quiet (according to the dentist) that not even the usual coughing and respiratory upheavals were in evidence. A doctor friend, not particularly religious, who was there as the guest of the dentist, told him afterwards, 'I've never witnessed or heard anything like it. It was so quiet that I was almost afraid to breathe.'

I asked the dentist, 'But, speaking that long extemporaneously, didn't Peter ramble or repeat himself?'

'Not once,' he answered. 'However you tie it, Catherine, when anyone can hold six hundred people *that* attentive for an hour and a quarter – that had to be God.'

What neither Peter nor the dentist knows is that 'There Is a Balm in Gilead' was one of the favourite songs of Peter's father. He had sung it in a quartet during his seminary days. He sometimes sang it as a duet in Westminster Church in Atlanta. When he was pastor of the New York Avenue Church in Washington, it was one of the favourite numbers of Charlie Beaschler's great massed choirs. Now, through that singer in Kansas City, God has used it again to bring His message to a hurting world.

2

Happiness Is . . .

As I've been pondering the subject of happiness this morning – an elusive and seemingly unattainable state for so many – I am led to these words of Jesus:

> If any man would come after me, let him deny himself and take up his cross and follow me. For whoever would save his life will lose it, and whoever loses his life for my sake will find it.

Matthew 16:24–25 RSV

I believe the secret of happiness lies imbedded in those words, painful though they appear to be. How else explain radiant people like the young man who sat in our living room and described how his six-year-old boy had died in his arms from leukaemia. Today this man finds fulfilment in giving himself totally to helping college students. Or the woman I visited recently whose husband had turned out to be a homosexual and demanded a divorce. Some years later, this woman also lost her eyesight. Yet she is a cheerful, loving person, fully self-supporting.

You might say that such people almost have a right to be unhappy. That they are not, lies in the way they spend themselves for others.

I have observed that when any of us embarks on the pursuit of happiness for ourselves, it eludes us. Often I've asked myself why. It must be because happiness comes to us only as a dividend. When we become absorbed in something demanding and worthwhile above and beyond ourselves, happiness seems to be there as a by-product of the self-giving.

That should not be a startling truth, yet I'm surprised at how few people understand and accept it. Have we made a god of happiness? Have we been brainwashed by ads assuring us 'Happiness is . . .' – usually a big, shiny, new gadget?

Perhaps our national preoccupation with happiness dates from these words in the Declaration of Independence:

> . . . All men are . . . endowed by their Creator with certain unalienable rights, [and] among these are life, liberty and *the pursuit of happiness* [italics added].

Now, I have always had immense admiration for Thomas Jefferson, author of these words. And until recently I never questioned them. But (and my apologies to you, Mr Jefferson) I do question them as I see more and more people interpret 'the pursuit of happiness' as a licence to grab for power or money or physical pleasure.

The truth, as I see it, is that not one of us has 'an unalienable right' to anything, not even to life itself. We did nothing to bring about our birth, and we are dependent for the next breath we draw on the grace of God. How arrogant and ungrateful we must seem to our Creator when we demand our 'rights'.

I think of Mary and Harold Brinig – a remarkable couple who found the true basis of happiness some years ago. Having moved to Chicago where they had no friends, they became irritable with each other and unhappy. While seeking help from the Bible one day, they were struck by these words of Jesus:

> You did not choose me, but I chose you and appointed you that you should go and bear fruit and that your fruit should abide. . . .

> John 15:16 RSV

Somehow that passage was like light penetrating their darkness: much of their unhappiness, they realised, was caused by self-centredness. Could Jesus be choosing them for service? But practically speaking, how could this happen in a big city like Chicago?

The first person they encountered after this revelation was the waitress who served them in a nearby restaurant. She apologised for giving slow service, admitted she was new in the city and miserable. They invited her to visit them in their apartment after work.

'You did not choose me, but I chose you. . . .' A widower in the next apartment was the second person they befriended. Soon a dozen people were meeting together once a week for conversation and prayer.

Out of these meetings grew a project called Adventures in Friendship. Before long, scores of people were involved in seeking the lonely and the shut-ins throughout the whole area. Needless to say, Mary and Harold Brinig had become so absorbed in the needs of others that their own life was enriched beyond anything I can describe. Happiness found them.

This Chicago experience prepared the Brinigs for a thirty-five-year team ministry at the Marble Collegiate Church in New York City that resulted in spiritually rejuvenated lives for thousands of people, including my husband, Len.

3

The Power of Let

While reading a manuscript by Mrs John Peters (wife of
the founder of World Neighbours), I was intrigued by
one episode in particular. Losing his footing in the bathroom, her husband struck his head on the ceramic soap
dish. One ear was almost severed and he was bleeding
profusely when Mrs Peters heard his cries and came to
his aid.

Despite her shock at the sight of so much blood, the
Spirit took over and enabled her to speak with authority.
She heard herself saying, 'Let the bleeding stop im-
mediately. Let there be no infection. Let there be no pain.
Let there be no scarring.'

Mrs Peters made no comment on the experience other
than to report that, gloriously, the bleeding stopped.
There was no infection. Almost no pain. No scars. But
something about these 'Lets' stuck like glue to my mind.

I realised that it was the same word God had used in
creating our world. '*Let* there be light,' . . . and so on.

Jesus to His disciples:

Let your light so shine before men, that they may see
your good works, and glorify your Father which is in
heaven.

Matthew 5:16 KJV

And if the house is worthy, *let* your peace come upon
it; but if it is not worthy, *let* your peace return to you.

Matthew 10:13 RSV

Paul used it too:

> *Let* this mind be in you, which was also in Christ Jesus.
> Philippians 2:5 KJV

What, I wondered, is the significance of this word for us?

Author Harold Hill gave me the missing insight. '"Let" is a word of tremendous faith with volumes of meaning poured into it,' he told me. 'It *assumes* the total love and good will of the Father. It *assumes* that heaven is crammed with good gifts that the Father desires to give His children. The "let" is saying, "Father, I give to You permission to do so-and-so for us down here on earth. I allow it."'

It also assumes an almost preposterous humility on God's part – that He should wait for our permission to bestow wonderful gifts on us! How amazing!

Worlds of meaning behind this three-letter word . . . *let*.

4

The Poverty Complex

I'm going through one of those 'money anxiety' periods this morning, Lord, so I know I've taken my eyes off You and placed them squarely on worldly matters.

The sad thing is that I know better. Only the other day I was expressing my incredulity over a famous financier who committed suicide when his wealth diminished from fifty million to ten million. It seemed inconceivable that a man could feel desperate about money when he still possessed ten million dollars. Wealth, clearly, is a matter of attitude.

So once again I go through the process of replacing fear with faith in connection with Your provision.

First, I need to remind myself that You control all of earth's material resources. Most of us do not really believe this. Yet from cover to cover the Bible declares it:

> The earth is the Lord's and the fullness thereof. . . .
> Psalm 24:1 KJV

> But my God shall supply all your need according to his riches. . . .
> Philippians 4:19 KJV

If I truly believe that I am a child of a King, then my fear will disappear. Worrying would be the sure sign that I did not believe God's ownership of earth's resources. To think myself a pauper is to deny either the King's riches or my being His beloved child.

Second, I can think about Mary Welch. Born in a log cabin on a run-down farm in west Texas, even after she became a Christian she found it difficult to shed her poverty complex. A turning point for her came when she was in St Paul, Minnesota, on a speaking trip as the guest of a wealthy woman. As she was preparing to take a bath before dinner, she drew her customary three inches of water in the tub.

Her hostess happened to look into the tub. 'You're not intending to take a bath in that tiny amount of water?'

'Why not? That's all I ever use.'

'This isn't Texas, Mary,' her hostess chided her. 'There's no shortage of water here. Minnesota has ten *thousand* lakes.'

Mary realised that she had just gotten a sharp insight about herself. She watched the water nearly fill the tub. Then she lathered herself with soap – marvelling at all she was wasting. That night before she went to sleep she asked God to register His Perfect Adequacy on her sub-conscious and clear out all her deep-rooted beliefs in shortages.

Soon after, Mary realised that even her skinny, ninety-pound body looked like a shortage of woman. She took a piece of soft soap and, in a full-length mirror, drew an outline of her ideal measurements. Then she packed most of her size-three dresses to send to an orphanage.

Her mother caught her at the packing and didn't approve at all. 'You've never had much. You worked too hard to get those clothes to give them away. Besides, suppose you *don't* gain weight?'

But Mary realised that she could not pray for one thing and make provisions for another. Furthermore, she had discovered what she calls the 'law of the Golden Initiative': the secret of receiving is to give – even out of poverty. In fact, the more sunk we are in visions of lack, the greater need we have to start giving.

So the dresses went off to the orphanage. 'And within

that year,' Mary reports, 'I measured exactly what I had pictured and prepared for – size nine.'

The third thing I'm to do is to remind myself of that moment of decision I faced some weeks after Peter Marshall's death in 1949. The trustees of his church gave me a bleak financial report of how little insurance money there was. They advised me to take a full-time job to support Peter John and myself.

You, Lord, encouraged me to write, with the promise that if I trusted You, all my needs would be met. I took Your challenge and how greatly have You blessed me! Thank you, Lord. Praise You! Forgive me for my lack of faith.

Forward, Like Gideon!

This morning, Len and I dragged ourselves out of bed at 6:00 A.M. for our morning prayer time. After the long drive from Evergreen Farm in Virginia to southern Florida, I'm exhausted. Our suitcases are still packed. But there's a meeting of our church committee on Christian education this afternoon that Len insists we attend.

I'm fighting off resentment as well as fatigue. I want to get back to my writing. Meetings drain me. Bore me. Len wants us to teach a class on the Holy Spirit this winter to a group that is resistant to what is happening across the country today, frightened by the excesses of some of the 'Jesus people', by speaking in tongues and so on. Len looks at this class as an adventure. I'm full of doubts as to whether we can handle it.

Is it coincidence that I have been reading the Book of Judges? Today it was the story of Gideon. Such fascinating reading! So jam-packed full of truths and insights!

For instance, Gideon certainly had no idea that he was anyone special in God's sight or in man's. He lived at a low point in Israel's history when the people had forsaken Jehovah and were worshipping idols.

Yet God sent an angel to Gideon with the message, 'The Lord is with you, you mighty man of [fearless] courage' (Judges 6:12 AMPLIFIED).

There's immense humour in this greeting. For the 'mighty man of courage' was at that moment hiding out in a winepress for fear of the Midianites.

And his reaction to the angel's appearance was doubt

and confusion. 'If the Lord is with us, why is all this befallen us?' (v. 13).

The answer was a strange one. The angel did not rebuke Gideon for answering back with unbelief. Instead, he repeated, 'Go in this your might, and you shall save Israel from the hand of Midian. Have I not sent you?' (v. 14).

Again Gideon sounds like anything but a hero. He replies, in effect, 'Who, me? Save Israel? Surely you must be kidding. My clan is the poorest in Israel and I'm the least in my father's house, the youngest son, the one everyone picks on.'

The Lord's answer is, 'Surely, I will be with you, and you shall smite the Midianites as one man' (v. 16).

Only after the angel disappears does Gideon seem to realise that he has actually been in the presence of an angel. His reaction to this, characteristically, is downbeat all the way. He might have been thrilled and begun praising God. Instead, he says, 'Alas, O Lord God! For now I have seen the Angel of the Lord face to face!' (v. 22).

Never on God's side, however, is there anything but patient understanding of Gideon's doubt and unbelief. 'Peace be to you; do not fear, you shall not die' (v. 23).

Then begins a series of clear-cut instructions from the Lord. First, Gideon is to tear down two idols.

The 'mighty man of courage' obeys, but does it at night because he's so scared of his own clan, even of his father and brothers.

In fact, his father sticks up for him before the towns-people.

But Gideon is full of doubt still. Only after elaborate further signs and reassurances from Jehovah will he consent to take command of the Israelite forces. And then the point of the story becomes clear: it is God's strength and His alone that delivers us. For God persuades Gideon to reduce his warriors from 22,000 to 300. And it is this small army that routs the Midianites.

The clear message for today that I receive from this reading is that God is going to show me that I can rely on Him alone – for physical strength as for every other need. So thank You, Lord, for the meeting I will go to this afternoon, hence no nap today. Thank You for the challenge of teaching a class on the Holy Spirit. Full speed ahead, O Gideon!

Small Needs

After the Bible study I gave last week on praying for all
our needs, no matter how small, one woman took sharp
issue with me.

'Asking for small things is being selfish,' she remon-
strated, 'and self-centred prayers just aren't answered. I
think we should pray only about *spiritual* needs. Besides,
the God who runs the universe can't be bothered with
individual wishes.'

I could only reply that this was not Jesus' viewpoint as
presented in the Gospels: both by teaching and by action
He impressed upon us that no need is too trivial for His
attention.

I've combed Scripture for examples and there are
many, such as: The wine needed at a wedding feast (John
2:1–11); a dying sparrow (Matthew 10:29); a lost lamb
(Luke 15:3–7).

These vignettes, scattered through the Gospels like
little patches of gold dust, say to us, 'No creaturely need
is outside the scope of prayer.'

As if to emphasise the same thought, the apostle Paul
adds:

> Do not fret or have any anxiety about anything, but in
> every circumstance and in everything by prayer and
> petition [definite requests] with thanksgiving continue
> to make your wants known to God.
>
> Philippians 4:6 AMPLIFIED

Now obviously not all our human wants are genuine

needs. Moreover, we are often so selfish and short-sighted that the granting of some wants would not be good for us. But I believe that Scripture invites us to talk over all our concerns and dreams with our Father, then leave the outcome to His wisdom.

Just before Christmas we had a wonderful example of His loving involvement in the everyday-ness of life. My son Peter was labouring to build an elaborate miniature horse stable for his daughter, Mary Elizabeth. Hour after hour, he closeted himself in the basement putting it together. Especially time-consuming was the process of covering the roof with tiny shingles of almost paper-thin plywood. As the laborious work of positioning and gluing proceeded, it became apparent that he was going to run out of shingles.

Peter called all manner of hobby stores in the area. Nobody had any.

He even called the company in Texas that made the shingles. Yes, they could get them to him in time by special plane service for about $100. Too costly.

Finally, Peter found a hobby store up the road that had half of one package. The owner's wife had been using them for some project and had that many left. This was still not enough to complete the roof, but Peter decided to pick up those that were available.

As he drove off I breathed up a quiet little prayer about this. Immediately I had a mental picture – a little drama really – of Peter walking into the hobby store and the owner saying, 'I have a surprise for you. I found another package of those shingles.'

Peter came back home beaming. What I had 'seen' as I prayed was exactly what had happened. He had more than enough to finish the roof.

A very small prayer request for what many would consider a superficial need. Yet this little episode gave all of us a heartwarming glimpse of the Father's careful provision for the small details of our lives – and of the adventure He means each moment in His world to be!

Homemade Bread

I am troubled about a quality of blandness in our nation today, a lack of creativity. It's apparent in our leaders. Most gear their lives to television ratings, are afraid to take stands on issues. Movies and stage plays focus on sex and violence, with little originality. Sex so dominates advertising and the arts that it has become commonplace, almost boring.

Jesus lashed out at the spiritless quality in the people of His time:

> I know thy works, that thou art neither cold nor hot: I would thou wert cold or hot. So, then, because thou art lukewarm, and neither cold nor hot, I will spew thee out of my mouth.
>
> Revelation 3:15–16 KJV

One of our new neighbours is no longer trapped in a bland way of life. Yet for the first twelve years of her marriage, Cynthia felt she was losing her identity in an endless procession of social events and chauffeuring of children.

During one cocktail party, Cynthia decided to limit herself to ginger ale and made some discoveries – not especially pleasant: 'I saw our crowd through new eyes,' she told me. 'No one was really saying anything. Most sentences were never even finished. There was a lot of laughter over – well, nothing at all. All at once I began to ask questions about what we call "the good life".

'What was so good about it?'

'But,' she continued, 'what was I to do? If my husband and I ducked those invitations, we'd be thought snobbish and eventually dropped. But if we went, we would have to drink, otherwise how could we stand the emptiness?'

In a search for answers, Cynthia set aside an hour each day for meditation. As she did this over a period of weeks there came to her the realisation that she was being met in this quiet hour, at her point of need, by something more than her own thoughts and her own psyche, by Someone who loved her and who insisted that His love must be passed on to her family and her friends.

Cynthia began to bake bread regularly, finding this ancient female ritual deeply satisfying. 'You can't imagine how many enemies I slay and repressions I get rid of as I knead that bread,' she says.

Instead of letting the children dash away from the dinner table for television, the evening meal has become a time for family sharing. Family Game Night once a week has become a creative substitute for television.

A new strength developed in Cynthia in regard to her children. I have heard her tell her astonished eleven-year-old that he is going to walk to Little League one way each practice day, and calmly state to her nine-year-old daughter that she certainly is not going to buy her any 'training' bras.

'I've discovered that real love for our children has to go beyond catering to their every whim – or we turn them into tyrannical little princes and princesses,' Cynthia said. 'They, too, have to find their own inner resources. And how can they, if I do for them the things that they could do for themselves?'

Recognising that some of her friends were as bored as she with the typical cocktail party, she began experimenting with some new types of entertaining. One evening after a buffet supper, a hand-picked group listened spellbound to a play on the radio, 'The Murder Trial of William Palmer, Surgeon'. Cynthia had supplied each guest with a paperback copy of the play to follow as they listened. The evening was a big hit, especially with the men.

'I realised one day that my church had little more meaning for me than did our country club,' Cynthia said. 'I called our pastor and asked if there was a Bible study.'

That's what brought Cynthia and her husband to our house, where eight couples were already meeting twice a month to find ways to relate the Bible to some everyday problems we were all facing. Out of this experience has come a new level of shared concerns for us all and the exciting discovery of answers sought out together.

As I ponder Cynthia's story, I've concluded that we don't have to settle for blandness in life; God, who is the Author of creativity, is ready to make a dull life adventuresome the moment we allow His Holy Spirit to go to work inside us.

Section Three

Christian Growth

There is a misconception in the minds of many believers that successful communicators of the faith speak from some Mt Olympus of perfection – that it is only because these Christian superstars have overcome their faults and weaknesses that they are able to minister to others in a mighty way.

Not true. Those most used of God often have struggled or are struggling with one or more major weaknesses. It is often just because of a weakness that these people have much to share.

Dr Norman Vincent Peale frankly admits that only due to his own fears and doubts and tensions was he able to minister so effectively to others with similar problems. A study of Christian leaders down through the ages reveals that most of them battled major weaknesses.

So it was with Catherine. The Lord gave her major gifts in the area of communication that catapulted her into the public eye. But when people tried to place her on a pedestal, she refused, knowing that God alone deserves to be exalted. Instead, she wrote openly about her struggles, her mistakes, her flaws.

In her journals she was ruthless with herself. The following excerpts indicate how hard she struggled to overcome certain weaknesses, how seriously she took the matter of our need to grow spiritually.

A lesson learned was an inadequately thought-through novel she began in 1969 and abandoned two-and-a-half years later. It was titled Gloria. The loss of time and energy on this manuscript weighed on Catherine for years.

LL

1

Dealing with a Major Mistake

Last week I needed to be alone for a few days to think and pray. The mistake I made in deciding to write the novel *Gloria* has shaken my confidence. The shelved manuscript is like a death in the family.

What went wrong?

I needed to find some answers about this – and about other troubling areas in my life. So I made arrangements to spend two days at the Cenacle, a Roman Catholic Retreat House several miles away in Lantana, Florida. Len dropped me off Sunday at 8:00 P.M.

The next morning after breakfast I sat for a while in a lawn chair out under an ancient mango tree. Through the curving trunks of the coconut palms I had a glimpse of the Intracoastal Waterway. The grounds were alive with bird calls.

A sound new to me was the creaking of the tall, tall bamboo that borders part of the property. The bamboo, too, was ancient. The slender branches writhed and creaked as they rubbed against one another in the barely perceptible breeze. The creaking reminded me of the grating of a long-unused hinge, as of a door being opened after many years. The foliage was still delicate and lacy as it was when the bamboo was young.

Leaf patterns were all across the grass. Squirrels raced up and down trees. A cardinal kept whistling, 'Cheer! Cheer!'

I had thought that I wanted guidance on certain family matters and whether there was some way to resurrect

Gloria. But when I talked briefly with Sister Forman at breakfast, her advice was to seek Christ and Him alone and let Him decide what He wanted to talk to me about.

That morning the first thought dropped into my mind was the single word *edification*. 'Think on edification,' He seemed to be saying, 'what builds the members of the family up in love, perfecting them into the body of Christ.'

The focus throughout the morning was largely on my home situation. (Perhaps the conclusion to be drawn is that it's essential that I get this right with Christ before I can write *anything* worthwhile.)

Soon I found myself turning to the book of John. As I read, the Holy Spirit showed me that I had fallen hook, line, and sinker for one of Satan's oldest and most-used tricks: looking steadily at the difficulty instead of at Jesus. I had listened, really paid attention to Old Scratch's suggestions – every one of them, I fear – as to the size and intractability of my problems. The Comforter told me that all of this had been Satan's technique for discouraging me unduly and that I must *never* fall for this temptation again.

Next I was shown that my husband, my children, and my grandchildren are not mine, but God's. He's not only as concerned as I am for them, but loves them far more than I ever could. Therefore, I was to take my possessive, self-centred hands off – strictly off. So, in an act of relinquishment, I did this.

Then came a beautiful touch. I was reading in the Psalms when suddenly these words leapt from the page:

The Lord will perfect that which concerns me . . . forsake not the works of Your own hands.

Psalm 138:8 AMPLIFIED

I could – and did – claim this promise promptly for my family. Years ago the Lord began a work in these lives. It's His business to perfect what He started. He had promised that He will. I've claimed and accepted that promise. It's as good as done. My heart is steadily rejoicing. Weights and weights have been lifted from me.

The focus that afternoon turned from my home situation to my failure with *Gloria*. What do You have to tell me about this, Lord?

I was led to this passage in Numbers:

> . . . the people . . . spoke against God and against Moses, and said, 'Why have you brought us up out of Egypt to die in the desert? There is no bread! There is no water! And we detest this miserable food!'
>
> Then the Lord sent venomous snakes among them; they bit the people and many Israelites died. The people came to Moses and said, 'We sinned when we spoke against the Lord and against you. Pray that the Lord will take the snakes away from us.' So Moses prayed for the people.
>
> The Lord said to Moses, 'Make a snake and put it up on a pole; anyone who is bitten can look at it and live.' So Moses made a bronze snake and put it up on a pole. Then when anyone was bitten by a snake and looked at the bronze snake, he lived.
>
> Numbers 21:4–9 NIV

It didn't take long for me to get the point: God told Moses that the people were to take that which had hurt them and lift it up to Him. He would then turn even a snake into blessing and victory. Thus the 'snake' in our life can be redeemed and turned to power.

In this way does God deal with our mistakes and sins. I had made a mistake in undertaking the novel *Gloria*. I had not heeded the advice of experts like Elizabeth Sherrill and Len; even my mother had expressed strong reservations. But God would find a way to turn a bad experience into good.

Even more to the point: when any one of us has made a

wrong (or even doubtful) turning in our lives through arrogance or lack of trust or impatience or fear – or what not – God will show us a way out. Therefore, I am to turn off all negative thoughts about this wrong decision and accept fully my situation as it is now, as God's will for me now. I am to place the present situation in His hands for Him to use fully for my spiritual growth and for the 'edification' of all concerned. Further, I am to do this joyfully.

2

The Servant Role

The message I am getting today from Jesus is the servant
role that He wants to play in the lives of every one of us.
The following passages reveal to me the extent of His
passion to *serve* us because He loves us so much:

> . . . the Son of man came not to be waited on but to
> serve, and to give His life as a ransom for many. . . .
>
> Matthew 20:28 AMPLIFIED

> . . . I am in your midst as one who serves.
>
> Luke 22:27 AMPLIFIED

In the early days of my walk with Him, when I was
experimenting day by day with hearing the Inner Voice, I
had a hard time believing that His guidance was for *my*
benefit, never His own. I still can hardly grasp this.

When He wrapped a towel around his waist, poured
water into a basin, and began to wash his disciples' feet
(see John 13:4–5), Simon Peter objected that this was
beneath the dignity of the Master. *We* the disciples are to
be the servants, I want to insist along with Peter. But
Jesus answered him, 'If I do not wash you, you have no
part in me.'

This is a stunning and stupendous thought. Unless I
can believe in *this much* love for me, unless I can and will
accept Him with faith as my servant as well as my God,
unless I truly know that it's *my* good He seeks, not His
glory (He already has all of that He can use for all
eternity), *then I cannot have his companionship.*

What an amazing revelation!

3

Why Do We Judge Others?

I am determined to dig in on the matter of my critical nature. I do not like it. It's negative; yes, often destructive. Jesus warned us not to be judgmental. So did Paul:

> Then let us no more pass judgment on one another, but rather decide never to put a stumbling block or hindrance in the way.
>
> Romans 14:13 RSV

I have tried to excuse myself by saying that one must evaluate situations and people. It won't wash. It still comes out judging, a haughty superiority, which is the opposite of love.

With Jesus' help I want to go back to my childhood to see if I can find the root cause for this fault of mine:

He is showing me a little girl who was supersensitive in the sense that she would rather die than be laughed at or found unacceptable by her peers, and most of all, by the adults around her. When she didn't make friends as quickly as other children, she tried to persuade herself that she was superior to others her age.

She got by with this superiority syndrome in school because she received top grades, especially in writing and speech courses. She yearned to be like classmates who were outgoing, witty, and popular, but since she had none of these personality traits, she convinced herself that these were lesser qualities while those of the mind and spirit were somehow on a higher plane.

When she left her small hometown for college, nothing changed in her approach to other people. Because she felt inferior socially, she looked with secret disapproval at those who danced, played cards, and went to drinking parties, all denied to her as a preacher's child.

Superiority breeds contempt. And contempt breeds criticalness. And my criticalness cut me off from other people. Even when I said nothing, made no comment at all, people would tell me they could feel my unkind judgment of them. I was miserable about this quality in me, yet trapped by it.

Along with all this, ironically enough, went an acute sensitivity to any criticalness of me. The Holy Spirit pointed out to me how *deeply* the least tiny bit of unacceptance rankles, causing a wound that festers on, year after year. Incidents, so small that a healthy reaction on my part should have been amusement and then prompt dismissal of the incident from mind, are remembered – still with an emotional sting attached – years later.

For instance . . . soon after I was married to Peter Marshall, I remember a woman friend commenting about my hands, 'Well, they aren't beautiful, but at least they're capable-looking.'

The pronouncement that my hands weren't pretty has stuck; ever since it made me reluctant to have a manicurist do my nails.

This is, of course, acute oversensitivity, which, in turn, is the sure sign of acute self-centredness . . . the same hypersensitivity and self-protectiveness that had led me to take refuge in an assumed superiority to others – with the accompanying right to stand in judgment on them.

Being oversensitive, I am quick to pick it up in others and relate to it. Once when a judge at the Junior Miss Pageant in Mobile, Alabama, I found myself intrigued by the contestant with the highest academic average of all fifty girls. When she came to the five judges for her ten-minute interview, I watched her with deep interest.

One question asked her was: 'If you could pick out one

person in any field of endeavour in our world today whom you admire most, whom would you pick?'

She hesitated a moment and then said loud and clear, 'Jesus Christ.'

Two of the judges responded almost simultaneously, 'Oh, we mean a living person.'

The girl felt rebuked. Her eyes filled with tears; she choked up and never could get herself under control during the rest of the interview. I ached for her. I wanted to hug her and tell her I loved her reply, that to me, as to her, Jesus *was* a living person.

Later, though, I wondered if her extreme sensitivity had caused her to put all her efforts into getting top grades – thereby avoiding, as I had, the far riskier confrontation of equal-to-equal.

How do we sensitive, critical people deal with our condition? I had one very direct answer from the Lord recently after I had loosed a blast of angry criticism at one of our national leaders at the luncheon table. God said to me, 'Do not criticise at all' (1 Corinthians 4:5 MOFFATT). 'You spread negativism around you and pollute your own atmosphere when you do so. Turn your criticism and your indignation to good use by praying for that leader right now.'

A good handle for me to grasp!

4

A Fast on Criticalness

The Lord continues to deal with me about my critical spirit, convicting me that I have been wrong to judge any person or situation:

> Do not judge, or you too will be judged. For in the same way you judge others, you will be judged, and with the measure you use, it will be measured to you.
>
> Matthew 7:1-2 NIV

One morning last week He gave me an assignment: *for one day I was to go on a 'fast' from criticism. I was not to criticise anybody about anything*.

Into my mind crowded all the usual objections. 'But then what happens to value judgments? You Yourself, Lord, spoke of "righteous judgment". How could society operate without standards and limits?'

All such resistance was brushed aside. 'Just obey Me without questioning: an absolute fast on any critical statements for this day.'

As I pondered this assignment I realised there was an even humorous side to this kind of fast. What did the Lord want to show me?

For the first half of the day, I simply felt a void, almost as if I had been wiped out as a person. This was especially true at lunch with my husband, Len, my mother, son Jeff and my secretary, Jeanne Sevigny, present. Several topics came up (school prayer, abortion, the ERA amendment) about which I had definite opinions. I listened to the others and kept silent. Barbed comments on the tip of my tongue about certain world leaders were suppressed. In our talkative family no one seemed to notice.

Bemused, I noticed that my comments were not missed. The federal government, the judicial system, and the institutional church could apparently get along fine without my penetrating observations. But still I didn't see what this fast on criticism was accomplishing – until mid-afternoon.

For several years I had been praying for one talented young man whose life had gotten sidetracked. Perhaps my prayers for him had been too negative. That afternoon, a specific, positive vision for this life was dropped into my mind with God's unmistakable hallmark on it – joy.

Ideas began to flow in a way I had not experienced in years. Now it was apparent what the Lord wanted me to see. My critical nature had not corrected a single one of the multitudinous things I found fault with. What it *had* done was to stifle my own creativity – in prayer, in relationships, perhaps even in writing – ideas that He wanted to give me.

Last Sunday night in a Bible study group, I told of my Day's Fast experiment. The response was startling. Many admitted that criticalness was the chief problem in their offices, or in their marriages, or with their teenage children.

My own character flaw here is not going to be corrected overnight. But in thinking this problem through the past few days, I find the most solid scriptural basis possible for dealing with it. (The Greek word translated 'judge' in King James, becomes 'criticise' in Moffatt.) All through the Sermon on the Mount, Jesus sets Himself squarely against our seeing other people and life situations through this negative lens.

What He is showing me so far can be summed up as follows:

1) A critical spirit focuses us on ourselves and makes us unhappy. We lose perspective and humour.
2) A critical spirit blocks the positive creative thoughts God longs to give us.
3) A critical spirit can prevent good relationships between individuals and often produces retaliatory criticalness.
4) Criticalness blocks the work of the Spirit of God: love, good will, mercy.
5) Whenever we see something genuinely wrong in another person's behaviour, rather than criticise him or her directly, or – far worse – gripe about him behind his back, we should ask the Spirit of God to do the correction needed.

Convicted of the true destructiveness of a critical mindset, on my knees I am repeating this prayer: 'Lord, I repent of this sin of judgment. I am deeply sorry for having committed so gross an offence against You and against myself so continually. I claim Your promise of forgiveness and seek a new beginning.'

5

Thou Fool

I visited my friend Virginia Lively in Belle Glade, Florida, on Sunday afternoon. Out of several hours of prayer together came – among other things – the conviction that my relationship with and attitude to B— needs to be corrected by Jesus, especially in the spiritual realm.

This morning, Lord, You brought to my remembrance Your words, 'Whosoever shall say to his brother . . . Thou fool, shall be in danger of hell fire' (Matthew 5:22 KJV).

Well, I have certainly been saying that of B—, and thinking it. How clearly I see this now, Lord, as the sin of spiritual and intellectual pride. So I confess this sin of mental and verbal judgment. I ask You to forgive me for my arrogance and to cleanse me. Bring my attitude toward, my every thought of, my every reaction toward, and my every word about or to B— in line with Your view of her.

Cleanse me of every holier-than-thou stance. Since I am 'hidden in Christ', then my opinion of anyone doesn't matter. Only Jesus' opinion matters.

Thank You, Lord, for Your acceptance of this confession. Thank You for Your forgiveness. Thank You for the beginning right now of a new relationship with B—. Thank You for dealing with her in Your all-seeing love. Thank You for lifting the burden of resentment and judging from me. I *do* feel tons lighter already. Thank You!!

Jesus Makes the Decisions

Yesterday I began trying to get back to a real Quiet Time in the early morning. My directive was, 'Never mind about reading. Spend the time getting in touch with Jesus directly.'

For a couple of days prior to this the Holy Spirit had dropped a curious clause from Scripture into my mind and heart: 'And the government shall be upon [Jesus'] shoulder . . .' (Isaiah 9:6 KJV). I had never thought of this in relation to the government of *my* life. Suddenly it spoke volumes to me . . . the responsibility of my life is now His, the burden *He* will carry. He will make the decisions, the right decisions. What a relief: what joy to turn it over to Him.

Yesterday I mostly just asked Him questions, knowing that sooner or later in His time, He will answer them. He well knows my questioning spirit. I don't think He minds that.

Having posed my questions, I left them there, in His hands . . . and felt sweet peace flow into my spirit.

A while ago I was told that I was to refrain from criticism for one month, a fast of the tongue. Now I am directed to extend this curbing of my faultfinding into the thought area.

The Spirit reminded me of Jesus' words, 'Sufficient unto the day is the evil thereof.' Clearly then, Jesus recognises the evil all around us in our daily walk. Simply, for the time being, I am not to let my mind dwell there. The Spirit also showed me that the tidiness of my possessions and papers has a direct bearing on my peace on the inside. Rather than let this chore weigh on me as an added pressure, though, I am to let Him direct me *when* to undertake straightening up my things.

The Dry Period

I've been off on a familiar barren road recently and need to get down on paper the steps I took to get back on the main highway. I'm talking about the *dry period*. The state is always much the same for me: shrivelled and lonely on the inside. I can't do any writing. I'm unable to accomplish much of anything, just going through the motions of life and barely able to do that. Worst of all – shut off from God.

In her book *Mysticism*, Evelyn Underhill points out that such experiences are a necessary part of the Christian walk.

For those who have trod the Christian way for some time, a spiritual and psychic fatigue occasionally creeps in and overcomes one. In this state one knows anew the helplessness of us humans. Yet here, for a time, we are in a worse state than at the beginning of our Christian walk. For at that early stage, along with the helplessness, there was the sure and wonderful knowledge of God's adequacy.

Now the skies seem totally deaf; no glorious light breaks through at all. Nothing, inside or outside, seems to work. If one can ride it through on sheer blind faith, just hanging onto the rock of salvation, *then* it has to pass, and we go on into an advanced state in the spiritual life.

The reason this dry state is necessary, she points out, is

that we have to find anew our need, become desperate in a new way, in order to get on with the next stage in our Christian development.

We know that physically and emotionally the developing self advances through a series of growth spurts interspersed with pauses on plateaus. Apparently, the same process holds in the spiritual life.

So the way out of this latest dry period for me began with an admission of my helplessness. And not just a grudging acknowledgment, but a trusting and expectant *acceptance*, relying on Jesus' promise that *His* strength is made perfect in *my* weakness (see 2 Corinthians 12:9).

Next, I was not only to bear this dry and barren stretch of life, but actually to *thank* God for it. My praise to Him lacked enthusiasm at first, but as always the Psalms supplied the words I could not. (Psalms 95, 100, 103 are some of my favourites.) Gradually my cup began to fill and my spirit to loosen.

The last step was to show someone I loved them; in this case it was a visit to a bed-bound neighbour.

Before going back to my writing, I asked the Holy Spirit for specific help in setting up the story sequences in my novel. Soon a wonderful thing began to happen. I could feel my creative nature thrusting down its rootlets in search of the life-giving Water at some deep level in my being. Bit by bit, episode by episode, I watched the lineaments of the story line emerging in my hand. It was as if I could see the bulbs I planted in the ground last fall begin their growth in the cold and the dark. Even the creative process that formed the earth, I reflected, began in *darkness*.

It takes acceptance and praise and outgoing love for me to emerge from a dry period, but, oh, the exhilaration that follows!

8

To Forgive . . . and Forget

This morning I had to face up to the fact that I still had a
bad attitude toward a woman who is constantly attacking
me and my writings. On taking it to the Lord, I received
two insights:

(1) The reason I am so upset is that *I haven't forgiven her
completely.* I've made stabs at this in the past, but as she
comes to my mind I have an almost physical sensation, as
of iron bars pressing against my chest. The Lord showed
me that on the other side of these bars was a woman, a
human being, who needed to be freed. So, on my knees
before Him, I went through a process of unreservedly
forgiving her by an act of my will. I confessed my feelings
about her and asked God to make the forgiveness real.

(2) My job was not finished, however, He told me, until
I can forget what she has done.

'But *how can* I do that, Lord?'

*Your will is greater than your memory, Catherine. Rebuke
the painful memory and cast it out in the name of Jesus.*

I was to '. . . bring into captivity every thought to the
obedience of Christ' (2 Corinthians 10:5 KJV). Then to ask
forgiveness for hanging onto these memories (we tend to
stab ourselves again and again with old, hurtful episodes), and ask for an alarm system on the door of my
mind whenever the memory tries to creep back.

From henceforth I am to look at this woman – *and at
anyone else who has ever hurt me* – with eyes of compassion
and love, concentrating on the potential they have for
good. Only thus will I be able to see them as Jesus does.

'But Lord . . . will this approach bring about changes in them?'

That's between them and Me. You will have peace.

The Key to Obedience

Am struggling this morning with the seeming contradiction between Jesus' constant stress on *obedience* as crucial to Christian growth, over against the reality of 'grace', which is the 'unmerited favour of God'.

Obedience would seem to be our going up the ladder step by step, not earning our way exactly, while continually dependent on still putting forth our own efforts. Whereas the teaching all through the Bible is that it is God who always takes the initiative with us. All of God's good gifts are given by pure grace; there is no way we can deserve a single one of them.

So – exactly where and how does obedience fit into this?

I'm beginning to see that the missing key here is Love. The chief characteristic of love is wanting to do what pleases the beloved. The analogy Jesus used most often was filial love: He meant His relationship to His Father to be the pattern for *our* relationship to Him (Jesus). Jesus' obedience was not the result of gritted teeth and grim determination, but the natural outworking of love: 'I do as the Father has commanded me, so that the world may know (be convinced) that I love the Father . . .' (John 14:31 AMPLIFIED).

When we truly love someone, our focus is on *him* or *her*, not on ourselves. And our constant thought is, 'What can I do to give this beloved person joy? To please him? To ease his path? To minister to him?'

It staggers my mind to think that I can in any way

minister to Jesus, or gladden His heart. Yet this is the gracious message of the Gospel, which always puts the emphasis on love:

'We love Him, because He first loved us' (1 John 4:19 AMPLIFIED).

God's grace, God's initiative.

'. . . If a person [really] loves Me, he will keep My word – obey My teaching' (John 14:23 AMPLIFIED).

Our natural, unforced response.

10

Worry: Be Gone

This morning I awoke full of worry about the future, with Len having resigned from his job as editor of *Guideposts*. Len and I were in agreement about this step, and he is enthusiastic about going into book publishing with John and Elizabeth Sherrill, but I see so many obstacles ahead, especially when his salary cheque stops coming.

Then the Lord directed me to the fourth chapter of Philippians, particularly to verse 8 (AMPLIFIED, italics added):

> . . . whatever is worthy of reverence . . .
>   is honourable and seemly . . .
>   is just . . .
>   is pure . . .
>   is lovely and lovable . . .
>   is kind and winsome and gracious,
> if there is any
>   virtue . . .
>   excellence . . .
>   anything worthy of praise,
> [we are to] think on
>   and weigh
>   and take account of these things –
> *fix* your minds on them.

Now this might seem to be the worst kind of not facing reality were it not for the fact that earlier in the same chapter Paul has already exhorted us (v. 6) to pray about *everything*, to pour our hearts out to the Heavenly Father with 'definite requests'.

My problem is that having done this, having laid my concern before the Father, I get the feeling that if I do not frequently return to it in my mind and keep 'worrying' it, much as a dog would a bone, then there certainly can be no chance of solving it. It's a feeling that it would actually be irresponsible or frivolous *not* to do this – wrong to think about other things, and go my merry way while a major problem faces us.

I slip into the worry stance in spite of telling myself over and over that God is the problem-solver, that we can confidently leave our situation in His hands. I know what I should do, yet emotionally and practically I do not act out this letting go. This morning God seems to be pointing out chapter four in Philippians as a blueprint for handling crises His way:

1) Regardless of any circumstances, we are to *rejoice in the Lord always*.
2) We are *not* to fret or have anxiety about *anything*.
3) We are to pray about everything, making our needs and wants known unto God.
4) We are to be content with our earthly lot, whatever it is.
5) We are to guard our thoughts, think only upon upbeat, positive things – nothing negative. If we will do the above, then we are promised:
   a) God's peace . . . shall garrison and mount guard over our hearts and minds in Christ Jesus.
   b) Christ will 'infuse inner strength into us' – that is, 'We will be self-sufficient in Christ's sufficiency.'

LL Note: God honoured our leap of faith into book publishing. Chosen Books, from its inception, produced books that made a major impact on both the Christian and secular world.

11

His Peace

This morning the Lord asked me to look up the Scripture verse 'the things that belong unto thy peace'. With the help of a concordance, I found it in Luke 19:41–42 KJV. The scene is a hill overlooking Jerusalem.

> . . . [Jesus] beheld the city, and wept over it, Saying If thou hadst known, even thou, at least in this thy day, the things which belong unto thy peace! but now they are hid from thine eyes.

Lord, what do You want me to understand from this? What are the things that belong to my peace?

Surely, this ties in with the 'rest' that was the other message given me this morning.

> There remaineth, therefore, a rest to the people of God. For he that is entered into his rest, he also hath ceased from his own works. . . .
>
> Hebrews 4:9–10 KJV

In the midst of disquiet about so many things in our life right now – my trying to make progress on my novel, the Chosen Books situation in general, my declining eyesight due to cataracts, poor sleep, etc., the message Jesus wants me to have today seems to be simply, 'Peace! Rest in Me. I am here to give you, Catherine, the precious gift of peace of mind and spirit.'

How glorious! He confirms it in Scripture after Scripture (italics added):

May grace (God's favour) and *peace* (which is perfect
well-being, all necessary good, all spiritual prosperity
and freedom from fears and agitating passions and
moral conflicts), be multiplied to you. . . .

2 Peter 1:2 AMPLIFIED

For though the mountains should depart and the hills
be shaken or removed, yet My love and kindness shall
not depart from you, nor shall My covenant of peace
and completeness be removed, says the Lord, Who has
compassion on you.

Isaiah 54:10 AMPLIFIED

Praise You, Lord Jesus! Praise You!!

The next day . . .

I discovered that the beautiful freedom the Lord gave
me in His gracious promises of 'peace' carried along with
it the joy of a moment-by-moment obedience.

That is, during the day I made the discovery that I had
departed from the habit of looking directly to Jesus for the
answer to small daily decisions; that the only way I will
keep a pliable, obedient spirit in the larger decisions, is to
look to Him and *to obey* in the smaller ones.

I had slipped badly on that. I'm always getting hung up
on the tension, or seeming tension, between freedom in
Christ Jesus and obedience.

James, however, makes this connection beautifully:

But the man who looks intently into the perfect law
that gives freedom, and continues to do this, not
forgetting what he has heard, but doing it – he will be
blessed in what he does.

James 1:25 NIV

Or to approach all this another way. I see that Satan has
small chance of getting at us – of accusing us and destroying our rest (as he has with me so often over 'small'

things like sleeping pills, or the lipstick issue I faced years ago on Cape Cod) when we are faithful in present-moment obedience, steadily looking to Jesus, asking, 'Shall I do this? Or not?' – and then obeying.

Thus this obedience *results* in liberty – and the two go hand in hand.

12

Idolatry

A couple of days ago Len and I had a heated discussion about the subject matter for the Tuesday evening Bible class and how we were going to teach it. He did not accept – or even understand – what I was saying, and it annoyed me that I could not get my point across.

That night I had a dream in which I was pursued by photographers. Flattered, I allowed them to take a series of pictures. When they appeared in print, I was horrified. The photos were obnoxious, nasty, almost obscene. To my eyes, the pictures clearly said, 'She's a big show-off.'

Through the dream I believe God was revealing to me my arrogance and self-righteousness about my *opinions*. I saw that this has always been one of my problems with the children, Linda especially. 'Love me, love my opinions!' Ideas are very, very important to me, and I consider *my* ideas uncommonly valuable.

How ironic that the very passage over which Len and I disagreed – the giving of the Law to Moses – included as the first Commandment of all: *Thou shalt have no other gods before me* (Exodus 20:3 KJV).

Before bedtime that night I confessed to God and to Len my idolatry of my own passionately held convictions.

13

Self-denial

Last night at bedtime I ate several pieces of candy, which
was wrong from every point of view: pure gratification of
self's momentary desire.

This morning I could not worship the Lord. Something
was coming between us. Then the Spirit spoke gently,
'Deny yourself . . . pick up your cross daily and follow
Me.' It was as if He were putting His finger on the words
'Deny yourself.' I had never noticed them particularly in
that passage. I wasn't even certain those two words were
there. So I looked up the verse; they were there all right. I
also got illumination on the rest of the passage: 'For
whoever wants to save his [higher, spiritual, eternal] life,
will lose [the lower, natural, temporal life which is lived
(only) on earth]' (Mark 8:35 AMPLIFIED).

I saw that Jesus is here simply stating a fact of life. If I
want to lose weight, I must give up the lower desire for
stuffing my mouth in order to attain the higher desire of a
fit, healthy body.

If I want to write a book, I must give up the use of my
time for other things.

For the first time I glimpse the rationale of certain
spiritual exercises, such as fasting.

Lord, teach me!

14

Self-denial: The Teaching Goes On

An insight today on how to make the denial of some small pleasure not only less painful but even an almost joyous event.

Up to this point in my life, whenever I've thought I was hearing the Lord's voice telling me to give up something that I loved, I could – and often would – drag my feet for weeks and months. Often I've had to pray the laggard's prayer, 'O Lord, make me willing to be made willing.' Almost always I've thought of obedience to the Lord as really quite painful.

But now after so many years of my Christian walk, a change is taking place within me. Jesus is becoming much more real to me as a person. I believe that what has been happening to me recently is the beginning of the direct fulfilment of this passage (italics added):

> The person who has My commands and keeps them is the one who [really] loves Me, and whoever [really] loves Me will be loved by My Father. And I [too] will love him and *will show* (reveal, manifest) *Myself to him – I will let Myself be clearly seen by him and make Myself real to him.*
>
> John 14:21 AMPLIFIED

For quite a stretch I've been getting the message that Jesus was displeased with my 5:00 to 6:00 P.M. 'Happy Hour', a time for relaxed reading or listening to music, when I sip a glass of sherry. At first I thought He wanted me to give up the sherry. Lately I've seen that it isn't so much what He wants me to give up, but that He wants me to be active physically during this hour, to walk or work in the garden. I had let myself become too lazy and sedentary, and too rigid about this 5:00 to 6:00 P.M. pattern. *I* like my ruts. *He* wants me active, and above all, flexible.

Then He began teaching me about *how* He goes about changing long-standing habits. It's part of the out-working of the great promise,

> This is the covenant which I will make with the house of Israel after those days, says the Lord: I will put my law . . . upon their hearts; and I will be their God, and they shall be my people.
>
> Jeremiah 31:33 RSV

I had never before tied this promise to the problems connected with habit changing. I have no addiction to alcohol or smoking, or sweets, for instance, but I ache for certain persons I know who do. I see now how He helps us with these ingrained patterns when we ask Him for help. What happens is that *our* tastes begin to change. Something that we liked a lot suddenly is not so appealing. When we understand *how* He works and that this *is* the Lord Himself working, then we can stop resisting our own changing tastes, thank Him, and flow with the new direction of the tide.

It's a marvellous plan only He could have thought of, for there is no pain in ceasing to do what we no longer care to do.

15

The Temptation of Things

I've been through a small siege of temptation to worldliness that I'm almost embarrassed to write about – and yet feel I should.

From the time I was a small girl I've loved pretty, feminine things, especially jewellery. Nothing very unusual or terribly wrong about that. For most of my life I could not afford jewellery, so it was no issue.

Even when in recent years I could afford some jewellery, the Depression syndrome that permeated my family for many years has kept me frugal. One day a cheque for several hundred dollars arrived that I hadn't expected. 'Now I can get those gold earrings,' I said to myself.

So I began making trips to jewellery stores looking for the exactly right earrings. Then an inner restlessness began to ruffle me. So I started to argue with God.

'Lord, are You telling me that earrings are too frivolous?'

Silence.

'It isn't as though I'm buying them from my tithe funds. I mean, the money is extra. I hadn't expected it.'

Silence.

'Lord I've spent much more for a rug or a piece of furniture without this guilt complex. Now, really, isn't this inner disquiet just my Puritan, Depression-born complex?'

Then came the gentle response:

I'm concerned over the inordinate amount of time you've given to this in your thought life.

At once I was led to the apostle John's comment on worldliness and his warning about the 'delight of the eyes':

> Do not love or cherish the world or the things that are in the world. If any one loves the world, love for the Father is not in him.
>
> For all that is in the world, the lust of the flesh [craving for sensual gratification], and the lust of the eyes [greedy longings of the mind] and the pride of life [assurance in one's own resources or in the stability of earthly things] – these do not come from the Father but from the world [itself].
>
> And the world passes away and disappears. . . .
> 1 John 2:15–17 AMPLIFIED

Here John is taking us into the higher reaches of spirituality. He doesn't use the word 'sin'; he doesn't mention Satan. He's concerned with whether we realise the extent of God's love for us – and how much love for God there is in us.

The crux of it: the love exchange between God and me is going to suffer if I focus too much on worldly things.

16

Fear of Man

The Lord is having me look at something this morning that is very unsettling. It came first through the following verse:

> The fear of man bringeth a snare: but whoso putteth his trust in the Lord shall be safe.
>
> Proverbs 29:25 KJV

I don't fear man in a physical way, but do I fear his disapproval of me? In other words, how much do I try to please other people instead of looking to God alone for His approval? Certainly, there is enormous pressure on all of us to be accepted and approved by others. But God wants us to resist this pressure. Consider the tragedy of the religious leaders of Jesus' day:

> Among the chief rulers also many believed on him; but because of the Pharisees they did not confess him, lest they should be put out of the synagogue: For they loved the praise of men more than the praise of God.
>
> John 12:42–43 KJV

Even Peter, soon to be leader of the earliest church, denied knowing Jesus at all following His arrest, simply to remain in the good graces of a motley crowd gathered around a bonfire. Peter was no coward. When the soldiers had come to seize Jesus, he had grabbed a sword and cut off the ear of one of them. So it wasn't his life

Peter feared for here, but the ridicule and judgment and opinions of others.

We are told that in our daily task – whatever our vocation or profession or daily round – we are to seek to please God more than man:

> Servants, obey in all things your masters according to the flesh; not with eyeservice, as menpleasers; but in singleness of heart, fearing God.
>
> Colossians 3:22 KJV

The thought comes that my tendency to be critical of others springs out of the soil of what-people-will-think. What we are, we see in others. I am judgmental, therefore I expect others to be the same.

Jesus was simply stating a law of life when He told us, '. . . judge [and] ye shall be judged: and with what measure ye mete, it shall be measured to you' (Matthew 7:2 KJV). Put this way, judging others constantly cultivates more soil for the thistles of fear-of-man to grow in.

Judgmentalism is an attempt to ward off this fear by standing in a superior place. Self thinks that when it can get there first and judge before others can state their opinions, it can forestall others' criticisms. Of course, self is mistaken, since the very opposite happens – judging draws the judgment of others.

Two passages of Scripture, personalised for this specific fear, are helping me overcome my exaggerated concern for man's approval:

> Fear not [the opinions of others]: for I have redeemed thee; I have called thee by thy name; thou art mine.
>
> Isaiah 43:1 KJV

> When thou passest through the waters [of ridicule], I will be with thee; and through the rivers [of rejection], they shall not overflow thee: when thou walkest through the fire [of contempt], thou shalt not be burned; neither shall the flame kindle upon thee.
>
> Isaiah 43:2 KJV

17

Immersed in a Horse Trough

I want to get down in my journal the fascinating experience Len and I had this past weekend. At the urging of our friend Virginia Lively we drove to Clewiston, Florida, about sixty miles from our home here in Boynton Beach. Virginia had gone through what she called a 'believer's baptism' in the Episcopal church there. She described it as 'a beautiful, cleansing, and healing experience' and urged us to consider doing it.

For months now I have read with fascination about the Jesus people, a California phenomenon. Most seem to be young, former members of the drug culture, who, after a 'believer's baptism' in the Pacific Ocean, experience an almost total change of lifestyle.

Virginia's conviction was that every Christian should have the opportunity of undergoing baptism *following* his or her personal decision for Christ. She had been baptised as a very young child in her own Episcopal church and had accepted this sacrament as valid, but she believes that, ideally, we should be 'dedicated' to God as babies, then have a 'water baptism' later when we are ready to accept Jesus on our own.

I spent a morning digging out Scripture references to baptism, coming on one archetype I'd never noticed:

For Christ . . . was put to death in the body but made alive by the Spirit, through whom also he went and preached to the spirits in prison who disobeyed long ago when God waited patiently in the days of Noah while the ark was being built. In it only a few people, eight in all, were saved through water, and this water symbolises baptism that now saves you also – not the removal of dirt from the body but the pledge of a good conscience toward God. . . .

1 Peter 3:18–21 NIV

Since the subject of baptism has always divided Christians, at first Len and I felt a certain wariness about accepting Virginia's invitation. Then John and Elizabeth (Tib) Sherrill (our close friends and associates at *Guideposts* magazine) arrived for a visit and expressed interest. All four of us had been baptised as infants, long before we could remember. We were convinced that the performance of this sacrament on our behalfs had been complete and theologically adequate in every way. We all agreed, however, that we didn't want to miss anything that the Lord might have for us right now. The Sherrills, LeSourds, my friend Freddie Koch, and her daughter Claudia drove from our home in Boynton Beach last Saturday for a spiritual adventure. In Clewiston we located the home of the Episcopal rector. Virginia Lively had arrived there a few minutes earlier.

The first thing that happened was between John Sherrill and me. Our relationship had become strained through some theological differences. While we sat together in the rector's living room, John began speaking about his fear of change. Twice when there had been major upheavals in his life he had developed cancer. He confessed apprehension of a recurrence in the face of upcoming changes in his and Tib's situation.

At Virginia's urging, he recollected his childhood and talked about the little-boy John – skinny, non-athletic, not popular with the 'in' crowd – and tears filled my eyes. How I identified with him there. A new love for John filled me and I went over and hugged him. The reconciliation was complete and almost instantaneous.

Next we went to the nearby Episcopal church, a small

sanctuary set in a grove of Florida pine trees. In the vestibule of the church had been placed a galvanised iron horse trough, the stickers from the feed store still visible on one end. A hose, connected to a water spigot outside, ran through the open screen door and was filling the trough. This was to be the setting for the baptism.

First, we sat down in the sanctuary and sang some appropriate hymns. The Episcopal priest, in slacks and sports shirt, prayed, then explained the significance of a believer's baptism: that it was not necessary for salvation, but an opportunity for confession, asking and receiving forgiveness, then making a new commitment of our lives to Jesus. This would open us to a fresh infusion of the Holy Spirit with the resulting new love and joy and power that comes when Jesus indwells us.

As we changed into bathing suits, each of us pondered the areas in our lives where confession and forgiveness were needed. This was done quietly with God, with our spouses, or openly with the rector. The Sherrills led the way, first Tib, then John being immersed.

Afterwards John said softly to Tibby, 'Now that we have left our old persons at the bottom of the horse trough and are new creatures, don't you think we ought to get married again?'

The two of them, barefoot, water dripping from their hair and bathing suits, stood before the altar, pledging themselves to one another again. Len and I followed . . . into the horse trough and then to the altar for a reaffirmation of our marriage vows, our eyes brimming with tears.

The next morning, after we got home, we found just outside our front door an elaborate 'Just Married' sign which Claudia Koch – who had been wide-eyed during the ceremonies – had made and sometime during the night left at our door.

Section Four

His Strength in Our Weakness

At one point during our courtship, Catherine voiced a concern over her health, saying she doubted that she had more than five years to live. I 'pooh-poohed' this, pointing to her own mother's robust health at age sixty-seven.

Both of us were wrong. Catherine lived twenty-three years more, but her death at sixty-nine was far short of her mother's life span (Mother Wood is now ninety-four).

And for all those twenty-three years, Catherine battled a debilitating emphysema that sapped her energy and sometimes left her gasping for breath after even so simple an exertion as climbing a flight of stairs. New York winters brought on severe bronchitis. Our move to Boynton Beach, Florida, doubtless prolonged her life, but it did not solve her health problems. Along the way she won a battle over sleeping pills – until her last years when sleeplessness once more turned her nights into a spiritual battleground.

Prayers for Catherine's healing throughout our marriage lifted her, strengthened her, but never totally healed her. 'Why?' she asked over and over. The enigma of why some are healed, some are not, frustrated Catherine all her life.

But she never stopped struggling for answers. And out of the struggle came – not the robust health she yearned for, but a daily, growing intimacy with God that became far more precious than any amount of physical stamina. Her constant companion on this closer walk . . . the Bible.

LL

1

Trusting God

Today this verse in Psalm 37 spoke to me:

> Commit your way to the Lord – roll and repose [each
> care of] your load on Him; trust (lean on, rely on and be
> confident) also in Him, and He will bring it to pass.
>
> Psalm 37:5 AMPLIFIED

This is my husband Len's favourite verse of the entire
Bible. He has leaned on this passage in recent years while
making the switch from editing a magazine to publishing
Christian books.

There is much in Scripture stressing our need to have
faith in God. The above verse takes us a step further. It
not only admonishes us to trust, it promises that when
we do, God will act in a supernatural way to answer our
need. Dwell on that for a moment. We trust, God acts. A
mind-blowing premise.

Yet total, all-out trust on our part is not as easy as it first
seems. There are periods when God's face is shrouded,
when His dealings with us will *appear* as if He does not
care, when He seems not to be acting like a true Father.
Can we then hang onto the fact of His love and His
faithfulness and that He *is* a prayer-answering God?

Can we get to the point Habakkuk reached: 'Though
the fig tree does not blossom, and there be no fruit on the
vines . . . Yet I will rejoice in the Lord . . . !' (Habakkuk
3:17–18 AMPLIFIED).

Can we, *at the moment* when His face is hidden, exult in

the God of our salvation? 'The Lord God is my strength, my personal bravery and my invincible army' (v. 19).

Last Saturday morning Len had a chance to demonstrate the principle of trust in a difficult situation. He awoke with a very bad throat condition; could hardly speak. Yet he was supposed to give a talk that morning at a men's prayer breakfast in the local Lutheran church.

Before he left for the church I anointed him with oil, placed my hand on his throat, and asked the Lord to do a healing work in Len for the glory of God.

During the breakfast preceding Len's speech, however, he told me later, his voice got worse and worse until there was little left but a croak. The Lutheran pastor suggested turning the gathering into a discussion group, giving Len the chance to bow out. But no, my husband would at least try.

So Len stood up and uttered a rasping, halting first sentence, literally plunging ahead on faith. Suddenly, he reported afterwards, his voice cleared. From then on, for thirty-odd minutes, the message poured out with no cough, hardly even a clearing of the throat. The Holy Spirit had simply taken over. In the question period afterwards, still no problem with his throat.

But when he returned home, Len's voice was once again a painful whisper.

What fascinated me in this episode is how biblical it is: as the symptoms get worse, the temptation is there to 'give up' and not to trust Jesus. We must resist that temptation in the midst of our very real human helplessness, 'roll' the entire burden onto His shoulders, as He bade us do, step out and *take the first step* with bare, no-evidence-at-all, faith.

And lo, He does take over gloriously, doing what we literally cannot do for ourselves.

2

Lord, I Resent . . .

Thank [God] in everything – no matter what the circumstances may be, be thankful and give thanks; for
this is the will of God for you [who are] in Christ
Jesus. . . .

1 Thessalonians 5:18 AMPLIFIED

Yesterday morning in my prayer time, God showed
me that if I wanted more vitality for my work hours, I
had to deal with the following resentments that were
smouldering inside me.

I resent my lack of social graces in certain situations,
which I'm inclined to blame on my childhood years when
I too often fled social encounters.

I resent the fact that I'm such a poor sleeper. I can see
that resentment produces tension and, of course,
accumulated tension through the day is one reason I'm
not sleeping better.

Here at Evergreen Farm there are so many stairs to
climb, and outside, hills and more hills, which I cannot
mount because of my breathlessness. This condition is a
constant embarrassment and the central thorn in my
flesh. I resent my damaged lungs.

I see this morning that there are deeper resentments
still: that of creeping old age, being progressively shut
down, as it were, and, of course, out there – death. Have I
not always resented the fact of death, even though I have
total belief in and expectancy about the life after death?

How can I come to terms with all this?

The answer came in the above verse. I am to praise God for *all* things, regardless of where they seem to originate. Doing this, He points out, is the key to receiving the blessings of God. Praise will wash away my resentments. I've known this, accepted it, even written about praise. But as I began praising Him yesterday, my efforts were wooden.

Then came these thoughts: I was to ignore my feelings and act on the principle. I was to do it despite the lack of joy – simply because God told me to. True praise grows out of the recognition and acknowledgment that in His time God will bring good out of bad. There is the intolerable situation on the one hand and the fulfilment of Romans 8:28 on the other hand. ('All things work together for good. . . .') By an act of will and through imagination and with faith, I am to turn my back on the bad and face the good, and begin actively to praise God for it as Scripture commands.

Shortly after this insight, my cleaning woman called in to say that she was not coming. Praised God for this, though mechanically.

Following that, joy began spilling over into the tiny everydayness of my life. Walked by a vase of beautiful roses from our garden and buried my nose in the fragrance, saying, 'Praise You, Lord, for such beauty!'

Stepped onto our patio for a moment to listen to the birds singing. 'Praise You, Lord, for all Your creatures.'

Then came the feeling that all these small acts put together – little trickles of praise – were running together, beginning to form a river of praise.

Continued to praise God for *all* things, good and bad. All setbacks, frustrations, and resentments.

Praise You, Lord, for my awkwardness in certain social situations.

Praise You, Lord, that I have trouble sleeping.

Praise You, Lord, for my weak lungs.

Praise You, Lord, for creeping old age.

Praise You, Lord, for the death that comes to all of us.

This morning I actually woke up with praise swelling in my heart. Only later did I realise I had slept through the entire night! Cannot remember when I last did this! Awakened by the coffee pot going on. Imagine! Praise God indeed!

Do I Really Want to Get Well?

My heart is heavy this morning as I think of Rosalind. She is almost bedridden now with asthma. We went to pray for her healing yesterday, but she was more interested in talking about her ailments than in receiving Christ's love and power. How tragic!

This morning I turned again to the Gospel of John for the story of the man at the Pool of Bethesda who had been ill for thirty-eight years. As I read, I pretended I was there in Jerusalem myself, watching in the shadow of one of those great arched colonnades around the long pool. I could shut my eyes and see the scene as if it were happening today.

The man in this account is a chronic invalid, probably in his fifties or sixties. The stone floor around the large pool is crowded with the pallets of the crippled and the blind. But this man has been there longer than any. He is now the old-timer; his illness has virtually become his career and status symbol.

Now Jesus appears, threading His way through the porticos. He looks into the eyes of the sick man: 'Do you want to become well?' (John 5:6 AMPLIFIED).

It seems a ridiculous question on the surface. Wouldn't anyone want to be healed of a physical handicap? But surprisingly the invalid begins to stammer excuses.

'Sir,' he replies to Jesus, 'it's just that I haven't anybody to put me into the pool when the angel of healing is present. While I'm trying to get there, somebody else always gets into the water first.'

As I read these words I knew that this sick man's problem was Rosalind's problem too. He thought he wanted healing, but even to his own ears his rationalisations must sound hollow. Yet those amazing eyes boring into his hold no contempt. Rather, Jesus issues a loving directive in a voice that rings with authority. 'Pick up your bed and walk.'

This is the moment of truth. I could picture the emotions moving across the pinched features: surprise, consternation, doubt, awareness, hope, then resolution. The man scrambles to his feet, picks up his bedroll, a well man.

How much this story says to me every time I read it – and can say to anyone who finds his fervent petitions unanswered. The principle here is: True prayer is dominant desire. If the person is divided in his real yearnings, he will experience emptiness and frustration.

I still remember vividly the three years in the 1940s when I myself was bedridden. Little by little I had come to enjoy my quiet life. I thought that I yearned for healing, but in fact I was not ready to shoulder the full responsibilities of vigorous health.

Only when I asked the Lord to mend my inner confusion was I able to go all-out in prayer. The healing of my physical disability followed.

Since that experience, I have been able to perceive this divided self as a major stumbling block to many people. I think of my friend in Washington, Jessie, who had been praying long and hard for her husband to be healed of alcoholism. Jessie was spiritually minded, her husband worldly and cynical. He was contemptuous of his wife's frequent trips to retreats and church meetings.

Several of us met regularly to pray with Jessie that her husband would encounter the living Christ for himself. Thanks to a group of vital Christian men, this came about, gloriously. John became a recovered alcoholic and a changed man.

The surprise was Jessie's reaction. Her criticism of John continued unabated. For the first time we, her friends, suspected the divided will in Jessie. Our suspicions were confirmed one night when one of the women suggested that Jessie thank God for so great an answer to our prayers for John.

Jessie could not do it. The words would not come. Then we understood. For years Jessie's prayers for John had gone unanswered because she had enjoyed standing above John on her pedestal marked 'spiritual'. Admired by friends for her suffering and patience with an alcoholic husband, she came to enjoy her martyr role. Therefore, the unsuspected desire of her deepest being had cancelled out the prayer of her lips for John's conversion. Only when she was able to see this divided self and surrender it to God was she able to work out a better relationship with her husband.

It is so clear to me this morning. The divided self can defeat us in every area. Like finding the right job. When we hear the job-seeker insist on a string of specific conditions regarding salary, hours, pension, geographic location – we will often find a cleavage in his aspirations.

Fortunately, there is something we can do about the contradictions inside us.

First, we can present our long-standing, unanswered prayers to God for analysis. If there is any division of will deep inside, He will put His finger on it. This will hurt. We will be shocked – even as the man at the pool was, even as Jessie was.

Second, we can acknowledge this inner inconsistency and present it, without cringing or making excuses, to God for healing, asking Him to bring our conscious and subconscious minds into harmony. At this point He will almost always issue us a directive as Jesus did the man at the poolside. He asks that we prove our wholeheartedness by obedience. The moment that we rise to obey Him, we discover a great fact: that the word of God and the work of God are one. His words *are* life – with power to restore the atrophied will to quicken pallid desire, to resurrect us from the graveclothes of a half-dead existence.

4

To Live in the Present Moment

I want to record this morning that I did something yesterday, November 5, 1978, I do too seldom. For a period of time I lived fully in the present moment. What a healing this was for my spirit.

It happened in church. Six members of our family were sitting in the same pew.

Beside me was my tall son Peter, then his beautiful wife, Edith, and their two children, Mary Elizabeth and Peter Jonathan; on my other side, Len – so faithful, so solid. And we were all healthy and together and of one mind in the Lord. Great surges of gratitude washed over me and I was happier than I have been in a long time.

The Spirit seemed to say, 'Bask in the moment. No matter that the future may hold problems. This is yours.'

I did bask. It was golden.

My thankfulness flowed beyond the church walls. I thanked Him for my mother – now eighty-seven – who is still with us with her serene, cheerful disposition. How blessed I am, Lord, to have had You choose such a woman to bear me! I thank You for her lifelong gentleness . . . her womanliness, her unwavering faithfulness, her vision that always could lift our dreams on wings and send them flying beyond drudgery or mundane circumstances.

And for Len's three children, grown now, all Christians, each on the right path to his or her own fulfilment. How grateful I am for what they have taught me.

At that beautiful moment God seemed to be shining a

light on each member of my family, saying, 'See what I have wrought. Enjoy them, be thankful for them, for everything I make is good.'

And my response this morning is to thank Him and praise Him in these words I find in His book:

Give thanks to the Lord, for he is good; his love endures forever.

Psalm 107:1 NIV

O Lord my God, you are very great; you are clothed with splendour and majesty.

Psalm 104:1 NIV

Shout for joy to the Lord, all the earth. Worship the Lord with gladness; come before him with joyful songs. . . . Enter his gates with thanksgiving and his courts with praise; give thanks to him and praise his name.

Psalm 100:1–2, 4 NIV

Thanks be to God! He gives us the victory through our Lord Jesus Christ.

1 Corinthians 15:57 NIV

5

Helplessness

When I was still not asleep last night about 1:00 A.M., I swallowed one mild sleeping pill. No sleep! At five minutes to three, feeling empty, I got up, went to the kitchen, ate two Ritz crackers with peanut butter, drank a paper cup full of milk, and went back to bed.

Still no sleep! About 4:00 A.M., I took a second sleeping pill. It had no effect at all. I saw dawn break and finally got up.

I got down on my knees and prayed something like, 'Lord, You have promised to talk to Your friends. Would you tell me what this is all about?'

I drank a cup of coffee in bed, had my Quiet Time – Bible reading, etc. No answer from Him. Dead silence.

Got down on my knees again and prayed. No response.

Or . . . was I simply not listening to the message He was speaking? As I was dressing, light began to dawn: He wants to demonstrate to me that I really am helpless without Him, that I really am dependent on Him *even for the sleeping pills to work.* Jesus put it this way:

> Apart from Me – cut off from vital union with Me – you can do nothing.
>
> John 15:5 AMPLIFIED

Since I am stubborn, He has been forced to bring this oh, so-very-basic truth home to me the hard way.

It was on the subject of sleep – the subject *I* wanted to

know about – that He was silent. He did not promise me a thing, not that I would sleep beautifully without the sleeping pills, nor that I would sleep *with* them, this afternoon or tonight; nothing. Apparently, He wants me to place this whole area trustingly into His hands, believing that He loves me and wants me to be full of the vitality that comes from adequate sleep. Total dependence, that's the all-important lesson He wants me to learn. For regardless of what I do or do not do, whether I'm in a period of trusting Him or of pulling away, *He* never forgets that I belong to Him, that my life has been paid for with a price. *He* never lets me go!

This is such a *tremendous* base fact to know and to build on and to lean on.

Praise God for this tough experience!

6

Spiritual Preparation for Surgery

This morning I can look back over the past weeks and see so clearly how God works in adversity. It began over a month ago with the doctor's words, 'You're going to need surgery. . . .'

The procedure was 'routine', he assured me, the problem most likely 'minor', but no casual approach could soften the impact of the next sentence: 'Of course, we never know what we'll find.' Statistics on cancer then followed. 'With this type of ovarian cyst, the percentage of malignancy is . . .'

Thus began a month's battle with fear. As I drove home from the doctor's office that beautiful September afternoon, the brilliant colour of the autumn leaves seemed tarnished. How is it, I marvelled, that bad news has a way of invading human life so suddenly? Trouble rings no warning bells. Adversity and sorrow stalk into life on rubber soles.

'Fear is lack of faith,' I told myself. 'It dishonours God.' But then I discovered that I could not handle fear any more than I could mastermind any other strong emotion.

As Len and I talked over my situation, our first reaction was the very human one: 'Is this operation really necessary?' However 'routine' such surgery might be for the doctor, my inadequate lungs make any use of anaesthesia a questionable risk. On the medical level, a second opinion seemed the wise course. We pursued this; the second examination confirmed the first.

Next came our conviction that we needed to pose the

same question in prayer: 'Lord, what is Your will? Do You want to handle my case through prayer alone?'

After all, Scripture provides clear directives and means of grace, which we ignore to our own detriment. From James 5:13–15: prayer with a group of fellow Christians, followed by the laying on of hands and/or anointing with oil by church elders or spiritual leaders. From 1 Corinthians 11:23–30: prayer at the altar rail of a church by a priest or pastor, with the laying on of hands and/or Communion.

How wonderful it is when God wants to move in this direct manner, and the way is clear for Him to do so! This is what happened to John Sherrill back in 1960 when a suspicious lump was discovered in John's neck and an operation scheduled to remove it. Since a melanoma cancer had been surgically removed from his ear two years before, John asked his rector for the ancient laying-on-of-hands ministry of the Episcopal Church.

Twenty-four hours later, when the famous cancer specialist at New York Memorial Hospital operated, all he could find was a tiny, dried-up nodule. No lump, no malignancy. I know of other instances equally dramatic, where God has chosen to heal without medical intervention.

In my case, a group of fellow Christians began to meet with Len and me for prayer at 7:30 each morning. My crisis was their crisis. After two weeks in which we sought God's healing, I went for still one more examination. The doctor found no change. More intensive prayer followed; with it came the assurance that I was to go ahead with the operation, that my lungs would withstand the strain, and that there would be no cancer.

Apparently this was one of those times when God wishes us to make use of the skilled hands of surgeons. (God may have other purposes too, of course, such as some personal contact in the hospital He wishes us to make for Him.)

The next step in preparation came over the long-distance telephone from a Christian physician in North Carolina. 'Over several years,' he told me, 'I have seen an incredible difference in the patient's post-operative condition between those who saturate surgery with prayer and those who don't. Most anyone facing surgery has fears. We can't just will them away. But God can handle our fears.

'Another thing,' he went on. 'Those undergirded with prayer often escape sticky little complications and just sail through the recovery. They even heal faster.'

What helped me most of all during those long hours the night before the operation were two Scripture verses. The first promise spoke to fear:

> Fear not; [there is nothing to fear]. . . . For I, the Lord your God, hold your right hand; I, Who say to you, Fear not, I will help you!
>
> Isaiah 41:10, 13 AMPLIFIED

The second Scripture was a promise from the Psalms:

> Though I walk in the midst of trouble, thou wilt revive me . . . thy right hand shall save me.
>
> Psalm 138:7 KJV

As I read these reassuring words, a clear picture was dropped into my mind, childlike in its simplicity: the Lord would be standing on the right side of the operating table, facing me, looking into my eyes.

Of course. He would have to be in that position since the Isaiah promise was that He would hold my right hand, and the promise from the Psalms was that by *His* right hand, He would save me. *How beautiful!* I thought.

At ten minutes to eight the next morning, Len and our daughter, Linda, who had flown down from Washington, arrived at my hospital room just as an orderly appeared to roll me to the operating room.

'A quick prayer,' Len said. He had no sooner said

'Amen' than the telephone rang. It was our dear friend, the Reverend Joe Bishop. 'I can't believe this split-second timing,' I told him. 'The orderly is here to take me to surgery.'

'Then time for one more prayer,' Joe said. His loving benediction was all around us as we left the room.

All through the corridors Len and Linda walked beside the stretcher, right up to the anteroom.

As I was wheeled into the operating room I was given a beautiful three-part promise, one from each Person of the Trinity:

God the Father would hold me in His everlasting arms.
Jesus would take my right hand in His.
From the moment I lost consciousness, the Holy Spirit
   would be my Breath of life.

After that, suddenly I found that fear was nowhere around.

LL Note: The cyst was benign. Catherine had a recovery as swift and uneventful as the North Carolina doctor predicted.

My Yoke Is Easy

For many years I have pondered the following words of Jesus, wanting to bear them out in my life, repeatedly falling short:

> Come to Me, all you who labour and are heavy-laden and over burdened, and I will cause you to rest – I will ease and relieve and refresh your souls.
>
> Take My yoke upon you, and learn of Me; for I am gentle (meek) and humble (lowly) in heart, and you will find rest – relief, ease and refreshment and recreation and blessed quiet – for your souls.
>
> For My yoke is wholesome (useful, good) – not harsh, hard, sharp or pressing, but comfortable, gracious and pleasant; and My burden is light and easy to be borne.
>
> Matthew 11:28–30 AMPLIFIED

Then at age sixty-five I was given a whole new perception of these verses through my friend, Roberta Dorr, author of the novel *Bathsheba*. During a visit at our home, she told me of the miracle-healing of her doctor-husband from supposedly incurable Hodgkins disease.

The diagnosis was made while her husband, David, was still in surgical residency. Having a laid-back temperament, David accepted the verdict of a very limited life span and went about his work.

But Roberta has a different nature – always seeking to understand, always questioning, always a fighter. She resisted the idea of losing her beloved husband and seeing their three small children grow up without a father. She and her husband had just filled out the final papers and were ready for an appointment to a hospital in Africa when the diagnosis was made final. Why, she asked over and over, had this happened?

No answer came. Until at last, with total relinquishment she asked God the right question, 'How do You want me to pray about my husband?'

One morning shortly afterwards, this thought was planted in her mind: 'Pray that your husband will be able to *use* for the good of others the medical training he has been given.'

As soon as Roberta prayed *this* prayer, the tremendous burden lifted from her heart. She had discovered that the yoke Jesus offered really did bring peace; by praying *His* prayer, sharing with Him His concern for all of suffering humanity, she was able to repose her load on His great strength. One year later the doctors at Johns Hopkins were astonished during a periodic test to discover no trace of disease in David. They were frank to say that they did not understand what had happened. Three years later, they dismissed him entirely, still unable to explain it. The disease never reappeared, but during the four years of 'waiting', David completed a surgical residency that was to change his life. Instead of going to Africa, he went to the Gaza Strip where he was desperately needed as a surgeon.

It was while the Dorrs were on a medical mission to the Middle East that Roberta had further illumination about what it means to be yoked together with Jesus. (The Dorrs spent a total of seventeen years in Yemen and Gaza.) Perhaps seeing double-yoked oxen working the fields helped bring the truth home to her.

Roberta had always thought of these verses in Matthew as a metaphor of Jesus helping her with *her* projects, *her* life – ploughing *her* field, so to speak.

Then one day the Lord said to her something like this:

'No, you have it all wrong – backwards. Drop your plans. At the beginning of each day simply ask to be yoked with Me for *My* work, to plough *My* field. Then you will find that the yoke fits perfectly and that the burden truly is light.'

I've thought a lot about Roberta's experience. First, David's healing. Did it happen in part because David was so involved in ministering to other people that he didn't have time to dwell on his own illness? Did he not only find refreshment in serving his Lord, but healing as well?

Not the whole answer, of course, but a clue toward that great mystery of how and why miraculous healings take place.

Second, there's much for me to ponder about the injunction Roberta received to 'drop her plans' and listen for God's plan for her.

Again I'm back to relinquishment. Time after time I've laid my concerns, questions, doubts, plans, on God's altar. The problem for me is leaving them there.

At age sixty-five I still have that determination to take charge of my life, to prove that I can still do everything I did when I was twenty. I still want God to applaud my good works. It's so ridiculous! No wonder I have trouble sleeping and breathing.

Meanwhile, God waits patiently for me to come to Him, forgetting my agenda, so that I can hear what He has in mind for me.

Is it possible for an opinionated woman in her autumn years to become like a child and sit at the feet of Jesus with one idea – to hear what He will say?

The Joy of the Lord Shall Be Your Strength

For weeks now I have been so discouraged about the quality of my writing that I wonder if I am capable of doing another novel. Is *Christy* to be the only one?

The new novel I've been working on is set in western Pennsylvania during the 1930s. So far it seems lifeless. The characters aren't real to me yet.

Yesterday was the low point as I struggled to get words on paper. I had a mental picture of myself as a lost, crying sheep at the bottom of a very deep pit. Then with startling clarity these words of Jesus flooded my thinking:

> I tell you the truth, I am the gate for the sheep . . . whoever enters through me will be saved. He will come in and go out, and find pasture.
>
> John 10:7–9 NIV

How like Jesus to rescue people like me, not because we have done, or are currently doing, one solitary thing to deserve it. I sought Him and last night He reached down and, with His shepherd's crook, physically and spiritually lifted me out of the pit. Today He is comforting me even as He puts renewed strength into me.

It happened through a dream, fragments of which remained in my mind upon awakening.

In the dream I had a basket in my hands decorated around the rim and sides with flowers and leaves. I was having to 'redo' the decorations. As I took off the old ones

I was surprised to find how easy they were to remove. But there was an even greater surprise: I *expected* the flowers to be artificial ones, but found them not only real flowers, but surprisingly fresh.

When I awoke there was a joy and a release springing from deep in my spirit and my heart was full of praise.

The message of the dream appeared to be not only my own readiness to begin work on the novel again, but even divine approval of the timing. And the ease with which the bunches of flowers were removed from the basket and the fact that they were *fresh*, seemed to say, 'The task of revision will not be as difficult as you have thought, and you will find the material fresh.'

I have long known that my writing is never truly on target unless I feel at some point, while in the process of getting words on paper, that certain hallmark of joy within. The scene I am attempting to write may be quite a serious one, but the touchstone of joy must be there – or else I'm working in my own strength, not His.

It will take a little while to turn around a habit of negative thinking about this book – but Jesus is beginning to do that for me this morning. In fact, He who *always* gives to us 'more abundantly than we could ask or think' has given me a glimpse of *His* vision for this novel.

I had been realising the last few days, as I have been doing a quick rereading of the words already written, that I am at the same point in this book I was with *A Man Called Peter* when I received the devastating critique: 'You haven't yet gotten *inside* the man Peter.'

It was after I fell into a pit of discouragement over that remark that God told me, 'No man's life has ultimate significance apart from what that man's life shows about God.' So I re-outlined Peter's story *that* way.

Now God is telling me to think of the novel like this: We are living in a time when evil and trouble seem rampant. Every person I know has *trouble* of some kind.

So I am to separate the strands of the different kinds of

trouble in the novel, and see what God's solution is to each one. For instance, we have

Economic trouble – I am writing of the Depression times, the 30s.

Emotional depression – Ken, the father, with his conviction that he is a failure.

Ecological trouble – powerful financial interests ignore environmental danger signs.

Natural disaster – the final flood. What is God saying here? To us today?

I'm going to have to listen to the Inner Voice *very* carefully to 'get' all this, but praise God, oh, how I praise Him for this revelation! For He is saying, 'Yes, yes, of *course* I want you to write this book. Yes, yes, it has an important message for our time.'

Oh, thank You, Lord. Thank You for the return of joy to my life!

9

The Intercessors

Yesterday this Scriptural passage seemed to leap out at me:

> And he [the Lord] saw that there was no man, and wondered that there was no intercessor. . . .
>
> Isaiah 59:16 KJV

Then came a rather startling bit of guidance from the Lord (I want to check this out with others). He seemed to be asking me to set up an intercession ministry that would consist chiefly of people with the desire and the faith to pray for others, and the time to devote to it – like many of the elderly, or handicapped, or those who earnestly want to be used by God but can't figure out *how* to be useful within the limitations of family demands, geographical location, etc.

To these intercessors would be forwarded the letters and requests we receive from those who need prayer – with names removed, of course – to whom it could mean everything to know that other people are lifting them up. My conscience hurts me when people write for prayer and I can give so little time to each one, for there are so many.

It would mean an incredible job of collation and feedback, a lot of postage, probably a newsletter with real input on the subject of intercessory prayer. Since this is a phase of prayer about which I know least, I'm surprised the Lord would lay this upon me.

LL Note: This was Catherine's first journal notation (June 1, 1980) about intercessory prayer; her guidance grew stronger with the passing weeks. From this single verse in Isaiah has grown the Intercessors prayer movement, launched in the autumn of 1980 as a part of the nonprofit organisation Breakthrough, Inc. (Lincoln, Virginia 22078). As of April 1, 1986, there were 1,500 intercessors enrolled to handle the thousands of prayer requests received each year. The newsletter (put out eight times a year) was being mailed to 12,000 people involved in intercession.

Section Five

Spiritual Warfare

Early in our marriage Catherine and I went through periods when we seemed to be up against a kind of unexplained opposition: there would be a series of breakdowns in our household equipment; times when all the children misbehaved for no apparent reason; work would be constantly interrupted; and we would feel a heaviness in our spirits. At first we tried to examine these happenings logically; then as we learned more about the dark powers and principalities at work in the world we realised that on occasion we were under a form of satanic attack.

When Catherine was writing Beyond Our Selves, *she reported the spirit of opposition in her office as being almost palpable. No wonder, since this book more than any other of hers helped people move from unbelief or an uncertain faith into making a commitment to Jesus Christ as Lord.*

As we learned more about 'the enemy' and his cohorts, we were able to pray against those dark spirits, reducing their effectiveness. But we were never free from them. In fact as the years went by, we accepted the fact that for all of us engaged in Christian service, there is never-ending spiritual warfare.

In the final years of her life, as her body weakened from a series of ailments, Catherine had a daily battle with the dark forces. Rebuking the enemy in the name of Jesus was the best weapon for reclaiming the creative atmosphere to do our work, to minister to others, to protect our home environment.

But we could never relax our vigilance.

LL

1

Fear

Last night I had a vivid dream. . . . While driving a car, I became terrified of what was ahead. With no clear idea of what the problem was, I could not seem to keep from doing the very worst thing possible – *closing my eyes as I drove.*

Then I was driving over a concrete road with about three inches of very clear water on it. There was still overwhelming fear in me. I awoke in panic.

As I pondered it this morning, the message of the dream would appear to be that my actual danger is very small – shallow water. Thus my real problem is fear itself. Fear of many things, including God Himself.

He scolded me for this – gently – this morning, reminding me that fear is one of Satan's tools. The *fear of God* – the wrong kind, that is, fearfulness rather than awe – is something I have struggled with for so many, many years. And I sense that many believing people are like me, unable to love and praise their Heavenly Father fully because of fear – often a fear of punishment.

Then I remembered something that Jesus did. Knowing that all people struggle with fear, He often prefaced what He was about to say to His fellow humans with the words, 'Fear not.'

Therefore my prayer is, 'Lord, I hand my fears over to You, fears of all kinds. Fear of You is actually a kind of blasphemy against Your character. I'm sorry. Forgive me.'

In answer to my prayer, a line from an old hymn, 'Take

it to the Lord in prayer,' began running through my mind. The Spirit said very clearly, 'Why do you think I am reminding you of these words? *Pay attention to every line of these verses*. Learn to bring everything directly to Me instead of allowing so many worrying wonderings.'

What a Friend we have in Jesus
All our sins and griefs to bear!
What a privilege to carry
Everything to God in prayer.
O what peace we often forfeit,
O what needless pain we bear,
All because we do not carry
Everything to God in prayer.

Have we trials and temptations?
Is there trouble anywhere?
We should never be discouraged –
Take it to the Lord in prayer.
Can we find a friend so faithful
Who will all our sorrows share?
Jesus knows our every weakness –
Take it to the Lord in prayer.

Are we weak and heavy-laden
Cumbered with a load of care?
Precious Saviour, still our refuge –
Take it to the Lord in prayer.
Do thy friends despise, forsake thee?
Take it to the Lord in prayer;
In His arms He'll take and shield thee –
Thou wilt find a solace there.
                    Joseph Scriven (1819–1886)

2

Fear of Death

A visit from Betty Malz this week has forced me to do something I keep putting off – examining my attitude about death.

After returning to life from twenty-eight minutes of being dead (*My Glimpse of Eternity*), Betty is so full of *details* of what life will be in eternity, as well as bubbling over with stories of remarkable answers to prayer, that being with her is like a feast.

Yet our conversation several nights ago highlighted my own wrong emotional orientation to death. Though I know intellectually that Jesus *did* conquer death, though I believe with my mind in immortality, my emotions deny this. Somewhere back in my childhood certain experiences planted firmly the conviction that death is our enemy, to be hated and fought every step of the way. By the time I was in my teens, I was writing poetry full of emotional rebellion about the brevity of our lives here and how pathetically unfair that is.

I slept almost none at all night before last, finding in myself a deep unrest about all this.

Yesterday morning as I prayed about it, I remembered a New Testament verse about those 'who for fear of death are in bondage all their lives'. This seemed such an exact description of me that I thought, *I'd like to take a look at that verse*. Whereupon the Helper clearly said (in my thoughts), *Look in Hebrews*.

So I turned to that book, not having the least idea *where* in Hebrews. I found the verse in the second chapter, fifteenth verse.

Verse fourteen talks about what Jesus did for us on the Cross:

> . . . that by [going through] death He might bring to nought and make of no effect him who had the power of death, that is, the devil.

Verse fifteen:

> And also that He might deliver and completely set free all those who through the (haunting) fear of death were held in bondage throughout the whole course of their lives.
>
> AMPLIFIED

How to the point! I decided that I had been in emotional bondage to the fear of death long enough, that Satan had used this as a way of stirring up doubt and confusion in me. All of which has interfered with my having full fellowship with the Father.

So I made a date with Betty Malz and Len for 4:30 yesterday afternoon and in prayer together we claimed my freedom, asking that Jesus fulfil His promise 'to deliver and completely set free'.

Last night at the church meeting where Betty spoke, one of the hymns we sang was 'Be Still, My Soul'. The words were like a Night Letter straight from the heart of God in answer to my claiming prayer in the afternoon (italics added).

> Be still, my soul – the Lord is on thy side!
> Bear patiently the cross of grief or pain;
> Leave to thy God to order and provide –
> *In every change* He faithful will remain.
>
> Be still, my soul – thy best, thy Heavenly Friend
> Through thorny ways leads to a joyful end.

Be still, my soul – thy God doth undertake
To guide the future as He has the past,
Thy hope, thy confidence let nothing shake –
All now mysterious shall be bright at last. . . .

3

Self-dissatisfaction

Last night I dreamed I was making a telephone call from a department store pay phone. There was immense trouble, though, about finding the number. I could not locate the yellow pages of the directory. Then I thought that I might have the number written in one of two notebooks in my handbag. But the two notebooks kept getting mixed up, and as I would find the page, someone else would push into the phone booth ahead of me, and my finger would slip out of place in the little notebook. Once I located the number, only to find it so blurry that I could not read it.

The message my unconscious seems to be playing back to me – confusion. Not enough order in my life, or even in my pocketbook.

This morning as I sought answers in prayer to a number of problems, the same spirit of confusion seemed to settle upon me. Quickly I asked for His help. After a few moments I was led to Psalm 78. These verses hit me:

> He divided the sea and led them through. . . . He guided them with the cloud by day and with light from the fire all night. He split the rocks in the desert and gave them water as abundant as the seas. . . . But they continued to sin against him rebelling in the desert against the Most High. They wilfully put God to the test by demanding the food they craved.
>
> vv. 13–18 NIV

. . . and his wrath rose against Israel, for they did not believe in God or trust in his deliverance.

vv. 21–22 NIV

Was I full of doubts and questions and criticism like the Israelites? Yes, I had to admit I was. How can I be free of this, Lord?

These words of reassurance came:

'Thou art my beloved child, Catherine. Rest in that love. . . . Simply rest in it. Bathe in it. Stop asking so many questions. Stop all this probing, taking your spiritual temperature. Does the Lord want me to do this? Or that? Is this right? Is that right? This is the source of the confusion you are feeling.

'You *are* My child, My disciple. I accepted you long ago – *as you are* – as you are growing.

'You are *still* accepted. Nothing is between us from My side, only yours! Grasp that by faith and all else will follow.

'The nervous probing is Satan's doing, to unsettle you, to confuse you, to knock you off the base of your belief.

'Let My joy flow through you unimpeded, even though you do not feel it at first. *Let it flow. Be not afraid.* That joy will sweep away your fear and uncertainties.

'Stop accusing yourself, Catherine. Turn any such thoughts over to Me instantly. They come from Satan, not from Me.

'Place yourself in My hands as though you were an infant. Let *Me* handle your questions, the tattered remnants of your unbelief, your growth in My *grace* – not My stringency.

'Grace . . . grace . . . grace. Love . . . love . . . love. I came *not* to judge or to condemn. *All* accusation comes from the enemy.

'Open the floodgates that My love can bathe you and that the living water may flow through you to others.'

4

Free from Bondage

Sarah, a woman in our Tuesday night group at church, told us the following experience.

For years she had been struggling to quit smoking. She would get down to two packs a week, then back up to three, endlessly defeated. Her conscience hurt her about the grip that cigarettes had on her.

Sarah sat on the front row the night Len did a Bible study on how the Holy Spirit can free us from any habit that binds us and keeps us from a close relationship to Jesus. The Scripture he focused on:

> For if you live according to the sinful nature, you will die; but if by the Spirit you put to death the misdeeds of the body, you will live, because those who are led by the Spirit of God are sons of God.
>
> Romans 8:13–14 NIV

In his talk, Len included alcohol, drugs, cigarettes, food, and sex as pitfalls for the compulsive personality. Sarah told us later that she began to associate Len with her cigarette struggle.

One night Sarah had a short, vivid dream in which Len was present. Then she saw a hand with a lighted cigarette between the fingers. The fingers began vigorously and repeatedly tamping out the cigarette. With that the dream ended.

When Sarah awoke the next morning she pondered whether the meaning of the dream could be as obvious as it seemed. Scarcely thinking, she reached for her package of cigarettes. There was a single cigarette left. She lighted it, but it tasted different, not at all good. She tamped it out and has had no desire to smoke since. Her tastes, her desire-world itself, had been transformed by the Spirit.

Later Len and I shared with the group the following steps we use in praying for someone in the grip of addiction:

1. In the name of Jesus move against the powers of darkness that have attached themselves to R—'s mind and will.

2. With Christ's authority, drive these forces back a day at a time. Persist. No matter how long it takes; refuse to be discouraged.

3. Once you have captured any piece of ground in R—'s mind from the enemy, occupy it with a declaration of faith, telling Satan he cannot return.

4. When R— has been released from an addiction, pray for his salvation and his infilling by the Holy Spirit.

We also suggested that anyone who, like Sarah, has been released from addiction, hold onto the following verse:

Stand fast therefore in the liberty wherewith Christ hath made us free, and be not entangled again with the yoke of bondage.

Galatians 5:1 KJV

5

Satan's Best Weapon

There is an oft-repeated story about the time Satan gathered his co-workers together for a strategy session. The purpose: find more effective ways to tempt Christians into sin.

One evil spirit said, 'Let's set before them the delights of sin.'

Satan shook his head. 'That works up to a point, but not with the strong believers.'

Another incubus suggested, 'We can show them that virtue is costly.'

Satan again shook his head. 'They know that the rewards are worth it.'

The third little demon had a knowing look in his eye. 'Let's bring discouragement to their souls.'

'Now you have it!' cried Satan. 'Discouragement is the weapon!'

How true it is! Right now I am worn down by lack of sleep. I thought I had won a victory over sleeplessness and dependence on sleeping pills six years ago. But lately I've been in the pit of despair. Nor has going back to a mild sleeping pill helped.

This morning I want to put on paper what it is like to try and sleep. I go to bed fatigued, yet am not able to let go. The sleep mechanism of the frontal lobe of my brain is apparently all askew. It's as if the stay-alert function is working overtime – night and day. Even at moments when, out of total weariness, I am about to drop off, the brain sends the message, 'Wake up!' and I jerk to.

There is a constant tiredness behind my eyes, lids are

heavy as if pressing the eyes back into the head.

I cannot find any comfortable position in bed. Make elaborate arrangements with pillows and sheet, but no sooner settled than I am moving again. What to do with the arms to keep them from aching? How to place my neck?

My face itches and I must scratch. There's a cramp in one leg and I flex and unflex my toes. The sheet is scratching my chin. Right arm is hot. Finally, I tumble to the fact that there can be no sleep until I lie perfectly still for a while. Yet it's agony to force myself to do so.

The nights seem endless. How can they be so long?

When I do – toward dawn – drop off, the 'sleep start' wakens me abruptly. A muscle in a leg gives a sudden jerk.

I have come to hate the bed, yet am drawn to it, always hopeful. Isn't it man's *natural* state to sleep? Lord, I'm exhausted and discouraged.

So many times discouragement has been the doorway through which the powers of evil have flooded into my situation. For discouragement says, 'My problem is bigger than God, who is not adequate to handle my particular need. So herewith I take my eyes off God, bow down before my problem, and give myself to it.'

In digging through Scripture on this subject, I have discovered that no matter how difficult the situation, Jesus' attitude was always a calm, 'Courage, My son, My daughter. Have no fear. There is nothing here that My Father cannot handle.'

It was not that Jesus minimised the problem, but rather that His faith was a magnet for God's power. He knew that *no* problem was any match for the Lord God Almighty.

I confess now that I am discouraged because I have been relying on myself rather than on You, Lord; I have expected something from myself and am deeply disappointed not to find it there. I want to think that I can handle things myself . . . succeed better . . . do more than others.

In *The Practice of the Presence of God*, Brother Lawrence writes that he was never upset when he had failed in some duty. He simply confessed his fault, saying to God, 'I shall never do otherwise, if You leave me to myself; it is You who must hinder my failing and mend what is amiss.' After this admission, he gave himself no further uneasiness about it.

What the devil wants us to do, of course, is to focus on our failure rather than on Jesus. For when we keep our eyes on Him, we find that no problem – of the 1st century or the 20th – has ever defeated Him.

Jesus never encountered a human situation that discouraged Him. Sickness and disease? Jesus healed a man blind from birth . . . a woman who'd had an issue of blood for twelve years . . . another bent double with arthritis for eighteen years. At not one of these cases did Jesus look with despairing heart.

Did sin get Him down? Never, no matter how heinous. Jesus insisted that He had come into the world not to condemn us, but to save us (John 8:15; 12:47). His attitude was that any time spent in condemnation, in wallowing in old sins and regrets, in recriminations, in kicking ourselves around, is wasted time.

The woman taken in adultery, He forgave and restored – immediately.

Zaccheus had spent a lifetime in greed and grasping. Yet Jesus told him, '*This* day has salvation come to thy house.'

Jesus' word in any situation was one of encouragement:

To the paralytic borne by four: 'Courage, My son!'

To the ruler of the synagogue whose daughter was dying: 'Have no fear, only believe and she shall get well.'

To Martha, grieving over her dead brother: 'Said I not unto thee, that if thou wouldst believe, thou shouldst see the glory of God?'

Hear that, Satan? In the name of Jesus, I kick you and discouragement out of my life.

6

The Other Side of the Mountain

Yesterday David Hill from Dallas telephoned and was on for forty-five minutes. David has had an escape from some sort of cult. He is unmarried, thirty-two or thirty-three, and has been a Christian for eight years. *What* a mature Christian he is for an eight-year-old!

He has had quite a bit of experience with spiritual warfare, and one of the helpful facts he gave me is that when we're engaged in these battles energy is sapped from us and we are *very* prone to depression. *Exactly* my state for the last two months!

He also painted a very vivid picture of Genesis 22. As Abraham and Isaac were toiling up Mount Moriah, Satan must have been tempting Abraham every few minutes. 'Surely you did not hear God correctly! Sacrifice your son and heir? Why should you do such an evil thing? Why, Isaac was God's special gift to you in your wife's old age. You're probably just getting senile, etc., etc.'

But at *that very moment* that Abraham was struggling with his thoughts, the ram was travelling up the *other* side of the Mount, and God was preparing the way of escape.

David's message was, God always is working on the 'ram part' – the escape, God's own way out.

Knowing the Enemy

How much better we will withstand Satan's assaults when we're wise to his tactics! Thus, these past few days I've been searching the Bible for insights as to the forces – within and without – arrayed against us.

The Serpent's Strategy:
First of all the serpent's objective was to call God a liar, to contradict His Word, to tell Eve – and us – 'His Word is not so.' It was because Eve believed the serpent as over against God that the Fall came (Genesis 3:2–4).

The serpent's second strategy was to tell Eve, in effect, 'God is out to take away or withhold something good from you.'

The third trick was to tempt the woman into letting the forbidden fruit play upon her senses. She put herself in the way of the temptation, walked around it, looked at it, toyed with it (Genesis 3:6).

Three curve balls – and Eve struck out.

The Immediate Results of her sin:
1. Eve wanted fellowship in her disobedience. She felt at once the sense of isolation that sin brings. Inevitably when we do wrong we want to drag other people down with us. So Eve gave the fruit to Adam to eat (v. 6).
2. Innocence was gone. Both the man and the woman knew they were naked.
3. They had no desire for fellowship with God; ran from Him; in fact, hid themselves from Him (Genesis 3:8).

4. They knew fear (v. 10).
5. They knew shame (vv. 7–10).
6. Each blamed his sin on someone else:
   Adam – on Eve (v. 12).
   Eve – on the serpent (v. 13).

The Far-reaching Results:
1. Woman is reduced to a subordinate position to man.

2. In sorrow and pain and difficulty will the reproduction process take place. Moreover, woman will be something of a slave to her sexual desire for her husband (v. 16).

3. Man shall till the ground, which will be stubborn in producing for him. He will get food by the sweat of his brow (vv. 17–19).

4. Death enters life – 'To dust thou shalt return' (v. 19).

5. Adam and Eve begin to wear clothing, symbol of perpetual loss of innocence (v. 21).

6. They are driven from the Garden and the Tree of Life (vv. 23–24).

How seriously did Jesus take demons?
Apparently very seriously indeed. When He sent the first group of disciples on the first mission, His charge to them was:

First: Preaching
Second: Casting out demons (Mark 3:14–15).
The demons always seemed to have recognised:
1. *Who Jesus was* (Mark 1:24, 34; 3:11; 5:7).
2. *That Jesus was against them all the way.*
3. *That they had to obey Him* (Mark 1:25–28, 5:12–13).

Jesus' dealing with demons:
1. He rebuked them (Mark 1:25).
2. He then gave them a direct order (Mark 1:25, 5:8).
3. He charged them not to reveal who He was (Mark 3:12).

The result for the possessed individual:
1. He is often buffeted and thrown about (Mark 1:26).
2. But the demon obeys Jesus and departs (Mark 1:26).

These further insights have come as I pondered Satan's inroads into my own heart and will:

1. When we rejoice over, or look for, or repeat with relish negative news, then we have placed ourselves on the side of evil.

2. It is possible to take this negative stance so often with regard to situations and persons that this becomes a way of life. Negative thinking is really a weapon of Satan. *We* call it 'realism'; Christ calls it 'not believing the truth'.

3. We do not realise how definitely our mind-set – that is, what the mind picks out from all the news to highlight – reveals *whose* side we're really on.

4. Even after we have accepted Jesus and asked Him to come and live within us, Satan will keep trying to persuade us that the flesh is dominant and must be obeyed. Satan will also feed us the lie that 'that's human nature' and there's nothing we can do about it.

5. The response to Satan's attacks had to be *faith*. When I became Jesus' woman, a series of marvellous things happened – whether the effects are visible yet or not. Among them, as I accepted the atoning work of Jesus for me, I was unshackled on the inside from my bondage to the flesh, freed from the ascendancy of flesh over spirit (Romans 8:2). Paul says that when we accept this wonderful liberation by faith, and begin to live it out, we find that the flesh now *has* to obey the spirit, that Satan has been subdued, overcome, deprived of his power (Romans 8:3). Realising this, we need only allow the Holy Spirit to lead the way, step by step, obedient act by obedient act, like a conquering General victoriously marching ahead (Romans 8:9–16).

8

Offensive Warfare

Yesterday I read a pamphlet by Ralph Mahoney, editor of *World Map Digest*, who makes the following powerful points about spiritual warfare:

1. 'On this rock I will build my church, and the gates of hell will not overcome it' (Matthew 16:18 NIV).

Now, gates are stationary. *They* are fixed in place, stay put. Therefore, the 'gates of hell' cannot move against us. So Jesus has to mean that His Church is to take the offensive against the citadel of Satan.

The picture (according to Mahoney) is of a victorious Church laying siege to hell and breaking down the gates to release its prisoners.

2. 'That enemy of yours, the devil, roams around like a lion roaring [in fierce hunger], seeking someone to seize upon and devour' (1 Peter 5:8 AMPLIFIED). Peter did not write those words to scare us to death, says Mahoney. For the key word is *like* the lion. Satan is always an imitator, a fake, a bluff, a counterfeit. He *isn't* a lion. His claws were drawn out at Calvary.

3. The real Lion is Jesus, 'the Lion of the tribe of Judah' (Revelation 5:5 AMPLIFIED). We Christians have no strength or ability in ourselves for fighting Satan, or for pulling down gates, or anything else.

But as we allow the Lion of Judah to live in us, we take on the nature of Him who is the real Lion. Our weapons – fickle and weak of themselves – pass through God and become mighty enough to make hell itself tremble with fear.

9

Conversations with God

LL Note: As she learned more and more about confronting Satan with his lies and deceit, rebuking him daily, and seeking to hear the voice of the Lord, the answers from Him became clearer and clearer. Here are excerpts from Catherine's 1981 journal:

'Lord, I need Your help in so many areas. How can I better hear Your voice?'

You need to begin listening in the absolute quiet as you did during that summer long ago on Cape Cod. Remember how you lay on the daybed in the living room, pen and notebook in hand, in absolute stillness? I spoke to you then — and will again.

A morning Quiet Time should be that — not simply reading in this book or that. What I, your Lord, have to say to you is more important than the best wisdom of any author.

'Lord, my novel goes so slowly. The words I put on paper seem so wooden. I need Your Help.'

I am glad you have asked Me to be your editor. Turn to Me each time you begin writing for specific directions. If you want real creativity, follow My inner directives.

Now, start reading 2 Corinthians and I'll have more to say to you.

'Lord, I wince at 2 Corinthians 2:9: obedience in all things. How do I achieve that? I feel like such a failure in that area.'

Child — you always take life too seriously — with too heavy a spirit, too anxious a mien. A true child of Mine has no need to worry so. You act as if you think you have to do everything yourself, as if I, your Burden Bearer, am not with you at all Do you really think that honours Me?

Do you not see the egotism in all this? Satan has gotten a toehold in this attitude-area in you, and you have failed to recognise it so that you can deal with it. He is the one who wants you burdened down, fatigued, feeling overwhelmed with work.

'Lord, what a gorgeous revelation! Thank You, thank You. . . . But how do I kick the old boy out and let You turn these wrong attitudes around?'

By recognising Satan's lies. For example, he wants you to think that your everyday life is monotonous and dull. The very opposite is true. Satan's aim is always to turn your eyes to the world. That's not for you. Even during that brief period in Washington when you thought you were making a little progress into Washington social life, it wasn't for you and would have garnered you husks had you achieved it. Forget it! Permanently! Your life is fascinating, with pleasant surprises every day. Praise Me for the richness of the life I have given you.

Each time you feel a negative attitude building up inside yourself, refuse to accept it. Recognise the satanic source of it, reject it, and turn to Me.

'Lord, there are doubts in me this morning. I admit it. Doubts that what I am writing down here is really You speaking and not just my wishful thinking or what I think You would say. How can I be sure?'

Proof in the world of the spirit never comes in the same way as in the material world. Don't try to transfer the techniques of what you call 'evidence' from the one realm to the other.

Trust the Holy Spirit to be the link between us, to speak My words, transfer them to you – and He will. Was there not a sureness and a joy and a knowledge of My benediction on you yesterday that you have not known in a long time?

'Yes, there was, Lord. But there are so many things I want and need to talk over with You that it's going to take all eternity to do it.'

Your endless curiosity, which at its best is real seeking, is from Me. Don't fight it. Those who seek Me, do find. Remem-

ber? 'The poor in spirit'. . . . *Always I am ready to receive any question. I bless you and love you beyond comprehension.*

'Lord, I know that discouragement is from Satan, that I have no business being discouraged under any circumstances. But I am troubled about my novel. I don't feel I can finish it. How do I keep from giving into those down feelings?'

Patience, Catherine, patience. Don't be dismayed. What's happening to you is only a ripple, a little wave on a big sea. This too will pass. The hostages do come home. The prodigal does return. Joy cometh in the morning.

Take a deep breath, look to Me, and be glad. Smile again. The sky has not fallen in.

In other words, keep at it.

'Thank You, Lord. And thank You that the Spirit gave me this verse from Psalm 31 yesterday: "My times are in Your hand" (v. 15 AMPLIFIED).'

'Lord, what I read in Tournier's *The Healing of Persons* is exciting to me because I have long sought the answer to the problem of "scruples", of why I am the sort of person who is always finding some one little thing wrong in my life that I am convinced stands between me and You. I feel very guilty about having to go back to sleeping pills, even though they are the mildest available. So, Lord, the question I ask today: Am I exaggerating a minor problem, my scruple of the moment – sleeping pills – in order not to have to face up to something much more important that You really want me to look at?'

Do you not see that your love of sleep and your desire to escape into sleep is, in large part – and always has been – because you are reluctant to give more of yourself in love for others?

'What a revelation, Lord! But how do I go about letting You change something as ingrained in me as this? It would be asking You to change a lifelong habit pattern. Also, I'd be afraid that going the people route really would knock out my writing.'

I told you that My yoke is easy and My burden is light, didn't I? My burden was and is and always has been love of people, love of you, Catherine. You've never believed Me that this burden is light. You'll find that this is so only as you allow Me to take you by the hand and lead you out. Are you willing?

'Yes, Lord.'

'Lord, are there other sins You want me to look at, which I have perhaps avoided facing up to, by the smoke screen of small "scruples"? What I long for is that love of You, and the realisation of Your love for me, become the motivating factor in my obedience.'

Ah, if only you knew how much I love you! If only you knew what love surrounds you from the 'cloud of witnesses' here with Me – your father, your brother, and Peter. If only you knew how many prayers are constantly flowing for you. How grateful you should be for the waves of good will flowing to you constantly from those who read your books.

Relax into My love. Allow Me to love you. There are times when a mother wants to hold her child. No words need pass between them, just the feel of love. This morning let Me love you like that. Let all spiritual strain and tension go. Relax in Me.

'How beautiful, Lord. I do!'

'Lord, is there any particular word You want to speak to me this morning?'

Your life has been unbalanced, Catherine, hence your boredom. You need to cook, to garden, to shop, to exercise more, to be with people more. The more you retreat into the idea-world away from people, the more unreal your Christianity and your relationship with Me will become – even though in such retreat you might think that you were being more spiritual.

'I had almost no sleep last night, Lord. This morning I am full of fears again.'

Read the 91st Psalm, Catherine, and absorb it into your bone and marrow and bloodstream and mind and heart and spirit.

I will deliver Catherine. . . .

I will set her on high because she knows and understands My name, has a personal knowledge of My mercy, My love, My kindness. You, Catherine, are to trust and rely on Me, knowing that I will never forsake you.

You, Catherine, will call upon Me, and I will answer you; I will be with you in trouble, I will deliver you and honour you.

One fearful of the water can never get over the fear by standing on the bank shivering, consumed by the fear. . . .

I will not force one to do anything. . . .

Take the first step toward Me. Trust My love for you. Trust . . . trust!

Section Six

The Final Victory

Early in 1982 Catherine realised her time on earth was limited. The emphysema in her lungs had been slowly reducing her vitality. Walking up a flight of stairs was a major undertaking. Talking to people, meetings, shopping drained her.

Saddest of all to see was how her growing breathlessness affected her mornings, the cream time for manuscript work she looked forward to so much. I would watch her go resolutely into her office at 9:00 A.M. Forty minutes later I would hear her return to our bedroom. Once I confronted her there as she lay listlessly on the bed.

Tears welled up in her eyes. 'I try to concentrate,' she said. 'The inner drive is gone. I don't have it anymore.'

Then she would rail at herself for being a quitter, get up, and try again. My dilemma was: Should I prod her into doing what was painful and hard, or let her drift into invalidism?

The answer soon became clear. Catherine's basic competitiveness, her battling nature, her spirit of adventure, and her curiosity about life could not, should not be allowed to die. Catherine would never have forgiven me if I had encouraged her to let go of all this.

So we waged spiritual war against the forces of darkness and the enemy's subtle enticements to give in to weakness. The coffee-pot alarm continued to be set for 6:30 A.M. The day began with an hour of Scripture reading, prayer, and journal entries. During the morning, work continued on the novel Julie. Commitments to our prayer and fellowship groups were kept. We ended the day in prayer, when I anointed Catherine with oil, taking a stand against ill health, asking for sharpness of thinking and a healing of body and spirit.

LL

1

His Unfinished Work in Me

Dreamed last night about death. I don't relish putting this one on paper, but since it *has* to be worked through with the Lord, I suppose I must.

I was in a country where certain citizens were being exterminated by order of the state. One got one's notice and came to a special 'office' in which were three booths, side by side. In one of these you were given a shot, like a dog being 'put to sleep'. Afterwards you were carted off to a back room where the bodies were stacked.

Apparently my number had come up. When I got to the office, I noticed that there were stacks and stacks of dirty dishes in the three booths. I sought to stall my death by offering eagerly to wash all the dishes. The attendant said, 'Sure, go ahead. I don't blame you. Just don't tell any of the others that I agreed.'

I started to wash a stack of plates, saying to myself, 'There's always the chance of something happening to intervene, a national emergency or something.' Then I woke up.

So now that I have put this dream on paper, Lord, what does it mean – and what do I do about it?

As I waited for some response, a name came to mind – *John Wesley*. Tuttle's book on Wesley was in the stack of unread books on my night table. I picked it up and soon discovered that Wesley and I shared a dread of death as the Great Enemy. Wesley's fear surfaced dramatically in 1735 during a crossing of the Atlantic to Georgia. There were heavy storms at sea and the small wooden ship at times seemed doomed. Most on board, including the crew, were terror-struck. The only ones who remained calm were a group of German Moravian Christians.

Seeing the strength of these Christians as they faced death, Wesley knew he must work through his problem. In reviewing his walk of faith, he realised he had espoused a life of *asceticism*, which took four forms:

1. Self-denial. (He lived frugally in order to give money to the poor.)
2. Solitude.
3. Works of charity. (Including visits to the terrible prisons of the time where he prayed with condemned men.)
4. Interior life as exemplified by the great mystics.

Now Wesley had to admit that while each of these disciplines had a place in Christian life, not one of them dealt with his fear of death. Finally he began to see that this fear was not from God, as the mystics maintained, but from Satan.

Soon after these discoveries John Wesley had his personal experience of the Holy Spirit at Aldersgate. He was back against the basic New Testament proposition: There is no road to God except via faith in the finished work of Jesus Christ on the Cross. Joy flooded in and gradually his fear of death dropped away as the totality of these triumphant words of Jesus sank into his being:

In My Father's house there are many dwelling places (homes). If it were not so, I would have told you, for I am going away to prepare a place for you.

And when (if) I go and make ready a place for you, I will come back again and will take you to Myself, that where I am you may be also.

John 14:2–3 AMPLIFIED

I know that the Holy Spirit has much unfinished work to do inside me about my attitude toward death. I need this, and I will myself to desire it.

2

Our Servant Role

I was the recipient of a beautiful and touching act last night that reverberates through my prayer time this morning. Myra Gertz, a friend and member of our church fellowship group, asked if she could drop in for a short visit.

As we talked I could see that she had something on her mind and was struggling how to say it. Finally she did.

'Catherine, I feel a bit foolish, but the Lord told me to come over and wash your feet. I don't know what this is all about and I've never done this before, but the Voice was very emphatic.'

I was startled. My inner reaction was, *Oh, no! Surely, this is not necessary.* But our group had been learning to respect these nudges from the Spirit. 'We certainly want to obey the Lord, Myra,' I agreed.

Soon she was on the floor in front of me with towels and a basin of water. She removed my stockings and shoes and gently began washing my feet.

Tears filled my eyes as I felt the presence of the Lord through Myra. He had instigated this, just as He had done with His disciples two thousand years ago.

I was the needy one all right. My fatigue level had never been lower.

'Catherine, the Lord wants you to know He loves you deeply,' Myra said as she finished drying my feet. 'May I pray for you now?'

'Of course.'

She did, asking for a healing in every part of me –

mind, spirit, emotions, and body. A deep feeling of peace spread over me. 'Thank you for being faithful, Myra,' I said as she left.

This morning I read through the Scripture account of this act by Jesus in the New Testament book of John:

> When he had finished washing their feet, (Jesus) put on his clothes and returned to his place. 'Do you understand what I have done for you?' he asked them.
>
> 'You call me "Teacher" and "Lord", and rightly so, for that is what I am. Now that I, your Lord and Teacher, have washed your feet, you also should wash one another's feet. I have set you an example that you should do as I have done for you. I tell you the truth, no servant is greater than his master, nor is a messenger greater than the one who sent him. Now that you know these things, you will be blessed if you do them.'
>
> John 13:12–17 NIV

I have set you an example that you should do as I have done for you. . . . Myra had been obedient to this instruction of Jesus, although I can imagine what she went through, wondering if it would seem over-emotional to me.

And it did, at first. But how I needed it. I was hurting. Jesus knew this, wanted to demonstrate His love for me and chose Myra as His vessel. If she had not been faithful, a beautiful inner healing experience would not have happened.

Body Language

> I beseech you therefore, brethren . . . that ye present
> your bodies a living sacrifice, holy, acceptable unto
> God, which is your reasonable service.
>
> Romans 12:1 KJV

Reading the Bible yesterday afternoon, I felt an inner
nudge to stop and reread this verse. I was conscious that I
resisted this idea of offering my body as a sacrifice. Why?
Because I suspected it could mean more speaking and
travelling, more stress and pressure, with consequent
loss of sleep at night, and no chance to recoup with
daytime naps.

What is so bad about this is that I'm not really trusting
the Lord with my physical body – and that's an awful
confession. God expects his followers to be willing to be
expendable; I've been circling around this point of total
trust in a kind of spiritual holding pattern, unwilling to
lay down my body as 'a living sacrifice'. I'm constantly
protecting myself, succumbing too quickly to the temptation to stop my work and lie down for a while.

The conviction then came that I must be willing – and
tell God so – to have the self with which I was born, the
particular bundle of talents, predispositions, preferences, tastes – all that constitutes me – nailed to the Cross
with Jesus, actually die and be buried with Him.

But, a voice inside me argued, *didn't I do just this when I
became a Christian?* Jesus assured me, however, that this
was a new step of dying to the self that so loves body

comforts and beautiful things, that longs to escape the demands and entanglements of other people.

Much of that self *I dislike* (Romans 7:15–25). But a lot of what constitutes 'me' I like very much. I've been 'me', and lived with 'me', and put up with 'me' a long time. To lay this self on the altar would indeed be a death.

I remembered Jesus' words about 'counting the cost' (Luke 14:28). Was I really willing to take myself to the Cross, die and be buried – not having any idea what sort of person would rise with Jesus on the third day?

I went through agony thinking about this, with a lot of tears.

Scripture says that Jesus resolutely and willingly turned His face to the Cross for 'the joy that was set before Him' (Hebrews 12:2).

I finally told Jesus that I was going forward with this because I knew He *was* going to have His way with me, now or in the next life.

I got down on my knees in my office by the daybed at 4:40 P.M. and offered up my body to Him as a living sacrifice.

As a result, I must now be obedient hour by hour, day by day, and *not* hold back. This means seeing the indwelling Spirit so residing in my mortal flesh that I am willing to spend myself totally for others, as He did. It means letting *all* self go – everything in my desire world – whenever it cuts across His higher priorities.

No wonder we can do no mighty works until the surrender is this complete. Until Jesus has been allowed to come and make His home in me like *that*, I will be praying for others, doing His work, in *my* name and in *my* nature rather than in His.

The apostle John puts it this way:

He laid down His [own] life for us; and we ought to lay [our] lives down for [those who are our] brothers in [Him].

1 John 3:16 AMPLIFIED

LL Note: Six months of creativity followed during which Catherine made an important breakthrough with her novel Julie, ministered to several in our prayer group, made several speeches. The two of us drove together from Florida to our farm in Virginia for a month, then flew back to Florida to continue work on her novel.

4

Self-pity

This morning I took to the Lord a matter that has troubled me for the past two years or so. Sudden tears. I've never been a person who cries often. I generally keep my emotions in check, perhaps more than I should. Recently though, bouts of unpredictable weeping.

The Lord has graciously shown me this morning the why of tears being just under the surface of these past weeks – *self-pity*. In reality, I am weeping for myself.

I weep because of what is happening to me physically. First, my energy level has again dropped to such a degree that it is literally a chore to put one foot before the other. Added to that, worse breathlessness than I've ever known. Sometimes even sitting or lying in bed, I wonder if I'm going to be able to take the next breath. This makes the stairs and hills at Evergreen Farm an agony.

Most puzzling, after years of battling sleeplessness, suddenly I can hardly stay awake. I must check out with the doctor whether this is an overreaction to the new arthritis drug they are giving me.

Or is it possible that, through lack of oxygen to the brain, I am coming into early senility? Hideous thought! For the first time since early girlhood I have no desire to read at night. During church yesterday, I could scarcely keep my eyes open.

Lord, help!

I am led to this verse:

. . . I know . . . Whom I have believed . . . and I am [positively] persuaded that He is able to guard and keep that which has been entrusted to me and which I have committed [to Him] until that day.

2 Timothy 1:12 AMPLIFIED

Since self-pity is a sin, then clearly it has to be dealt with as a sin. A sin because since I belong to Jesus, it is He who has control over my life. Thus He overrules everything that He 'allows' to happen to me – overrules it for *good*.

My part is to trust Him as a loving Heavenly Father in each of these adverse circumstances. I am to watch expectantly for the 'good' . . . the new adventure He has for me . . . the open door I am to go through toward the better way to which He is leading me.

So, given all that, what is there to have self-pity about?

I see that there is a self-discipline to practise during the days ahead: Each time I am tempted toward despairing self-pity, I am to rebuke it, reject it, and turn immediately to praise.

5

Crisis Time

On July 9, 1982, Catherine was so weak that we had her taken by ambulance to Bethesda Memorial Hospital in Boynton Beach, Florida. Tests showed an alarming carbon dioxide content in her body because of shallow breathing, and she was placed in the Intensive Care Unit. Respirator tubes led through her mouth to her lungs; she was fed through an IV tube in her nose. Machines handled all her body functions. Family members could visit her for no more than fifteen-minute periods three times a day.

Because the tubes in her mouth and nose made it hard to wear glasses, she found it difficult to read the small print of her Bible. A grey 10 by 7-inch notebook that she had filled over the years with Bible promises (see p. 202) in large handwriting became her spiritual lifeline.

The prognosis for her recovery was not good. Doctors could offer no hope that her breathing capacity would improve enough for her to be taken off the respirator. It appeared that Catherine's last days would be spent in the Intensive Care Unit, unable to speak, communicating only through a note pad. Here is a sample of her scribbled comments as the painful weeks passed:

I never knew how frustrating it can be not to be able to speak a word.

I can only move my head about six inches because of that tube in my nose. Lying all night in that one position is torture.

Each little thing is so difficult. It's tough to be getting weaker and weaker and thinner and thinner.

The progress from day to day depends on the blood gases test they take . . . they're running out of places on my arms to draw blood, I bruise so easily.

Remember those old-fashioned cardboard fans people used in church? See if you can find one at home. It gets so hot here at night.

This has been a lonely day. Shifting personnel each with little knowledge of my situation. Sense some are hostile toward Christians. Wish I was a better witness to them for Jesus.

I'm taking twice as many breaths per minute as I should. How do I retrain my body?

I feel that something has to give today. I'm so miserable that I don't see how I can take much more.

It seemed that the Lord was promising me last night that Romans 8:28 would be fulfilled and that I was to begin praising Him. 'I believe. Help my unbelief.'

Had a crisis with the IV. They spent two hours trying to get it to work. When I began praying they found the answer.

Prayed about my dread of nights. Discovered why I can't really relax. I'm a chronic thinker and a 'what-if-er'. Prayed to change.

Imagine, four weeks without a shampoo! I dare not look in the mirror. Will be horrified.

Last night the simple thought, 'Be still and know that I am God,' pulled me through.

On July 24 at 7:30 A.M., my telephone rang: a male nurse reported that Catherine wanted to see me right away. 'Don't be alarmed,' he said. 'It's not a medical emergency. Your wife has something to tell you that she feels is important.'

I awoke Peter and Jeff (the family members then on hand) and we drove immediately to the hospital. Catherine greeted us with great excitement in her eyes and reported through written notes that during the night she had felt the Lord's presence there in her Intensive Care cubicle! With His presence came the assurance that she was being healed.

Confirmation came in the next blood tests, which showed a definite decrease in the carbon dioxide content in her body. Day by day the improvement continued. Just as doctors had been unable to explain Catherine's sudden loss of breathing capacity, so too were they baffled when it returned. One doctor said it had to be the power of prayer.

One by one the tubes came out. The ventilator was wheeled away. On August 11, Catherine was moved out of the Intensive Care Unit; she had been there thirty-two days. Nine days later, on August 20, a rejoicing husband brought her home.

Catherine had been through a dehumanising process in Intensive Care and had lost twenty-five pounds. The recuperation was agonisingly slow as members of the family took turns coming to Florida to help her recover. Meanwhile, Catherine resumed her journal entries.

LL

Crucified with Jesus

In many ways my thirty-two-day stint in the Intensive Care Unit of Bethesda Hospital was a crucifixion experience. Soon after I arrived there, the Lord reminded me of the act I had performed (through Romans 12:1) of offering forever my defective body, along with all my faculties, as a living sacrifice on His Cross.

While lying on my back, hour after hour, unable to read or talk, I had plenty of time to reflect on the study I did awhile ago on the 'Humanity of Jesus'. Through it I saw that His humanness for thirty-three years on earth was *real*; that He was as helpless, as 'out of control' of circumstances, as we are. All this was in order for Him to be the Wayshower, the true and very practical Captain of our salvation.

I also perceived that during this earthly walk, *the* guiding principle of Jesus' life was 'what pleases My Father in heaven, never what *I* want to do.'

In the intervening months since I made this study, several things have been happening: (1) the Holy Spirit has been doing a steady softening and melting process within me. This has meant that the plights of other persons presented to me, mostly through correspondence, have been laid on my heart with a new urgency; (2) During this same period my own circumstances have not only been taken out of my control, but also have gone in directions contrary to anything *I* would wish.

At what point in the Christian walk are we *actually*

'crucified with Him'? At what point is the mortal self dead on His Cross and buried with Him?

In my case, I concluded, dying to self has been going on for some time. For me it has been a slow, torturous, lingering death indeed – no doubt because I have been resisting all the way. I'm reasonably sure that it need not be this drawn out and this painful, if the believer really understands what is going on and why, and assents to it in his will. Yet I do think it's something we have to walk through all the way and *feel*. Death on a Cross hurts.

Early the morning of July 24 (fifteen days after entering the hospital) the climax came for me. I was in a semi-conscious, dreaming state when I felt myself literally hanging on the Cross with Jesus. There was no pain from the nails in my hands or feet; only a suffocating, crushing weight on my chest as my entire body dragged downwards. I knew I was close to death, but strangely there was absolutely no fear.

As the weight on the rib cage grew unendurable, however, I was aware of a dark presence, as well as that of Jesus. A fierce struggle with some evil force ensued. Again and again I rebuked the dark power and ordered him to be gone. He didn't leave easily, but leave he did at last.

Then – so gently – Jesus picked me up and removed me from the Cross. As He did so, three words came to me: 'The Great Exchange.' Later I realised this is what theologians call 'the substitutionary atonement', meaning that every sinful thing in our lives was dealt with in Christ's finished work on His Cross. At the moment I knew only that the crushing weight had lifted from my ribs.

I awoke the next morning very excited, feeling that a miracle had taken place in my body. This is the note saved by Len I wrote to the nurse:

Please grant me this one request! I want to see my family, now! My husband first. Please call him. 732-6352.

My husband, my son Peter, my son Jeffrey. I want all of them. I want no medication before they get here. I'll 'calm down' to suit you.

When Len, Peter, and Jeffrey arrived, through notes I told them about my death, that at one point in my struggle with that dark force, it seemed my body parts were burnt up and lying in pieces around the room. The turning point came when way down deep I cried, 'Jesus! Lord. My Lord.' And He came and was with me. And He healed me.

My family was very responsive, but I think they wondered if it was an hallucination brought on by low oxygen levels in the brain. The key would be the next blood gases test.

When the doctor arrived at my bedside the next day, he was all smiles. 'The carbon dioxide is way down!' he reported. And then we all celebrated!

What transpired on the Cross two thousand years ago has taken on sparkling new meaning for me. We are accustomed to thinking that Jesus carried only our sins on the Cross, but Scripture makes it equally clear that He bore all our sicknesses and diseases there too. . . .

When evening came, they brought to Him (Jesus) many who were under the power of demons, and He drove out the spirits with a word, and restored to health all who were sick; And thus He fulfilled what was spoken by the prophet Isaiah, He Himself took our weaknesses and infirmities and bore away our diseases.

Matthew 8:16–17 (Isaiah 53:4) AMPLIFIED

Len asked me the other night what I considered the chief significance of my crucifixion experience.

'I'm not sure yet,' I replied. 'I was close to death and the Lord returned me to life. He must have had a reason.'

'Do you know what that might be?'

'There are a number of things I'm supposed to do. Finish my novel was one. Even more important: work on some bruised relationships.' Then it struck me. 'I've had a crucifixion, but not a resurrection.'

Len wouldn't accept this. 'You emerged from a dark valley into the light. Wasn't that a resurrection?'

'Not entirely. My breathing was restored to what it was last spring, but that's far from normal. My lungs have still not been completely healed.'

'Consider this, Catherine,' Len replied. 'You've operated with little more than half your normal lung power for almost forty years. But look at all you've accomplished. Maybe, like Paul, God's given you a thorn in the flesh for a reason.'

Lord, how much more I have to learn!

7

Doing Grief Work

How grateful I am for Robert Bonham's[1] visits during my recuperation! What a sensitive counsellor and friend! His gifts of wisdom and discernment are balm to my spirit.

After I told him how discouraged I am over the slowness of my recovery and the suspicion that my voice may be permanently damaged, it came out last week that Bob feels I am doing *grief* work.

The minute he spoke the word 'grief', it rang a bell within me. He said that whenever we encounter a major shift or change in life, of necessity it involves separation from things well-known and comfortable (whether completely desirable or not), and this entails loss.

When I asked him to spell this out as he saw it in my situation, he ticked off the following:

Loss of identity in the Intensive Care Unit (ICU). Rings, bracelets, etc., removed and placed in hospital safe. Only individuation is a plastic identification bracelet on patient's left wrist.

Loss of dignity. Emergency conditions in ICU rule out privacy. Tendency on part of nurses is to deal with bodies not persons.

Loss of speech for so long. Respirator tubes in mouth mean communication is curtailed.

---

[1] At the time the Reverend Robert Bonham was Director of the Christian Institute of Healing at New Covenant Church, Pompano Beach, Florida.

The possibility of loss of life. Death is common and frequent in ICU. Dependency on machines underscores the fragility of life.

Loss of mental ability and memory. Reduced oxygen in brain brings on confusion.

As he talked a flood of emotion ran through me. I saw the physical stripping of possessions that takes place in any hospital as more devastating than I had acknowledged. It says, in part, that any so-called success one has had is now of no consequence. That comes off too. Raiment is a hospital gown – the same garment for everyone. One is just a *body* headed for life or death.

I know now what my husband Peter meant when he was asked what he had learned from his first heart attack. His reply, 'I have learned that the kingdom of God can go on without Peter Marshall.'

In the same way I learned in the hospital that everyone can get along quite well without my opinions or 'insights' or teaching. Even my wedding ring, symbol of marriage to Len, the closest earthly relationship, was taken away. The experience left me feeling not only helpless but worthless – a digit. The danger here, of course, is that this sense of nonentity can lead one into the pit of despair. It can render one unable not only to accept God's unqualified love, but also the love of other people.

Bob's complete assurance that 'this too will pass' was very heartening. He had no answer, though, to my question as to what I can do to make the grief work shorter. Simply that I am to trust God and listen.

This morning I had this word from the Spirit. He tells me to praise and rejoice. He brings to mind the Scripture song we've sung so often at church:

Rejoice in the Lord always; again I will say Rejoice.

Philippians 4:4 RSV

Rejoice!

That I can enjoy music again through my stereo record-player. I actually got up and played the piano a bit –
'Breathe on me, breath of God. . . .'

Rejoice!

Telephoned T. and confessed my lack of love and understanding about several matters. A time of renewed fellowship and reconciliation.

Rejoice!

For patient Len and faithful family . . . for the Intercessors . . . for all who prayed . . . for my doctors and the hospital personnel.

Rejoice!

Linda and I are so close now. She drove down to be with me for a week, bringing a gift of four mats and four napkins for the dining-room table. 'Use them,' she urged. The point is that Len and the doctor have insisted on my getting out of bed and eating at the table.

Rejoice!

Mary Moncur discovered a tree with mangos out of season. Also fresh grapefruit. And our lime tree is so full that Mary will spend all morning squeezing and freezing them.

Praise You, Lord, for Bob Bonham giving up half of every Saturday to be with me.

Praise You, Lord, for bringing out all the fears that are clinging around the fear of death – so that I can deal with them.

Praise You, Lord, for allowing me to have those experiences in Intensive Care, and for pulling me back from death.

8

Receiving Love

God continues to heal me. This morning He gave me a walloping message about the fact that I have not always been able to receive other people's love and so cannot receive Jesus' love. This revelation was sparked by a hassle with Len last night in our bedroom when I was complaining about members of the household who are shielding me about family situations, finances, and decisions that involve my manuscripts and affairs.

Len became quite agitated; finally with tears in his eyes he said, 'Catherine, the doctors have told us that you need time to recover from being at death's door. What we're doing is for your protection, out of our love for you. Don't you realise that we almost lost you?' With that, his voice broke with a show of emotion such as I have rarely seen in our marriage.

This morning I awoke with the full impact of Len's deep feeling sweeping over me. How often, I wondered, do men in our society shortchange themselves and their families by letting a 'macho' front cover up a sensitive nature underneath? The conviction came too, though, that I have not been open enough to love. I've often had trouble accepting the feelings Len did express. The affection and gratitude of friends and readers, too.

'Read 1 Corinthians 13,' the Spirit nudged.

Those verses lay it out for me even more stringently than Len did last night:

Love is patient, love is kind. It does not envy, it does not boast, it is not proud. It is not rude, it is not self-seeking, it is not easily angered, it keeps no record of wrongs. Love does not delight in evil but rejoices with the truth. It always protects, always trusts, always hopes, always perseveres.

1 Corinthians 13:4–7 NIV

I see further that, while my act of laying my body on the altar as 'a living sacrifice' was a good first step, it was not enough for: 'Though I give my body to be burned and have not love, it profiteth me nothing' (v. 3).

Now comes further revelation, even as I write. Following the 1944 experience of Jesus' healing Presence in my room after I was bedridden for almost three years, I nevertheless lacked something. I've always supposed it was sufficient faith to make the healing complete.

But suppose it was *love* that was missing, not faith. Oh, obedience was not altogether there either, but obedience would have followed love.

'Lord, I rejoice. Lord, I capitulate. Lord, let Your love – and Len's and the love of those around me, each member of my family, and all the love of far-flung friends through my books – *take over*.'

Grief Work Continued – The Healing of Memories

Today I shared with Bob Bonham what I have only flicked at with Len: that is the strange negativism I'm feeling about myself. Lately I keep seeing the underside of things, tend to concentrate on the downbeat.

I'm aware too of a loosening of the hold that *things* have on me. I could care less about fixing up Evergreen Farm or the Florida house – redecorating, repairing, restoring – whereas I used to be very much on top of all of this.

Bob interpreted these observations positively by telling me that this is a normal part of recuperation, that the 'grief work' needs to go on. He sees too that God is showing me how to *die of self*. The indifference to *things* is simply one manifestation of this. As the culmination of this process, Bob sees that self will eventually be given back to me in a new way.

Even as I write this, the Spirit gives me a further insight – I am to take the lassitude, the wanting to lie down and take oxygen, the lack of motivation and will power to get on with diaphragm exercises, as part and yet another proof of this 'death'. The crucifixion experience at the hospital was real.

The above, positively seen, is that Catherine is dead and my dependence upon *Jesus'* motivation and *His* strength is more real than ever.

After reassuring me that my negativism is a part of the recovery process, Bob Bonham then sought to lead me through the healing of some memories that lie at the root of my fear of physical death.

Bob asked me to begin this session by seeking 'contact' with Jesus. For example, I might ask to feel the touch of His hand on mine. Then I was to let Jesus lead me back to the memory He wanted to heal.

The first one, curiously, was the time I was walking in the woods as a young girl and stepped on something in the leaves. To my horror I saw that it was a dead bird. The dread of that experience has obviously clung to me ever since.

The second was the time our family went to a relative's funeral in Johnson City, Tennessee. The body of Uncle John Herndon was in a coffin open for viewing. This was my first look at a dead person. The stark coldness of my uncle's face numbed me.

The third was a real surprise – the 'living death' of my grandmother Sarah Wood for whom I was named. Grandmother, for the last part of her life, stayed in her bedroom, where she would allow no window opened. To me she appeared sealed in a tomb.

Bob had me continue to seek contact with Jesus who repeatedly reassured me that death was a doorway experience, that the body was shed as an old, worn-out garment while the inner person, the essential being, went joyously through the door into eternal life.

The whole process took over an hour.

After Bob Bonham left I remembered that Agnes Sanford in her book *The Healing Gifts of the Spirit* had a chapter entitled 'The Healing of the Memories.' I found the book in my library, turned to that chapter and was stopped by this sentence:

'The truth is that any wound to the soul so deep that it is not healed by our own self-searching and prayers is inevitably connected with a subconscious awareness of sin.'

We find the same connection in the Bible! Jesus died for

our *sins*. Yet in Isaiah 53:4 we are told, 'Surely he hath borne our griefs.'

So there is a sense in which sin equals, or is tantamount to, grief.

Which is why the healing of memories is bound up with the forgiveness of sins.

While pondering all this, I recalled my mother's statement to me several years ago, how it distressed her, after Peter's death, the way I would spend hours talking over lofty 'spiritual matters' with our housekeeper while my nine-year-old son, Peter John, playing alone in his bedroom, desperately needed my attention, time, and love.

A picture came to mind. It is an actual photo. Peter John is half-squatting on the floor of his bedroom, his toys around him, his big eyes solemn, bewildered, seeking.

With sudden tears I confessed my 'heavenly-mindedness' as a sin and asked Jesus' forgiveness.

Next I asked Jesus to go back in time and take that little boy with the hurt, bewildered eyes in His arms. Then to sit there on the bedroom floor beside him, playing with him, ministering the healing needed to Peter John's lonely heart.

'Thank You, Lord, that all time – past, present, and future – is "right now" with You. Therefore, that little boy is available to Your healing presence, even as the little girl Catherine is. I claim especially Your power to "cleanse me from all unrighteousness". Thank You for Your great promise "to restore . . . the years that the locust has eaten" (Joel 2:25 AMPLIFIED), both for Peter and for me.'

After this prayer I felt the love of Jesus washing over my body like a benediction.

What the Spirit has been doing for me through Bob Bonham is remarkable. Each time I believe I have plumbed the depths of peace and joy in the Christian life, there is more . . . more . . . more! My spirit bounds and leaps and overflows with thanksgiving so that I struggle for any way at all to express it! The fact that Jesus would love each individual *that much* – me – regardless of worth, regardless of performance turned in, regardless of anything, is *so* amazing. No wonder He was raised to the right hand of the Father and crowned with glory and honour!!

10

Keeping My Eyes Upon Jesus

Fell on my face yesterday. Breathing was laborious. Did very little walking. Could not do the exercises. Was discouraged and disheartened and bored.

I knew the cause of all this. A letter came from my doctor, putting names and tags to my 'chronic' illness for use in Medicare forms. It sounded so final that I began looking at *this*, accepting it, settling down to it.

I also opened the door to fear. Not so much fear of death because I've actually, finally worked through that. This time it was a fear that I would let down the readers of my books who expect me to be an example of victorious faith.

In my session with Bob Bonham we traced the roots of this fear of letting people down, back to my childhood. What came out was that my father's praising me so highly when I played the piano for his prayer meetings, or made top grades in school, eventually created in me the feeling that I *had* to achieve in order to have his love.

As the years passed this feeling was extended to other members of my family, to friends, even to God. Added to this was the belief that because I have been so public in my life as a Christian, if I did not measure up to what Jesus expected of me, I would not only let Him down, but that people 'out there' would think less of *Him*; that Jesus' reputation would actually suffer.

Put in so many words, this is obviously ridiculous! But that's what came out. So yesterday was a total setback for me.

This morning I sought the Lord's forgiveness and was told something like this, most emphatically:

'Catherine, take your eyes off yourself, off your symptoms, off your fears and centre your attention on Me. Look at *Me*. Keep looking at Me.

'Allow Me to be your Doctor. This is My will. I *do* know how to give you health. I made you. I know how to mend you.

'Why do you think I healed everyone who came to Me in the days of My flesh? Out of overflowing mercy. I had only to see any human being blind or crippled or sick or in pain to want to set the wrong situation right as quickly as possible.

'I have told you in My Word (Hebrews) that as man's High Priest I am able – and want – to "*run*" to the assistance of those who cry to Me.'

In my answering prayer, I said, 'Lord, I do cry to You. I give You permission to change me on the inside, to strengthen my flabby spiritual muscle, to reverse the direction of my gaze, to make me eager to look at You only.

'I know You want a resurrection thrust inside me and an end to my doubts and negative thinking. In the wake of this will come new life and health. If not on this earth, then I will go into the next life with the differentness that You want for me.'

Then Jesus led me to the sixteenth chapter of John where I was stopped by this magnificent verse:

> . . . it is profitable – good, expedient, advantageous – for you that I go away. Because if I do not go away, the Comforter (Counsellor, Helper, Advocate, Intercessor, Strengthener, Standby) will not come to you – into close fellowship with you. . . .
>
> John 16:7 AMPLIFIED

These are the blessed functions of the Holy Spirit promised by Jesus:

> *Counsellor* (He gives wisdom to the simple.)
> *Helper* (He lifts us over every obstacle.)
> *Advocate* (He is our personal lawyer to 'take us on' and plead our case.)
> *Intercessor* (He stands before the throne of grace.)
> *Strengthener* (He gives us vitality and courage.)
> *Standby* (He is always at our side.)

How can any one of us get along without any of those things!

Then glorious verse 33 (italic added):

I have told you these things so that *in Me* you may have perfect peace and confidence. In the world you have tribulation and trials and distress and frustration; but be of good cheer – take courage, be confident, certain, undaunted – for I have overcome the world. – I have deprived it of power to harm, have conquered it [for you].

11

Resurrection

Thanks to Pastor Robert Bonham and the ministry of other loving friends and family, Catherine made good progress during September, October, and November 1982. To my amazement she decided we should accept the invitation to fly to Cape Cod to spend Thanksgiving with her son Peter, his wife, Edith, and their three children, Mary Elizabeth, thirteen, Peter Jonathan, nine, and David Christopher, two. Mother Wood, ninety-one, insisted she would go too.

There were moments of hilarity en route. Since Catherine and her mother both needed wheelchairs to traverse airport terminals, I took over when porters were not available, jockeying both wheelchairs through gates and up and down ramps.

It was Catherine's first visit to the Marshalls' new home, a joyous family time with four generations interacting, sometimes peacefully, sometimes through tensions that bubbled with creativity.

At Christmastime, our own home was the scene of another family reunion. Chet and his wife, Susan, arrived with our new grandson, Jacob LeSourd, joined by Linda and Phil Lader and our younger son, Jeff. Christmas had been a time when the perfectionist in Catherine ran her ragged with holiday preparations. Now for the first time in twenty-three years, Catherine let others run the show and simply enjoyed herself. Gift-giving and elaborate meals had been reduced, allowing more time for games and family talk.

At the beginning of 1983 Catherine set several goals for herself. An 800-page draft of the novel had been completed, but needed months of work to sharpen characterisation.

She wanted to resume writing for each issue of The Intercessors *newsletter.*

And do an article about her mother for a Guideposts *series on aging.*

At the end of January, however, she underwent a cataract operation. From her journal:

February 9th . . . I am staggering under what the eye surgeon said to me yesterday during a routine checkup following the cataract surgery: 'You are sick from head to toe.' I did not have to accept this verdict, but I did. Now I really have to ditch it – with the Spirit's help and by God's grace. This verse has truly helped me:

And if the Spirit of Him Who raised up Jesus from the dead dwells in you, [then] He Who raised up Christ Jesus from the dead will also restore to life your mortal (short-lived, perishable) bodies through His Spirit Who dwells in you.

Romans 8:11 AMPLIFIED

February 24th . . . Have hit a new low. I am quite out of breath – indeed, gasping for air – just in walking from room to room. My doctor could find no obvious cause for the trouble yesterday. Today it hit me. . . . Once again the doctors neither know what is wrong, nor how to help me. So . . . I am backed up against Jesus' help.

March 9th . . . In my Quiet Time, this thought: my hospital experience of the crucifixion was centred on the matter of breathing. This morning the Holy Spirit reminded me once again: 'Jesus took your breathing problem into His own body on the Cross so that from henceforth *He* is your life-breath.'

With great heaviness of spirit I drove Catherine to Bethesda Memorial Hospital on March 11, where she was admitted for more tests. We made light of it. 'Just a few days,' I assured her.
Silently, however, I was recalling another hospital episode

*almost twelve years before. A daughter, Amy Catherine, had
been born to Peter and Edith Marshall and been given her
grandmother's name. The baby, however, was genetically damaged in lungs, kidneys, and brain. Doctors at Children's
Hospital in Boston offered no hope.*

*Friends from around the country gathered to pray for little
Amy's healing. God answered the prayers, but not the way we
expected. Healings occurred . . . in the people who came to
pray. Amy Catherine died.*

*Catherine was desolate for months. 'What went wrong?' she
wept.*

*Eventually, she saw it – nothing went wrong! God is a
sovereign God. We can plead with Him, bargain with Him, rail
at Him, and claim anything and everything in His name. In
return God overwhelms us with His blessings, but retains the
decisions about 'times and seasons' in His hands.*

Here is Catherine's last journal entry made in the hospital:

March 12th . . . The blood test yesterday showed carbon
dioxide level in my blood too high, but not dangerous;
not enough oxygen in the blood, however. Another
problem seems to be anaemia.

This morning Jesus told me once again: 'Keep your
eyes off yourself and look steadily at Me. I love you. I
know how to mend you.'

*That very day Catherine was taken to the same Intensive Care
Unit where she had spent so many weeks last summer, and put
on a respirator. Shortly after midnight on March 18, Catherine's heart stopped beating. The Lord had come to take her with
Him to experience the joyous resurrection she missed last
summer.*

In the hours and days that followed, the Lord seemed to
place all of us in the family under His special love and
protection; plus a necessary degree of numbness. The
calls, letters, cards, flowers, and food that flowed in
warmed and nourished us.

Two triumphant occasions followed: the burial service in National Presbyterian Church, Washington, DC, conducted by its pastor and Catherine's close friend, Dr Louis Evans, Jr, with her son, Peter John Marshall.

And the memorial service at the New Covenant Presbyterian Church, Pompano Beach, Florida. Pastors George Callahan along with Dr William Earnhart (church elder and Catherine's personal physician) shared their memories of a great lady.

Robert Bonham, the man who for so many hours ministered healing to Catherine as pastor and friend, spoke these words at this same service:

'During Catherine's funeral in the National Presbyterian Church, my eyes went to some beautiful stained glass windows through which the sun was shining. I thought of Jesus telling His disciples, "You are the light of the world." Catherine as a 20th century follower put her light on a lamp stand so that all might see.

'I looked at the glass in those windows and thought about all the pieces therein. There were dark pieces and light pieces, all kinds of colours blended together. I thought about the suffering experiences that Catherine had early in her life and recently in the hospital. These were deep, deep colours. Her body never was able to keep up with her mind and her spirit. It always hauled her back.

'There were, of course, the brighter colours, the rose tints of love and warmth – the giving of her heart to those in her family and to everyone she touched. Those colours went out across the United States and throughout the world. I remember years back when I was at the University of Illinois, one of the professors there had a hydrocephalic child. He told me that he had called Catherine up long distance and had asked her to pray for his child. She did and the child was healed. All the way to Illinois, and other places far and near, went those pieces of radiating light – warm, bright, healing colours falling on the lives of people.

'There were so many pieces in her life – the books that she and the Lord wrote – the articles for *Guideposts* and other magazines. She wrote nothing that did not have all of her heart and mind in it as well as the heart and mind of Christ. Starting *The Intercessors* not long ago, she and Leonard mobilised prayer warriors across the nation to bring help to many people. Her family represents warm, glowing pieces of glass in the mosaic of her life. Likewise her many friends who kept calling when she died and could not believe that this had happened.

'A surprising thing about a stained glass window is that when the light is not shining through, it comes across as dull. Have you ever looked at a stained glass window when there is no light behind it? You cannot see what is in it. Catherine always had Christ's light shining through her life. As the light of Jesus radiated through the stained glass mosaic of her life, all of us who were within sight of it got blessed.

'When the sun goes down, the horizon stays bright for a long time. There is going to be a long afterglow to Catherine Marshall LeSourd's life. The books that were written will go on to become classics in Christian literature. The articles will go on helping people. There are things she has written that will yet find their way into print to bless us. Her touches on our lives will live on, ministering to my children, and my children's children.

'In the last page of her book *To Live Again*, Catherine wrote these words as she faced life without her husband, Peter: "At moments when the future is completely obscured, can any one of us afford to go to meet our tomorrows with dragging feet? God has been in the past, then He would be in the future, too. Always He had brought adventure, high hopes, unexpected friends, new ventures that broke old patterns. Then in my future must lie more goodness, more mercy, more adventures, more friends. Across the hills, light was breaking through the storm clouds. Suddenly, just ahead of the car an incandescent, iridescent rainbow appeared, hung there shimmering. I hadn't seen a rainbow for a long time." And then Catherine's last sentence, "I drove steadily into the light."

'Catherine is doing that right now – moving steadily into the Light.'

Catherine's Scriptural Lifeline

Early in her marriage to Len, Catherine formed the habit of copying into a grey 10 by 7 inch notebook the Bible verses that helped most in health or household crises. Over the years the pages filled to become a kind of scriptural lifeline. In the summer of 1982, when she was in the Intensive Care Unit, too ill to read the handwritten entries herself, a member of her family or close friend would read them to her. Here are 41 verses[1] to which she clung with ever-growing assurance:

Behold, I am the Lord, the God of all flesh; is there anything too hard for Me?

Jeremiah 32:27

The grass withers, the flower fades, but the word of our God will stand for ever.

Isaiah 40:8

He has bestowed on us His precious and exceedingly great promises, so that through them you may escape (by flight) from the moral decay (rottenness and corruption) that is in the world because of covetousness (lust and greed), and become sharers (partakers) of the divine nature.

2 Peter 1:4

God is faithful – reliable, trustworthy and [therefore] ever true to His promise, and He can be depended on;

---

[1] All passages from the Amplified Bible unless otherwise noted.

by Him you were called into companionship and participation with His Son, Jesus Christ our Lord.

1 Corinthians 1:9

So shall my word be that goeth forth out of my mouth: it shall not return unto me void, but it shall accomplish that which I please, and it shall prosper in the thing whereto I sent it.

Isaiah 55:11 KJV

And if the Spirit of Him Who raised up Jesus from the dead dwells in you, [then] He Who raised up Christ Jesus from the dead will also restore to life your mortal (short-lived, perishable) bodies through His Spirit Who dwells in you.

Romans 8:11

So too the (Holy) Spirit comes to our aid and bears us up in our weakness; for we do not know what prayer to offer nor how to offer it worthily as we ought, but the Spirit Himself goes to meet our supplication and pleads in our behalf with unspeakable yearnings and groanings too deep for utterance.

Romans 8:26

And we know that all things work together for good to them that love God, to them who are the called according to his purpose.

Romans 8:28 KJV

I know that whatsoever God doeth, it shall be for ever: nothing can be put to it, nor anything taken from it: and God doeth it, that men should fear before him.

Ecclesiastes 3:14 KJV

For the Lord is our judge, the Lord is our law-giver, the Lord is our king; He will save us.

Isaiah 33:22

For I, the Lord your God, hold your right hand; I, Who say to you, Fear not, I will help you!

Isaiah 41:13

For God's gifts and His call are irrevocable – He never withdraws them when once they are given, and He does not change His mind about those to whom He gives His grace or to whom He sends His call.

Romans 11:29

When the enemy shall come in like a flood, the Spirit of the Lord will lift up a standard against him and put him to flight – for He will come like a rushing stream which the breath of the Lord drives.

Isaiah 59:19

But God is faithful [to His Word and to His compassionate nature], and He [can be trusted] not to let you be tempted . . . beyond your ability and strength of resistance and power to endure, but with the temptation He will [always] also provide the way out – the means of escape to a landing place – that you may be capable and strong and powerful patiently to bear up under it.

1 Corinthians 10:13

The Lord redeems the life of His servants, and none of those who take refuge and trust in Him shall be condemned or held guilty.

Psalm 34:22

Though I walk in the midst of trouble, You will revive me; You will stretch forth Your hand against the wrath of my enemies, and Your right hand will save me.

Psalm 138:7

The Lord also will be a refuge and a high tower for the oppressed, a refuge and a stronghold in times of trouble [high cost, destitution and desperation].

Psalm 9:9

And He will establish you to the end – keep you steadfast, give you strength, and guarantee your vindication, that is, be your warrant against all accusation or indictment – [so that you will be] guiltless and irreproachable in the day of our Lord Jesus Christ, the Messiah.

1 Corinthians 1:8

He will swallow up death in victory – He will abolish death forever; and the Lord God will wipe away tears from off all faces; and the reproach of His people He will take away from off all the earth; for the Lord has spoken it.

Isaiah 25:8

Fear not; for I am with you; do not . . . be dismayed, for I am your God. I will strengthen and harden you [to difficulties]; yes, I will help you; yes, I will hold you up and retain you with My victorious right hand of rightness and justice.

Isaiah 41:10

I have called you by your name, you are Mine. When you pass through the waters I will be with you, and through the rivers they shall not overwhelm you; when you walk through the fire you shall not be burned . . . nor shall the flame kindle upon you. For I am the Lord your God, the Holy One of Israel, your Saviour . . .

Isaiah 43:1–3

For though the mountains should depart and the hills be shaken or removed, yet My love and kindness shall not depart from you, nor shall My covenant of peace and completeness be removed, says the Lord, Who has compassion on you.

Isaiah 54:10

For thus saith the Lord God, the Holy One of Israel; In returning and rest shall ye be saved; in quietness and in confidence shall be your strength.

Isaiah 30:15 KJV

In the world you have tribulation and trials and distress and frustration; but be of good cheer – take courage, be confident, certain, undaunted – for I have overcome the world. – I have deprived it of power to harm, have conquered it [for you].

John 16:33

I assure you, most solemnly I tell you, the person whose ears are open to My words – who listens to My message – and believes and trusts in and clings to and relies on Him Who sent Me has (possesses now) eternal life. And he does not come into judgment – does not incur sentence of judgment, will not come under condemnation – but he has already passed over out of death into life.

John 5:24

Do not fret or have any anxiety about anything, but in every circumstance and in everything by prayer and petition [definite requests] with thanksgiving continue to make your wants known to God. And God's peace . . . which transcends all understanding, shall garrison and mount guard over your hearts and minds in Christ Jesus.

Philippians 4:6–7

But they that wait upon the Lord shall renew their strength; they shall mount up with wings as eagles; they shall run, and not be weary; and they shall walk, and not faint.

Isaiah 40:31 KJV

Whoever takes a drink of the water that I will give him shall never, no never, be thirsty any more. But the water that I will give him shall become a spring of water welling up (flowing, bubbling) continually within him unto eternal life.

John 4:14

My sheep hear my voice, and I know them, and they follow me: And I give unto them eternal life; and they shall never perish, neither shall any man pluck them out of my hand. My Father, which gave them me, is greater than all; and no man is able to pluck them out of my Father's hand. I and My Father are one.

John 10:27–30 KJV

Keep and protect me, O God, for in You I have found refuge, and in You do I put my trust and hide myself . . . my body too shall rest and confidently dwell in safety.

Psalm 16:1, 9

In the day when I called, You answered me, and strengthened me with strength (might and inflexibility) [to temptation] in my inner self.

Psalm 138:3

Now the Lord is the Spirit, and where the Spirit of the Lord is, there is liberty – emancipation from bondage, freedom.

2 Corinthians 3:17

(For the weapons of our warfare are not carnal, but mighty through God to the pulling down of strongholds;) Casting down imaginations, and every high thing that exalteth itself against the knowledge of God, and bringing into captivity every thought to the obedience of Christ.

2 Corinthians 10:4–5 KJV

Behold God, my salvation! I will trust and not be afraid, for the Lord God is my strength and song; yes, He has become my salvation. Therefore with joy will you draw water from the wells of salvation.

Isaiah 12:2–3

Rejoice in the Lord always – delight, gladden yourselves in Him; again I say, Rejoice!

Philippians 4:4

Although the fig tree shall not blossom, neither shall fruit be in the vines, the labour of the olive shall fail, and the fields shall yield no meat; the flock shall be cut off from the fold, and there shall be no herd in the stalls: Yet I will rejoice in the Lord, I will joy in the God of my salvation. The Lord God is my strength, and he will make my feet like hinds' feet, and he will make me to walk upon mine high places.

Habakkuk 3:17–19 KJV

Heal me, O Lord, and I shall be healed; save me, and I shall be saved; for You are my praise.

Jeremiah 17:14

Thou wilt keep him in perfect peace, whose mind is stayed on thee: because he trusteth in thee.

Isaiah 26:3 KJV

Our inner selves wait [earnestly] for the Lord; He is our help and our shield. For in Him does our heart rejoice, because we have trusted (relied on and been confident) in His holy name.

Psalm 33:20–21

. . . for He (God) Himself has said, I will not in any way fail you nor give you up nor leave you without support. [I will] not . . . in any degree leave you helpless, nor forsake nor let [you] down [relax My hold on you]. – Assuredly not!

Hebrews 13:5

For I am persuaded beyond doubt – am sure – that neither death, nor life, nor angels, nor principalities, nor things impending and threatening, nor things to come, nor powers, Nor height, nor depth, nor anything else in all creation will be able to separate us from the love of God which is in Christ Jesus our Lord.

Romans 8:38–39